Reluctant Partner

The Complete Story of the French Participation in the Dardanelles Expedition of 1915

George H. Cassar

Helion & Company Limited

Also by the same author

The French and the Dardanelles: A Study of Failure in the Conduct of War (London, 1971)
Kitchener: Architect of Victory (London, 1977)
The Tragedy of Sir John French (Newark: 1984)
Beyond Courage (Ottawa, 1985)
Asquith as War Leader (London, 1994)
The Forgotten Front: The British Campaign in Italy (London: 1998)
Kitchener's War: British Strategy From 1914 to 1916 (Washington DC, 2004)
Lloyd George at War, 1916-1918 (London, 2009)
Hell in Flanders Fields: The Canadians at the Second Battle of Ypres (Toronto, 2010)
Trial By Gas: The British Army at the Second Battle of Ypres (Washington DC, 2014)
Kitchener as Pronconsul in Egypt, 1911-14 (London, 2016)

Helion & Company Limited
Unit 8 Amherst Business Centre
Budbrooke Road
Warwick
CV34 5WE
England
Tel. 01926 499 619
Fax 0121 711 4075
Email: info@helion.co.uk
Website: www.helion.co.uk
Twitter: @helionbooks
Visit our blog http://blog.helion.co.uk/

Published by Helion & Company 2019
Designed and typeset by Battlefield Design (www.battlefield-design.co.uk)
Cover designed by Paul Hewitt, Battlefield Design (www.battlefield-design.co.uk)
Printed via Jellyfish Solutions (www.jellyfishsolutions.co.uk)

Text and maps © George H. Cassar
Images © as individually credited

Front cover: 1st Division commander General Joseph Masnou (1855-1915) inspects advanced trenches at Cape Helles. (*L'Illustration*, 17 July 1915)
Back cover: Bound for the Dardanelles, General D'Amade presents new regimental colours whilst in transit. (*L'Illustration*, 6 May 1915)

Every reasonable effort has been made to trace copyright holders and to obtain their permission for the use of copyright material. The author and publisher apologize for any errors or omissions in this work and would be grateful if notified of any corrections that should be incorporated in future reprints or editions of this book.

ISBN 978-1-911628-92-7

British Library Cataloguing-in-Publication Data.
A catalogue record for this book is available from the British Library.

All rights reserved. No part of this publication may be reproduced, stored in a retrieval system, or transmitted, in any form, or by any means, electronic, mechanical, photocopying, recording or otherwise, without the express written consent of Helion & Company Limited.

For details of other military history titles published by Helion & Company Limited contact the above address or visit our website: http://www.helion.co.uk.

We always welcome receiving book proposals from prospective authors.

Contents

List of Illustrations	v
List of Maps	vi
Abbreviations	vii
Acknowledgements	viii
Preface	x

1	The French State and Army, 1870-1914	15
2	The Search for an Alternate Theatre of War	28
3	The French Succumb to Churchill's Folly	41
4	Genesis of Military Cooperation	59
5	Assumption of Victory	76
6	Conduct and Aftermath of the Naval Attack on 18 March	88
7	Kum Kale and Krithia	100
8	Hanging On	127
9	Last Throw of the Dice	143
10	L'Affaire Sarrail	161
11	Dardanelles or the Balkans?	179
12	End of the Adventure	194
13	General Review and Reflections on the Dardanelles Campaign	215

Appendix I	221
Appendix II	223
Bibliography	224
Also by the same Author	231
Index	232

To the memory of the dedicated educators who shaped my professional career:

Dr Alfred G. Bailey
Dr James K. Chapman
Dr Robert Vogel

List of Illustrations

The first Viviani Cabinet. Messimy is on the right at the end of the second row. (BnF)	i
Raymond Poincaré. (BnF)	i
Alexandre Millerand. (BnF)	ii
Victor Augagneur. (Open source)	iii
Théophile Delcassé. (BnF)	iv
Aristide Briand. (BnF)	v
General Joseph Galliéni in civilian clothes while serving as Minister of War. (BnF)	vi
French troops arriving in the Dardanelles pose for posterity. (BnF)	vi
Rear-Admiral Émile-Paul Guépratte. (Open source)	vii
Poincaré decorating two French soldiers near the front. (BnF)	viii
A French soldier carrying a wounded comrade from the front line. (Open source)	ix
Turkish captives marching to Sedd-el Bahr with a Zouave escort. (Open source)	x
A French 75 artillery gun at Cape Helles during the Third Battle of Krithia, 4 June 1915. (Open source)	x
Joffre chatting with a few members of the French delegation at the railway station in Paris, all of whom are waiting for the train which will take them to Calais for a conference with the British. (ILN)	xi
French troops firing at Turks in an opposing trench. (BnF)	xi
General Joffre acknowledges the cheers of the crowd on leaving the War Office with Lord Kitchener during his visit to London in October 1915. (ILN)	xii
A French soldier surveying the scene behind barbed-wire. (Open source)	xii
Admiral Guépratte boards a French destroyer prior to an offshore reconnaissance of the Gallipoli Peninsula. (*L'Illustration*, 6 May 1915)	xiii
French troops resting in a trench. (BnF)	xiii
General d'Amade. (Open source)	xiv
General Gouraud is standing with his foot resting on a gun and next to him is his successor General Bailloud. (BnF)	xiv
General Henri Gouraud with General Hamilton several days before he was seriously wounded. (ILN)	xv
General Maurice Sarrail at his headquarters in Salonica with his chief of staff. (Open source)	xvi
Sedd-el Bahr French cemetery. (BnF)	xvi

List of Maps

1. The Turkish Empire in 1914 — xii
2. The Allied Naval Attack at the Dardanelles, 18 March 1915 — 90
3. Theatre of Operations — 102
4. The French Diversion at Kum Kale — 107
5. The British Landings in April and August — 113
6. The First Battle of Krithia, 28 April 1915 — 115
7. The Turkish Night Attack, 1–2 May 1915 — 118
8. The Second Battle of Krithia, 6–8 May 1915 — 121
9. The Third Battle of Krithia, 4 June 1915 — 139
10. The Battle of 21 June 1915 — 147

Abbreviations

AMAE	*Archives du Ministère des Affaires Etrangères*
AMG	*Archives du Ministère de la Guerre*
AMM	*Archives du Ministère de la Marine*
AN	*Archives Nationales*
ANZAC	Australian and New Zealand Army Corps
BNA	British National Archives
BnF	*Bibliothèque nationale de France*
CEO	*Corps Expéditionairre d'Orient*
EMA	*État-Major de l'armée* (Army General Staff)
FO	Foreign Office
GHQ	General Headquarters (British Army Headquarters)
GQG	*Grand Quartier Général* (French Army Headquarters)
IWM	Imperial War Museum
LHCMA	Liddell Hart Centre for Military Archives
SHD	*Service historique de la Défense*
WO	War Office

Acknowledgements

This book could not have been written without the help of many individuals and institutions, so it is a pleasure to recall all their kind efforts on my behalf. First, I would like to thank my colleagues and friends at Eastern Michigan University for their encouraging support and advice. In particular I would like to express my gratitude to Steve Ramold with whom I discussed the project at various stages and shared his extensive knowledge of military history; to Jim Egge, my department head, whom I frequently interrupted and distracted from his administrative duties, to act as my sounding board; to Jesse Kauffman who gave me incisive criticism and shrewd suggestions based on his own writing about the Great War; and to Roger Long who shared with me his broad knowledge of India and the Middle East during the war years. The department secretary, Rachelle Marshall, to whom I owe more than I can say, patiently attended to my endless requests, some of which went well beyond the call of duty. Special appreciation goes to John Shubsda, data analysis at Eastern, whose technical expertise solved my countless computer glitches; and to his co-worker David Zylstra, College Technology Specialist, who led me through, as I am not computer savvy, the publisher's list of instructions and requests. Mehmet Ya Ya, a native of Turkey, and current member of the Economics department here, kindly helped locate remote places in Anatolia (mentioned in the text) for my maps.

Whilst I grew up speaking French and can translate the language without difficulty, my entire education, unlike that of my sisters Carole and Sylvie, was in English speaking institutions. As I never formally studied French and do not write the language well, I invariably turned to Geneviève Pedan, a good friend and member of the language department at Eastern Michigan University to come to my rescue. I want to express my deep gratitude to Geneviève for composing the many letters to the archivists and librarians I contacted in France.

Beyond Eastern I would like to acknowledge the kindness of Christopher Bell for his valued input. Peter Hart graciously allowed me to borrow a number of excerpts of eyewitness testimony of participants in battle from his *Gallipoli* volume. I am indebted to Professor Halpern, for the right to reproduce a lengthy piece from his study, *The Naval War in the Mediterranean*, as well as providing me with helpful information relating to the French navy. Thanks are also due to my sisters Carole and Sylvie for their patience in helping me to decipher the sometimes unclear (to me) handwriting of President Raymond Poincaré. Rachel Trudell-Jones with the assistance of Stephanie Sambrook turned my rough sketches into the excellent maps that appear in this book. My greatest debt, as usual, is to my wife Mary who has tolerated without complaint my frequent absences from home, while I was abroad engaged in research or absorbed in the writing process in my office at the university.

My project owes much to local libraries and to archival repositories in France and Great Britain and to the unfailing courtesy and guidance of their personnel during my visits. I cannot mention everyone by name but a few individuals deserving more than an anonymous vote of thanks include Jean-Philippe Dumas who allowed me to examine the papers of General Gouraud while they were in the process of being catalogued; William Spencer, Principal Military Specialist at the British National Archives; Lianne Smith, Archives Service Manager at King's College, London; Andrew Powers, Assistant Librarian at Eastern Michigan University; and Tim Utter, Manager of the Clark Library at the University of Michigan. To each I owe my heartfelt thanks.

I also am indebted to the following institutions for graciously giving me permission to quote from material to which they own the copyright: in Paris to the *Archives Nationales* and the *Service Historique de la Défence* in Vincennes; in the United Kingdom to the Trustees of the Imperial War Museum; the Masters, Fellows and Scholars of Churchill College; and the Trustees of the Liddell Hart Centre for Military Archives, King's College. Crown copyright material in the British national archives is reproduced by permission of the Controller of Her Majesty's Stationary Office.

Preface

While searching for a topic to complete the requirements of a doctoral thesis at McGill University in the mid-1960s, my supervisor, Professor Robert Vogel, who was a keen chronicler of the two world wars, suggested that I look into the possibility of investigating the French involvement in the Dardanelles campaign of 1915. He pointed out that the French sent a full-fledged expeditionary force with a staff and command structure. Yet most books overlooked or barely mentioned the French, assuming that their contribution was insignificant. It is true, he added, that as junior partners they were under the command of the British and played no part in the planning process, the selection of the landing sites on Gallipoli and decisions affecting the execution of the plans. However appearances do not always tell the whole story and he suspected that the French role in the Dardanelles was more important than given credit. He believed that it would make an excellent thesis topic if I could gain access to the French official records. I took his advice and journeyed to Paris where I had interviews with the chief archivists at the Ministries of Marine, Foreign Affairs and War. They were all kind and sympathetic and, although subject to restrictive guidelines, indicated that they would go as far as they could to help. Presumably it meant that I would be allowed to see some of the official documents, but it was clear that the personal collections of key politicians deposited in their repositories, except in one or two instances, were closed to researchers. I was still uncertain whether I could find enough material in the government archives to produce an acceptable thesis, but I decided to take a chance and fortunately it paid off. After I left the university, I made some revisions in the manuscript and sent it to Allen and Unwin which published it in 1971 under the title of *The French and the Dardanelles: A Study of Failure in the Conduct of War*.

It is understandable that readers may want to know why I have produced another volume on a matter that I had addressed nearly half a century ago. I was inspired to do so by a sense of unfinished business. *The French and the Dardanelles* was confined to essentially examining Anglo-French high policy or "the war behind the war," partly because the source material for a broader account was unavailable and partly because, as a novice in the field of military history, I lacked the experience to discuss and analyze the French side of the land operations. The limited scope of the work obviously ruled out exploring other aspects of a complex subject. Moreover, I made what I considered in hindsight some errors in judgement. Only a few need to be acknowledged here. One was to include material that had only slight relevance and should have been left out. Another was to devote, in certain circumstances, more attention to the British than I should have. It is true that they oversaw the enterprise and supplied most of the forces and resources so obviously they could not be ignored. Still their role needed to be reduced to the bare minimum – just enough to make the matter under discussion intelligible.

For years I have been aware of the flaws in the book and, with retirement looming, I realized that if I planned to make major revisions in the narrative, I could not delay the task any longer. Happily, the current research conditions were excellent. Since *The French and the Dardanelles* first appeared many helpful specialized studies have been published and, even more important, all the official French documents for my period are accessible as are the papers of prominent politicians in archival centres in Paris. On top of this, a set of volumes containing the incoming and outgoing war correspondence at the Ministry of Foreign Affairs has been published and the President's journal containing his daily notes are available online.

This new work was written with an eye to correct the earlier sins of omission and commission and to place the French at the centre of events. I excised parts of the old narrative so that the focus on the French is much sharper. I enlarged on themes introduced earlier, in particular on the issue of war aims in which the Allies were more absorbed in advancing their own political interests than in seriously considering the needs of the campaign itself. I extended my research into areas not examined before - such as the French role in the naval and military operations. The book also seeks to place the campaign within the context of the war in France as it depicts the struggle between the army high command and government over control of military policy and the flow of resources to the distant fronts.

Whilst the French were content to follow Britain's lead in the first half of the campaign, their dissatisfaction with the manner in which it was conducted convinced them that they must take on the responsibility of finishing the job. Overcoming the opposition of GQG, the French cabinet decided to augment its forces in the Dardanelles by four divisions in preparation for the next major assault. Just as the troops were prepared to leave, the Central Powers attacked Serbia and caused the French to cancel their plans. Instead they opted to send forces to the Balkans to help Serbia and placed unrelenting pressure on the British government to follow suit. The British were already involved in four theatres and, as their resources were stretched to the limit, opposed embarking on another venture, especially one they judged was doomed to fail. They held out for as long as they felt they could but, in the end, yielded in the interest of preserving the Alliance. The train of events that the French had set in motion made it impossible for the British to continue to reinforce the Dardanelles campaign. Their only option was to pull out.

In summary this study fills an important gap in the voluminous library of histories and commentaries on one of the most controversial campaigns in the Great War. It presents a more accurate and, with the inclusion of an immense quantity of new material, a much fuller account than the previous version. It covers the French involvement at all levels – political, diplomatic and military. It is hoped the new narrative will provide a more balanced treatment of the French impact on the ill-fated Dardanelles expedition which continues to grip the popular imagination.

A word on the French archival sources. Since I first approached the subject many years ago, the archives at the Ministries of Marine and Foreign Affairs were transferred, the former to the *Service historique de la Défence* in Vincennes and the latter to a new building in La Courneuve at the edge of Paris. In both places I was unable to locate some of the material I had used in my earlier work, even with the help of the current archivists. Thus I retained the reference numbers for documents consulted prior to the move.

George H. Cassar
Ann Arbor, Michigan

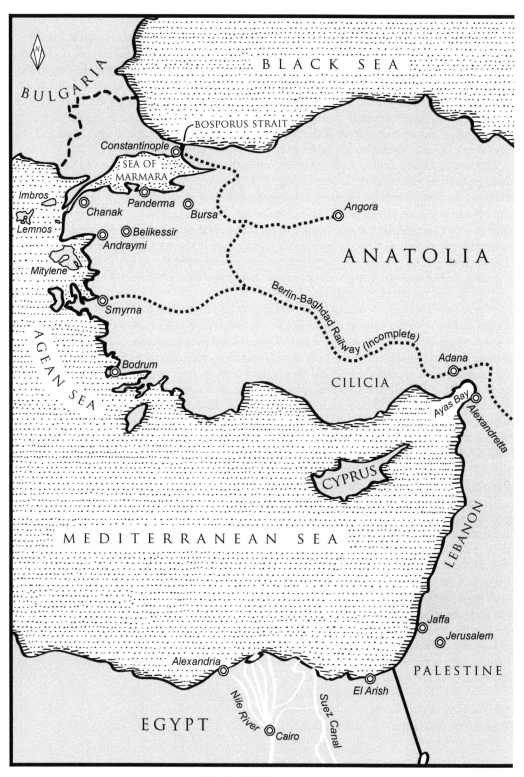

1. The Turkish Empire in 1914

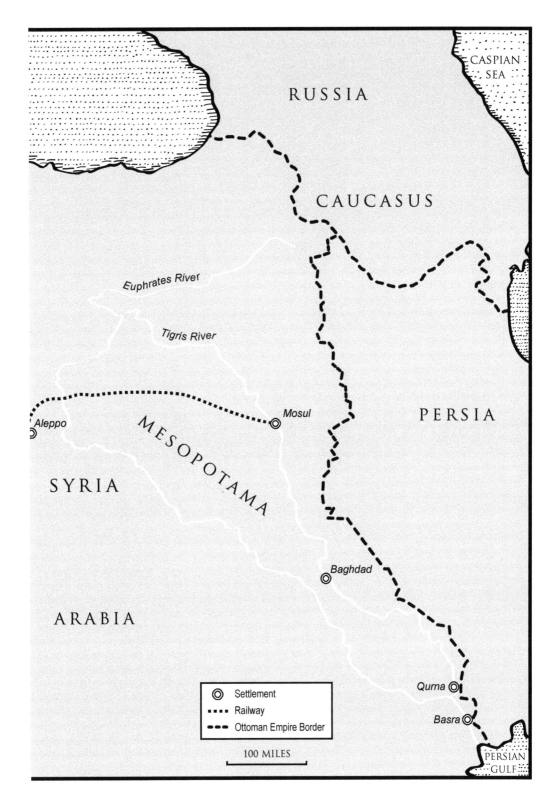

1

The French State and Army, 1870-1914

The pattern of civil-military relations established after the downfall of Napoleon in 1815 extended to the eve of the Great War without significant change. The army throughout the long period confined itself to military matters and was politically neutral, seeing itself as an arm of the state and obedient to civil authority. There had been revolutions in 1830 and 1848 that had toppled the monarchical regimes of Charles X and Louis Philippe respectively, but these had been politically inspired and executed. The army played a more active political role on 2 December 1851, when the President, Louis Napoleon, unable to persuade the legislators to amend the constitution that would have allowed him to run for reelection, staged a *coup d'état*. He sent army units to disperse the National Assembly and to arrest its leaders. The event was not a military revolution as has been alleged by some writers. The hierarchy of the army had not planned nor been responsible for the coup, but as agents of the government were merely obeying instructions from their constitutional chief. A year later a plebiscite allowed the head of state to end the republican experiment as he inaugurated the Second Empire and assumed the title of Napoleon III. The 18-year rule of Napoleon came to an end when he blundered into a war with Prussia. Poorly led, with a chaotic mobilization effort and no strategic plan for the war, the French army suffered a crushing defeat at Sedan on 2 September 1870. The news that Napoleon and over 100,000 French troops had surrendered to the Prussians led to the immediate collapse of the Imperial regime and a call for the establishment of a republic.[1]

A provisional government was installed and feverishly sought to turn the tide of war but it was beyond hope and, after Paris capitulated on 28 January 1871, an armistice was signed. Early the following month a National Assembly was elected by universal manhood suffrage to negotiate peace terms as well as to draft a constitution for the country. Of the more than 600 deputies, the Assembly contained 400 monarchists as opposed to about 200 republicans. The appearance of a conservative landslide was misleading, however. Since during the electoral campaign the

---

[1] For the period between the fall of Napoleon I and the overthrow of Napoleon III see Pierre Chalmin, *L'Officier français de 1815 à 1870* (Paris: Librairie Marcel Rivière, 1957); Raoul Girardet, *La société militaire de 1815 à nos jours* (Paris: Perrin, 1998), chs. 1-4; Guy Chapman, "The French Army and Politics", *in* Michael Howard (ed.), *Soldiers and Governments* (London: Eyre and Spottiswoode, 1957), pp. 54-59.

republicans had wanted to continue the futile and unpopular war, most Frenchmen voted for conservative candidates.

The settlement with Germany had barely been concluded when severe friction developed between the National Assembly, now sitting at Versailles, and the Paris Commune.[2] The government tried to resolve the differences through conciliation but when that failed decided to subdue the city by force. As is often the case in a civil war, the fighting was extremely brutal for the hatred between the two sides was at white heat. Government troops, after laying siege to the city, broke through its defences on 21 May 1871. In a final act of desperation, the Communards set fire to a number of public buildings and executed hostages, including the Archbishop of Paris. Attacking troops, in turn, shot everyone caught carrying a rifle and executed thousands of prisoners. An estimated 20,000 Communards and sympathizers were killed and thousands more were deported to penal colonies overseas.[3]

The action of the army in suppressing the Communards was in keeping with its traditional function to preserve order, not depart from political neutrality. It would play no further role in the political events that shaped the destiny of the country until the Dreyfus Affair. Burning for revenge, it could only think of rebuilding itself for the next inevitable confrontation with Germany. Anxious to wipe the stain of defeat and recover the lost provinces of Alsace and Lorraine, the general public lent its wholehearted support to the army's revival. The nation's pulse was felt in the National Assembly which introduced new measures that provided the essential framework for modernizing the army. The laws in 1872, 1873 and 1875 demonstrated that the soldiers and politicians had learned the lessons of 1870. They established universal military service and fixed the term for all eligible young men at five years; abolished substitutions which had released the sons of the wealthy in the past; created a cadre of reserves that was lacking in 1870; set up a structure of command and reorganized the army, so that it could expedite deployment in the field on the outbreak of war.[4]

The unity of the politicians in embracing the military reform measures contrasted sharply with their differences over the nation's future form of government. Although the royalists enjoyed a large majority in the National Assembly and a restoration seemed inevitable, it turned out they were unable to agree between the two claimants to the throne.[5] As an interim measure they appointed Field Marshal Patrice de MacMahon as president for seven years and granted him extensive powers. A devoted monarchist, MacMahon was expected to step aside as soon as the impasse was broken.[6] But the monarchists continued to check each other and the Assembly finally got on with its work and passed a series of laws known collectively as the Constitution of 1875. Nominally republican, the constitution could, with slight modification also operate under a monarchy.

---

2   The name refers to the municipality of Paris (*commune de Paris*).
3   The reasons that led to the break in the relations between the two sides and the ensuing fighting are well covered in John Merriman, *Massacre: The Life and Death of the Paris Commune* (New York: Basic Books, 2014), one of the most recent studies of the tragic event.
4   Paul-Marie de la Gorce, *The French Army: A Military-Political History* (New York: George Braziller, 1963), pp. 7-9; David B. Ralston, *The Army of the Republic* (Cambridge, MA: MIT Press, 1967), pp. 29-63.
5   Gordon Wright, *France in Modern Times* (New York: Norton, 1987), pp. 219-222.
6   Douglas Porch, *The March to the Marne: The French Army 1871-1914* (Cambridge: Cambridge University Press, 1981), p. 13; François-Christian Semur, *MacMahon* (Paris: Gawsewitch, 2005), ch. 20.

The constitution provided for a government consisting of a president and a bicameral legislature with the senate elected indirectly and the chamber of deputies elected directly by universal manhood suffrage. As head of state, the president enjoyed wide powers. He was commander-in-chief of the army and he had the right to select the prime minister, preside at cabinet meetings, dissolve the chamber of deputies with the support of the senate, order new elections, appoint ministers, initiate legislation and negotiate and sign treaties.[7]

In December 1875, the National Assembly, its work done, disbanded to make way for the new constitutional system. In the first elections the republicans won a substantial majority in the chamber of deputies and narrowly missed gaining control of the senate. After months of frustration MacMahon embarked on a controversial course in a bid to halt the growth of republicanism. On 16 May 1877, MacMahon, invoking his legal right as president, forced the moderate republican prime minister to resign and in his place chose a monarchist but the chamber refused to approve of him. Leaving it up to the public to resolve the dispute, MacMahon dissolved the chamber of deputies with the consent of the senate and scheduled new elections. He threw himself into the campaign in an effort to influence the voters but the new elections reaffirmed the sizeable republican majority in the chamber and he was forced to accept a republican cabinet much like the one he had dismissed earlier. There were calls from some impassioned high-ranking anti-republican officers for a military coup, but MacMahon had too much regard for the constitutional process to defy popular will and so he allowed the new government to do its work without interference.[8] The final blow came a year and a half later when senate elections brought a republican majority and rendered his position untenable. He resigned in January 1879 and was replaced by Jules Grévy, an able but colourless republican politician. Much as the leading officers in the army regretted MacMahon's departure, they recognized that it was their duty to cast aside their sentimental attachments and become loyal servants of the new regime.[9]

The crisis of 16 May, was a turning point in the history of modern France for it established the ascendancy of republicans and the domination of the legislature over the presidency. Beginning with Grévy, most of the president's powers fell into disuse and he became largely a ceremonial figure. The real authority lay with the prime minister and his cabinet, themselves accountable to a majority in the chamber of deputies, the dominant house.

Republican France did not possess a strongly rooted two-party system like the British but rather a host of small, loosely organized factions divided according to a principle such as clericalism or varying shades of republican thought. Since no one group was strong enough to command a majority in the chamber, cabinets could be formed only by putting together coalitions which were subject to collapse the moment one or more of the parties withdrew. Between 1875 and 1914 France had no fewer than 50 different cabinets. The rapid change of ministries made it difficult to tackle controversial problems and impossible to frame long-term plans. Still the political scene was not as chaotic as it seemed on the surface for often the new

---

7   For a brief account of the constitution see Charles Sowerwine, *France Since 1870* (New York: Palgrave, 2001), p. 31.
8   Porch, *March to the Marne*, pp.13-15. For a full account of MacMahon's presidency see Semur, *MacMahon*, chs. 21-24.
9   Ralston, *Army of the Republic*, p. 77.

cabinet contained the same politicians as the previous one and so would be unlikely to radically change the direction of policy.

Although the republicans had broken the back of the monarchists and were in firm control of the government, they were ever-mindful of a revival of Caesarism. For many it was not enough that under the law the minister of war administered as well as supervised the army. There was a lack of continuity as ministers of war changed frequently and some, given the office for political reasons, were content to fall into the comfortable routine of administrative work. It was felt that an additional safeguard was needed to steer army recruits in the right direction. As it was, conscription laws tied young men in the country to the army for a period of five years – longer in case of a war – during which their values were apt to be subverted by officers faithful to clericalism and monarchism. The only way to free French manhood from the alleged corrupting influence of reactionary officers, so the thinking ran, was to republicanize the military command.[10] Efforts to accomplish that goal never succeeded in the long run and only served to strain the relationship between army leaders and the state.

In the 1880s, an economic downturn, a financial scandal involving the president's son-in-law, and a series of weak and unstable governments, shook the public's faith in the new republic's institutions. Many on all sides of the political spectrum crystallized around General Georges Boulanger, viewing him as a strong man capable of lifting the country out of the doldrums and laying plans for a successful war of revenge against Germany. Highly ambitious, charismatic, and striking in appearance with his red hair and blond beard, Boulanger had been wounded in Italy in 1859 and again in the Franco-Prussian War, in addition to serving at various places in France's colonies. Although he professed to be a devout republican, earlier in his career he had regularly attended mass and was conservative in sentiment and practice. In 1886 he was appointed minister of war and used the office as a platform to build a personal following. He improved the living conditions and food of the ordinary soldier; won the admiration of businessmen by sending troops to control a strike; stood up to Bismarck and prohibited the heads of former reigning families from entering the army and navy and depriving those already in the service of their commands. When the ministry fell in 1887 he was assigned to an obscure military command but was later dismissed from the army for intriguing with conservative monarchists. His military career at an end, he was now free to campaign actively in politics, seeking to add to his reputation by making frequent public appearances and promising what each group desired. He reached the height of his popularity in 1889 when he gained a spectacular victory in a parliamentary by-election in Paris. Conditions were ripe for a *coup d'état*, but Boulanger wanted to gain power by legal means. In desperation the government circulated rumours of his imminent arrest for supposedly conspiring against the state and that he would shortly be put on trial before the senate. Boulanger lost his nerve and fled across the border to Brussels where two years later he shot himself in the head on the grave of his mistress. It is important to note that the army had remained out of the picture and, as Boulanger knew all along, would not help him. In fact, most members of the general staff despised him.[11]

The Republic had survived the threat from Boulanger but only through sheer luck. Much of the credit was owed to the pro-monarchical military establishment which had refused to rally

---

10 Porch, *March to the Marne*, pp. 46-49.
11 De la Gorce, *French Army*, p. 18.

behind Boulanger, maintaining the army's traditional political neutrality despite attempts to have its top commander replaced in favour of republican sympathizers. Breathing a sigh of relief, republican politicians allowed the army a high degree of autonomy within its sphere of competence. The relationship between the two institutions rested on the assumption that politicians would not meddle in strictly military affairs and the soldiers, as always, would keep out of politics. The unwritten rule was shattered when a far greater danger than Boulanger broke out, a sorry event that embittered and divided French opinion for years and nearly destroyed the republic.

It began in 1894 when Captain Alfred Dreyfus, a French general staff officer of Jewish descent, was convicted by a military court of delivering classified information to a foreign power, presumably Germany. As punishment he was sentenced to life imprisonment on Devil's Island, a notorious penal colony off French Guiana in South America. Almost two years later Colonel Georges Picquart, the new head of Intelligence, launched his own investigation which revealed that Dreyfus had been convicted on forged evidence and that the real culprit was a certain Major Ferdinand Esterhazy, a dubious character known to have significant gambling debts. When he reported his findings to his superiors they refused to reopen the case, evidently to protect the army's prestige and maintain the high esteem in which it was held by the French people. When Picquart insisted, he was transferred to a post in Algeria. Before leaving he passed his evidence to a sympathetic high ranking member of the senate who lobbied to have the matter investigated further.

Once the issue entered public print it assumed national proportions with newspapers ranging themselves on one side or the other. Celebrated novelist Emile Zola wrote a long article which he released to the press under the heading *"J'accuse."* In it he castigated the highest levels of the French Army for obstruction of justice and anti-Semitism and for wrongly convicting to life imprisonment a soldier they knew was innocent. The resulting uproar over the Dreyfus affair sometimes took the form of open clashes in the streets. As a rule, the defenders of Dreyfus were republicans whereas those in the opposite camp were anti-republicans – that is, monarchist, clericalists, army officers – and anti-Semites. In a new trial in 1899 the judges excluded evidence in Dreyfus' favour and again found him guilty, but the President of France, Paul Loubet, pardoned him ten days later. Eventually Dreyfus was completely exonerated and reinstated in the army with the rank of major.[12]

The impact of the Dreyfus affair was felt immediately on the political life of the country. For one thing it united a loose gathering of progressive republicans into an organized body known as Radical Socialists, or Radicals as they preferred to be called, the first formal party in France. The Radicals became a dominating force in French politics from 1902 until the outbreak of the First World War and were usually an indispensable part of every coalition government. They were a grouping of the middle left and liked to think of themselves as the party of the republic. They drew their support from the lower middle class, small independent businessmen, farmers and minor civil servants. Party doctrine committed them to anti-clericalism, anti-militarism and anti-Caesarism, while championing egalitarianism, private enterprise and private property. Although the Radicals abhorred the principles of Marxism, they did not hesitate to join hands with the extreme left to thwart a perceived right-wing threat to the republic.

---

12   Ruth Harris, *Dreyfus* (New York: Henry Holt, 2010), is a good recent account of this episode.

In the elections of 1902, the Radicals and the socialists[13] gained the greatest number of seats in the chamber. The Radicals' popularity stemmed from their ability to convince many voters that they had forestalled a clericalist-monarchist plot to establish an authoritarian regime and that they must be kept in office to preserve the democratic institutions of the republic. They wasted no time in striking against ecclesiastical power in collaboration with the socialists who were no less antagonistic towards the church. A wave of anti-clerical legislation followed, culminating in the separation of church and state in 1905.

Simultaneously the reformers opened a campaign to restrict the army's freedom and purge it of officers deemed disloyal to the republic – which meant those attending mass or suspected of royalist sympathies. Left to implement this assignment was the zealous and dedicated Minister of War, General Louis André, whose strongest claim to the post was his known attachment to republicanism and anti-clericalism – practically unique among high ranking officers in the army. André's first priority was to republicanize the general staff and officer corps. To that end he altered the system of promotion, transferring it from military authorities to the ministry of war. Henceforth political rather than military qualifications would be the criteria in deciding which officers would be promoted. The consequences of such action was that a number of top generals, including the chief of the general staff, resigned rather than have subordinates of dubious qualification imposed on them by the Minister of War. Their replacements were either mediocre or inexperienced and the only thing in their favour was their absolute loyalty to the republic. Ideology also determined the officers who would staff the military schools to instill cadets with the desired values.[14] André encouraged officers to spy on each other and employed Freemasons to operate an intelligence service. He kept a card file indicating which officers went to church, sent their children to Catholic schools, or freely expressed anti-republican views. André's sordid system was eventually exposed and produced such an outcry in parliament and the press that he was forced to resign.[15]

André's efforts towards reshaping the general staff and officer corps had broken the monarchial monopoly but it had come at a high cost. The prestige of the army declined, discipline grew lax, the morale of the officers in regiments fell sharply, applications for officer training schools decreased and many who were discriminated against resigned their commission or retired. The blows against the army continued after André left office with a further reduction in the term of military service as perhaps the most damaging in the long run. A law in 1889 had lowered national service from five to three years and reduced the loopholes that had permitted exemptions. To limit the time conscripts would be under the authority of professional officers, new legislation in 1905 again lowered the length of service to two years with no exemptions. The army shrank from 615, 000 men to 540,000.[16] The decline in the size of the army and the reduction in the period of active training, together with the relaxation of the disciplinary code, was coming at a time when Germany was becoming more menacing than ever.

---

13 The socialists were divided and remained so until 1905, enjoying a brief period of unity until the Great War.
14 Porch, *March to the Marne*, pp. 76-80. For a recent biography of André see Serge Doessant, *Le general André* (Paris: Editions Glyphe, 2009).
15 Ralston, *Army of the Republic*, pp. 269-80; Doessant, *André*, chs 19 and 20.
16 Alistair Horne, *The Price of Glory*, (New York: Harper Colophon, 1967), p. 9.

France ended its long period of diplomatic isolation in 1891 when it signed a friendly entente with Russia in which the two nations essentially agree to work to maintain the peace of Europe. The new friendship was confirmed three years later by a defensive pact. The French position was further strengthened in 1904 by a rapprochement with Great Britain, hitherto second only to Germany as a serious rival. Under the terms of the Entente Cordiale the two states resolved all outstanding colonial disputes. The Entente Cordiale was not a defensive alliance and would not have assumed the character of one if Germany had conducted itself with more restraint. With the encouragement of Paris, Britain and Russia ended their long-standing mutual antagonism and concluded an entente which resolved most of their colonial differences and opened the door for wider cooperation. Thus by 1907 the British drift into the Franco-Russian camp created the cornered relationship known as the Triple Entente, which was now ranged against the Triple Alliance of Germany, Austria-Hungary and Italy.

From 1905 on the European scene was marred by a series of crises, each of which then seemed highly threatening. Although in each instance a temporary solution was found and major warfare avoided, these crises tended to solidify the respective alliance systems and widen the gulf separating them. It all but ensured that any serious dispute among members of the two rival groups that unraveled would break out into a general war.

The French seemed oblivious to what was happening outside their country. The pervasive spirit of anti-militarism had given rise to pacifism which was fed by a recently united Socialist party and militant trade unions. The Radicals returned to power stronger than ever in the general elections of 1906 but their alliance with the increasingly rigid Socialists collapsed and they were driven to collaborate with moderate groups. French cabinets had to grapple with a host of internal, new and controversial problems during the period between 1906 and mid-1911 and consequently adopted a policy of diplomatic *laissez-faire*.[17] But German sabre-rattling caused Paris to refocus its attention on foreign affairs. On 1 July 1911, the Germans dispatched the gunboat *Panther* to the port of Agadir as a clumsy attempt to protest France's intention to convert Morocco into a protectorate. Berlin's action in precipitating a crisis over Morocco caught the newly formed French government by surprise.[18] The ministry was headed by Joseph Caillaux, the 48-year-old Radical leader. Born into a wealthy family whose patriarch was a former conservative politician, Caillaux excelled at his studies and, upon obtaining a law degree, joined the finance ministry as deputy inspector. Elected to the chamber of deputies he established a reputation as a financial expert and served as minister of finance in two administrations before becoming prime minister. His untiring energy, aggressiveness, and shrew financial mind gained him nation-wide renown and independence of behavior which he was sometimes inclined to push too far. An arrogant and unprincipled pragmatist, he pursued a course that was not always consistent with Radical tradition. He was regarded by his contemporaries with varying admiration and dislike but no one disputed his immense influence in politics.[19]

In seeking to defuse the Moroccan crisis, Caillaux adopted a conciliatory attitude towards Germany. He thought that in return for modest concessions it was possible to resolve all

---

17 D.W. Brogan, *The Development of Modern France* (London: Hamish Hamilton, 1967), p. 443.
18 John F.V. Keiger, *France and the Origins of the First World War* (London: Macmillan, 1983), p. 35.
19 On Joseph Caillaux see Dominique Jamet, *La Chute du President Caillaux* (Paris: Pygmalion, 2013); Enno Franzius, *Caillaux: Statesman of Peace* (Stanford: Stanford University Press, 1976); Jean-Claude Allain , *Joseph Caillaux* , 2 Vols. (Paris: Imprimerie Nationale, 1978, 1981).

differences with Germany but he was opposed by a few hardliners in the cabinet, including the foreign minister. As a result Caillaux conducted secret negotiations behind the backs of the cabinet ministers and president, and in November 1911 reached a settlement with the Germans, although it did not go as far as he would have liked. In return for a free hand in Morocco, Paris ceded a large slice of the French Congo to Germany. If Caillaux viewed this as the first step towards better relations with Germany, he misjudged the mood of his countrymen. Fierce attacks in the press and chamber of deputies for mishandling negotiations brought down his government in January 1912.

Germany's bullying tactics had shaken the French public's complacency and produced a wave of anti-German feeling across the country. It included not only ordinary citizens and moderate politicians but a large segment of Radicals and a few independent socialists. In reaction to the new attitude, the country turned to Raymond Poincaré, an intensely patriotic conservative republican, to succeed Caillaux. Originally from Lorraine and a lawyer by training, Poincaré, was elected to the chamber of deputies at the age of 27 and between 1887 and 1906 held ministries in education (twice) and finance. Outwardly cold, widely respected for his integrity, relentless in pursuit of his goals and with an infinite capacity for hard work, he became the symbol and chief spokesman of the nationalist revival between 1911 and 1914. After a year he decided to forgo the premiership and run for the office of president which he won by a narrow margin.[20]

For Poincaré the return of Alsace-Lorraine to France was an article of faith but there is no evidence that he was pushing for an armed showdown with Germany. Rather it is likely he believed that war would come sooner or later and that, for France to have a chance to win, it required strengthening ties with its allies and building up its army. Poincaré was closely involved with foreign affairs and he played a key role in breathing new life in the faltering alliance with Russia. While Paris promised to lend Russia more diplomatic support, it sought more precise commitments from London. Although unable to extract a promise from the British to provide military assistance in case of a European war, Paris did reach an agreement with them to delineate their mutual naval responsibility.

The growing maritime strength of Germany had driven the British Admiralty to propose concentrating most of the Royal Navy in home waters to guard against the threat to the country's security. However such a move would imperil British communications through the Mediterranean in the event of war against the Triple Alliance. It was seen that the best solution to keep the Mediterranean secure without weakening the fleet at home was to work out an arrangement with the French.

Prior to 1914, the centerpiece of the French government's naval strategy was to maintain superiority in the Mediterranean in order to keep open the ties with its colonies in North Africa. Naval talks began in earnest in the middle of 1912 and led to a convention on 10 February 1913. While the British assumed responsibility for the defence of the lower and upper English Channel, the Mediterranean was divided into an eastern and western basin with operational zones assigned to each navy. Should circumstances require it, the remaining British ships in the Mediterranean would join the French fleet and act under the orders of the French naval commander. The naval convention was vague on details and considered provisional and

---

20 On Raymond Poincaré, see J.F.V. Keiger, *Raymond Poincaré* (Cambridge: Cambridge University Press, 1997); Gordon Wright, *Raymond Poincaré and the French Presidency* (New York: Octagon, 1967); and François Roth, *Raymond Poincaré* (Paris: Fayard, 2000).

non-binding.[21] The British wanted to avoid a formal commitment so the terms did not require the two governments to decide whether or not to come to the aid of the other in case of an unprovoked attack by another power. The British may not have felt they incurred any obligation to assist their ally in case of war but the French read the matter differently. Britain's defence of the North Sea in the absence of the French fleet was an implicit obligation to help France against a naval attack in a future war with Germany.[22] Otherwise, as Poincaré told Lord Bertie, the British ambassador in Paris, there would have been no point to engage in naval talks and France would simply have kept "their best ships to face Germany in the Channel."[23]

A major tenant of Poincaré's domestic policy since 1912 was to rescue the army out of the abyss it had fallen and restore it as the focal point of French pride. The men around Poincaré, especially the successive war ministers, pushed hard to introduce reforms. The army was depoliticized which improved morale and efficiency in the officer corps; discipline was strengthened; more money was made available to buy weapons; and a law was passed keeping conscripts in service for three years instead of two in order to offset the disparity in numbers between the French and German troops. The old system in which the war ministry exercised tight control over the army to protect against a coup was changed with much of the authority turned over to the general staff. Henceforth the general staff would control all aspects of the army as well as determine military policy and its head was answerable only to the government through the war minister. Technically the war minister did not renounce his supervisory powers over the army but, with only politicians occupying the office, it is difficult to see how any of them would have dared overrule the chief of the general staff. In short as long as the government had the legal authority over the army in practice, it recognized that too much interference in technical matters would hamper the work of the general staff and damage national interest. The accommodation between civil and military leaders would prove durable and effective during the remainder of the pre-war era.

The late renaissance obviously had a tonic effect on the French army but not to the extent of significantly narrowing the gap between it and its Teutonic rival. The acquisition of big guns heavier than the more mobile and fast-firing 75mm – regarded by many as an all-purpose artillery piece – was hampered by bureaucratic complacency, ministerial instability and an absence of funds. A good deal of dead wood (from the anti-military period) remained among army commanders and officers on the general staff. The relentless Radical assault on the army in the aftermath of the Dreyfus Affair had not only caused many officers to resign but, too often, rendered those that remained timid and indecisive. The sad state of the high command naturally undermined the efficiency of the army. Training was poor, especially in reserve units; reports evaluating army officers were compiled haphazardly and tended to skirt over their deficiencies; and military inspections and manoeuvres were held infrequently. But nothing was more destructive than the army's doctrine of warfare, that is, if it can be so dignified.

---

21 Paul G. Halpern, *The Mediterranean Naval Situation 1908-1914* (Cambridge,: Harvard University Press, 1971), pp. 107-09.
22 Arthur J. Marder, *From the Dreadnought to Scapa Flow*, Vol. 1 (London: Oxford University Press), pp. 304–09.
23 Great Britain, Foreign Office, *British Documents on the Origins of the War 1898-1914*, ed. by George P. Gooch and Harold Temperley, Vol. 10, pt. 2 ((London: HMSO, 1938), p. 606.

The important thing to remember about the army's military doctrine is that it sprang from mid-level officers and moved upwards rather than filtered down from the high command. Part of the problem lay with the manner in which the military system was structured. Legislation during the first decades of the republic allowed the government to control the army and its military planning. The Superior Council of War (*Conseil supérieur de la guerre*), set up in 1872 and reorganized in 1888 to widen its remit, was under the chairmanship of the president and included politicians and senior generals. The role of the generals was to voice army concerns and to provide the government with technical military advice on such issues as mobilization, concentration, training and defence.[24] Because the politicians worried about a military coup, they refused to appoint a commander-in-chief of the army during peacetime. Instead they selected a general as chief of staff and another to sit on the Superior Council of War as its vice-president. The former ran the day to day activities of the army in close concert with the minister of war while the latter was the designated commander of French forces in case of war. The arrangement allowed the minister of war to maintain control over the army but at the expense of its efficiency, especially as the two high-ranking military officials, instead of cooperating, worked independently of one another.

Early French military analysts seeking to draw lessons from the war of 1870-71 ascribed their county's defeat to the adoption of a defensive-minded attitude against an enemy that had placed its reliance on an offensive strategy. Thus was born the gospel of attack under all circumstances, known as *offensive à l'outrance*, with emphasis laid on the psychological impact of fearless infantry assaults. Victory was reserved for an army which, by sheer dint of will to conquer, seized the initiative and opened with a vigorous offensive without due concern for strategic or tactical principles. The theory of the offensive gained wide currency in the army, particularly among junior staff officers. The new school found a high priest in Colonel Louis Loyzeau de Grandmaison, chief of the operations branch of the general staff, whose views are summed up in the following excerpt: "In the offensive, imprudence is the best of assurances … Let us go even to excess and that perhaps will not be far enough… For the attack only two things are necessary: to know where the enemy is and to decide what to do. What the enemy intends to do is of no consequence."[25]

The advantage of morale in battle was seen to be unaffected by the improvement in firearms. "Firepower does not weaken the offensive spirit," General Bazaine-Hayter, a corps commander wrote in 1906. "Never forget that a defensive battle will seldom bring victory. However powerful weapons become, the victory will go to the offensive which stimulates moral force, disconcerts the enemy and deprives him of his freedom of action."[26] If nothing else, common sense should have dictated that the defence, manned by entrenched soldiers armed with magazine rifles and backed by machine guns, would enjoy a clear advantage.

The cult of the offensive triumphed because there was no direction from above. A general staff that had been beaten down and emasculated, with its members, or at least some of them, chosen on the basis of political ideology and devoid of the requisite skills and training, simply lacked the confidence to formulate a coherent strategy. The lack of direction and timidity of the

---

24 Elizabeth Greenhalgh, *The French Army and the First World War* (Cambridge: Cambridge University Press, 2014), pp. 10-11.
25 Cited in Horne, *Price of Glory*, p. 12.
26 Cited in Porch, *March to the Marne*, p. 226.

high command, more than anything else, allowed the doctrine of the offensive to fill the army's doctrinal vacuum.

The one person who represented a threat to the fervour of the offensive was General Victor Michel, vice-president of the Superior Council of War and designate commander-in-chief in case of war. Michel anticipated the Schlieffen Plan, reasoning that the Germans would invade France by wheeling through Belgium west of the Meuse rather than risk attacking its formidable defensive positions in the south. He proposed to leave a covering force facing Alsace-Lorraine and concentrate the bulk of his regular troops, bolstered by reserves along the Franco-Belgian border, and await the enemy. In this way, the French army would be deployed to stop the German sweep through Belgium and, once the main axis of the assault had been identified, launch a counterattack.

Michel's new strategic plan aroused the fierce opposition of Loyzeau de Grandmaison and his disciples who argued that wars were not won by adopting a defensive strategy. The general staff never seriously considered his proposals and the Superior Council unanimously voted them down in July 1911.[27] Attacked from all sides, Michel's position became untenable when he lost the confidence of Adolphe Messimy, the war minister. Messimy began his career as a soldier, attending the military academy (école de guerre) at Saint-Cyr and after graduation became a line officer. His promising military career ended when he resigned from his post as captain in 1899 in protest at the army's refusal to reopen the Dreyfus case. After a brief stint as a journalist he turned to politics and was elected to the chamber of deputies in 1902 as a Radical Socialist. He became minister of the colonies in 1911 and in the same year was appointed minister of war in the government of Joseph Caillaux.

Messimy explained in his memoirs that he knew Michel only by reputation before he held several interviews with him between 2 and 10 July 1911. To his dismay, he found Michel hesitant, ill-informed and seemingly bewildered at the prospect of coping with the crushing burdens that might fall on his shoulders at any moment. Any lingering doubts Messimy may have entertained disappeared after he consulted with the nation's senior generals, all of whom considered Michel unfit for command and one went so far as to say that he was a "national danger."[28] Messimy's unequivocal endorsement of the army's faith in the doctrine of the offensive may also have been a factor in his decision to sack Michel. Messimy chose in his place General Joseph Joffre, who was relatively unknown even within the army.

Joffre was 59-years-old and possessed a less than spectacular record when he assumed command of the French army on 28 July 1911. Son of a village cooper, he attended the école polytechnique and, although an indifferent student, earned a commission as an engineer. Widowed at a young age, he carried out a variety of assignments in the colonies with credit, demonstrating organizational skills and a capacity to handle responsibility. He returned to France in 1900 and, after commanding first a division then a corps, became director of engineers. He moved on in 1910 and served as director of support services which gained him a seat on the Superior Council of War. Joffre was a trained and competent engineer, an expert on the operation of the French railway system and understood the logistical requirements of

---

27 Ralston, *Army of the Republic*, p. 330; Jan K. Tanenbaum, *General Maurice Sarrail 1856-1929* (Chapel Hill: University of North Carolina Press, 1974), pp. 26-27; Robert A. Doughty, *Pyrrhic Victory: French Strategy and Operations in the Great War* (Cambridge: Harvard University Press, 2005), pp. 13-14.
28 Adolphe Messimy, *Mes Souvenirs* (Paris: Plon, 1937), pp. 74-75.

the army. The same could not be said about his qualification as a strategist and tactician for he had not attended the *école de guerre*. In addition he lacked general staff training and had never commanded an army.[29] Such limited command experience normally would have ruled out anyone aspiring to reach the very top rung of the French army and, needless to say, his appointment came as a surprise. However after Joffre's main rivals were eliminated for one reason or another, Messimy found him acceptable because he possessed proven organizational ability, was free of supposedly embarrassing religious and political affiliations and echoed the same strong conviction of the offensive school of military theorists.

The departure of Michel opened the way for Messimy to make radical adjustments in the high command. The most far reaching change was the merging of the functions of the commander designate and chief of the general staff in one person. Two years later another reform was introduced when a report by a different minister of war led to the establishment of guidelines defining the relationship between political and military leaders in wartime. For our purpose the relevant part of the regulations were spelled out in the opening paragraph:

> The government, which has responsibility for the vital interests of the country alone has the authority to fix the political objective of a war. If the struggle extends to several frontiers, it designates the principal adversary against which the greater part of the national forces should be directed. It consequently distributes the means of action and all types of resources and places them entirely at the disposition of the generals charged with being commander-in-chief of the various theaters of operations.[30]

The government in fixing its arrangement with the army maintained civilian supremacy but refrained from interfering in field operations. Specifically, it reserved for itself the right to lay down political objectives and, while envisaging a multi-theatre war, selected the commanders for the various fronts. It committed itself to furnish the men, supplies and equipment required to attain objectives, while leaving it up to the commanders to devise strategy and control operations.[31] What the government failed to understand is that by granting the generals unfettered strategic control over operations, it was forfeiting its power to arbitrate the flow of resources between the fronts.

Chief among Joffre's duties in preparing the French army for war, seen as inevitable by many of his countrymen given Germany's continued aggressive behavior, was to replace Michel's discredited war plan. Joffre initially favoured invading Germany through Belgium where the flat terrain would facilitate his advance. But this scheme was ruled out because it would have violated Belgian neutrality and damaged, perhaps irreparably, relations with Britain which had a treaty with Belgium guaranteeing its territorial integrity. Instead Joffre adopted an offensive blueprint known as Plan XVII, the last in a long line of French strategic proposals. The idea was to send four French armies, ranged along the Franco-German frontier, into Alsace and Lorraine, passing on either side of the German fortress of Metz. Once a breakthrough had been achieved and the lost provinces regained, no other objectives were stipulated though French commanders were told to exploit what opportunities presented themselves. In finalizing

---

29 Doughty, *Pyrrhic Victory*, p. 15; Greenhalgh, *French Army*, p. 15.
30 Cited in Doughty, *Pyrrhic Victory*, p. 44.
31 Ralston, *Army of the Republic*, p. 331.

offensive plans, the French general staff made two major miscalculations: The first did not take into account the difficulty of mounting an offensive across the rugged terrain of eastern France. The other was the failure to take adequate measures to counter the German thrust through Belgium. The French were aware of the general outline of the Schlieffen Plan and assumed that the German incursion into a Belgium was merely a feint as they lacked the manpower to go beyond the Meuse.[32]

Plan XVII was formally accepted by the government in 1913 though Joffre continued to make modifications until the summer of 1914. Once everything was in place the vagaries of politics threatened to rob Joffre of the supreme moment of his career.

The decline in nationalist fervour was evident in the general elections in the spring of 1914 when the Radicals captured the greatest number of seats in the chamber of deputies. Poincaré refused to call upon Caillaux, who had campaigned against the three-year-law the previous year, to head the new ministry. Given the predominance of the left in the chamber, it was not easy for the President to find someone who would preserve the law and attract the necessary political backing.[33] He turned to René Viviani, an independent socialist, who succeeded on his second attempt to form a government with the collaboration of a sizeable number of Radicals. The price demanded for their support was the removal of Joffre in favour of General Maurice Sarrail who was currently in charge of the VI Corps. Sarrail was the darling of the left for his known adherence to socialist principles, a rarity among the senior officers dominating the French army. With the assent of the Prime Minister, Messimy, back at rue Saint-Dominique (the Ministry of War) for a second time, agreed in July to make a change in the leadership of the French army and to install Sarrail as the new commander in the following autumn. But he ran out of time before he could initiate the change. What prevented Joffre's removal from command was the outbreak of the Great War, triggered by events in the Balkans.[34]

32 Doughty, *Pyrrhic Victory*, pp. 36-43; Greenhalgh, *French Army*, pp. 19-21.
33 Keiger, *Raymond Poincaré*, pp. 162-63.
34 Tannenbaum, *Maurice Sarrail*, pp. 34-35.

2

The Search for an Alternate Theatre of War

The crisis that broke out in the summer of 1914 was not much different from some of the ones during the past decade. It sprang when a young Serbian nationalist assassinated the Archduke Francis Ferdinand, presumptive heir to the Austrian throne, and his wife while they were on a visit to Sarajevo on 28 June 1914. Normally the act, as heinous as it was, would not have been seen as sufficient to provoke a general war. There had been several such assassinations in the past, not to mention that Francis Ferdinand was not a popular figure back home. The only difference this time was that none of the powers backed down.

Few outside the government in France paid much attention to the unfolding drama. The Balkans were far away and there was every reason to believe that diplomacy would resolve this dilemma as it had with the others in the past. Actually there was more interest in a sensational murder at home than with the assassination of the Archduke. For nine days beginning on 20 July the country was riveted on the trial of Henriette Caillaux, wife of the former prime minister. On 16 March 1914, Mme Caillaiux shot and killed the editor of *Le Figaro*, Gaston Calmette, for publishing certain embarrassing letters which had passed between herself and her future husband while he was still married to his first wife. On 28 July an all-male jury acquitted her on grounds that she had acted "under temporary uncontrolled passion."[1] On the same day the Austrian government declared war on Serbia, setting in motion the events that would produce one of the great catastrophes in world history. On 31 July Germany declared war on Russia and, with a wider conflict suddenly looming, the French government ordered the mobilization of the army the next day. Germany took the decision out of the hands of Paris by declaring war on France on 3 August. Britain joined its partners on 4 August when German troops invaded Belgium.

Despite the turbulent situation in Europe over the last decade, the outbreak of war came as a shock to the French people. In some of the cities nationalist groups gathered in support of the conflict, viewing it as an opportunity to regain Alsace and Lorraine but they constituted only a small minority of the general public. France's interest in colonial expansion since the last quarter

---

1   For further details of the episode see Peter Shankland, *Death of an Editor: The Caillaux Trial* (London: William Kimber, 1981); and Edward Berenson, *The Trial of Madame Caillaux* (Berkeley: University of California Press, 1992).

of the nineteenth century had absorbed the attention of most of its citizens. They had almost forgotten the nature of armed conflict, imagining that this phenomenon belonged to the past. As late as the summer of 1914 the French socialists, a potent political force, who were committed to pacifism, urged workers not to take up arms in the event that the country was drawn into a capitalistic war. If the French had not been reconciled to the loss of Alsace-Lorraine they thought less and less of a recovery by force. In truth they could hardly welcome a showdown with Germany which had far surpassed their country in population and industrial strength.

Yet the mood in the country changed overnight and the spirit of pacifism disappeared. It was evident that nationalism trumped all other considerations. The social and political divisions that had characterized the Third Republic since practically its inception disappeared suddenly, as if a fairy godmother had waved a magic wand. The overwhelming majority of French people came together and backed the war effort. Even the socialist and trade union leaders, instead of protesting, responded approvingly of the call to arms. There were no strikes or anti-war demonstrations; crowds gathered at the rail stations to cheer the soldiers about to leave for the front; and volunteers flooded the recruiting centers in their eagerness to defend the homeland. The most dominant members of the cabinet had anticipated that the number of draftees refusing to report to duty might reach as high as 15 percent and they were ecstatic when it turned out to be a mere 1.5 percent.

Poincaré recognized that the country was about to be sorely tested in the coming weeks and that only by mobilizing all its people could it hope to survive. On 4 August he drafted a speech and made a dramatic plea for a *union sacrée*, whereby the political parties would end partisan strife and join hands in a fraternal alliance of all Frenchmen.[2] Under the constitution the President was forbidden from addressing the legislature directly so his message was read separately to the senate and to the chamber of deputies.[3] The unprecedented show of unity was immediate. In the chamber lifelong enemies shook hands or embraced and in passionate, emotional speeches vowed to fight together until victory was achieved. There were shouts of "*Vive la France*" and "*Vivre la République*." Poincaré himself arranged a truce with the choleric Georges Clemenceau, his most severe critic inside and outside the chamber.[4] It was not easy to placate Clemenceau and before long the two men were at loggerheads again.

On the afternoon of 4 August, the chamber concluded its business and ratified the president's decree issued two days earlier that a state of siege existed – which he was empowered by law to declare in the face of an imminent peril – and adjourned until the next regular session scheduled for 22 December 1914, leaving the cabinet to govern as a quasi-dictatorship.[5] The legislators had accepted the general assumption that a strong government, unhampered by parliamentary process, was the only effective way to run the war which was expected to be over in a few months or perhaps only weeks. They agreed to maintain the state of emergency in France for the duration of the war or until it was revoked by a decree of the president, acting on the

---

2   Keiger, *Raymond Poincaré*, pp. 187-89; Roth, *Raymond Poincaré*, pp. 292-93.
3   Keiger, *Raymond Poincaré*, pp. 187-88.
4   Poincaré, Notes journalières, 6 August 1914. The incident is not reported in his published memoirs.
5   Jean Marie Mayer, *La vie politique sous la Troisième Republique* (Paris: Seuil, 1984), pp. 236-37; Keiger, *Raymond Poincaré*, p. 201.

recommendation of the cabinet.⁶ In abdicating its authority, the chamber expected the ministry to oversee the activities of the army high command.

As president prior to the war, Poincaré had operated in a way that was not much different from his predecessors after 1879. But realizing that under the circumstances normal procedures were apt to fly in the face of common sense when quick action and centralized authority were vital, he altered the spirit of president-cabinet relations.⁷ A brilliant lawyer he knew how far he could go in invoking the full powers of his office as laid down by the constitution. There were instances at the start of the war when he acted on his own but all of his edicts had to be countersigned by the cabinet. As a rule his efforts were directed at coordinating the war effort and guiding and influencing cabinet action. He resisted calls from his supporters to exceed the limits of his constitutional jurisdiction and become an all-powerful war-time leader. He was a rare politician who placed the county's interest above everything else and was instrumental in maintaining French morale and the spirit of national unity.

A high priority for Poincaré during the early days of the war was to put in place a ministry to represent all the major parties to give effect to his theme of a *union sacrée*.⁸ On the surface Poincaré's choice to retain Viviani to head the wartime ministry would appear to be a peculiar one. It is true that Viviani was congenial, a moderate member of the left and a superb orator, but on the debit side he tended to fall apart under pressure and lacked strength of character, conviction and experience in administration with the result that he had to place too much reliance on his colleagues for guidance.⁹ Poincaré evidently did not consider Viviani's mediocrity a political liability. In the first place he would be able to dominate the prime minister and through him have more influence in the cabinet's decision-making process. Then too it was expected that Viviani would excite no jealousy under which rival ambitions might unite, thus he could always depend on a working majority in the chamber.

Viviani's broadened ministry excluded the conservative right but found a place for the Socialist party. The president was able to influence the selection of a number of cabinet officers but Viviani, in one of his rare instances of unwavering conviction, overruled his proposal to add two conservatives.¹⁰ All in all the cabinet consisted of a remarkable collection of personalities.

At the age of 52 and prominent on the national political scene in recent years, Aristide Briand accepted the call to head the portfolio of justice. As a young lawyer, he was ardently anti-clerical, championed labour rights and syndicalism, and in 1902 was elected to the chamber as a socialist deputy. He first attracted attention by his skillful handling of the law for the separation of church and state. Thereafter his rise was rapid and, as he moved upward, he drifted increasingly to the centre. He held several ministerial posts and before the war had served as prime minister on four occasions, beginning in 1909-10, during which he broke up a railway strike by the novel expedient of conscripting the workers into the army. Briand was not a strict doctrinaire after his break with the extreme left, refusing to identify with any political group but maintaining friends

---

6   France, assemblée nationale, *Journal officiel de la republique française* (Paris, 1915), 8 August 1914, p. 7126.
7   Wright, *Raymond Poincaré*, p. 142.
8   Wright, *Raymond Poincaré*, p. 144.
9   As far as I know, the only biography of Viviani in print is Jean-Marc Valentin, *René Viviani 1863-1925* (Limoges: Pulim, 2013) and frankly on the period of his premiership it is of little value.
10 Wright, *Raymond Poincaré*, p. 146.

and connections in all camps. His dialectic power, flexibility, intuition and ambition, combined with his thorough understanding of politics and diplomacy, allowed him to move in and out of the prime minister's office on ten separate occasions, a distinction unmatched by any politician in the history of democratic France.[11]

Adolphe Messimy who had served as minister of war in the first Viviani administration was sacrificed in favour of Alexandre Millerand. A moderate socialist for much of his career, Millerand passed into the nationalist camp when he held the same post in Poincaré's cabinet in 1912-13. An able politician and administrator, he strongly supported the three-year service law and worked hard to restore the prestige and morale of the army and provide it with the necessary armaments for the coming war. During his tenure in the second Viviani ministry he allowed the high command to function without close civilian supervision. He was content to concentrate on the administrative side of his office and leave the generals to formulate strategy and manage operations. He had absolute faith in Joffre and often acted as a buffer between him and the government. He has been harshly criticized by historians, with justification, for allowing himself to be reduced to a mere mouthpiece for Grand Quarter Général (French Army Headquarters).[12]

Théophile Delcassé returned to the ministry of foreign affairs, a post he had held at one time for seven consecutive years (1898-1905) in five different administrations. An excellent manager of men, shrewd and calculating, Delcassé had achieved amazing success in strengthening France's international position and restoring the balance of power in Europe. In 1914, however, the 62-year-old Delcassé was in the twilight of his political career. As a central figure in French politics for more than twenty years, the strain of his burdensome responsibilities had sapped his vitality and spirit. The clearness of vision and sense of dexterity which had been so conspicuous in his earlier diplomatic career were no longer apparent. Although Delcassé's last tenure in office was a failure, he was one of the most outstanding statesmen in the Third Republic.[13]

The new cabinet was well received by the general public, not surprising in view of the depth of its talent. The incoming members for the most part had served in previous administrations and quickly found their place in the department they headed. Poincaré met informally with key members of the government singly or as a group but details of what transpired were not recorded, not even in his daily journal. In fact, the same veil of secrecy characterized cabinet meetings for no minutes were taken and comparatively few memoranda were circulated. Moreover, there was no prepared agenda or order of business.

The cabinet faced immense responsibilities, not the least of which was management of the higher direction of the war. Despite the crises that had brought Europe to the edge of war on several occasions prior to August 1914, no serious thought had been given to devise a supreme command structure adapted to cabinet government to coordinate or reconcile opposing views on

---

11   For details of Briand prior to the war see Bernard Oudin, *Aristide Briand* (Paris: Perrin, 2004), chs 1-8; Georges Suarez, *Briand*, Vols. 1 and 2 (Paris: Plon, 1939) and Gérard Unger, *Aristide Briand* (Paris: Fayard, 2005), chs. 1 and 2.
12   On Millerand before his appointment in 1914 as minister of war see Marjorie M. Farrar, *Principled Pragmatist: The Political Career of Alexandre Millerand* (Oxford: Berg, 1991), chs. 1-6; and Jean-Louis Rizzo, *Alexandre Millerand* (Paris: L'Harmattan, 2013), chs 1-8.
13   Louis Claeys, *Delcassé* (Pamiers: Acala, 2001), chs. 1-13; Charles Zorgbibe, Delcassé, (Paris: Editions Olbia, 2001), chs. 1-3; and Charles W. Porter, *The Career of Théophile Delcassé* (Philadelphia: University of Pennsylvania Press, 1936), chs 1-5, are good accounts of Delcassé's pre-war life and career.

strategy. The old *Conseil supérieur de la guerre* had been founded as an advisory and consultative body. Its main function, as we have noted, was to assist in preparing for war. But this was a peace-time organization, not geared to war conditions, and after the outbreak of hostilities it was allowed to lapse.[14] Thus until the creation of the *Section d'études de la défence nationale* in August 1915, there was no body to coordinate grand strategy with political aims.

At least the relationship between the government and the high command had been established a day before the war broke out. The arrangement, as can be seen, was similar to the one laid down the previous year:

> The political direction of the war properly belongs to the government. The conduct of operations is the exclusive domain of the commander-in- chief. Furthermore, the state of siege confers upon the chief of the army the most extensive powers over all the territory, this authority in the zone of the armies being delegated *ipso facto* to the general in chief.[15]

The intent, as always, was to maintain civilian supremacy over the military without impinging on the commander-in-chief's unfettered authority over the conduct of operations. Thus the first Viviani ministry (which was not replaced until 26 August) had no compunction about providing the commander-in-chief with absolute control in the war zone, assuming that it would not extend appreciably outside of enemy-held territory. If a French victory had been achieved in what was expected to be a brief war, arrangement between the government and the military would have worked without friction. But what actually happened had not been foreseen.

The objectives of both the government and the military were in harmony during the opening weeks of the war. Left unhindered, Joffre rolled out Plan XVII. The terrain over which the French had to advance was hilly and an even greater hurdle to overcome was that modern technology had made old fashion attacking tactics obsolete. German defenders occupied the high ground and, backed by an ample supply of machine-guns and heavy artillery, brought the entire French drive to a standstill after inflicting horrendous casualties. With the collapse of Plan XVII, Joffre had no option but to order a general retreat.

Another egregious mistake by the French high command was the conviction in the prewar period that the Germans lacked the necessary regular troops to invade France through Belgium. The French general staff refused to believe that in so complicated a movement the Germans would use reserve units as well. The Germans evidently had more faith in their reserve forces than the French did in theirs. The Germans got off to a fast start and cut a wide swath through Belgium, overcame resistance, and broke into France.

As the German advance threatened Paris, Joffre made it clear that he wanted the government to leave the city as soon as possible. Poincaré pleaded against abandoning the capital but the cabinet, influenced by Millerand that it could not afford the risk of investment by the enemy, as had happened to the government in 1870-71, voted to move to Bordeaux. Joffre's motive in pressing for the departure of the political leaders is unclear. He may have been genuinely concern for their safety, but that sentiment did not resonate with a cynical observer who suggested it was likely born out of a desire "to develop the omnipotence of GQG."[16] Whatever Joffre's reason,

---

14 Pierre Renouvin (1893-1974) to author, 20 September 1968.
15 Messimy, *Mes Souuvenirs*, p. 232.
16 Cited in Jere C. King, *Generals and Politicians (*Berkeley: University of California Press, 1951), p. 28.

there can be no doubt that the high command, far from the watchful eye of politicians was free to act much more independently.[17]

The flight of the government to a safer locale was deemed a cowardly act by the general public and played up with sardonic humour by the press. Given the derisive nickname of "free runners", the politicians were portrayed as departing hurriedly for a hegira to Bordeaux. The ultimate insult may have come from General Joseph-Simon Galliéni, the governor of Paris, in a proclamation to the city's inhabitants: "The members of the government of the republic have left Paris in order to give a new impulse to national defence. I have received the mandate of defending Paris against the invader. This mandate I shall fulfil to the end."[18]

Whilst the French nation heaped scorn on the politicians, the overconfident commander of the First German Amy, Alexander von Kluck, made a fateful decision. Instead of swinging west of Paris, as called for in the Schlieffen Plan, he turned south-east to try to cut off the retreating French forces. In the process he exposed his army's right flank to the Sixth French Army which had been hastily created to defend Paris. Galliéni, the first to recognize the golden opportunity, alerted Joffre who drew up his forces along the Marne River north-east of Paris and prepared a counter-attack. As von Kluck turned to meet the unexpected French threat, he allowed a thirty-mile gap to open between himself and the neighbouring Second Army. Standing by chance before the gap, the British Expeditionary Force, with elements of the nearby French Fifth Army, moved cautiously forward, encountering little opposition. The German high command, fearful that its two armies on the extreme right might be destroyed, ordered a general retreat. Crossing over ground they had won in recent weeks through bitter fighting, the Germans halted when they reached the high ground behind the Aisne River and dug in.

The "Miracle of the Marne" elevated Joffre to near demigod status in the eyes of the French people and until the summer of 1915 had the effect of holding back the government from confronting him on his conduct of subsequent operations or matters that fell within its purview.[19] Joffre deserves credit for his imperturbable calm and for holding things together during the retreat, as well as for his courageous decision to stake everything on one last battle, but his victory owed more to good fortune and to the incompetence of the German high command than to his tactical wizardry. In the months that followed the Marne, Joffre would experience plenty of military setbacks but no major success.

The French victory on the Marne had irretrievably dislocated the Schlieffen Plan and forced the Germans into a two-front war, thereby significantly diminishing their chances of winning the war. In August 1914 the conventional wisdom was that the war would not last long, negating the need to escalate the conflict, and in the process, of contracting additional obligations. The likelihood of a protracted struggle, however, drew the belligerents to southeast Europe as each side burst into complex and conflicting diplomatic activity to enlist new allies.

Of all the neutral states in that region, the far-flung Turkish or Ottoman Empire was the most prized, offering a wide-range of strategic possibilities. As masters of the Dardanelles Straits, the Turks could at any moment sever Russia's communications with the Mediterranean. The Ottoman Asiatic provinces also provided a base from which to attack or threaten British

---

17   Keiger, *Raymond Poincaré*, p. 208.
18   Cited in King, *Generals,* pp. 28-29.
19   Roy A. Prete, S*trategy and Command: The Anglo-French Coalition on the Western Front 1914* (Montreal and Kingston: McGill-Queen's University Press, 2009), p. 52.

power in Egypt and India. Equally important was the character of the Sultan, who as spiritual leader of Islam, had the authority to proclaim a holy war or jihad against infidels. Indeed, Turkey would greatly benefit whatever side could win it over. Germany, with its long and intense studied efforts to cultivate the friendship of Turkey, held a definite advantage.

Imperial Germany's interest in Turkey began a generation before 1914 when it planned to secure economic control of Mesopotamia, an incredibly backward region but fertile and rich in mineral deposits. Before the Germans could achieve their objective, it was necessary to collaborate with Austria-Hungary which lay in-between the regions they ultimately wanted to dominate. Such a *Mitteleuropa*, knit together into an economic federation under Germany's leadership, would provide it with an empire equal to Britain and Russia. The foundation of this German edifice was the proposed construction of a railway line, linking Berlin, Constantinople and Bagdad and running all the way to the Persian Gulf.

Gradually and inconspicuously the Germans usurped Britain's predominant position in the Ottoman capital. The construction of a railroad linking Berlin to Baghdad started in 1903; a leading German bank provided loans to bolster the Turkish economy; German trading and industrial enterprises were set up in Turkey; Krupp, the largest arms manufacturer, contracted to supply and equip the Ottoman army; and a German military mission was sent to reform the Ottoman army.[20] The Turks for their part believed that they had found a powerful friend willing to organize the finances of their nation, help to reconstruct their industrial system and provide active support against the unfriendly encroaches of Russia.

Germany's growing political, economic and military influence in the Ottoman Empire confirmed fears among the Entente partners in the west of its long-range ambitions to establish a political hegemony in the Middle East. The extension of German power in that region, with its rail connections, as Dr Paul von Rohrback – a native son and best known of the Teutonic imperialist writers – observed in *Die Bagdadbahn* would make Egypt vulnerable to a land attack. The British had always been very sensitive to anything which threatened their control over Egypt. Without Egypt and the link to the east provided by the Suez Canal, Britain would be in danger of losing India as well as its possessions in Central and East Africa.

The French were even more alarmed because their interests in the Middle East, broader than those of any western power, would be directly menaced. French connections in that part of the world were centuries old, dating back, it was alleged, to the time of Charlemagne. In 1535 Francis I and Suleiman the Magnificent concluded a treaty in which the French were granted far reaching rights and privileges. The accord, know thereafter as "Capitulations", provided the basis of a prolonged collaboration between France and Turkey that would last until the start of the 20th Century. A treaty in 1740 confirmed the exclusive rights given to the French in the Turkish Empire. So sacred were they held in France, that Napoleon III defended them in the Crimean War and they became matters of agreement at the Congress of Berlin in 1878. A strong Ottoman Empire was a conscious aim of France and the maintenance of its integrity became a cornerstone of French foreign policy decades before Britain gave serious thought to the Eastern Question.

Partially on account of historical precedents and partly on account of juridical rights under treaties with both sultans and popes, the French government assumed the role of protector of

---

20 A.L. Macfie, *The End of the Ottoman Empire 1908-1923* (London: Longman, 1998), p. 99.

Christians regardless of nationality, in the Ottoman Empire. It established particularly strong bonds with the Maronites (inhabiting modern Lebanon) who had fought with the crusader armies. Since the period of the crusades, French religious orders had carried on missionary and educational work on an increasing scale and this activity was not the least bit hampered by the separation of church and state after the establishment of the Third Republic. Government funds were still available to build Catholic missions, hospitals and educational institutions throughout the sultan's realm. Indeed, it may be said that by 1914 French had become the language of culture and literature of all educated classes in the Levant.

France's economic and financial penetration was likewise strong and increased significantly in the latter stages of the 19th century. It held the bulk of Turkey's public debt, supplied experts to many posts, controlled the Imperial Ottoman Bank and the *régie des tabacs*.[21] In Syria, the French obtained a monopoly on transport facilities and by 1914 controlled all but two railway lines. The cultivation of silk worms in Turkey was of special concern to French textile manufacturers. French funds also flowed freely into public works programs, harbor, facilities for chemical products and gas and electrical plants, big business and practically every important concession or enterprise.

Over the succeeding years several organizations interested in Ottoman Empire affairs sprouted in France. These groups actively supported the government's Middle Eastern policy and were constantly alert to anything that might undermine France's predominance in that part of the world. They fervently believed that the wide diffusion of French capital, language, thought and influence there would indissolubly tie the people to France and create a bond of everlasting friendship. After the outbreak of the Great War they were joined by a segment of the press in urging that the government take prompt and adequate means to safeguard French interests in the eastern Mediterranean.[22]

The government did not need to be reminded of France's extensive political, cultural and economic involvement in the Ottoman Empire. Yet during the immediate prewar period France, as well as Britain, rejected Turkish overtures to enter into an alliance lest it offend the Russians.[23] Thereupon Turkey became increasingly entangled with Germany and on 2 August 1914, the two countries signed a treaty of alliance. It must not be supposed, however, that the bonds linking the two countries together were forged in steel. Berlin had been drawn into the partnership rather reluctantly as it was skeptical of Turkey's military strength. On the other hand the Turkish government contained a small pro-German element but the majority favoured a policy of armed neutrality.

Unaware of the secret pact between Berlin and Constantinople, the Entente powers in the west hoped to keep Turkey neutral. But relations deteriorated rapidly after the First Lord of the Admiralty Winston Churchill, looking to reinforce the Royal Navy with the prospect of war likely, suddenly commandeered two modern battleships (on 3 August) which the Turkish government had ordered from British shipyards and paid for them by popular subscription. The

---

21 A French company known as *Régie* was granted a monopoly over tobacco sales. The profit was supposed to prevent the tottering Ottoman state from sinking further into debt.
22 On France's pre-war policy in the Middle East see especially Christopher M. Andrew and A.S. Kanya-Forstner , *The Climax of French Imperial Expansion 1914-1924* (Stanford: Stanford University Press, 1981), ch. 2.
23 William Hale, *Turkey's Foreign Policy 1774-2000* (London: Frank Cass, 2000), pp. 32-33.

incident was roundly condemned in Constantinople and strengthened the pro-German clique within the Ottoman government.

Once it became apparent that the war would not be over in a few months, Germany abandoned its indifference towards Turkey and pressured it into opening a front against the Russians. While the Turks vacillated, two German warships, the heavily-armed battleship *Goeben* and lighter cruiser *Breslau*, outmanoeuvred French and British ships in the Mediterranean which expected them to head for Gibraltar or the Adriatic. Instead they made a run eastward and, on reaching Turkish territorial waters on 10 August, were allowed to sail up the Dardanelles Straits towards Constantinople. To disguise what was clearly a breach of neutrality, the two ships were turned over to the Turks through a fictitious sale. A German Admiral (Wilhelm Souchon) was appointed to command the Turkish navy, a move that increased the chances that the alliance would be implemented in the near future.[24]

Turkey was on the mind of Poincaré when he visited the headquarters of General Louis Franchet d'Espèrey in Champaigne on 6 October 1914. A graduate of Saint-Cyr, Franchet d'Espèrey spent much of his career outside of France, taking part in operations in Indo-China, China and Morocco. Prior to the Great War, he served as a military attaché in the Balkans and knew the area quite well as he had made extensive private tours through Greece, Serbia and along the Dalmatian coast. Resolute, energetic and independent-minded, he was placed in charge of the Fifth Army several weeks after the war broke out and played a crucial role in the French victory at the Marne.[25]

Poincaré mentioned in the course of their discussion the likelihood that Turkey would soon join the Central Powers. This gave Franchet d'Espèrey an opportunity to push for an external plan that had been germinating in his mind. He pointed out that if the war in France degenerated into a stalemate it might be advisable to engage the Central Powers in other sectors as a means to weaken Germany. He favoured opening a new front in the Balkans to strike, in cooperation with the Serbs, Austria from the rear.[26] This was the first time that anyone had called for such an operation, although several men would later claim credit for that dubious honour.[27] Poincaré was sufficiently impressed to ask the general to set down his views in detail in a memorandum.

Franchet d'Espèrey worked on the memo in-between his normal duties and, by his own admission, the finished product in the latter part of November was not to be considered an exhaustive investigation.[28] The plan was ambitious and aimed to restore the war of movement. It envisaged landing five divisions at Salonica and from there transport them up the Vardar Valley to Belgrade (642 kilometers/399 miles distant) in readiness for an advance in the spring of 1915

---

24 Paul G. Halpern, *A Naval History of World War I* (Annapolis: Naval Institute Press, 1994), pp. 54-58.
25 Pierre Gosa, *Un Maréchal Méconnu: Franchet d'Espèrey* (Paris: Nouvelles Editions Latines, 1999), chs. 6-25.
26 Raymond Poincaré, *Au service de la France,* Vol. 5 (Paris: Plon, 1928), p. 360.
27 In my earlier volume, *The French and the Dardanelles*, I had concluded that Briand was the first person in France to introduce the idea of a diversion to the Balkans. I have since revised my opinion even though the evidence remains unclear. A good deal of ink has been spilled as to who initially came up with the proposal and a case has been made by various writers for the following: Briand, Galliéni and Franchet d"Espèrey . After wading through the sea of literature on the subject, I concluded that it was Franchet d'Espèrey and he alone followed up with a memorandum containing his strategic views.
28 Commandant Maurice Larcher, *La grande guerre dans les Balkans* (Paris: Payot, 1929). Part of the memorandum is reproduced in the book's appendix (annexe no. 3).

The Search for an Alternate Theatre of War   37

on Budapest and Vienna. The French thrust was expected to drive a wedge between Turkey and its allies and establish contact with the Russians through Romania. Franchet d'Espèrey identified two major obstacles before the army could reach its destination in Serbia: limited harbor facilities and the inadequacy of the single railroad track. His solution was to utilise Kavalla (a Greek Macedonia seaport) as an additional base and to send engineers to double the rail line from Salonica to the interior. The suggestion on the former point made good sense but the same could not be said about his views on the latter one – which defies explanation in view of his knowledge of the Balkans and its landscape. How could he believe that enough material, engineers and vital workers could have been spared from the Western Front to double the railway line, much of it through mountainous country, in a timely fashion. At any rate Franchet d'Espèrey estimated (on the assumption that the obstacles referred to could be overcome) that it would take about two months for all the troops to reach the concentration area in Serbia.[29]

Franchet d'Espèrey assigned an officer on his staff – who also happened to be deputy on his way to Paris – for the opening of the new parliamentary session,[30] to turn the document over to the President. When the plan reached Poincaré on 1 December, no action was taken because the Austrians were applying heavy pressure on Serbian forces and the next day occupied Belgrade unopposed. Still the Serbian leadership, calculating that Austrian forces were overextended and exhausted after a month of campaigning over rugged terrain, launched a counterattack. The Serbs caught the Austrians unprepared, regained control of Belgrade and sent them streaming back across the Austrian border.[31] By 15 December the liberation of Serbian soil was complete, and it was not long after the news reached Paris that there was renewed interest in the Balkan scheme.

When the cabinet ministers returned to Paris at the end of December 1914, they learned, much to their dismay, that power once relinquished is not so easily retrieved. As the "Victor of the Marne", Joffre's fame had reached such exalted heights at home that he became politically untouchable. During the government's refuge in Bordeaux, Joffre was able to exercise complete control over the strategic and operational direction of the war and he had become too fond of his freedom to return to a system where he would be constantly badgered by the government to disclose details of his future plans or hampered by its restrictions. Thus he insisted that the government authorities rely on the reports he submitted, implying that he would be the judge of what they were required to know. His contempt for the politicians may be inferred from a note he sent Galliéni: "I should be obliged if you would send the government no information concerning the operations. In the reports that I send them, I never make known the aim of current operations, nor my intentions."[32]

Millerand considered it vital that he be in complete accord with the Generalissimo and he never questioned his strategic decisions or pressed him for military information to which the government was entitled. Joffre accepted in theory the concept of divided responsibility established by Messimy, but in practice he refused to allow Millerand to intrude in any way in

29   Gosa, *Franchet d'Espèrey*, pp. 153–54; Alan Palmer, *The Gardeners of Salonica* (New York: Simon and Schuster, 1965), pp. 20-21.
30   After the chamber adjourned in August many of its members joined army units but returned for the start of the new session in December 1914.
31   John Keegan, *The First World War* (New York: Vintage Books, 1998), pp. 152-54.
32   Joseph-Simon Galliéni, *Mémoires* (Paris: Payot, 1920), p. 172.

strategic and operational matters. He conceded that ultimately the commander-in-chief was responsible to the government which can replace him if it disapproved of his action but he knew too well that his iconic status put him beyond the reach of politicians.[33] No government would have dared to remove him or force his resignation without inviting its own demise and upsetting public confidence in the army. Jean de Pierrefeu, an officer at GQG, was not far off the mark when he wrote: "After the victory of the Marne, there was in reality only one power in France, that of Joffre and his staff."[34]

When parliament reconvened in December 1914 it sought to exert some control over the military through the agency of various commissions created in both the chamber and senate. These parliamentary representatives carried out investigations pertaining to national defence in secret and were empowered to inspect the front and to call in ministers to answer questions at any time. Parliament wanted to avoid public debate on controversial political and military questions which it feared would undermine the Viviani administration and reignite internecine partisan political strife while the country was fighting for its survival. But Joffre was no more cooperative with the commissions than he was with the government. He not only hindered their investigation but prohibited them from entering the war zone without the permission of GQG.[35]

Following the Marne miracle, the war of movement gradually gave way to siege warfare as each side spread northward to outflank the other in a series of bloody but indecisive battles. The so-called race to the sea created a twisted front along a line extending some 450 miles, from the Swiss Alps to the North Sea. As the fighting ended in stalemate on reaching the English Channel, both sides fortified their defences. What emerged was a different and unprecedented type of warfare. When the armies could not get around one another they tried to break through. The advance in modern technology had given the defence a substantial advantage. All things considered equal, the attackers always suffered much heavier casualties than the defenders. The Germans quickly realized the obvious and were content to act on the defence. The French persisted, determined as they were to expel the invaders from the homeland.

There was no shortcut to victory and the cost would have been high even if a sensible strategy had been employed in the early stages. Joffre was correct to perceive that the war could only be won on the Western Front, but he was wrong to cling obsessively to the notion that, by adopting the prewar and outdated tactical concept, a breakthrough was attainable after a series of preliminary attacks had worn down the Germans. Joffre lacked breadth of vision to carry out a judicious policy of attrition or make crucial adjustments in light of the failure of his methods. Sending masses of battle-worn infantry, with no equipment other than a rifle and imbued by an indomitable spirit, against a strongly entrenched and well-armed enemy was not a prescription that would produce victory. The heavy artillery fire that preceded every attack rarely caused much damage since German trenches were deep enough or provided with boom-proof shelters. Once the barrage subsided and the signal to go over the top was given, the Germans could rapidly re-deploy machine guns back into position and cut down the advancing columns as they picked their way through the entanglements. There were instances when French troops

---

33 Field Marshal Joseph Joffre, *Personal Memoirs*, Vol. 2 (New York: Harper, 1932), p. 397; Doughty, *Pyrrhic Victory*, p. 110.
34 Jean de Pierrefeu, *French Headquarters, 1915-1918* (London: Bles, 1924), p. 115.
35 King, *Generals*, chs. 2 and 3; Richard M. Watt, *Dare Call it Treason* (New York: Simon and Schuster, 1963), ch. 7.

managed to capture the enemy's first line. but they were unable to move forward. The Germans would open up with their artillery and a little later counterattack just as the advancing French forces were becoming exhausted, sending the survivors scurrying back across no man's land littered with the dead or dying bodies of their comrades. Increasing the number of attacks only added to the butcher's bill. No wonder the politicians were desperate to find a novel approach to the war.

On 1 January 1915, Poincaré and Viviani, in accordance with time-honoured tradition, drove to extend their good wishes to the presidents of the two parliamentary chambers. On the way over, Viviani did not conceal his distress over Joffre's recent operations in Champagne which he considered were a dismal failure. He went so far as to reproach Joffre for having no strategic plan and merely reacting to events day after day.[36]

The two men returned to the Elysée (presidential residence) where they were joined by the other members of the cabinet for lunch. The festive atmosphere dissipated quickly as the ministers engaged in a long discussion centering on the disheartening military situation in France. Viviani repeated what he had said to the president earlier in the morning. Briand, although somewhat guarded, expressed himself in the same vein. It seemed reasonable to him to look elsewhere than the main front to weaken Germany. He maintained that GQG's military policy of assaulting the enemy's line was unsound for, apart from the terrible human costs, the chances of producing decisive results were remote.[37] Both he and Viviani wondered whether it was possible to prepare, in collaboration with the English, an expeditionary force of 400,000 to 500,000 men to strike Austria from the rear through Serbia. The idea would be to land along the Adriatic coast or at Salonica, advance on Budapest, and from there on to Vienna, and, while on the move, attempt to raise the Slavs under the domination of the Dual Monarchy. Poincaré warmly endorsed the scheme which he claimed was practically identical to the one Franchet d'Espèrey had recommended to him earlier.[38]

The interest of the three politicians had been heightened by Serbia's victory over the Austrians and also by reports that, in addition to Franchet d'Espèrey, other senior French generals, notably Galliéni and Edouard Castelnau (then in command of the Second French Army), fretting over the stalemate, favoured opening another front where the chances of victory appeared brighter. It was pointed out that great benefits would accrue from a successful diversion in the Balkans: that it would boost morale at home, likely provoke the Slavs and Czechs to revolt against the Austrians, and possibly draw Italy and Romania into the conflict on the side of the Allies.[39] The other members of the government, except for Millerand whose reaction is not recorded, were equally enthusiastic. A decision was taken to confer with Joffre as soon as possible. There was no intention of imposing a strategic plan on the commander-in-chief, merely invite his views on the merits of a diversion in the Balkans.[40] Poincaré asked Briand to remain behind after Viviani and the others had left, and for an hour or so, the two further discussed the Balkan plan.[41]

36 Poincaré, *Au Service*, Vol. 6, pp. 1–2.
37 Archives du Ministère des Affaires Etrangères (AMAE): Briand papers, PAAP, Vol. 23. Briand's account of the meeting on 1 January 1915.
38 Poincaré, *Au Service*, Vol. 6, p. 2.
39 (AMAE): Briand papers, Briand's account of the meeting on 1 January 1915.
40 Poincaré, *Au Service*, Vol. 6, p. 3.
41 (AMAE) Briand papers, Briand's account of the meeting on 1 January 1915.

On 7 January 1915, Joffre was invited to the Elysée for lunch, during which Poincaré had arranged to have the other members of the government present. At the end of the meal, the doors to the room were closed and a long discussion about the war followed. Viviani thought that to escape from the immobility on the main front it might be useful to affect a diversion through the Balkans. Briand amplified the case advanced by Viviani. Poincaré weighed in and without identifying Franchet d'Espèrey outlined his plan of campaign. Joffre listened calmly to what was said until given the floor. Although not brilliant, he was articulate and a forceful speaker. In his opening statements he left no doubt that he was opposed to the operation and proceeded to list a number of reasons to support his case. In the first place he claimed that he could not spare a large force – which he estimated would require 100,000 men – in view of reports that the Germans had been reinforced in the west by 24 divisions and obviously intended to attack in the near future. Secondly that it would be difficult to supply an army of 100,000 men as it pushed deeper inland and farther away from the coast. Lastly, the war could only be won by beating Germans, not Austrians. At this point Briand asked Joffre if he thought that a decision could be reached in France. Joffre was certain that it could, though he was not sure how long it would take. Briand observed that the recent offensives had not produced any gains. Joffre's explanation was that "the time was not propitious."[42] Briand remained unconvinced but neither he nor the others asked Joffre why the attacks continued if the right moment was not at hand. In the end they saw that Joffre was so fixed in his conviction that there was no point in continuing the discussion.[43] To be fair, at this early stage in the war, before large numbers of British units had completed their training and were ready to reinforce their comrades on the Western Front, it would have been extremely difficult, if not impossible, to find enough French troops to make such an operation feasible.

The compelling reason among the French politicians for advocating the dispatch of an expedition to the Balkans a week into 1915 was the belief that the war could not be won, or at frightful costs if at all, by conventional frontal assaults in the west. Although at this time the ministers were unwilling to override Joffre's veto lest he resign, as he had threaten to do in the past whenever his views were challenged, it was a proposal they would bring to fruition later in the year. In the interim the British, acting independently, embraced a different peripheral strategy, one that concentrated initially on sea power to knock Turkey, now an active ally of Germany, out of the war.[44] How the French were drawn into the operation is the subject of the next chapter.

---

42 (AMAE): Briand papers, PAAP, Vol. 23; Briand's account of the meeting on 7 January 1915.
43 Poincaré, *Au service*, Vol. 6, pp. 8-9; (AMAC): Briand papers, Briand's account of the meeting on 7 January 1915; Doughty, *Pyrrhic Victory*, p. 109.
44 Without informing the other members of the cabinet, the Turkish ministers of war and marine, leading advocates of the alliance with Germany, authorized Souchon to attack Russian Black Sea installations. On 29 October 1914, the Turkish fleet, with *Goeben* and *Breslau* in the vanguard, bombarded four Russian seaports, destroying several ships. Russia responded by declaring war on Turkey on 2 November and three days later France and Britain followed suit.

3

The French Succumb to Churchill's Folly

After nearly four months of the war in 1914 the slaughter on the Western Front had surpassed all calculations and, with the prospect of a breakthrough as remote as ever, the level of anxiety among the politicians in London was no less than that of their counterparts in Paris. The War Council,[1] charged with the control and direction of the war, was intent on finding a solution to the dilemma. Apart from the Prime Minister, H.H. Asquith, its most dominant members were Winston Churchill (First Lord of the Admiralty) and Lord Kitchener (Secretary for War). Only forty years old, Churchill had enjoyed a meteoric rise in politics since entering parliament in 1900. Possessing considerable intellectual gifts and powers of argument, he was also impulsive, arrogant and self-centered with a mania for self-advertisement.

Kitchener had little in common with his colleague at the Admiralty. Before Kitchener took over the War Office, he had served in the outer posts of the empire for nearly forty years as a soldier and administrator and his long list of accomplishments brought him immense fame and influence. He was inarticulate, rarely made decisions in haste, kept his emotions in check and shunned the spotlight. Accustomed to exercising absolute authority wherever he was posted, he did not fit easily in a structured system of collective responsibility.

At the end of December 1914 and the start of the new year several members of the War Council, each acting without reference to one another, produced papers in which they pointed out that the existence and probable continuation of the stalemate in the west imposed the need to find a new theatre of war where Germany could be effectively weakened by striking at its allies. One by David Lloyd George, the Chancellor of the Exchequer, calling for an attack on Austria-Hungary via Salonica or a landing along the coast of Syria to cut the communications of the Turkish troops threatening Egypt, drew some attention in the early stages of the discussion.[2] Nevertheless the plan that gained the most traction was Winston Churchill's idea to force the Dardanelles Straits by ships alone. The origins of the Dardanelles campaign has been and continues to be the object of intense scrutiny as the British, and to a lesser extent the Australians,

---

1   Formed at the end of November 1914 by the Prime Minister, it was a special committee of the cabinet. The War Council did not meet regularly and its decisions were not binding on the cabinet and so liable to be thrashed out again by the full body.
2   For the details see David Lloyd George, *War Memoirs*, Vol. 1 (London: Odhams Press, 1938), pp. 219-26.

never seem to tire of writing about that forlorn adventure. As a detailed account lies outside the scope of this study a brief summary for our purpose will suffice.

The story began on 2 January 1915 when the Foreign Office received a telegram from the Grand Duke Nicholas, the Russian army commander, requesting a demonstration to relieve Turkish pressure on his forces in the Caucasus. With no troops to spare, Kitchener asked the Admiralty to stage a demonstration, preferably in the Dardanelles, though he realized it would not have much effect in inducing the Turks to divert forces from the Caucasus.[3] At that very moment, however, the Turkish army's flanking movement in the midst of a blizzard near Sarikamish badly miscarried and by 5 January the debacle was complete. Of the more than 100,000 men involved, only 12,000 survived to return home.[4] On 5 January Kitchener was apprised of the Russian victory which was announced in several London dailies that evening. As the reason for a naval demonstration had disappeared, Kitchener gave the matter no further thought.[5] Churchill on the other hand hit on the idea of using only ships to blast a passage through the Dardanelles Straits and force Turkey to surrender.[6]

The Dardanelles was a long tortuous channel linking the Aegean and the Sea of Marmora. Extending 41 miles in length, from its mouth at Cape Helles to where it reaches the Sea of Marmora, the Dardanelles averages between three and four miles in width and closes to three-quarters of a mile at The Narrows. The currents produced by the tidal action in the Black Sea and Sea of Marmora make the waterway among the most difficult and potentially hazardous in the world. Ships must await the right conditions before entering the Straits. The stretch of water is flanked on the west by the Gallipoli Peninsula and on the east by the coast of Asia. Turkish fortifications, running along both shores, formed three lines of resistance known as "Outer," "Intermediate" and "Inner" defences.[7] A hostile fleet advancing into the Straits would thus be exposed to the enfilading fire from the batteries in Asia and the Gallipoli Peninsula.

Since the days of Nelson, a belief persisted in the British navy that it was foolish for ships alone to challenge coastal fortifications. In 1807 Vice-Admiral Sir John Duckworth beat the odds and successfully led a squadron through the Dardanelles Straits but was unable to reach Constantinople.[8] After the Turks multiplied and strengthened their forts along the Straits in the late 1880s, naval experts considered a purely naval attack not only injudicious but almost certain to fail. Indeed, investigations by both the Admiralty and War Office before the Great War concluded that even an amphibious operation entailed serious risks.[9]

---

3   Winston S. Churchill, *The World Crisis*, Vol. 2 (New York: Charles Scribner's Sons, 1951), pp. 85-86.
4   Robert Rhodes James, *Gallipoli* (London: Batsford, 1965), pp. 17-18.
5   George H. Cassar, *Kitchener's War: British Strategy from 1914 to 1916* (Washington, DC: Potomac Books, 2004), p. 123.
6   The full story of Churchill's role in initiating the naval operation can be followed in many works on the subject, but few are as well researched and written than Christopher M. Bell, *Churchill and the Dardanelles* (Oxford: Oxford University Press, 2016).
7   Brig.-Gen. C. F. Aspinall-Oglander, *Military Operations: Gallipoli*, Vol. 1 (London: William Heinemann, 1929), pp. 31-32.
8   Eight miles from the city, the ships ran into a head wind and stalled. After waiting a week for a favourable wind Duckworth decided to withdraw. On the return passage he retained all his ships, but enemy batteries along the Straits inflicted 150 casualties among his men. Aspinall-Oglander, *Gallipoli*, Vol. 1, pp. 25-26.
9   Aspinall-Oglander, *Gallipoli*, Vol. 1, pp. 25-31.

Churchill believed that the advances in technology proved otherwise. If the Germans using heavy howitzers of 5.9-inch and 8-inch calibre could reduce the Belgian strongholds, it seemed to him a reasonable deduction that the powerful salvos of the 12-inch and 15-inch guns on British ships, lying outside the range of the antiquated Turkish artillery, could smash the forts to bits. Thereupon Churchill asked Vice-Admiral Sackville Carden, who commanded an Allied squadron at the entrance of the Dardanelles, whether he considered forcing the Straits by ships alone a practical operation. Carden replied that he doubted that the Straits could be rushed but that they might be forced by extended operations with a large number of ships. That was all the information that Churchill needed to make a case for a naval attack. He was anxious to bolster his sagging reputation – which had taken a hit in recent months – by engineering a dramatic coup. His imagination fired up, he became convinced, on the basis of intelligence reports, that the Turkish government would surrender, or a popular revolution would occur the moment the ships arrived before Constantinople. Churchill outlined his scheme in the War Council on 13 January and gave the impression that he had the support of his naval advisers which was not exactly the case – they were at best lukewarm or coerced into not opposing it. The bait that hooked the War Council was Churchill's assertion, often repeated, that if the attack proved too difficult it would be treated as a demonstration and abandoned without loss of face. Backed by Kitchener, Churchill received authorization to prepare for a naval expedition to bombard and take the Gallipoli Peninsula with Constantinople as its objective.[10]

Churchill had a major obstacle to overcome before he could continue to move forward with his plan. It will be remembered that in February 1913 an Anglo-French agreement had divided the spheres of naval responsibility, laying down that the British assume general direction of naval operations in the Straits of Dover and North Sea while the French fleet take over the predominant role of defending the Mediterranean. Still given the ambiguity and uncertainty of the arrangement, it left the two governments with their hands relatively free. Circumstances changed once Britain actively joined the Entente, so it was essential to replace the prewar strategic script. Accordingly, in a naval convention signed on 6 August 1914, the two partners made a written commitment to one another. There was also a clause which provided for the withdrawal of all the British armoured ships except one from the Mediterranean as soon as the *Goeben* and *Breslau* were destroyed.[11] A day after Britain declared war on Germany, the Admiralty ordered its Mediterranean fleet to pursue and sink the two German ships. The *Goeben* was faster and more heavily armed than any British battle cruiser in the Mediterranean but its guns were slightly less powerful (11-inch as opposed to 12-inch).[12] As already noted the British cruisers and French fleet were unable to catch up to the German warships before they found refuge in Turkish waters. On 22 September 1914 at the request of the Admiralty, the French Minister of Marine Victor Augagneur, dispatched two ships under Rear-Admiral Emile-Paul Guépratte to reinforce Vice-Admiral Carden's squadron in the vicinity of the

---

10 British National Archives (BNA): Cabinet papers, CAB 42/1, Minutes of the War Council, 13 January 1915.
11 Service historique de la Défence (SHD): Archives du Ministère de la Marine (AMM), Es 11, La convention navale entre la France et la Grande-Bretagne, 6 August 1914; Paul G. Halpernn, *The Naval War in the Mediterranean 1914-1918 (Annapolis: Naval Institute Press, 1987)*, pp. 26-27.
12 Marder, *From the Dreadnought*, Vol. 2, pp. 20-21.

Dardanelles.[13] In principle the French naval commander-in-chief Vice-Admiral A. P. Boué de Lapeyrère was responsible for the entire Allied fleet in the Mediterranean but in practice his jurisdiction never extended over the British naval division which acted separately and on the direct orders from London.

Britain and France had entered the war as associates but with no real tradition of alliance or even friendship. On the contrary their relationship before the twentieth century was often troubled and they tended to be rivals rather than friends. Between 1689 and 1815 they had been mortal enemies and clashed numerous times and, as recent as 1898 during the colonial scramble to carve up Africa, they came perilously close to armed conflict. Their collaboration since 1904 had been rather smooth, inspired as it was by the German menace. There was no guarantee, however, that the present alliance would survive once Germany was defeated. As it happened the Anglo-French partnership would endure unbroken throughout the war but there were moments when the old fears and rivalries would resurface. The earliest signs occurred even before the stalemate set in on the Western Front at the close of 1914.

A group of influential French parliamentarians and officials in the government, believing that the partition of the Ottoman Empire was inevitable, wanted the Viviani ministry to be ready to claim Syria (which at the time also included much of present-day Lebanon, Israel, Palestine and Jordan) for France. The French pressure group had heard rumours that the British intended to extend their sphere of control from Egypt to Syria. The last thing that these expansionists wanted to see was the British accorded unrestricted freedom to occupy Syria, just as a generation earlier, French idleness had cleared the way for their move into Egypt. They pointed to the landing of British troops at the head of the Persian Gulf on declaration of war with Turkey, followed by their occupation of Basra and a few weeks later Qurna to the north, seemingly on their way to sweep across Mesopotamia. It was reasonable to assume that Syria, lying between Egypt and Mesopotamia, would be Britain's next target. It was thus vital to act quickly to forestall the British. France, it was pointed out, did not need to send more than a handful of troops. One plan called for the landing of between 1,500 and 2,000 mountain troops at some point in Syria and, aided by some 30,000 Lebanese Christians, would have no difficulty in routing the demoralized Turkish defenders.

The idea received more attention from the government than it deserved, especially after the newly appointed British High Commissioner in Egypt Sir Henry McMahon, meeting with representatives of the Foreign and War Ministries in Paris on the last days in December 1914, gave rambling and vague responses to questions relating to London's military intentions in the Middle East. They were unaware, however, that McMahon was rather slow witted and wrongly concluded that he was covering up the fact that the British were trying to steal a march on the French. The discussion with McMahon reached the ears of the cabinet ministers, the majority of whom felt or argued that abandoning Syria to Britain would damage France's standing as a great power. Millerand, notwithstanding his socialist origins, had supported the prewar nationalist revival and sided approvingly with the interventionists. Delcassé saw no value in a Syrian expedition but gave his reluctant consent after it was pointed out that the government's inaction would infuriate public opinion and that the object was not to open a new theatre but to

---

13   SHD: AMM, Xa 1, Saint-Seine to Augagneur, 20 September 1914; and Xa 32, Augagneur to Saint-Seine, 22 September 1914.

show the French flag to preempt British intrusion. Everyone appeared to be on board when the cabinet authorized Millerand to make secret preparations to assemble an expeditionary force. Millerand indicated that he would only use second-rate troops, identifying them as territorials and Africans.[14]

Back at the War Ministry, Millerand assigned the general staff to investigate possible landing sites and to determine the number of troops each would require. Before the report was submitted, the French government had been drawn into a British-led operation that would turn out to be far more ambitious than its members had anticipated. A central player in the preparatory stages of the collaborative undertaking was Victor Augagneur.

It would be difficult to find a more unlikely person to head the Ministry of Marine than Augagneur. A pathologist with an international reputation, he found a second career in politics later in life. In 1904, at the age of 49, he was elected to the chamber of deputies as a moderate socialist and a short time later took on the duties of the governor of Madagascar. He returned to the chamber in 1910 and the following year served as Minister of Public Works in the Caillaux administration and in June 1914 Viviani appointed him to take charge of the Department of Public Instruction. A skillful, strong-minded, and energetic administrator, his record of accomplishment came to an end when, lacking a solid background in naval affairs, he became Minister of Marine in August 1914.[15]

Turkey's involvement in the conflict upset earlier calculation that the Mediterranean would not be the scene of major naval action. In the belief that an invasion of Egypt was now imminent, the Admiralty transferred Rear-Admiral Richard Peirse from the Indian zone to take over command of the warships that were concentrating in Egyptian waters to defend the Suez Canal.[16] The French understood the importance London attached to the defence of Egypt and raised no objections when the British arbitrarily took charge of the eastern end of the lake. To keep an eye on the movement of Turkish troops southward and also with a view to future operations, British ships on patrol pushed well-beyond Egyptian waters, seemingly on the way to take over the entire coastal strip from El Arish to Alexandretta. Since the French had already acquiesced in the removal of the Egyptian areas from their general command of the Mediterranean, they were alarmed at the prospect of further encroachment, especially at the Royal Navy's patrols off Syria which lent credence to their suspicion that it was the focal point of the British government's Imperial ambitions.[17] Indeed, even before the war, the French were convinced that the British were making secret arrangements to move into Syria in the event of the collapse of Ottoman power in the region. Although the British Foreign Office had always insisted that it was neither feasible nor desirable for His Majesty's Government to entertain expanding into Syria, lingering French apprehensions remained.[18]

---

14 Andrew and Kanya-Forstner, *Climax of French Imperial Expansion*, pp. 65-66, 70.
15 As far as I know there is no comprehensive biography of Augagneur and, try as I might, I was unable to determine whether he left any private papers.
16 Julian Corbett, *Naval Operations*, Vol. 1 (London: Longmans, 1920), p. 73.
17 (AMAE): in section under the heading Opération des Dardanelles, carton 4, dossier 1, Augagneur to Delcassé, 10 January 1915.
18 George H. Cassar, *Kitchener as Proconsul of Egypt, 1911-1914* (London, Palgrave Macmillan, 2016), pp. 225-26.

Accordingly, on 28 December 1914, Augagneur sent a long memorandum to the Admiralty, in which he proposed that the naval zones in the Mediterranean be revised. He prefaced his idea by laying down that it was necessary to maintain a fleet in the vicinity of the Dardanelles to keep a strict watch until the *Goeben* was destroyed. That said, he suggested that the naval forces operating at the entrance of the Dardanelles and on the coast of Asia Minor and Syria as far south as Jaffa, should fall under the responsibility of Vice-Admiral Boué de Lapeyrère. Anglo-French ships on patrol in the Red Sea and on the coast of Egypt would be placed under the direction of Rear-Admiral Peirse who would enjoy an independent command.[19] Churchill objected to the idea of transferring command of the Dardanelles from British to French hands and declined to give the matter further consideration.

When Augagneur failed to receive a reply he asked the French naval attaché in London, the Comte de Saint-Seine, to sound out the Admiralty on the matter. Saint-Seine replied several days later (8 January 1915) that, in spite of daily visits to the Admiralty, he had been unable to elicit information as what the First Lord had in mind.[20] Augagneur's annoyance turned to anger on receiving a telegram from Boué de Lapeyrère the next day, explaining that Pierse was supposedly unaware of the earlier Anglo-French agreement regarding the Mediterranean and had assumed that policing the coast of Syria was linked to his own duties as commander of the Egyptian naval zone.[21] Thereupon Augagneur produced a second paper, much sharper in tone, insisting on prompt settlement of the respective spheres of action for the two navies in the Mediterranean along the lines he had indicated earlier.[22]

By the time Churchill began to feel the heat from across the channel, he had become involved in the drama unfolding in the Mediterranean. Since he wanted the British to retain naval command in the Dardanelles, he asked Grey to tell Paul Cambon, French ambassador in London, that the "Admiralty think the present arrangements had better stand for the time being."[23] Churchill had no sooner received the War Council's unofficial stamp of approval for his naval operation against the forts guarding the route into the Sea of Marmora on 13 January, than he conceived of yet another scheme. He proposed to strike at Alexandretta at the same time as the naval attack on the Dardanelles. He explained to Kitchener that "if we are checked at the Dardanelles, we can represent that operation as a mere demonstration to cover the seizure of Alexandretta." He added, "I believe this aspect is important from an Oriental point of view."[24] Even before Churchill received the formal consent of Kitchener and the other members of the War Council for his subsidiary operation, he handed Saint-Seine his long-delayed reply to Augagneur on 16 January. It ran as follows:

> The British Government find it necessary to take offensive action against Turkey in the near future. The Admiralty have in consequence decided to attack the Dardanelles forts and force, if possible, a passage into the Sea of Marmora. It is proposed to achieve this by a

---

19 SHD: AMM, Es 11, Mémorandum par Augagneur, 28 December 1914.
20 SHD: AMM, Xa 2, Saint-Seine to Augagneur, 8 January 1915.
21 SHD: AMM, Ca 20, Boué de Lapeyrère to Augagneur, 9 January 1915.
22 SHD: AMAE, under the heading Opération des Dardanelles, carton 4, dossier 1, Augagneur to Delcassé, 10 January 1915; and AMM, Es11, Delcassé to Cambon (copy), 13 January 1915.
23 BNA: Grey papers, FO 800/88, Churchill to Grey, 10 January 1915.
24 BNA: Kitchener papers, PRO 30/57/72, Churchill to Kitchener, 20 January 1915.

gradual and methodical reduction of the forts by naval bombardment taking three or four weeks, if necessary ...

The Admiralty do not wish, in view of this very important operation, that any change in the local command in that portion of the Mediterranean should be made at the present time. They hope however that the squadron of French battleships, together with the French submarines and destroyers and the sea plane ship *Foudre*, will cooperate under a French Rear-Admiral.

The War Office also considers it necessary during the month of February to occupy Alexandretta and the surrounding district in order to cut the Turkish rail communication at this most strategic point.[25]

Attached to the memorandum when it arrived at the Ministry of Marine the next day were two letters from Saint-Seine. The first reported a conversation with Cambon who enthusiastically endorsed the idea of forcing the Straits, and urged that measures be taken to avoid discussing in public, or even in the cabinet, the text of Churchill's proposals. The other, cited immediately below, sought to justify the Admiralty's case against readjusting the naval zones in the Mediterranean and to allay French fears concerning British intentions in the Levant:

As Mr. Churchill was handing this document to me, he expressed the wish to have brought to your attention the tremendous military and political interest attached to an energetic and prompt action against the Turks ...

The Admiralty hopes that the Russian Black Sea fleet will contribute to the success of the operation by guarding the exit of the Bosporus in order to prevent the escape of the German-Turkish fleet and also by attacking simultaneously the defences of the northern part of the Bosporus if conditions are favourable. Nevertheless, the Admiralty wishes to communicate directly with the Russian Admiralty at a time thought to be appropriate and asks that you observe absolute discretion concerning this matter. This secret is, by the way, one of the most important ingredients of success. What makes the operation relatively simple is the absence of submarines in the area. The arrival of submarines would bring considerable danger. But information held to be of value by the Admiralty confirms that there are no shipyards on the shores of the Sea of Marmora able to assemble submarines sent by rail. Nevertheless these [submarines] could be sent by sea from Austria if the enemy suspected that there was a project under way to force the Dardanelles.

The First Lord's answer emphasizes that the accords concluded on 6 August between the two Admiralties in order to divide the spheres of action in the Mediterranean had been drafted at a time when Germany and Austria were our only adversaries. The entry of Turkey in the coalition has rendered them obsolete as far as the Levant is concerned and necessitates their revision ... The First Lord has told me repeatedly and with insistence, that his greatest desire was to avoid doing anything that could offend the French government and to remain loyally, sincerely and without questioning in complete harmony with it. He also told me, and authorized me to reveal to you, that the British government considers that

---

25 Churchill College Archives Centre (CCAC): Churchill papers, CHAR 2/74/47, Churchill to Augagneur, 16 January 1915.

occupation of enemy territory by British forces is essentially provisional and does not give exclusive territorial rights to Great Britain. All Allied conquests belong to the Allies.[26]

Churchill's proposition received a frosty reception in Paris. In the first place the French had no desire to cover up the decomposing Ottoman corpse and in the past, they had continually tried to check the rapid progress of its disintegration. There lingered a genuine fear in Paris that should the Turkish Empire collapse, the relative strength of France in the Middle East might be weakened rather than strengthened.[27] For that reason the policy of the Third Republic remained unchanged, despite the fact that Turkey was fighting on the side of the Central Powers. If it became impossible to keep the Turkish Empire intact, then the French proposed to claim Syria, Palestine, Cilicia and Alexandretta.[28]

Augagneur had known since 7 January that the Admiralty was toying with the idea of forcing the Straits by ships alone but he fully expected to be consulted before the British decided to go ahead with the scheme.[29] He was therefore incensed when the project was presented to him as a *fait accompli*, especially as it ignored French privileges in the Mediterranean. Immediately he concluded that the English were trying to chip away at those rights in a bid to regain command of the lake. For the French, control of the Mediterranean was so vital that it could not be left to a friendly power to secure it. Not only was it needed to protect their North African colonies, reportedly coveted by the Germans, but also to screen the transport of their African armies to France.

No less resented was Churchill's justification to occupy Alexandretta, a seaport in southwest Turkey which the French had long regarded as being with their sphere of influence. It was the centre of the cotton growing belt and both the caravan routes from the desert and the oil pipeline from Mosul terminated there. Much of the seaborne trade of northern Syria and upper Mesopotamia passed through this port which had rail connections with the main Turkish system. Alexandretta was the gateway to Asia Minor and a vital link in France's strategy to dominate the Mediterranean.[30]

When Churchill gave notice of an intended landing at Alexandretta, Augagneur strongly suspected that it was not so much out of military necessity as it was for a desire to gain a foothold in Asia Minor. To defer to British ambitions would be to provide the base for a future rival. It would also invite other European powers to move into Ottoman territory and further threaten France's cultural and economic primacy in that part of the world. For Augagneur, an ardent

---

26 SHD: AMM, Es 11, Saint-Seine to Augagneur, 19 January 1915.
27 AMAE: Delcassé papers, Vol. 25, Note sur la question soulevées par le forcement des Dardanelles, 5 March 1915. The note is unsigned but almost certainly represents the views of Delcassé.
28 W.W. Gottlieb, *Studies in Secret Diplomacy during the First World War* (London: Allen and Unwin, 1957), pp. 80-81; Maurice Paléologue, *An Ambassador's Memoirs*, trans. by F.A. Holt, Vol. 1 (New York: George Doran, 1924), p. 193; Lady Algernon Lennox (ed.), *The Diary of Lord Bertie of Thame, 1914-1918*, Vol. 1 (London: Hodder & Stoughton, 1924), pp. 106, 120; A.J.P. Taylor, *Politics in Wartime* (London: Hamish Hamilton, 1964), pp. 180-81; A. Ribot (ed.), *Journal de Alexandre Ribot et correspondances inédites 1914-1922* (Paris: Plon, 1936), p. 8; Poincaré, *Au Service*, Vol. 6, p. 94.
29 SHD: AMM, Xa 2, Saint-Seine to Augagneur, 7 January 1915.
30 Stephen H. Roberts, *The History of French Colonial Policy 1870-1925* (London: Frank Cass, 1963), pp. 591–92; Étienne Flandin, "Nos droits en Syrie et Palestine, "*La revue hebdomadaire*, 29 May 1915, pp. 17-32.

colonialist, the imperial factor overruled everything else. Determined to bar the intrusion of British power in the Levant, Augagneur issued a stiff rejoinder through the French naval attaché:

> The Minister persists in claiming the execution of the convention of August 6, and the entire direction of the operations in the Mediterranean for the French command. Under these conditions any operation must be planned and directed by us. The Admiralty cannot adopt a plan in which we would assume the role it would assign to us. Do insist firmly on this line of thought.[31]

Churchill had anticipated some resistance from Paris but not an outright rebuke. He was bewildered and upset that Augagneur should choose this critical moment to invoke the Anglo-French accord of 6 August which had been concluded at the beginning of the war. Such an arrangement, he felt, was subject to modification or cancellation by either signatory at any time owing to the new conditions created by Turkey's entry into the conflict. In a mood of exasperation, he poured his heart out to Edward Grey, the Foreign Secretary of State:

> It is absurd for the French to claim that we are to make no movements into the Mediterranean except by their directives and under their command. That would be to inflict on Gr. Britain, as the forfeit for her services to France, conditions which could not be extorted from her by any power by war. The French ships placed under our direction have done little or nothing in the Channel and foreign waters and we are ready to release them at any time. The French fleet moreover has itself done nothing in the Mediterranean. We are quite capable of conducting the Dardanelles operation without any assistance and I only suggested French co-operation out of loyalty and politeness ... All plans for the attack on the Dardanelles are moving forward and I have every expectation of opening fire on the 15th [February]. I hope I may count on you to see me through with these people.[32]

Although Churchill felt that French demands were unreasonable, he had no choice but reach an accommodation with them if he expected his operation to come off. Indeed, his own colleagues in the War Council would not have supported him over French objections. From the outset of the war, the British were determined to maintain unity of purpose which they deemed indispensable to eventual victory. It became a central aim of British policy to avoid doing anything that would so exasperate the French that it might endanger the Alliance. Thus whenever disputes threatened to get out of hand, the British invariably capitulated even when it went against their own national self-interest.

The obvious question confronting Churchill was how to approach his French opposite number. The more he thought about it, the more he believed that he could win over Augagneur in a face-to-face encounter. Accordingly, Churchill proposed to Augagneur (via Cambon) that they meet in London so that they could iron out their differences.[33]

---

31 SHD: AMM, Xa 37, Augagneur to Saint-Seine, 21 January 1915.
32 BNA: Grey papers, FO 800/88, Churchill to Grey, 24 January 1915.
33 AMAE: Cambon papers, under the heading Voyages des ministres et des personalities, carton 10, Cambon to Delcassé, 22 January 1915; SHD: AMM, Ca 9, Augagneur's testimony before the Marine Commission, 18 July 1917.

Augagneur later explained his reasons for agreeing to meet with Churchill: (1) a disagreement with the Admiralty which had planned to employ French minesweepers in the Straits without informing him: (2) to put an end to the encroachment of the British Admiral [Pierce] on the Syrian coast in violation of the convention of 6 August 1914.[34]

Augagneur must have realized at some point that it would serve no purpose to insist that the French navy should take the lead in attacking the Dardanelles. Even if the British had been willing to accept a subsidiary role, the plain truth was that the French navy, occupied mainly with transporting African troops to France and blockading the Austrians in the Adriatic, lacked the strength to force the Dardanelles. Augagneur later admitted as much when he was interviewed by the Marine Commission.[35]

Before crossing the channel, Augagneur wanted the cabinet to authorize his mission. In these circumstances it became impossible to refrain from disclosing the intended operation in the Dardanelles as Churchill had requested. At a meeting of the cabinet on 23 January, the Minister of Marine revealed that the British Admiralty were organizing, independent of the French navy, an operation in the Dardanelles. He went on to say that, in view of the Anglo-French naval accord, the right of command in the Mediterranean belonged to France. Therefore, the British could not undertake an enterprise there without the prior consent of the French government. The cabinet ministers decided without a lengthy debate that Augagneur should journey to London to discuss with Churchill a project which they maintained would require close study before it could be accepted.[36] The next day Augagneur communicated directly with Churchill and accepted his invitation, adding:

> May I remind you that in my telegrams ... I recommended that you bring to the attention of the British Government the interest that we have in the region of Alexandretta, as well as in Syria itself. An operation in this region, similar to the one our naval attaché attributes to the thinking of the British Admiralty could only take place with our agreement and co-operation.[37]

The meeting was scheduled at the Admiralty for the afternoon of 26 January and Augagneur arrived at the appointed time, accompanied by his *chef de cabinet*, Henri Salaun, a talented high-ranking naval officer (*capitaine de vaisseau*). Churchill, on hand to greet Augagneur, led him to a private room where they could talk more freely. As neither Churchill nor Augagneur could speak the other's language, they had to work through an interpreter. Unfortunately, no written record of their discussion exists but from Churchill's letter on 27 January containing the results of the conference and Augagneur's testimony before the Marine Commission on a number of occasions, it is possible to piece together a sense of what took place.

The first order of business was devoted to readjusting the naval spheres in the Mediterranean in accordance with the original French demands and Churchill's pledge to abandon, at least for

---

34 SHD: AMM, Es 11, Augagneur to Rear-Admiral Marie-Jean-Lucien Lacaze (then Minister of Marine), 26 February 1917.
35 AN: Série C7532, dossier 1106, Augagneur's testimony before the Marine Commission, 19 March 1915.
36 Poincaré, *Au Service*, Vol. 6, pp. 29-30.
37 SHD: AMM, Xa 37, Augagneur to Churchill, 24 January 1915.

the present, a landing at Alexandretta.[38] Thus patrol of the Syrian coast, including Alexandretta and as far south as Jaffa, would be the concern of the French, while control of naval operations in Egyptian waters and in the Dardanelles would remain in British hands. As for Alexandretta should any future operation become necessary there, it would be undertaken jointly after the details had been worked out through regular channels.[39] Churchill was enough of a pragmatist to realize that he must dampen French speculation about British aims in the Levant. In any event, the unlikelihood that he could get the necessary troops from Kitchener made it futile to create an incident when more serious matters, including the fate of the Dardanelles operation, rested on preserving friendly ties with the French. Well might Churchill declare to Grey after the meeting: "I think it important to let the French have what they want even about Alexandretta. It will be fatal to cordial co-operation in the Mediterranean and perhaps elsewhere, if we arouse their suspicions … in the region of Syria."[40]

A discussion of the Dardanelles campaign followed and took up the rest of the meeting. Churchill explained the reasons that had prompted the British government to want to send a naval fleet to breach the Dardanelles and that, in the view of Vice-Admiral Carden, this could be accomplished by a step-by-step destruction of the shore batteries. He painted a glowing picture of the tremendous political and military benefits that would accrue from a successful attempt to force the Straits: Turkey would capitulate, the southern sea-route to Russia would be cleared; the Balkans would probably be weaned from their neutrality and the back door to Germany would be opened.

Churchill strengthened his case by showing Augagneur a telegram from Petrograd which the Foreign Office had sent over that morning. While the Grand Duke Nicholas regretted that Russia could not assist in the forthcoming operation in the Dardanelles as the inferiority of its navy gave little hope of achieving anything meaningful, he nevertheless attached the greatest importance to its success. He explained that forcing the Straits would paralyze Turkey, influence the attitude of the Balkan states and assist Allied operations. Churchill did not consider that the absence of Russian help would jeopardize the success of the enterprise. Still he almost certainly pointed out, as Grey suggested in his covering note, that failure to go ahead with the operation would disappoint Russia "and react most unfavourably upon the military situation."[41]

Augagneur remained dubious of the ability of the navy to open a passage unassisted. He alluded to a report recently conducted at his request by French naval intelligence which had concluded that a purely maritime enterprise to force the Dardanelles was unlikely to succeed.[42] Augagneur added that he had also consulted Vice-Admiral (Marie-Jacques-Charles) Aubert, the chief of the general staff of the French navy, just before leaving for London and was told unequivocally that a fleet attacking the Straits would accomplish nothing unless accompanied by a military landing on the Gallipoli Peninsula.[43]

---

38   NA: Série C7531, dossier 1022, Augagneur's testimony before the Marine Commission, 18 July 1917.
39   SHD: AMM, Es 11, Churchill to Augagneur, 27 January 1915.
40   BNA: Cabinet papers, CAB 19/28, Churchill to Grey, 26 January 1915, appended to Churchill's testimony before the Dardanelles Commission. The letter is in the full and unpublished version of the Dardanelles Commission Report.
41   Churchill, *World Crisis*, Vol. 2, p. 155.
42   SHD: AMM, Ca 9, Augagneur's testimony before the Marine Commission, 18 July 1917.
43   SHD: AMM, Ca 9, Augagneur's testimony before the Marine Commission 18 July 1917.

Churchill endeavoured to calm the apprehensions of his French counterpart, observing that the vast improvement in gunnery had reshaped naval thinking regarding the old adage of ships versus forts. The potentialities of a ship like the *Queen Elizabeth* – the most powerful battleship afloat had been added to Carden's squadron – with its 15-inch guns, rendered a task hitherto impossible now comparatively easy or at least quite practical. The First Lord was confident that the Turks would give up the struggle and retreat once the forts at the entrance of the Straits were demolished. He indicated that in case the ships encountered unexpected opposition, the operation would be called off, followed by a public announcement that it was a feint for a strike elsewhere.

Augagneur's limitations in a field in which he was a novice was a fatal barrier in assessing whether the naval operation rested on a firm strategic and tactical premise. He did not request tangible evidence that breaking through the Dardanelles would cause the regime to collapse in Constantinople. On top of this, he had no way of knowing that the First Lord overestimated the effects of naval guns miles away against targets on land and underplayed the danger from mines, the enemy's mobile guns on minesweeping operations, and the disadvantage the ships would face when moving closer to engage shore batteries. If he was unconcerned about fully understanding the technical aspects of the operation, it was because he had been assured that if resistance at the Straits proved insurmountable, the attack would be abandoned.

Vice Admiral A.P. Bienaimé, an acidulous critic of French naval policy, subsequently raked Augagneur over the coals for, among other things, journeying to London without Vice-Admiral Aubert who could have provided the requisite technical expertise.[44] Some members of the Marine Commission doubted that Augagneur, in view of his vague answer to an inquiry, had even consulted Aubert before he left for London. Aubert could have shed light on troubling questions, but he was never interviewed. He died in June 1915. Still his views were well known on the issues that counted most.[45]

There are two plausible reasons for Augagneur's decision to leave Aubert behind. As will be discussed more fully later in the chapter, he thought that by leaving the planning process exclusively in the hands of the British – contrary to the expectations of the French cabinet which wanted a close examination – he could insolate himself from a possible naval failure. In the second place the relationship between Augagneur and his naval chief was strained, due at least in part because of their political differences – Aubert was very conservative. Aubert had already made his opinion clear about the idea of a purely naval attack, so Augagneur saw no value in bringing him along. He knew that he could draw expert advice from his *chef de cabinet* whenever he required it. Still, although Salaun was present during the talks, he lacked Aubert's standing and experience and would have been reluctant to offer his views, unless solicited, knowing that his chief during the negotiations was influenced as much, if not more so, by political considerations.

Augagneur may have taken it for granted that a successful naval operation would pay handsome dividends but it was not among the reasons he listed for acquiescing in Churchill's plan. As he told the Marine Commission, he was swayed by two compelling factors. First Churchill's assurance that if the ships encountered unforeseen difficulties in the Straits they

---

44 Vice-Amiral Amédée-Pierre-Léonard Bienaimé, *La guerre navale 1914-1915: fautes et responsabilités* (Paris: Jules Tallandier, 1920), pp. 176-82.
45 Vice-Amiral Henri Salaun, *La Marine française* (Paris: Les Editions de France, 1934), p. 173.

would be recalled, and the affair portrayed as a simple demonstration to avoid the moral consequence of a defeat. The Minister of Marine maintained that if he had been kept informed of the fleet's inability to deal with the forts in the preliminary stages of the bombardment, he would never have agreed to the naval attack on 18 March. Second, Augagneur was under the erroneous impression that Churchill had the full backing of the naval as well as civil authorities in England.[46] The determination with which the First Lord tried to press the naval scheme upon his acceptance convinced him that his failure to cooperate might affect Anglo-French relations.[47] To the two reasons Augagneur cited, a third must be added. It was a curious omission on his part given the emphasis he had placed on France's imperial rivalry with Britain. In any case he derived immense satisfaction from compelling Churchill to accept his proposal which thwarted the British from establishing themselves in an area of French interest.

Churchill did not seek French participation in the attack, other than requesting minesweepers and other auxiliary vessels, but indicated, presumably out of courtesy, that he would welcome the assistance of the French squadron currently in vicinity of the Dardanelles. Augagneur saw that France could not disassociate itself from the venture. He did not trust Churchill's assertion that territory conquered by any of the Allies was provisional and subject to revision at the end of the war, and knew too well that possession, as the old saying went, was nine-tenths of the law. He told the Marine Commission in retrospect: "Not to take part in the operation would have been, in case it succeeded, to witness the appearance of the English fleet alone before Constantinople. For us French who are deeply engaged in the Orient, as you are aware, it would have been a very painful renunciation of our national pride and perilous for our interests."[48] Augagneur would not commit himself on the extent of French naval participation until he had consulted with the leading members of his government.

The meeting ended on an amicable note and the two men shook hands. Each had more or less gotten what he wanted. Churchill won his case that the British be allowed to control the planning and execution of the Dardanelles operation. Augagneur consolidated French claims to command in the Mediterranean and off the coast of Syria and gained a role for France in an expedition that promised huge political and military benefits if successful. The seizure of Alexandretta was postponed, and should such action become necessary at a later date it was to be undertaken only after an understanding between the two governments.

The next day Churchill drew up a memorandum containing the results of the meeting which he later submitted to his French counterpart.[49] Cutting short his work day at the Admiralty on the 27th, Churchill, being the good host, provided Augagneur with a tour of London and in the evening had him over to his home for dinner.

Churchill had always appeared confident about the outcome of the Dardanelles campaign but in moments of reflection he could scarcely overlook the fact that the fleet would be embarking upon a task for which there was practically no precedent in naval warfare. A slight miscalculation or error in judgment might fatally compromise the operation. Although the fleet would possess the element of surprise that advantage could be nullified by indiscretions

---

46 Churchill had actually extracted from the Admiralty naval experts no more than lukewarm consent in support of the purely naval attack. Marder, *From the Dreadnought*, Vol. 2, p. 246.
47 SHD: AMM, Ca9, Augagneur's testimony before the Marine Commission, 18 July 1917.
48 SHD: AMM, Ca 9, Augagneur's testimony before the Marine Commission, 18 July 1917.
49 SHD: AMM, Es 11, Churchill to Augagneur, 27 January 1915.

at home. Secrecy was therefore deemed an essential requirement for the fleet's success. In London, Churchill tried to persuade Augagneur to conceal the news of the impending naval attack from the French government. Naturally Augagneur refused to endanger his career to accommodate Churchill's incomprehensible request, insisting that it must be left to the Prime Minister and others to decide.[50]

Churchill was not content to leave the matter up in the air. On 29 January he called in the French ambassador and urged him to use his good offices to convince Augagneur to withhold all information about the coming naval attack to all but a few key members of the French government. Always mindful that it was his duty to eliminate differences apt to upset the close bond between the two powers, Cambon replied that he would do what he could. Accordingly, he addressed a personal letter to Augagneur in which he stressed that secrecy was vital if the fleet was to attain its objective and, perhaps deviating slightly from Churchill's request, suggested that only those ministers likely to be involved, that is, the prime minister, and ministers of war and foreign affairs, should be told.[51]

Augagneur received the note as he was about to leave for Viviani's office. With the Prime Minister, he discussed his arrangement in London and the two men agreed that only Delcassé should be taken into their confidence. Millerand was to be shut out as there was no desire to arouse the ire of Joffre who considered himself in charge of grand strategy – unlike the British War Council, the French had as yet no mechanism in place to control the higher direction of the war. Both Viviani and Delcassé readily endorsed French naval participation in the Dardanelles operation, for they wanted to ensure that the country's imperial interests were protected. They might have reacted differently if they had known that the experts at the Ministry of Marine were adamantly opposed to the idea of a purely naval attack. On the other hand, they may have believed, like Augagneur, that no great harm would occur for the attack would be broken off and treated as a simple demonstration if the bombardment proved ineffective.

On 30 January Augagneur spoke briefly in the cabinet about his trip to London. He declared that he was highly pleased with the results, pointing out that command of the Mediterranean, especially along the coast of Syria, would remain in French hands. No mention was made of the Admiralty's plan to force the Dardanelles or of the French intention to support it.[52] Presumably Cambon's plea for secrecy had resonated with the Minister of Marine, at least for the time being.

Augagneur was more forthcoming when he visited the President in the afternoon. He showed Poincaré the confidential letter Churchill had sent him after their interview in London.[53] He explained that Churchill was adamant that the French navy should take part in some degree with the attack in the Dardanelles which was set to begin around 15 February. He went on to say that Churchill was confident that the forts would be destroyed without difficulty and the mines swept with the trawlers provided by France. Poincaré recognized that the naval attack involved considerable risk but he was comforted by the knowledge that it could not lead to

50 SHD: AMM, Ca 9, Augagneur's testimony before the Marine Commission, 18 July 1917.
51 AMAE: Cambon papers, under the heading Conférences des Alliés, carton 10, Cambon to Augagneur, 29 January 1915.
52 Bibliothèque Nationale de France (BnF): Poincaré's papers are in the BnF with the codes NAF 15992–16063. Poincaré's daily journal (notes journalières). See <http://gallacia.bnf.f//> and Poincaré, *Au Service*, Vol. 6, p. 33.
53 SHD: AMM, Es 11, Churchill to Augagneur, 27 January 1915.

disaster because the ships would be recalled if success appeared unlikely. Augagneur confided that he had no illusions about the chances of the ships to break through the Straits but he did not think it was his place to try to dissuade the British as they were prepared to assume nearly all the risks.[54] Whatever may be said about Augagneur's conduct of naval affairs, there was nothing wrong with his political instinct. His apparent *volte-face* in the presence of Poincaré, after he had willingly signed on with Churchill several days before, showed that he was sufficiently astute to disassociate himself from the enterprise in the event that it failed. He knew that the established opinion of experts at the Ministry of Marine strongly deprecated unsupported naval action against the forts. To have acted contrary to the solicited advice of Aubert and his staff would have been, in the event the ships ran into trouble, tantamount to committing political suicide. Thus by keeping them out of the picture, Augagneur could represent the expedition, as having been conceived, planned and executed by the English and lay the entire blame at their feet. On the other hand, if the fleet overcame the resistance of the Turkish forts and appeared before Constantinople, he could claim part of the credit by virtue of the role the French ships had played in the assault.

In a memorandum dated 31 January and forwarded to the Admiralty, Augagneur concurred in the statements in which his British counterpart had made on the 27th and announced that the French government would place four battleships, as well as a number of auxiliary vessels, at Carden's disposal.[55]

It is remarkable that Augagneur elected to keep Vice-Admiral Boué de Lapeyrère in the dark about his understanding with Churchill. Augagneur's conduct is perplexing especially since Boué de Lapeyrère's subordinate, Rear-Admiral Guépratte, was involved in the operation. It was only when Guépratte made inquiries about the supply of munitions that Boué de Lapeyrère first suspected that something was afoot. He sent Admiral Jules Docteur, deputy-chief of his naval staff, to see Carden to try to discover what was going on. Docteur had a long interview with Carden who under orders to remain silent, spoke vaguely of a grandiose project relating to the Dardanelles, regretting that he could not divulge specific details. Carden's immediate subordinates, however, talked more freely behind their chief's back and let word out that the Admiralty was laying plans for a naval attack on the Dardanelles. On receiving the report, Boué de Lapeyrère was naturally indignant that he had been kept out of the loop, but he struggled to contain his emotions while seeking an explanation from his superior. In a cable to Augagneur on 31 January, he revealed his latest findings and registered his disappointment that the operation would take place outside his command and without an opportunity for some of his ships to participate in it. His enthusiasm for the project might have been tempered if he had been acquainted with its details. The message sent was carefully worded but traces of the Admiral's bitterness were evident. The main part of the text ran as follows:

> Your lordship probably is aware of this project, but in as much as it is very new to me and of great military importance, I would like Mr. Herr [a naval officer on his staff] to talk to you in case you do not know its details. To my astonishment at not having been informed of the situation, while my subordinate Rear-Admiral Guépratte secretly knew of it, would

---

54 Poincaré, *Au Service*, Vol. 6, pp. 33-34.
55 SHD: AMM, Es 11, Augagneur to Churchill, 31 January 1915.

be added a profound deception, if I saw this operation, quite tempting and quite feasible, take place outside my command and without having an opportunity to participate in it, with several of my battleships, at least as compensation for all the weariness we have been subjected to in the last six months.[56]

Augagneur immediately replied:

> I am pleased to enclose herein a copy of a letter which has been addressed to me by the First Lord of the Admiralty on January 27th.
>
> I have given in principle my adhesion to the proposals contained in this letter, and, in particular to the cooperation of the French battleships operating in the Dardanelles to an action which will take place around February 15th in the Straits under the command of Vice-Admiral Carden.
>
> In the … telegram sent to you today, I ask that you find out from Admiral Guépratte the main points of Admiral Carden's project, and I would be thankful to receive your personal opinion on it.[57]

At the same time Augagneur signaled Guépratte, requesting specific information on how Carden proposed to reduce the forts along the Straits: "You undoubtedly must have had conversations with Admiral [Sackville] Hamilton Carden about the conditions under which this action can be undertaken, I would be grateful if you notified me immediately of the outline of your common plan of attack as well as your personal opinion on the matter."[58] Guépratte's reply two days later contained a brief description of the battle plan and concluded in optimistic terms: "Am in complete agreement with VA Carden and have absolute confidence in success, the consequences of which will be incalculable."[59]

Seeking relevant data from both Boué de Lapeyère and Guépratte is undeniable proof that Augagneur was unaware of the particulars of the naval operation before consenting formally to collaborate with the British. It was only after he sent off the two telegrams that he received a memorandum from the Admiralty (2 February), disclosing Carden's precise step-by-step plan of attack in the Dardanelles.

Carden's initial objective was to silence the forts at the entrance, then send minesweepers to clear the channel to enable his ships to sail up to Kepez Bay, methodically smashing the intermediary defences along the way. This would be followed by piecemeal destruction of the forts at The Narrows, the last and most formidable obstacle before the fleet entered the Sea of Marmora. The Admiralty proposed to send two battalion of marines to act as landing parties to complete the destruction of forts seriously damaged by the navy's guns. The Admiralty continued to believe that the destruction of the forts one by one would have a moral effect on those not yet under attack, leading the Turks to lose confidence in their German advisers and withdraw, an attitude that might be felt in Constantinople.[60]

---

56   SHD: AMM, Ed 108, Boué de Lapeyrère to Augagneur, 31 January 1915.
57   SHD: AMM, Ed 108, Augagneur to Boué de Lapeyrère, 31 January 1915.
58   SHD: AMM, Ed 108, Augagneur to Guépratte, 31 January 1915.
59   SHD: AMM, Ed 107, Guépratte to Augagneur, 2 February 1915.
60   SHD: AMM, ES 11, Churchill to Augagneur, 2 February 1915.

After Augagneur looked over the report from the Admiralty, he forwarded it to Aubert for his appraisal. The Minister of Marine had no illusions about what to expect. He had been told by Aubert, possibly before going to London but certainly after his return, that without military assistance the fleet was unlikely to accomplish any lasting results. Although Augagneur acknowledged Aubert's right to be heard (as was standard practice on all matters relating to naval strategy), he was not bound by his recommendations.

What troubled Aubert the most about Carden's plan was not the method of attack but the inattention given to a crucial and what seemed to him an elementary factor, namely what would follow should some ships break into the Sea of Marmora. Aubert's comments are contained in the following appreciation:

> A salient feature revealed by the reading of the diverse English memorandum is that in this expedition, initiated and directed by the English, the beginning is clear but the end cannot be foreseen.
>
> In most expeditions against cities, the attack and destruction of the defences comes first and are followed by the landing of the troops who take over the place and thus by force become its masters.
>
> In this case nothing similar happens. The destruction of the forts at Chanak and Kilid Bahr is expected to produce an effect on the morale [of the defenders] as is explicitly indicated in Mr. Churchill's last memorandum.
>
> It is believed that the slow and irresistible destruction of the forts by battleships that cannot be reached effectively by their fire will have a great influence on the morale of those in the forts that have not yet been attacked and might also destroy the trust of the Turks in their Germanic advisers; and it is possible that the reversal of German domination in Constantinople will result from it.
>
> Here is what is clear. Politicians are qualified to know what they can attain from the start of military action. I am not qualified to do so. I can only state that Mr. Churchill's memorandum stops with the destruction of the forts at Chanak and Kilid Bahr.
>
> What will be the ensuing military action?
>
> Let us suppose it to be as favourable as possible and let us admit that the Allied fleets arrive in view of Constantinople. The question is: what comes next?
>
> The Turkish government will probably be gone. We do not possess the necessary landing forces. What is to be done? Once more the problem seems to belong, at this time, in the domain of the politician, since military action has not yet been determined.
>
> That is what we desire to establish.
>
> From a technical point of view, the general method of attack appears to be good.[61]

It is significant to observe that Aubert was the first Allied naval expert to identify a glaring omission in the naval plan of operation. He had the good sense to ask what the fleet was supposed to do should it manage to reach Constantinople. How did the navy expect to capture and hold Constantinople? His meaning was clear. Since a military force was needed to garrison the Ottoman capital why not have it ready to cooperate in the naval attack. Contrary to Carden,

---

61   SHD: AMM, Ed 109, Aubert to Augagneur, 7 February 1915.

Aubert was unwilling to accept on faith the Admiralty's conviction that a Turkish collapse would occur once the fleet anchored before Constantinople.

As the report was unpalatable to Augagneur, he concealed it from his colleagues. He obviously envisaged no problems as he told Churchill: "I have read the memorandum that you sent me on February 2. The provisions contained therein raise no objections on my part. They appear to have been conceived with prudence and foresight, permitting a withdrawal without suffering loss of prestige should the continuation of the operation present difficulties."[62] The First Lord's constant reminder that the ships could be recalled at any moment appeared to Augagneur to limit the danger to a justifiable risk. For good or for ill the die had been cast.

---

62   CCAC: Churchill papers, CHAR 2/81/14, Augagneur to Churchill, 9 February 1915.

4

Genesis of Military Cooperation

As Millerand had requested, the general staff at the War Ministry submitted its investigative report on the proposed expedition to Syria on 1 February. It examined three types of operation and listed the pros and cons of each option. It rejected both a simple naval demonstration and a major military expedition and instead recommended a "restrained intervention," involving landings at five key points in Cilicia, Lebanon and Syria. The plan called for 25,000 combatants in the initial stages, to be subsequently joined by contingents from Syria and elsewhere. The object of the mission was to secure the areas of particular interest to France in case the Ottoman Empire broke up, afford a measure of protection to the Christian minorities, assist Arab nationalists and cut off Turkey's 4th Army (under Djemal Pasha) in Syria from its main supply base.[1] The report was filed and not given any consideration. As noted in the previous chapter, it was submitted after France became involved in the Dardanelles campaign.

At the beginning of February plans for a naval attack on the Dardanelles were moving ahead on the assumption that no troops would be available to cooperate in the forthcoming operation. Churchill held firm to the notion that the navy alone could silence the forts guarding the Straits and he saw no need to bring pressure to bear on Kitchener for military assistance. Churchill's only concession to allay the anxiety among his senior naval advisors at the idea of a purely naval operation had been to commit two battalions of marines to be used as landing parties to complete the destruction of the batteries once the Turkish forts were silenced. It did little to reassure the Admiralty experts, however.

During preparations for the naval attack, troops from various quarters suddenly became available. A subcommittee of the War Council, which had been appointed on 8 January 1915 to find an alternative theatre for the first divisions of the New Armies – which would be ready in a few months – had recommended a landing at Salonica in order to help Serbia. A report had reached London that an Austro-Hungarian army was set to again invade Serbia. Kitchener was inclined to favor a show of force in the Balkans, hoping especially to induce the Greeks to abandon their neutrality. The pro-Entente Greek Prime Minister Eleutherios Venizelos was apparently leaning towards intervention on condition that Romania could be persuaded to

---

1 SHD: Archives du Ministère de la Guerre (AMG), Considérations Générales, 1 February 1915, carton 2, dossier 5, in section under the heading of Turquie.

collaborate and the Allies provide a modest contingent to guarantee against a flank attack from his country's arch enemy Bulgaria. Millerand, who arrived in London on 22 January to urge the Asquith government to reinforce the Western Front with more divisions to ward off an expected German attack, was unsympathetic to the idea of sending an Anglo-French force to the Balkans in support of Serbia.[2]

Whilst in Paris on an unrelated matter, Lloyd George discovered that Millerand had not reported to the French cabinet that the British were considering extending the war to the Balkans. Lloyd George repaired the omission and, taking it upon himself to lobby the leading French politicians – Briand, Viviani, Delcassé and Poincaré – found them in a receptive mood. The interest in France reawakened, Delcassé crossed the channel to further discuss the matter with the British. He lunched with Grey, Asquith, Kitchener and Churchill and suggested that to relieve pressure on Serbia an Anglo-French landing at Salonica should take place with each country contributing a division.[3] With momentum building for the strategic diversion, the general sentiment in Paris was that winning over Greece was worth the price of several Anglo-French divisions. Millerand struck the only discordant note, claiming that the two divisions were absolutely required on the main front.[4] Poincaré suggested that the French division could be made up of troops from the interior (depots) and he thought that Kitchener would have no difficulty in supplying a division without affecting those he had already promised to send to France. The cabinet voted on 4 February to participate in the Balkan venture pending Joffre's approval. When Millerand sounded out Joffre about the cabinet's decision, he gave his reluctant consent.[5] The French Generalissimo evidently saw the value of a very modest investment to entice Greece, with its substantial army, to join the Entente.

At this point a piece of bad news derailed the whole arrangement with Greece. Bulgaria had accepted a loan from Germany, a sign interpreted in the western capitals and elsewhere that its adhesion to the Central Powers was imminent. The Greeks were unwilling to plunge into battle unless a clear understanding had been reached with Romania. Since the Russians had been driven back on the east Prussian front and, in addition, forced to withdraw from Bukovina, it was not the moment to approach the Romanians. Hence the Balkan project was dropped. In London all eyes were now fixed on the Dardanelles.

As soon as it became evident that troops would be available, naval opinion at the Admiralty mounted increasingly in favour of a military landing on the Gallipoli Peninsula to coincide with the naval attack. If troops could be spared for an operation in the Balkans, why could they not be used in the Dardanelles? Kitchener began to relent somewhat and on 9 February agreed that if "the Navy required the assistance of land forces at a later stage, that assistance would be forthcoming."[6] On 16 February an even more important development occurred. At an informal gathering of the upper echelon of the War Council, the decision was taken to send the 29th

---

2   Lord Hankey, *The Supreme Command 1914-1918*, Vol. 1 (London: Allen and Unwin, 1961), p. 274.
3   Aspinall-Oglander, *Gallipoli*, pp. 63-64; Hankey, *Supreme Command*, Vol. 1, pp. 276-77; Lloyd George, *War Memoirs*, Vol. 1, pp. 241-45; Lennox (ed.), *Diary of Lord Bertie*, Vol. 1, pp. 107-09.
4   Poincaré, *Au service*, Vol. 6, pp. 42-43.
5   Poincaré, *Au service*, Vol. 6, pp. 44-46.
6   BNA: Cabinet papers, CAB 42/1, Minutes of the War Council, 9 February 1915.

Division, originally earmarked for France, to the Greek island of Lemnos[7] and to direct General Sir John Maxwell, commander-in-chief of the British forces in Egypt, to prepare units of the Australian and New Zealand Army Corps (Anzac) where they were completing their training, for possible use at the Dardanelles. There was yet no definite decision to employ these troops as Kitchener and his colleagues remained confident that the ships alone could master the Straits. They were emergency forces, ready to strike where opportunity might offer.

The Foreign Office communicated the change of policy to the French government the next day. The note, sent through Lord Bertie, the British Ambassador in Paris, read as follows: "As the naval forces require the support of the army in their attack against the Dardanelles forts, we are preparing to send a division to Lemnos as soon as possible."[8] Whether it was an oversight or done deliberately, the note did not invite French military participation. It is known that Kitchener was not anxious to see the involvement of French land forces in the operation. He told Churchill on 20 February: "I have just seen Grey and hope we shall not be saddled with a French contingent for the Dardanelles."[9] An avowed imperialist, Kitchener wanted Britain to be in a position to claim certain areas of the Ottoman Empire which were of vital French interest. Before the war he had fixed his sight on Syria, except for the Christian areas which were pro-French, even though neither Asquith nor Grey were willing to disturb the government's good relationship with Paris.[10] With the French now as allies, he naturally had to abandon his quest to eventually bring Syria under British control. On the other hand he was adamant that Britain's position in Egypt would be untenable if any other power held Alexandretta.[11] He knew that the French also coveted the port and in recent years had maintained that it was part of Syria and thus within their sphere of interest.[12] But he believed that Britain's occupation of Alexandretta would ensure its future possession. Kitchener underestimated the degree to which the French attached to Alexandretta and imagined that they could be persuaded to give up their claim if compensated with former German colonies.[13]

It was not until 13 February that the full cabinet in Paris was informed of the impending naval assault in the Dardanelles.[14] The first important issue facing the ministers was to decide whether to send troops to assist in the operation. Their highest priority was of course to ensure the security of France and it was seen that collecting even a small contingent for service abroad could only be achieved at the expense of the Western Front. Yet it was feared that the absence of French troops in the Dardanelles would allow the British an unobstructed path to establish themselves in the Levant. The matter was aired in the cabinet on 18 February and the ministers,

---

7   By an informal arrangement with the Greek Prime Minister the English received permission to use the island of Lemnos in the Aegean, some 50 miles from Gallipoli, as a naval base for the operation.
8   AMAE: under the heading Opération des Dardanelles, carton 4, dossier 1, Bertie to Delcassé, 17 February 1915.
9   Cited in Churchill, *World Crisis*, Vol. 2, p. 182.
10 Cassar, *Kitchener as Proconsul,* p. 225.
11 BNA: Cabinet papers, CAB 42/1, Minutes of the War Council, 10 March 1915.
12 Lennox, (ed.), *Diary of Lord Bertie,* Vol. 1, p. 135.
13 Jukka Nevakivi, "Lord Kitchener and the Partition of the Ottoman Empire", in K. Bourne and D.C. Watt (eds.), *Studies in International History* (London: Longmans, 1967), pp. 324-26.
14 Abel Ferry, *Les Carnets Secrets 1914-1918* (Paris: Bernard Grasset, 1957), p. 56.

despite lacking information about the precise function of the military forces, agreed to match the British division with one of their own.[15]

After the meeting, Delcassé informed Cambon of the cabinet's decision and asked him to inquire whether the naval operation would be postponed until after the arrival of the army divisions.[16] This was the first time that the possibility was raised, now that troops were to be sent, of waiting for a combined attack. But Churchill, captivated by the mirage of success, persisted in ignoring every difficulty. He replied: "Naval operations will proceed continuously to their conclusion, as every day we add to the dangers of the arrival of German or Austrian submarines and any lull in the attack would prejudice the moral effect on the Turkish capital."[17] Beyond this, Cambon and other key French officials in London could not get any definitive answers regarding the use of military forces. Would the troops disembark during the bombardment or after the forts had been reduced? Would they land at all if the naval assault failed? Would land operations subsequently be undertaken in the neighbor of Constantinople or confined to the Gallipoli Peninsula itself? Grey told Cambon that the Anglo-French divisions would be sent only after the effects of the naval bombardment could be determined, at which time the two governments would confer and decide on a plan of action. From another source (unnamed) Cambon learned that a landing would take place only if the damage caused by the naval bombardment suggested that there was a high chance of success.[18] Colonel Arthus de la Panouse, the French military attaché in London, for his part approached Kitchener and was given a different version of the planned operation. According to the Secretary for War there was no question of trying to occupy the Gallipoli Peninsula which he believed was well defended by the Turks. Rather he proposed to use the division sent to assist the fleet in mopping up operations and, for that elementary task, he did not think that French troops would be necessary.[19] The French were bewildered at the inability of the British leaders to speak as one voice. The fog that was rapidly enveloping the entire enterprise should have raised a red flag. Thoughtful planning had been sacrificed in the interest of haste.

During the third week in February troubling events on the eastern front further complicated matters. News that the Russians had experienced severe reverses in Poland and in Bukovina raised fears among the soldiers in France that the Germans would transfer massive forces for an all-out assault in the west. In these circumstances GQG insisted that without the crack British 29th Division it could not guarantee the inviolability of the main front. Under mounting pressure

---

15 France, Ministère de la Guerre, État-Major de L'Armée, Service Historique, *Les armées françaises dans la grande guerre: Expédition des Dardanelles* (Paris: Imprimerie Nationale, 1923), p. 18. This is the French official history of the campaign. Henceforth it will be referred to as France, *Expédition des Dardanelles*.

16 AMAE: under the heading Opération des Dardanelles, carton 4, dossier. 1, Delcassé to Cambon, 18 February 1915.

17 BNA: Kitchener papers, PRO 30/57/59 (copy), Churchill [?] to Grey, 18 February 1915. The answer was forwarded to Cambon.

18 AMAE: Cambon papers, underthe heading Orient correspondence, carton 10, Cambon to Délcassé, 19 February, 1915.

19 De la Panouse to Millerand, 20 February 1915, in France, Ministère de la Guerre, État-Major de L'Armée, *Les armées françaises dans la grande guerres*, Service Historique (Paris: Imprimerie Nationale, 1924), tome 8, Vol. 1, annexe no. 1. This companion volume to the Official French History of the campaign contains many documents relating to the Dardanelles Operation. Henceforth it will be referred to as France, *Les armées françaises*, together with the tome, volume and annexe numbers.

Kitchener decided to hold back the 29th Division, at least until the crisis on the eastern front passed, and instead proposed to send to the Dardanelles the 30,000 untried and ill-equipped Australian and New Zealand units from Egypt. This elicited a sharp protest from Churchill who had changed his tune since winning over the War Council by his glowing enthusiasm and confidence about the capacity of the fleet to silence the forts guarding the Straits without the active involvement of the army. He claimed that, although he was still optimistic about the navy's ability to get through on its own, he wanted experienced troops concentrated nearby to assist to clear unexpected obstacles or reap the fruits of victory. Churchill had some support in the War Council, but Kitchener stood his ground, confident that only minor military action would be necessary to silence the concealed batteries and complete the destruction of the forts. Although he felt that the Anzac units would suffice to provide the fleet with all the help it would require, he did go as far as to say that he would later send the 29th Division if its absence threatened to jeopardize the operation.[20] The only thing left was to wait for the results of the naval operation which had just gotten under way.

Carden opened his attack on the forts at the mouth of the Straits a few minutes before 10 am on 19 February and ended at dusk, causing only slight damage to the forts and no direct hits on either the guns or mountings. As long as the ships were moving, marksmanship was inaccurate. The only way the Straits would be cleared was by short-range individual engagement with each of the Turkish guns. Bad weather and poor visibility hampered the operation and it was not until the 25th that the bombardment was resumed.[21] At close range, the fleet's results were more encouraging as the enemy guns on either side of the entrance were put out of commission. Parties of marines sent ashore on 26 February and succeeding days to complete the destruction of the forts and gun batteries obtained mixed results. There were instances when they achieved their mission but at other times, they were driven back by the defenders who had scurried back to the forts after the fleet's fire had lifted.

While this was going on, the fleet, embarking on the next phase of its operation, engaged the intermediate forts with little effect. Manoeuvring inside the narrow Straits, the ships were obliged to keep moving and consequently even had trouble in targeting enemy guns situated in place. Then there were the elusive mobile batteries which, although presented little danger to the battleships, wreaked havoc on the minesweepers whose task it was to clear the channel. And until the minefield was swept the path through the Straits would remain blocked. As a stalemate set in, Carden was becoming increasingly pessimistic about the ability of the navy to accomplish the job alone.

In the interim Churchill, acting on his own, issued a communiqué to the press on (Saturday) 20 February, announcing the start of the naval attack on the Dardanelles forts. It was an incomprehensive move on the part of the First Lord who had urged French political leaders repeatedly to maintain the utmost secrecy lest it compromise the operation. The press in London and Paris instantly concluded that the objective was to force the Dardanelles and threaten Constantinople. The military correspondent of *The Times* wrote that since much was at stake, both militarily and politically, the attack on the Dardanelles "having begun, it must be successfully carried through at all costs."[22] In Paris the media reached the same conclusion. The *Gaulois*

20 BNA: Cabinet papers, CAB 42/1, Minutes of the War Council, 19 February 1915.
21 Marder, *From the Dreadnought*, Vol. 2, pp. 233-34.
22 *The Times*, 22 February 1915.

explained: "The advantages of an operation which will render us masters of the Dardanelles and the Bosporus are too evident not to have been conceived."[23] It had been understood in the War Council from the beginning that no public statement would be released so that if the naval attack proved unsuccessful, it would be treated as a demonstration and abandoned without loss of face.[24] By drawing the attention of the world to the naval attack, Churchill took that option out of the hands of the War Council, not to mention that he alerted the Turks and gave them an early start to prepare their defences. What had prompted the First Lord to break his pledge to his colleagues? Was it to influence the wavering Balkan states to join the Entente? Was it to pressure Kitchener to send the 29th Division to the Dardanelles which he had indicated he would do on the 16th but changed his mind three days later? I am more inclined to believe, however, that Churchill whom Asquith, had described as "devoured by vanity," was motivated by selfish reasons.[25] He wanted to parade his master plan before the British people and, as he expected an eventual victory over the Turks, was laying the groundwork to reap the lion's share of the credit. Whatever the reason, Churchill made it certain that there would be no going back should the naval attack run into unforeseen difficulties.

The reaction to the First Lord's public announcement barely elicited a murmur at the War Council meeting on 24 February. None of the members openly rebuked Churchill for his indiscretion, although some had grumbled about it privately before the meeting.[26] If Churchill was spared a dressing down, it was because the War Council remained confident of an impending naval victory. It was only after disaster struck that the full implications of Churchill's injudicious statement became apparent and then belatedly, he was the subject of sharp criticism.   Lloyd George for one expressed his bitterness to his mistress when he accused Churchill of making it impossible for the War Council to contemplate quietly withdrawing the navy from the scene if things went awry.[27]

With the cat out of the bag, speaker after speaker in the War Council felt compelled to urge a modification of the policy by sending the army to ensure passage of the fleet into the Sea of Marmora. Kitchener weighed in as well, indicating that if the navy could not force the Straits unaided the Army should see the business through. He went on to say: "The effect of a defeat in the Orient would be very serious. There could be no going back. The publicity of the announcement had committed us."[28] After Turkey's entry in the war the Sultan had called for

---

23 Cited in the *Manchester Guardian*, 22 February 1915.
24 Churchill's own parliamentary secretary later admitted that the War Council intended that "very little should be said publicly" about the action of the fleet, and "that if the operation proved unsuccessful, it should be treated as a feint and the real objective described as Alexandretta." He added, "Winston's *communiqués* to the Press wittingly or unwittingly obscured this programme." Lord Riddell, *War Diary, 1914-1918* (London: Nicholson and Watson, 1934), p. 204. Hankey remarked that after the press announcement "it was felt that we were now committed to seeing the business through." Hankey, *Supreme Command*, Vol. 1, p. 283. See also Tom Curran, *The Grand Deception: Churchill and the Dardanelles* (Newport, NSW: Big Sky Publishing, 2015), pp. 86-89.
25 Michael and Eleanor Brock, (eds.), *Margot Asquith's Great War Diary 1914-1916* (Oxford: Oxford University Press, 2014), p. 79.
26 Lady Violet Bonham Carter, *Winston Churchill: An Intimate Portrait* (New York: Harcourt, Brace & World, 1964), p. 294.
27 A.J.P. Taylor (ed.), *Lloyd George: A Diary by Frances Stevenson* (New York: Harper & Row, 1971), p. 50.
28 BNA: Cabinet papers, CAB 42/1, Minutes of the War Council, 24 February 1915.

a jihad and there were fears among the ministers, especially Kitchener, that any loss of face in the Muslim world would inspire a revolt or, at the very least, serious trouble in India and Egypt.

The reaction in Paris to the release of the Admiralty communiqué came almost instantly. Besieged by the French press for a statement, Augagneur gave a brief interview to the *Petit Parisien* which appeared on Sunday. The gist of what he said ran as follows: "The French fleet and the British fleet bombarded the outer forts [of the Dardanelles] … I can say nothing more, further action depending on the commanders of the fleets."[29] Augagneur was furious with Churchill but the damage had already been done and he could only hope that the Anglo-French fleet succeeded in its mission.

At the same time the French had to deal with another distraction. They suspected that London may have deliberately deceived them as to the time and number of troops it planned to send to the Dardanelles. On the 20th Cambon wrote to Grey, reminding him of their interview on the previous day. Cambon then had been informed that the naval attack on the forts had just started and that the despatch of the Anglo-French troops for Lemnos was contingent on the outcome of the bombardment. If effective and the chances of a successful operation appeared favourable, it would be left to the two governments to devise a plan on how best to employ the troops and that such an understanding could possibly be reached the following week. Within 24 hours, however, Cambon learned that the British had decided to send 40,000 men – 10,000 marines plus 30,000 Australians and New Zealanders – to assist the fleet. This force, he was led to believe, was to be placed at the disposal of Vice-Admiral Carden, who could call on it at any time without requiring an understanding between the two governments. Cambon naturally wanted Grey to explain the contradiction between what he was initially told and the new arrangements adopted by the Admiralty and the War Office.[30] Grey's reply, couched in the following terms, was less than candid:

> I hear there is a misunderstanding as to what I said to you about sending troops to Lemnos.
> What I said was that the decision to send a division from England, which was communicated to the French Government some days ago, had been suspended till it was seen how the naval operation which were to begin at once progressed.
> Subsequently I hear at the Admiralty that the naval brigade would go from here and that this is entirely under Admiralty control. As the Admiral in charge of the operations may require early military assistance to make good his operations against the forts, 30,000 men of the Australian and New Zealand contingents now in Egypt have been placed at his disposal and will proceed as he requires them.
> If the French Government wish to send French troops, their presence and cooperation would be welcomed.[31]

Grey's tortured explanation that it was a misunderstanding rang hollow with the French. They remained suspicious that the British, having downplayed the expected role of troops, were possibly trying to get a head start and arrive in Constantinople before they could. So urgent was the need to act quickly that Joffre had not been informed of the cabinet's decision to send troops

---

29 Cited in the *Manchester Guardian*, 22 February 1915.
30 BNA: Grey papers, FO 800/57, Cambon to Grey, 20 February 1915.
31 BNA: Grey papers, FO 800/57, Grey to Cambon, 20 February 1915.

lest he delay the process by his anticipated objections. When Millerand approached Joffre and presented the issue as a *fait accompli,* his request for the necessary troops was nevertheless turned down.[32] The Generalissimo was not trained to link political objectives to military strategy, viewing the diversion as a waste of manpower. He cited his ongoing operations in Champagne and his planned attack further north in the spring in cooperation with Sir John French (the British c-in-c) as reasons why he could not permit the levy of troops from his front. Confronted by Joffre's refusal, Millerand instructed the general staff at the Ministry of War on 22 February to assemble the division from the depots in France and North Africa.[33] These soldiers were not under the jurisdiction of Joffre who held them in low esteem.[34] His attitude can be inferred from his reaction to Kitchener's request for information about the French division on the way to the Near East. His reply was brief and dismissive: "The Government has informed me that it is organizing a division for the expedition with troops from the interior. It will not comprise any unit serving on or destined for the Western Front."[35]

The new division was formed with lightning speed and, with its first elements ready to embark on 3 March, consisted of Europeans, French colonials, Foreign Legionaries and Senegalese.[36] Designated Expeditionary Corps of the Orient (*Corps Expéditionnaire d'Orient*), professional military experts shared Joffre's opinion of its inferior quality. As the men lacked training and discipline, they had been used to replace the casualties and sick at the front. They were adequate as long as they were intermingled with regular forces but to send them alone against seasoned forces was deemed unthinkable. All the same the government had no other option and besides it did not expect its troops to be involved in heavy fighting.

At the War Ministry the preferential choice to command the division was General Louis-Hubert Lyautey, the brilliant resident-general of Morocco, but Delcassé would not allow him to leave on account of the unsettled conditions and the threat of jihad in that colony.[37] Millerand selected General Albert d'Amade, an officer who had fallen from grace during the opening weeks of the war. The 59–year old d'Amade belonged to an old aristocratic family from the southwest of France and his wife, Nelly de Ricaumont, was equally of noble heritage. He was a graduate of the war college at Saint-Cyr and his varied service included a stint in China as a military attaché and later in London in the same capacity and finally in Morocco where, in command of an expeditionary force, he achieved his greatest fame by winning a series of victories over indigenous nationalists in the north-central part of the country, followed by highly successful pacification measures. Back in France he continued his steady advance professionally and in April 1914 was appointed a member of the Superior Council.

At the outbreak of the war he was placed in charge of the Army of the Alps but on Italy's declaration of neutrality he was appointed to command a group of territorial divisions formed to hold the line between Dunkirk and Maubeuge as best he could against the wide sweep of the

---

32 Joffre, *Personal Memoirs,* Vol. 2 (New York: Harper & Brothers, 1932), pp. 369-70.
33 France, *Expédition des Dardanelles,* pp. 18-19.
34 Imperial War Museum (IWM): Wilson papers, entry in the diary of Gen. Henry Wilson (British liaison officer with GQG), 25 February 1915.
35 Joffre to Gen. Victor Huguet (Head of French Mission at GHQ), in France, *Les armées françaises,* tome 8, Vol. 1, annexe no. 9.
36 France, *Expédition des Dardanelles,* pp. 18-19.
37 CCAC: Esher papers, entry in his War Journals, 25 February 1915.

German invasion. D'Amade's force was in no condition to stand its ground, much less undertake a counteroffensive, as it was weak numerically, ill-trained and equipped, and composed of old men. He was told by French headquarters that if the pressure became too intense, he was to retreat in the direction of Rouen. When the governor of Lille refused to support him as he was supposed to, d'Amade gave the signal for his army to fall back before it had engaged in any major fighting. According to GQG, d'Amade had a clear field opposite his front and his territorial divisions were in a position to throw themselves against the flank and rear of von Kluck's First Army. Certain contemporary commentators attributed d'Amade's inaction to wanting to spare his division from Memers to please his (then) friend Joseph Caillaux, who represented the district.

The retreat swept by Amiens before stopping briefly at Rouen and, leaving the city uncovered, continued into Normandy. By all account the retreat was poorly coordinated which may explain why GQG lost contact with d'Amade and his men for several days. An investigation (by the Ministry of War) judged the withdrawal to have been "inexcusably precipitate" and further criticized d'Amade for leaving behind rifles, munitions and provisions. Joffre was so displeased by d'Amade's conduct that he relieved him of his duties following the battle of the Marne. To recover his honour, d'Amade sought another command, even in the Foreign Legion, but he was relegated to minor posts. It was apparent that he was slowly being prepared for retirement, much to his dismay. Yet thanks to the intervention of the French President he received an active command when the Expeditionary Corps of the Orient was created.

The obvious question was why did Poincaré exert himself on behalf of a little known general who had shown neither courage nor leadership skill in his only important assignment in the opening weeks of the war? According to the most plausible explanation, it was the President's way of repaying the d'Amades for their kindness towards his wife Henriette. Elegant and attractive, Henriette (formerly Benucci) was of Italian origin and had been married twice before she entered into a relationship with Poincaré in 1901. Her first marriage to an irresponsible American of Irish heritage ended in divorce and her second, to a wealthy and considerably older French lawyer, never had a chance to prosper as he died less than two years later. Henriette married Poincaré in 1904 in a civil ceremony and, after discovering that her first ex-husband had died, the union was religiously solemnized in 1913. Henriette was often slandered in the press and snubbed by the ladies from the upper crust of French society on account of her obscure background and previous marriages. Nelly d'Amade was one of the few aristocratic women who took the time to reach out to the First Lady and it was not long before they became good friends. The French President, who was devoted to his wife, appreciated Nelly d'Amade's graciousness and took a liking to both her and her husband. Closing his eyes to the General's military shortcomings, he applied pressure on Millerand, a close personal friend, to give him another command. Millerand had reservations about d'Amade's competence but, in selecting him to take charge of the Expeditionary Corps, he was influenced by other factors besides the President's entreaty. The demands on the commander would at best be modest as the army was only expected to play a limited role in the operation; the General was one of the few senior officers who could be spared from France; and he was charming, easy to get along with, and spoke English fluently, assets that increased the chances that collaboration with his British counterpart would be conducted in a cordial atmosphere. Thus fortuitous circumstances had restored a career that was, for all intents and purposes, over. For d'Amade the appointment had been unexpected, and he was excited at getting another chance to atone for his earlier failure.[38]

On 24 February Delcassé asked Cambon to transmit an announcement to the Foreign Office that a French contingent of 400 officers and 18,000 men under the command of General d'Amade would be ready to embark for the Near East on 2 March (as it happened, they began leaving a day later). Moreover, Cambon was to try to persuade His Majesty's Government to accept an arrangement that would place a French general in charge of the land operations. Delcassé pointed out that the probable numerically superior size of the British force should not determine the choice of a commander-in-chief. After all the French had renounced their claim to the naval enterprise despite the fact that they had more ships than the English in the Mediterranean. It was therefore only fitting that in the interest of fair play London should yield control of the military operations to the French.[39]

Cambon wrote back immediately that several days earlier Colonel de la Panouse had sounded out Kitchener on the question of appointing a supreme commander in case troops were needed to support the fleet's action. Kitchener had replied curtly that since the operation was essentially naval in character and directed by a British admiral, conduct of the land forces should be left to the British general. The inference here was unmistakable. The operation was a brain child of the British and, as they supplied most of the naval and military resources, they had the most to lose. Thus it followed that that they should be left to exercise undisputed control. To strengthen his case, Kitchener referred to the situation on the western front where he alleged that 350,000 British soldiers were under the orders of the French Generalissimo. To be fair the circumstances were not exactly analogous. Sir John French, though usually framing his plans to coincide with those of Joffre, enjoyed a separate command.

Cambon recognized that to bring the matter up with Kitchener again would serve no purpose and, in a letter to his superior, tried to alleviate the irritation that was certain to develop in French government circles. If the authorities in Paris expected a reciprocal gesture from the English for having yielded the naval command, Cambon questioned France's right in the first place to claim the entire Mediterranean, observing that the accord of 6 August 1914 had been concluded before Turkey's entry into the conflict. He recommended that Carden be given provisional command of the troops until such time as military operations assumed significant importance. If and when this occurred, the issue of determining a military chief could be raised again.[40]

Cambon's suggestion did not strike the right chord at the French War Ministry. Millerand wanted a clear and definite understanding from the start. He abhorred a system of divided leadership which was apt to cause enormous delays, endless discussions, duplication of work and preclude the possibility of formulating or executing any consistent military policy. He

---

38 Jacques Puntous, "Albert d'Amade: Portrait Intime", *Mondes et Culture*, Vol. 66, no. 1 (2006), pp. 596-610; Emile Mayer, chapter entitled "D'Amade", in *Nos chefs de 1914* (Paris: Stock, 1930), is sharply critical; Article under the title of "Mistakes in the Dardanelles", in the *New York Times*, 16 May 1915; AN: C7544, Vol. 8, Commission du Budget, 22 June 1915; Joffre, *Personal Memoirs*, Vol. 1, pp. 116-17, 160, 183, 211, 220, 274; Poincaré, *Au Service*, Vol. 5 , pp. 261–62, 268, 289, 310; Keiger, *Raymond Poincaré*, pp. 102-3, 158.
39 AMAE: under the heading Opération des Dardanelles, carton 4, dossier 1, Delcassé to Cambon, 24 February 1915.
40 AMAE: under the heading Opération des Dardanelles, carton 4, dossier 1, Cambon to Delcassé, 24 February 1915.

was reminded by the unfortunate precedent of the Crimean War as well as by the reigning situation on the Western Front, an allusion to the instances in which the differences between Joffre and Sir John over military planning placed an unnecessary strain on their relationship. Millerand was therefore convinced that the issue could not be delayed until troops were in the midst of a major operation. If immediate acceptance of the principle of a single command for the Allied army meant that an Englishman would be assigned to the post, he was prepared to acquiesce in such an arrangement. The fact that d'Amade, in whom he had little faith, was the other alternative undoubtedly made it easier for him to want to reach an accommodation with Kitchener. Millerand conveyed his views to Lord Esher (Kitchener's military representative in Paris) who was often used as a go-between.[41]

Kitchener naturally recognized that dual control of strategy was contrary to every sound military dictum and he was glad to hear that Millerand was eager to reach a mutual understanding over a supreme commander. It suited him even more that his French counterpart did not object to the appointment of an English general, especially since he was not about to consider anyone who was not directly under his jurisdiction. He selected as head of military operations Lieutenant–General William Birdwood, a former subordinate and currently the Anzac commander. Millerand accepted Kitchener's choice even though Birdwood was practically unknown at the War Ministry and junior in rank to d'Amade. It was agreed that as long as the operations were primarily naval, the overall direction of the Anglo-French forces would rest with Vice-Admiral Carden.[42]

Of greater consequence to Millerand than the haggling over a supreme commander for the Dardanelles was the need to arrange a meeting with Kitchener, preferably in Paris so that Joffre could also attend, in order to consider common problems of which two required immediate attention. First, Kitchener had not yet made an announcement on the future employment of Britain's New Armies and there was considerable apprehension in Paris that these civilian units, currently under training, might ultimately be sent to the Near East instead of France. At the moment the French were trying to coax Kitchener to despatch the 29th Division to France. Apparently, the last remaining regular division had become in the eyes of the French "a symbol of Britain's future attitude with regard to the Western Front."[43] Second the exact nature of the operations to be undertaken in the Dardanelles had yet to be defined. There was not much point in accumulating troops on the spot until it was established how they would be used and where they would disembark.[44]

Kitchener declared that he would be willing to confer with Joffre and Millerand on condition that neither the future disposal of the New Armies nor the nature of the military operations envisaged in the Dardanelles be included in the agenda.[45] Given the unpredictable nature of war, Kitchener did not wish to leave himself open to future recriminations because he was

---

41 BNA: Kitchener papers, 30/57/59, Esher to Kitchener, 25 February 1915.
42 AMAE: under the heading Opération des Dardanelles, carton 4, dossier 1, Cambon to Delcassé, 25 February 1915; SHD: AMM, Ed 107, Cambon to Delcassé (copy), 26 February 1915; SHD: AMG, under the heading Engleterre, CEO-CED, carton 70, de la Panouse to Millerand (copy of a note sent to him by Cambon), 25 February 1915; BNA: Bertie papers, FO 800/167, Bertie to Grey, 2 March 1915.
43 Aspinall-Oglander, *Gallipoli*, Vol. 1, 71n1.
44 AMAE: under the heading Grande-Bretagne, carton 1, dossier 2, Delcassé to Cambon, 7 March 1915.
45 AMAE: under the heading Grande Bretagne, carton 1, dossier 2, Cambon to Delcassé, 9 March 1915.

compelled to go back on a commitment. A case in point was his indecision regarding the deployment of the 29th Division. Originally promised to France, Kitchener instead chose it to assist the fleet in the Dardanelles, then countermanded his order in view of the potentially critical military situation in France caused by Russian reverses, and finally on 10 March allowed it to proceed to the Aegean as conditions on the eastern front had improved. Kitchener, as justification for his stated position, later told Cambon: "I had promised you my 29th Division; I was unable to give it to you since it is en route to the East; You reproached me with it and I have no intention to expose myself to similar difficulties."[46] Kitchener's proviso was certain to deprive the conference of much of its value and the French, on receiving his initial response, were at a loss to understand why he refused to make his intentions clear.

There was a sense of urgency in the air. Joffre was complaining bitterly that without the New Armies he would have to interrupt plans for the next phase of his campaign; and Millerand was becoming increasingly uneasy about the whole Dardanelles adventure after receiving several ominous signals from Lieutenant-Colonel Maucorps, Head of the French Military Mission in Egypt. A former military attaché in Constantinople, he was thoroughly familiar with the Dardanelles and the state of its defences. He believed there was practically no chance of the fleet getting through alone and, even if it did, the unarmoured supply transports would be exposed to severe fire from the concealed guns which warships could not be relied on to destroy. On 25 February he submitted a report to the War Ministry which he also made available to Maxwell. In it he was adamant that the fleet could not force the Straits without military assistance and advocated a landing in the vicinity of Besika Bay on the Asiatic side as presenting the least difficulty. He claimed that the Gallipoli Peninsula would be a tough nut to crack as it had been converted, specifically at obvious landing sites such as Bulair at the neck of the Peninsula, into a fortress complete with trenches, barbed wire and gun emplacements. It was garrisoned by 30,000 men and commanded by Djevad Pasha, an excellent and energetic officer.[47]

Three days later Maucorps submitted a second paper to Millerand in which he described, on the basis of information fed to him by Maxwell and his staff, the British units earmarked for the Dardanelles, and concluded by insisting that, if a disaster was to be avoided, an Anglo-French force in the vicinity of 80,000 men would be required to help the navy get through.[48] Maucorps was a man whose judgment could not be discarded lightly but Millerand hesitated to speak out in the belief that the initiative rightfully belonged to the English. He expected to be able to express his views once he was informed of the decisions taken by the British government but, in the days that followed, London made no effort to define the intended role of the army in the operation. What little information he possessed was contained in a note sent by the French naval attaché to Augagneur on 5 March. It ran as follows:

> The War Office having asked the Admiralty to deal directly with the French Government regarding the disposition of the troops to be used at the Dardanelles, the First Lord asks me to let you know that he considers it essential that from March 18th these troops should

---

46 AMAE: under the heading Grande Bretagne, carton 1, dossier 2, Cambon to Delcassé, 22 March 1915.
47 Maucorps to Millerand, 25 February 1915, in France, *Les armées françaises*, tome 8, Vol. 1, annexe no.10.
48 AMAE: under the heading Opération des Dardanelles, carton 4, dossier 1, Maucorps to Millerand, 28 February 1915.

be in immediate readiness either to be disembarked at Bulair or sent through the Straits to Constantinople according to circumstances. The British military forces will be on that date in their transports near the scene of action. It is therefore indispensable that the French force should be there too, so that if necessary, the most powerful effort can be made.

It is of course not possible to predict the date at which the Straits will be opened, as the weather and the degree of Turkish resistance are uncertain factors, but since the War Office is making all its preparations for the 18th [March] the day of embarkation of our troops should be calculated accordingly ... The order to embark could on the other hand be postponed if operations proceed less rapidly than expected.[49]

The Admiralty was giving notice that it expected the troops massed by a certain date and ready for action but there were no details as to their employment. On 11 March Maucorps again sounded a note of warning to Millerand, this time revealing the gist of an appreciation by Maxwell who considered the Peninsula to be heavily fortified everywhere and, as a result, doubted that the ships alone could get past the forts. Foreseeing difficulties in bringing together sufficient forces on the scene, Maxwell conceded that it might even become necessary to abandon the enterprise. In these circumstances he advised a landing in Syria to avoid loss of face in the Muslim world.[50] In hindsight it is known that both Maxwell and Maucorps overestimated the strength of Turkey's military readiness but at the time, with the Germans firmly entrenched on French soil, it increased Millerand's anxiety to avoid large-scale military operations in the Dardanelles.

On 11 March Millerand wrote despairingly to Delcassé, observing that it was imperative to obtain more information on key questions from London. Had the British commander-in-chief decided on a plan of action and, if so, what was it? In particular did he propose to disembark in the north of Gallipoli to block the Bulair isthmus? Did he envisage the landing of French and British troops at or in the neighbourhood of Constantinople? Had he considered previous or subsequent operations and what were they? Millerand added that he did not need to emphasize the difficulties created in his department by his ignorance of vital details and of the consequences that might arise. The number of troops required in the Dardanelles would depend on the plan adopted. That being the case, he could not risk dissipating the French army's strength by allotting to the new campaign a force much larger than the one already collected.[51]

The next day Delcassé forwarded Millerand's inquires to Cambon with instructions that he was to obtain the requisite information but in a manner that would not offend the English.[52] Cambon immediately headed in the direction of the Foreign Office on the assumption that the mild-mannered Grey could fill him in on the details. To his surprise, he discovered that Kitchener had been unduly secretive about his future plans and revealed nothing pertinent to Grey, not even Millerand's proposal for a conference.[53] Grey appeared surprised when told

---

49 SHD: AMM, Xa 3, Saint Seine to Augagner, 5 March 1915.
50 Maucorps to Millerand, 11 March 1915, in France, *Les armées françaises*, tome 8, Vol. 1, annexe, no. 25.
51 Millerand to Delcassé, 11 March 1915, in France, *Les armées françaises*, tome 8, Vol. 1, annexe no. 24.
52 AMAE: under the heading Opération des Dardanelles, carton 4, dossier 1, Delcassé to Cambon, 12 March 1915.
53 Kitchener tended to be overly cautious and his mistrust of his colleagues' discretion caused him to reveal as little classified information as possible.

that Millerand had been kept in the dark about the military plans for the Dardanelles and gave assurances that he would try to persuade Kitchener to agree to meet with French leaders. Less than 48 hours later at 10 Downing Street, the French *chargé d'affaires* (A. de Fleuriau) in London was able to elicit a similar promise from Asquith.

Both Asquith and Grey independently appealed to Kitchener to induce him to hold talks with the French. Kitchener offered no resistance, possibly because he had finally made some important decisions and was in a better position to answer questions and supply information requested earlier by the French. On 11 March he had appointed General Ian Hamilton, an accomplished professional with 42 years of active service in the army, to replace Birdwood as c-in-c of the Allied force. The possible entry of Russian troops into the campaign (as will be discussed in the next chapter) and the announcement that d'Amade would lead the French division, made it desirable that a general of greater reputation and seniority be given the command.

From the written orders Kitchener gave Hamilton on 13 March, it can be seen that there was still no intention of forcing the Dardanelles by a combined operation. The troops were to be used to occupy the Peninsula following an essentially uncontested landing and perhaps later for an assault on Constantinople. There were to be no operations of a serious nature until the fleet had exhausted every effort to penetrate the Straits. If a major landing became unavoidable, none should be attempted before the entire force available had assembled. The military occupation of the Asian side was to be strongly deprecated, the orders concluded. On the last point, Kitchener left no room for discretion. He had warned Hamilton on the previous day not to become involved in any extensive campaign in Asia which he felt would place an unjustifiable strain on the resources of the country.[54]

On 15 March Kitchener met with Colonel de la Panouse and brought him up to date on what actual decisions he had taken. Later in the day the French chargé d'affaires, who had carried an investigation on behalf of Cambon, conferred briefly with de la Panouse before sending a telegram to the Quai D'Orsay. It was in response to Delcassé's note of 12 March but evidently meant for Millerand:

> Lord Kitchener has not yet arrived at a plan in regard to the operation against Turkey. He considers that the action of the Allied forces has not yet progressed far enough to take a decision on what should be done after the forcing of the Dardanelles.
>
> At the present time Admiral Carden feels that the navy alone cannot force a passage through the Straits. The Turks have constructed numerous defences which cannot be destroyed by naval guns and which can only be captured with the co-operation of the Expeditionary army.
>
> For the moment, therefore, it is necessary to seize the Gallipoli Peninsula, establish a solid defense, and from there bombard the works on the Asiatic side. As to the means to be employed to achieve this end it is up to Admiral Carden [and] Sir Ian Hamilton to choose them.

---

54   Great Britain, *First Report* of the *Dardanelles Commission* (London: HMSO, 1917), pp. 34-35; Aspinall-Oglander, *Gallipoli*, Vol. 1, pp. 89-90; James, *Gallipoli*, p. 54.

It will be only after opening the Straits to admit the fleet that it will be possible to think about subsequent operations, the nature and importance will depend above all on the attitude of the Ottoman government and the movement of its army.

Lord Kitchener will discuss willingly all these questions, as well as those concerning the operations in France, with you and General Joffre. He hopes, if the British Government consents, to be able to go to Chantilly [Joffre's Headquarters] next Monday, March 22nd or Tuesday 23rd.[55]

The information in the report was vague, confusing and contradictory. There was mention of the seizure of the Gallipoli Peninsula but no indication of when or how the effort would be made. Kitchener inferred that military action would begin after the navy had forced a passage through the Straits, but Carden was no longer optimistic about the naval prospects and was hopeful that landing parties would be available to silence the concealed guns to assist the fleet's action. Here was another example of the muddle surrounding the entire enterprise. Apparently, it was still unclear in certain quarters of London whether the initial attack would involve only the navy.

Millerand made no comments about the report, notwithstanding its obvious unreliability. Whatever reservations he may have felt privately, were likely overshadowed by the announcement of Kitchener's imminent visit to Paris. Until the meeting occurred, Millerand hoped to gain a clearer knowledge of British war plans from d'Amade who had just arrived on the scene.

Before leaving on his mission, d"Amade had reported to the Ministry of War on 2 March to receive his instructions. He was to cooperate with the Allied fleet and British troops in the operation to force the Dardanelles, in keeping the waterway open and in any subsequent action directed against Constantinople and the Bosporus. In the event that the British deemed it necessary to undertake further operations, he was required to refer the matter to the Minister of War. Finally, he was to take his orders from Vice-Admiral Carden who would be in supreme command in the Dardanelles.[56] With only a vague description of his responsibilities and little other relevant information, d'Amade and his staff left for Bizerte (Tunisian port) where the French division was concentrating.

D'Amade's task in preparing the French division to take the field was compounded by his uncertainty about the plan of operation. All he knew was that he must have his troops ready before 18 March to seize any advantage that might be gained by the fleet. In the absence of specific instructions from Paris, d'Amade turned to General Birdwood, who had not yet been replaced as the British c-in-c, in the hope that he might shed some light on essential questions:

> Admiral Carden, having the direction of operations and knowing the general goal to be attained, I consider that the plan of operation of the land forces which I am charged to concert with you is directly linked to the instructions of the Admiral. I beg you to inform me
> 1. What you know of these instructions?
> 2. What military measures do you expect to take to prepare for them?

---

55 De Fleuriau to Delcassé, 15 March 1915, in France, *Les armées françaises*, tome 8, Vol. 1, annexe no. 29.
56 Millerand to d'Amade, 2 March 1915, in France, *Les armées françaises*, tome 8, Vol. 1, annexe no. 17.

74 Reluctant Partners

3. What assistance were you hoping the French contingent would bring to the joint operation?
4. What point of debarkation have you reserved for your troops?[57]

Back came Birdwood's answer: "There is up to now no order from Admiral Carden and the only instructions that I have received is to stand ready to leave when told to do so; neither one of us can do anything for the moment – I might receive my instructions from Lord Kitchener when all the plans are finished.[58]

Since the preliminary arrangements for the departure of the French troops had proceeded smoothly, d'Amade set sail for Mudros harbor (on the island of Lemnos) on the first convoy on 10 March; the second convoy, already stocked and self-supporting, was scheduled to leave three days later and wait at the entrance of the Dardanelles.[59] On arriving at Mudros on 15 March, d'Amade sent word to Carden, asking if he had any plans for the employment of French troops.[60] Carden replied that it was up to General Hamilton to decide when the troops would be thrown into action.[61] By then d'Amade had learned from Rear-Admiral R.E. Wemyss, commandant of the base at Lemnos, that Hamilton had been appointed to take charge of the Allied army. Until that moment, d'Amade was under the impression that being senior to Birdwood, the supreme command was to devolve upon him, and, accordingly, was preparing detailed plans for a landing in the Bay of Adramyti on the western coast of Turkey, to be followed by an advance into Asia.[62] These plans were near completion when he was told that he would be taking orders from Hamilton, an announcement that was subsequently confirmed by Millerand.[63] The immediate result, apart from personal consideration, was to nullify all the administrative work that d'Amade and his staff had undertaken.

On 17 March Wemyss took d'Amade over to the Greek island of Tenedos, located off the Straits, to meet Hamilton. The two soldiers arrived at about the same time. As it happened d'Amade and Hamilton were old acquaintances – as they had first met in London in 1901 – and greeted one another in the manner of good friends. In the course of their conversation, d'Amade asked Hamilton if he had any specific instructions. Hamilton replied that his written orders from Lord Kitchener made it clear that he was not to undertake any military operations until the fleet had exhausted every effort to break through the Straits unaided and until the full assembly of his force.

D'Amade and Hamilton then attended a conference, called by Vice-Admiral J.M. de Robeck, Carden's sudden replacement, on board the *Queen Elizabeth*.[64] Besides de Robeck, d'Amade and Hamilton, the other personalities present included Weymss and Guépratte, commanding

---

57 SHD: AMG, CEO–CED, carton 6, d'Amade's telegram was sent through Maucorps (as Birdwood at the time was in Egypt), 5 March 1915.
58 SHD: AMG, CEO–CED, carton 8, Maucorps to d'Amade, 8 March 1915.
59 SHD: AMG, under the heading Angleterre, CEO–CED, carton 70, Millerand to de la Panouse, 8 March 1915.
60 SHD: AMG, CEO-CED, carton 6, d'Amade to Millerand, 15 March 1915.
61 SHD: AMG, CEO-CED, carton 6, Carden to d'Amade, 16 March 1915.
62 Albert d'Amade, "Constantinople et les détroits", *Revue des questions historiques*", vols. 98-99 (1923), pt. 1, p. 24.
63 Millerand to d'Amade, 16 March 1915, in France, *Les armées françaises*, tome 8, Vol. 1, annexe no. 31.
64 The reason for Carden's departure will be explained in chapter 6.

the French squadron. De Robeck explained that, while he was confident the battleships could knock out the big guns inside the forts, he was worried about the enemy's mobile howitzers which could not be located and, firing from concealed positions, were certain to hamper minesweeping operations. And should the fleet get through, these same guns would harass the supply ships that would follow. All-in-all, de Robeck was optimistic about the chances of the navy getting through without requiring large-scale military assistance.[65] The discussion was rather one-sided, and few questions were asked. D'Amade had secretly and for sometime harboured serious doubts that the navy could do the job alone, but he was apparently won over by de Robeck's bearing and air of calm confidence.[66]

The hour was near at hand when the power of the fleet versus the forts guarding the waterway was about to be put to the test. But before that happened, the politicians in the Allied capitals were distracted by another matter. Concluding that victory was a foregone conclusion, they began to discuss plans to carve up the Ottoman Empire.

---

65 Marder, *From the Dreadnought*, Vol. 2, p. 245.
66 D'Amade, "Constantinople", vols. 98-99, pt.1, p. 25.

5

Assumption of Victory

Since the days of Peter the Great, Russia's interest in expanding its naval reach had led to regional conflicts with the Ottoman Empire. In the 19th Century when it became apparent that the Ottoman Empire was in decline, Russia made a determined bid to acquire Constantinople and the Straits on several occasions, but England and France collaborated to arrest its advance lest it grow too strong and interfere with their own designs in Asia. Russia gained a fresh opportunity to fulfil its historic mission when Turkey embraced the cause of the Central Powers in November 1914. The Tsarist government, led by its Foreign Secretary, Serge Sazanov, did not want to forfeit what could be the last chance for Russia to gain possession of the Straits, seen as vital for its security and export trade. Sazanov recognized that surmounting the opposition of his western allies would prove to be a significant challenge. In truth, despite the recent alliance, it would have been asking too much to expect that the two powers which throughout the 19th century had serious political differences with Russia, resulting in open conflict on one occasion, to suddenly become indifferent to the incorporation of the Straits into its empire. Therefore Russian leaders planned to move slowly and await the right moment to press their claim to the Straits. In the interim they avoided divulging Russia's precise war aims with reference to Turkey.

A few days after Turkey's entry in the war Sazanov told the French Ambassaor in Petrograd, Maurice Paléologue, that he favoured leaving Constantinople in the hands of Turkey but he was rather vague about the fate of the Straits.[1] Yet in his own memoirs he admitted that from the outset of the war he worked to find a resolution of the Straits question in Russia's favour but that he was amenable to internationalizing Constantinople.[2] On 21 November Paléologue was received in audience by Tsar Nicholas who was somewhat more definite in his views. In discussing broad war aims, he wanted for his empire a guarantee of free passage through the Straits (though he was unsure as to the method) and the expulsion of Turkey from Europe with a neutral Constantinople under the auspices of an international regime.[3] The Russian leaders calculated that that by advocating the establishment of an independent regime in

---

1   Ronald P. Bobroff, *Roads to Glory: Late Imperial Russia and the Turkish Straits* (London: Taurus, 2006), p. 118.
2   Serge Sazanov, *Fateful Years, 1909-1916* (New York: Frederick A. Stokes, 1928), pp. 245-46.
3   Paléologue, *Memoirs*, Vol. 1, p. 193.

Constantinople, which was an important financial centre and the seat of the Orthodox Church, they would be reducing France and Britain's opposition to their bid to possess the Straits.[4]

Sazanov awaited the reaction of his allies. He expected the French to be less obdurate that the British. After all France was a close ally and Delcassé, a former ambassador to St. Petersburg (named changed to Petrograd after the outbreak of the war), was known to be pro-Russian, while the British had a long tradition of opposing Russia's installation at the Straits as presenting a threatening naval base.[5] But attitudes do not always remain constant. Grey took the first step towards reversing the status quo. On 9 November 1914 he declared to Count Alexander Benckendorff, the Russian Ambassador in London, that subject to the defeat of Germany the fate of Constantinople and the Straits should be settled in conformity with Russian desires.[6] Grey had received a disquieting report from the British Ambassador in Petrograd, Sir George Buchanan, that a group of Russian officials, including the elder statesman Serge Witte, were looking for ways to end the war through mediation. Although they did not represent the views of the Tsarist regime, Grey felt the need to dangle before the Russians their most cherished prize to ensure their continued commitment to the war. A few days later King George reinforced Grey's comments, telling Benckendorff that "as for Constantinople it is clear that it must be yours."[7]

Grey's pledge to the Russian Foreign Ministry was made without prior consultation with the French government. Subsequently he did notify Delcassé (through Lord Bertie) of his reason for acting unilaterally. He explained that it was intended to allay any suspicions in Petrograd that Britain would continue to resist Russia's efforts to achieve its historic ambition. But the form it would take, he added, must be subject to agreement by the Allies at the end of the war.[8] Delcassé had already stated his views on the matter to Alexander Isvolsky, the Russian Ambassador in Paris. On 7 November he suggested that "it would do well to develop a common plan of action of the Entente in regard to Turkey in view of the complexity of the interests involved."[9]

To Sazanov's dissatisfaction, neither France nor Britain offered clarification of their position that would have definitively met Russia's expectations. In these circumstances he could not be certain that Russia's prize objective could be achieved through diplomacy. Of course, Russia could have avoided any potential danger to foreign control of the Straits simply by seizing them and Sazanov advocated such a course in December 1914, but the Stavka (Russian high command) adamantly refused to divert forces from its main operations against Germany and Austria.[10]

There was practically no movement among the powers towards a resolution of the Straits question for the next two months. On 20 January 1915 Buchanan and Paléologue informed

---

4   Sazanov, *Fateful Years*, p. 245; Bobroff, *Roads to Glory*, p. 119.
5   Sazanov, *Fateful Years*, pp. 252-53.
6   Harry Howard, *The Partition of Turkey* (New York: Howard Fertig, 1966), p. 120.
7   Howard, *Partition*, p. 120.
8   BNA: Bertie papers, FO 800/177, Bertie to Grey, 22 November 1914.
9   Howard, *Partition*, p. 120.
10 Sazanov to N.N. Ianouchkevitch (Chief of the General Staff), 21 December 1915; Ianouchkevitch to Sazanov, 25 December, 1915, in Russia, *Constantinople et les détroits*, trans. by S. Volski, ed. by G. Gaussel and V. Paris and annotated by G. Lozinski, Vol. 2 (Paris: Editions Internationales, 1932), pp. 3-5.

Sazonov of the plan to force the Dardanelles and capture Constantinople. Sazanov was stunned by the intended action of his allies. He recalled in his memoirs:

> I was very much in sympathy with the idea of the French and British troops driving in a wedge between Turkey and the Central Powers, but I intensely disliked the thought that the Straits and Constantinople might be taken by our Allies and not by the Russian forces … I had difficulty in concealing from them how painfully the news had affected me.[11]

Sazanov was convinced that when the time came to enter into thorough negotiations with the British and French, diplomatic pressure was unlikely to be sufficient for Russia to gain control of the Straits unless aided by the simultaneous presence of its forces in the region. Thus the next day he again tried to prevail upon the Stavka to undertake a strike from the Bosporus, even though he had been told by different sources that detaching the requisite number of divisions from the main fronts was out of the question. He asked the Stavka to study carefully whether Russia could play a useful role in the capture of the Straits if progress was satisfactory and, if not, he suggested that it would be better to request that the allies defer their projected operation against the Dardanelles.[12] Sazanov so mistrusted his allies that he had no desire to see them overthrow the Turkish regime by themselves.

Sazanov's plea made no impression on the Grand Duke Nicholas, the Russian army commander, as his military situation was still unstable. The Grand Duke thought that any assault against Turkey would help dissipate its strength and ease pressure on the Russian front in the Caucasus as well as determine the attitude of the Balkan states. Still he maintained that at least for the time being he was unable to assist either with troops or ships in the Allied operation. At any rate he did not deem it advisable to become embroiled in a hazardous adventure. The Russian high command had regarded the forcing of the Dardanelles by the Anglo-French navy to be an almost impossible task. It added that even if the ships managed to get through, annihilate the Turkish fleet and intimidate Constantinople they would not be able to take possession of it: no landing force that could be spared would be capable of defeating the Turkish army. Still from the military point of view the operation would be useful and "very desirable" and "we risk nothing by encouraging the English to realize their projects."[13]

Sazanov was pondering his next move when he received a message from Delcassé who was looking for an ally to frustrate Britain's suspected designs in the Levant. The French authorities were convinced, not only that the Asquith government coveted most of the region but that its naval operation in the Dardanelles was, in fact, a cover "to bid for the last link in the British power chain encircling the future Levantine Empire from Cyprus and Suez to Aden and the Persian Gulf."[14] Although the French had not as yet precisely defined their own aims in the Levant, they had already decided that there were certain areas they intended to claim in the event, the break-up of the Ottoman Empire became inevitable. Thus if it came to settling a conflict of interest with the British, they understood that they would be at a disadvantage. The

---

11 Sazanov, *Fateful Years*, p. 255.
12 Sazanov to his representative at Stavka, Prince N.A. Koudachev, 21 January 1915, in *Constantinople*, Vol. 2, pp. 26-27.
13 Koudachev to Sazanov, 25 January 1915, in *Constantinople*, Vol. 2, pp. 27-30.
14 Gottlieb, *Studies in Secret Diplomacy*, p. 103.

English could argue that having organized the Dardanelles operation and borne the brunt of the fighting, they had priority to select any part of Turkish territory they coveted. In so doing they were bound to oppose any French claim to territory that they desired.

To offset the preponderant strength of the British in the Dardanelles and in the process neutralize their bargaining power, Delcassé sought to entice Russia to participate actively in the campaign. On 20 February Delcassé sent a note to Petrograd, announcing that a proposal was under study to concentrate military forces in Lemnos in order to use them to assist the Anglo-French fleet. He indicated that the bombardment of the Turkish forts at the entrance of the Straits had begun the previous day and appeared to have succeeded. He anticipated that the task of overcoming enemy resistance at the Straits would be slow and take at least three and possibly four weeks. He expressed the hope that the Russian navy would launch an attack from the Bosporus to coincide with Anglo-French action in the Straits. Delcassé added that in the event of success the three Allied fleets would appear simultaneously before Constantinople which he stressed would be very important from the military and especially the political point of view.[15] Several days later he urged that Russian support be extended to include land forces as well.[16]

The messages were sent without reference to the British who coincidently and simultaneously made similar overtures to Sazanov. Of France's two allies, Delcassé was more distrustful of the British. At this time he remained under the impression that the Russians, in view of the previously stated opinion of their leaders, only favoured free passage through the Straits and converting Constantinople into a neutral city.

Allied solicitation for Russian assistance sharpened Sazanov's focus to obtain troops from the Grand Duke and he pushed hard after receiving a report that the fleet might break through the Straits sooner than expected. He begged the Stavka to divert the brigade earmarked for Serbia to the Dardanelles where it would be more useful, insisting that it was vital for Russian troops to be part of the entry of Allied forces into Constantinople.[17] As he was not optimistic about the outcome of his latest appeal, he turned to the Tsar to intercede on his behalf. It turned out to be unnecessary as the Stavka had a change of heart. The high command decided to send troops from the Caucasus, rather than those destined for Serbia, to join in the ground action in the Dardanelles, as well as direct the Black Sea fleet to be ready to move towards the Bosporus. Sazanov's persistence had paid off. It was with a sense of jubilation that he notified London and Paris that his government would soon mount an attack against Turkey from the east.[18]

Still, the likelihood that the Allied fleet would break into the Sea of Marmora before Russian troops could be assembled and transported to the scene, induced Sazanov to approach London and Paris for a written commitment to endorse Russia's territorial aspirations.[19] The indefinite pledges by France and Britain thus far were deemed inadequate. Sazanov was under increasing pressure from governing circles and in the Duma to obtain concrete assurances before naval and military action ended. On 1 March the Russian Foreign Minister called in Paléologue

---

15   Isvolsky to Sazanov, 20 February 1915, in *Constantinople*, Vol. 2, pp. 44-45.
16   Isvolsky to Sazanov, n.d. but either 24 or 25 February 1915, in *Constantinople*, Vol. 2, p. 49.
17   Sazanov to Koudachev and to Gen. V.N. Mouraviev (on the Russian general staff), 28 February 1915, in *Constantinople*, Vol. 2, pp. 52-53.
18   Sazanov to Isvolsky, 3 March 1915, in *Constantinople*, Vol. 2, p. 57.
19   Bobroff, *Roads to Glory*, p. 130.

and Buchanan and laid his cards on the table. He claimed that until a few weeks ago, he still thought "that the opening of the Straits did not necessarily involve the definite occupation of Constantinople" but now "I have to admit that the whole country demands that radical solution." He reminded them of the promises made by Grey and George V in the fall of 1914 but that "the hour for plain speaking had come." As he felt that the Russian people were entitled to know that they could count on the good faith of their allies, he wanted them "to say openly that they agree to the annexation of Constantinople by Russia when the day for peace arrives."[20] In the interim he wanted the governments of Britain and France to condition their public to the idea of ceding Constantinople to Russia and to deflect the potential outcry by pointing out that all the allies were contributing equally to the common goal and consequently when it came to divide the war spoils it was only fair that each should see its vital interests met.[21]

Two days later Paléologue was invited to dinner at Tsarskoe Selo (royal country palace) and after rising from the table he and Nicholas engaged in a long conversation. The Tsar claimed that, while the opinion he had expressed last November had not changed, circumstances compelled him to be more precise. He went on to say that the question of the Straits had absorbed the attention of the Russian people to the highest degree and that the way to reward their sacrifice was to grant them "their time-honoured ambition." The only practical solution, as he saw it, was to incorporate Constantinople and southern Thrace into his Empire.[22] He made no pronouncement as to the eventual disposition of the Straits.

Before London and Paris could react to the Russian demands, they became absorbed by the Greek government's offer on 1 March to land three divisions on the Gallipoli Peninsula. Spurred on by the belief that the triumph of the Allies was inevitable, the Venizelos government seemed ready to abandon its neutrality and send the Greek army into the field. Although promised Smyrna and a substantial portion of the hinterland, the Greeks had an emotional attachment to Constantinople, the ancient capital of the Byzantine Empire and site of St. Sophia cathedral (converted into a mosque after 1453), still a revered symbol of Orthodox Christianity.

The first link in the chain of the Entente strategy of drawing in the wavering Balkan states was on the verge of being forged. Sazanov, however, was certain that Constantinople would fall without the need of outside arms and he was not keen on allowing the Greeks, in view of their known pretentions, to join the expedition. He feared that once the Greeks installed themselves in the city no amount of Russian pressure would compel them to leave. He suspected that the English were bent on placing the Greeks at the Golden Horn to act as an offset to Russian claims and to buttress their arguments for internationalizing Constantinople and the Straits. The consequence of such an arrangement, as clearly shown by the example of the Suez Canal, would give control of the Straits region to the strongest maritime power – i.e. Great Britain. Therefore on 2 March he indicated to London and Paris as well as Athens that his government was unwilling to allow Greek troops to enter Constantinople.[23]

---

20 Paléologue, *Memoirs*, Vol. 1, p. 295.
21 Sazanov to Isvolsky and Beckendorff, 17 February 1915, in *Constantinople*, Vol. 1, p. 166.
22 Paléologue, *Memoirs*, Vol. 1, pp. 296-97.
23 Sazanov to E. P. Demidov (Russian Ambassador.at Athens), 2 March 1915, in *Documents diplomatiques secrets russes 1914–1917*, trans. by J. Polonsky (Paris: Payot, 1928), p. 266. Copies of the telegram were sent to the Foreign Office and to the Quai d'Orsay.

London hastened to appeal the decision, arguing that Greek military contribution would ensure success against Turkey. Buchanan claimed that he had persuaded Sazanov to reconsider when Paléologue took it upon himself to intervene. Acting before receiving instructions from the Quai d'Orsay, he told Sazanov that in his opinion it would be a grave mistake to permit the Greeks to participate in the expedition. Paléologue had clearly exceeded his authority even though he presumably believed he was echoing the official French line. This diplomatic blunder was not unique during Paléologue's term as French ambassador to Russia. Any competent diplomat would have, as Bertie told Delcassé in reporting the incident, "held his peace if he had not received instructions to support his British colleague." Delcassé remarked that "it was not by a long way the first stupidity that M. Paléologue had committed." He expressed a willingness to recall Paléologue if the Foreign Office so desired.[24] Tempting though it may have been, the Foreign Office did not act upon the offer.

Delcassé was of two minds about the benefit of an alliance with the Greeks. He foresaw that their participation in the conflict would create complications, not the least was the danger of a rift with Petrograd. The Russians were reeling backwards under the heavy blows administered by the Germans and to override their veto would have dampened their fighting spirit and possibly have led them to negotiate a separate treaty with Berlin. Above all the whole hearted effort and the entire strength of Russia were essential to avoid a defeat in France. Then too Delcassé, shared Sazanov's concern over the possible establishment of the Greeks in Constantinople under the aegis of Britain. Finally Greece intended to maintain ties with Germany and wage war only against Turkey. King Constantine's dynastic ties with the Kaiser and his conviction of Teutonic invincibility ruled out a conflict with Germany. Since Greece's value would be diminished if it did not intend to wage war against Germany, Delcassé attached greater importance to Bulgarian cooperation. He saw that its adhesion to the Entente would cut off Turkey from Germany and Austria, safeguard Serbia and open the Mediterranean to the Russians. Any chance of enlisting Bulgaria as an ally would be significantly diminished if an understanding was reached with Greece. The relationship between the two states was marked by intense hostility.

All things considered, Delcassé would have preferred to wait upon events before reaching an arrangement with the Greeks. On 4 March he contacted the British Foreign Office (through Cambon) with a piece of advice:

> The French Minister for Foreign Affairs thinks progress of Anglo-French fleet may be such as to [enable it to] appear before Constantinople without necessity of landing troops, except a small body to hold the Bulair lines. There might consequently, not be any occasion for military co-operation with Greece ...
>
> If the Greek Government offer co-operation in the Dardanelles expedition they should be told that co-operation of Greece in the war must be entire and she must give active support to Serbia.[25]

If Delcasse was lukewarm to the Greek offer, neither was he ready to completely turn his back on it. At the same time that he approached Grey, he replied to Sazanov's note (sent on 2

---

24   BNA: Grey papers, FO 800/75, Buchanan to Grey, 14 March 1915; and Bertie to Grey, 9 March 1915.
25   Delcassé to Grey, 4 March 1915, cited in Churchill, *World Crisis,* Vol. 2, p. 203.

March), advancing a case that he hoped would make Greek cooperation less objectionable to the Russians. He argued that if the Greeks wanted to act in concert with the Allies, their forces must take part in the general war. He believed that the Greeks could render great service to the common cause by concentrating their efforts in support of Serbia. He added that there was no evidence that the British were encouraging the Greeks to send troops to the Dardanelles.[26]

Sazanov was too astute to fall for such a contrived line of argument but he had to be comforted by the tepid response from Paris. It was evident that his allies were not acting in unison and as long as one hesitated to push too far it was easier for him to manoeuvre a way out of the diplomatic impasse. In the final analysis the differences between Russia and its western partners were over quickly because the Greeks themselves settled the issue.

Petrograd's resentment and protest over Greek participation in the Dardanelles had reinforced Constantine's reluctance to embroil his country into so dubious a conflict. Venizelos' decision to offer three Greek divisions to the British on 1 March had been made without royal consent. At a Crown Council between 3 and 5 March, the King and his leading generals refused to endorse the Prime Minister's action. As a result of the rebuke, Venizelos submitted his resignation on 6 March and was succeeded by M. Gounaris who was committed to a policy of benevolent neutrality.

The episode involving the Greeks spurred Sazanov to formally stake out Russia's territorial claims without further delay. To that end he drew up a list of specific demands, much more extensive than those he and the Tsar had outlined a few days before, and submitted them in writing to Paléologue and Buchanan on 4 March. In the aide - memoire Russia laid claimed to the entire left bank (European) which included the Bosporus, the Sea of Marmara, the Dardanelles and Constantinople, southern Thrace as far as the Enos-Midia line and territory along the Asiatic coast. On top of this, it requested a number of islands, among which were Imbros and Tenedos lying outside the entrance of the Dardanelles. In return it promised that Russia would protect British and French interest in areas that fell under its possession as well as view with good will their desires in other regions of the Ottoman Empire and elsewhere.[27]

The Russian note, which went well beyond what the French had been led to expect, chilled the diplomatic atmosphere in Paris. If Russia had its way, it would become a naval power in the Mediterranean and be in a position to dominate the Middle East. The French were not keen on seeing another power challenge their influence in that part of the world. In addition they worried that if Russia gained all that it desired, it would lose interest in the war. Delcassé wanted the Straits to be demilitarized and policed by an international force and Constantinople declared a free city. He suggested to Isvolsky that to avoid misunderstandings the three foreign ministers should meet to decide the complex issues relating to the partition of the Ottoman Empire.[28] Sazanov replied that he could not absent himself from Petrograd and made it clear that nothing less than possession of Constantinople and the Straits would satisfy the Russian people. The matter appeared to be non-negotiable and by insisting that it be resolved quickly, Sazanov assured his allies free navigation of the Straits and protection of their economic interests.[29]

---

26 Isvolsky to Sazanov, 4 March 1915, in *Constantinople*, Vol. 2, p. 107.
27 Bobroff, *Roads to Glory*, pp. 131-32; Howard, *Partition*, pp. 127-28; Sazanov, *Fateful Years*, pp. 256-57.
28 Isvolsky to Sazanov, 6 March 1915, in *Constantinople*, Vol. 1, pp. 187-88.
29 Sazanov to Isvolsky, 7 March 1915, in *Constantinople*, Vol. 1, pp.190-91.

On 8 March Paléologue delivered the formal French response to the Russian aide-memoire submitted four days earlier. In it the Russian government was informed that it could count on the goodwill of the French in resolving the fate of Constantinople and the Straits. It stated, moreover, that this question, as well as others involving Allied interests in the Near East and elsewhere, should be decided definitively in the peace treaty at the end of the war.[30] During a conversation with Isvolsky the next day, Delcassé revealed that, while he would not contest Russia's claim to Constantinople, he insisted that the question must be part of the overall settlement of the war and not by a special accord.[31] This implied a lengthy delay as Delcassé gave no indication that he was ready for a general discussion of war aims – at least partly because he did not trust Paléologue to represent France skilfully.[32] Yet 24 hours later Lord Bertie and Isvolsky reported to their respective governments that Delcassé seemed ready to support Russia's historic dream. According to Bertie, Isvolsky had warned Delcassé that obstructionism by France and Britain might drive Russia to come to terms with Germany, an often repeated diplomatic threat.[33] Had the French Foreign Minister really changed his mind overnight? If so he would have faced formidable opposition at home. Bearing in mind that Delcassé was an experienced diplomat and politician, not a priest, it is reasonable to assume that his new stated position was in reality a ruse to stretch out the negotiating process with the Russians. Benckendorff had warned Sazanov that he would find the French far more difficult to deal with than the English. His prediction proved to be accurate.

The British Foreign Office shared the French belief that the Russian demands were much too excessive and yet did not hesitate to give Benckendorff a reassuring sign on 10 March. Grey was convinced that continued objection on the part of His Majesty's Government would so demoralize the Russians that even the loyalty of the Tsar might not suffice to keep them in the war. There were several other factors that encouraged Grey to reverse Britain's century-long policy of opposing Russia's most cherished goals. A recently discovered investigation conducted by the Admiralty in 1903 had concluded that Russian possession of Constantinople and the Straits would not fundamentally alter the strategic position in the Mediterranean.[34] Since the start of the war, moreover, there was an evolution in public opinion at home in favour of Russia's national aspirations. Then too the British had no intentions of establishing a permanent foothold in the area. Finally it was seen that relinquishing the Straits to Russia would be the best guarantee to inhibit the resumption of Germany's *Drang nach Osten* and safeguard British interests in the Levant.[35]

By now the British authorities had determined that the breakup of the Ottoman Empire was inevitable. While they had yet to formulate a definite set of war aims, they did periodically discuss schemes of partition and areas which they thought should come under British control.[36] They and their partners all presupposed a victory over the Turks.

---

30 Delcassé to Sazanov, 8 March 1915, in *Documents*, pp. 255-56.
31 Isvolsky to Sazanov, 9 March 1915, in *Constantinople*, Vol. 1, pp. 198-99.
32 C.J. Smith, *The Russian Struggle for Power 1914–1917* (New York Philosophical Library, 1956), p. 224.
33 Bobroff, *Roads to Glory*, p. 133.
34 Hankey, *Supreme Command*, Vol. 1, pp. 289-90.
35 BNA: Cabinet papers, CAB 37/128, The Dardanelles: Note by the War Office, 28 May 1915.
36 See for example Cassar, *Kitchener's War*, pp. 147-52.

Grey was unaware of the French position on the Russian aide-memoire when on 12 March he formally accepted on behalf of His Majesty's Government all of Russia's demands, asking in return for a number of concessions. These included, among other things, that no impediment be placed in the way of their own territorial claims; the establishment of a free port in Constantinople for goods in transit outside of Russia; freedom for ships passing through the Straits; and a pledge not to hinder any state offering to join the Entente on reasonable terms. The British conditions did not affect Russia's domination over the coveted area and were promptly approved.[37]

Britain's acceptance of the Tsarist regime's aide-memoire of 4 March touched off a violent outcry in Paris where feeling in certain influential circles ran high in opposing Russia's predominance over Constantinople and the Straits lest it imperil France's considerable investments and cultural ties in the Turkish Empire. The reversal of Britain's traditional Middle East policy, however, cut the ground from underneath Delcassé's feet. In the past Britain and France, though pursuing their special aims in the Sultan's realm, had enough in common to jointly resist the expansion of Russia to the Mediterranean. Now without that vital support Delcassé understood, if few in the government did, that France could not hope to hold out alone indefinitely. While continuing to assure Sazanov of France's steadfast backing, Delcassé used different tactics to play for time, no doubt in the hope that the British and French would soon arrive in Constantinople and be in a commanding position to exert pressure on Petrograd to revise its demands. As already noted, he suggested that the details of Russia's eventual acquisition of the requested territory should be worked out after the defeat of Germany; as well as proposing (on more than one occasion) a meeting of the three Allied foreign ministers to discuss the partition of the Ottoman Empire. He followed up by prolonging the negotiations with Sazanov to gain Russia's consent to France's annexation of Syria, parts of Palestine, Cilicia and Alexandretta. Lastly, as he was anxious to settle the question of a wartime administration of Constantinople, proposed a council of three commissioners, one from each of the interested Allied powers, to exercise control.

It worked for a while but at a certain point Delcassé realized that he could no longer continue to drag his feet. Sazanov's patience was wearing thin and, as we shall see, the operation in the Dardanelles was encountering more difficulties than anticipated. Thus Delcassé now faced the daunting task of waging a fight on behalf of Russia's demands against powerful and well entrenched adversaries in the country. These included elements of the press, all those who had financial interests in Turkey, as well as Maurice Bombard, former ambassador at Constantinople, a majority of the cabinet, among them, Briand, Marcel Sembat (Minister of Public Works) and Poincaré. The latter, a fervent exponent of France's traditional Eastern policy was especially implacable. A case in point was the following entry in his memoirs after he learned that Russia's demands included Constantinople and the Straits:

> This is the first time to my knowledge that Russia has advanced her claim to Constantinople. She had always declared that she held no such ambition and since the start of the war she had only asked for the freedom of the Straits, neutralization of Constantinople and a point on the Bosporus ... Thus far Russia has not participated in the Dardanelles operation. The

---

37 Smith, *Russian Struggle*, pp. 225-32.

troops she promised are nowhere in sight and if Constantinople were to fall it would not be due to Russia. Nor could she ignore, moreover, that Romania would never accept to be bottled up and the Greeks would rather see the Turks than the Russians at Constantinople. Russia will thus irritate two nations whose goodwill is precious to us, perhaps even necessary. Finally, as soon as Russia is assured of Constantinople, she will undoubtedly lose interest in actively pursuing the war against Germany.[38]

Poincaré conferred with Delcassé and at his suggestion took the unusual step of writing directly to Paléologue on 9 March, underlining the damage that would be done if Petrograd's territorial demands were met. In particular it would threatened French economic interests in Asia Minor and elsewhere, risk converting Russia into a naval power and deter interested neutral nations from joining the Entente. Poincaré considered any measure that increased Russia's strength acceptable only if France derived equivalent advantages from the war. That being the case, he urged Paléologue to try to persuade Sazanov and the Tsar to put off all idea of a separate peace and to defer the distribution of Ottoman spoils until the final settlement.[39] If there was the slightest chance that the Russian leadership could have been brought around to conform to the President's wishes, it would have required someone on the scene with more resolve and negotiating skill than Paléologue.

Despite marshalling all conceivable arguments, especially dwelling on the absence of Russian forces to take part in the operation, the opponents of appeasing the Tsarist government were eventually forced to bow before the grim force of reality. It helped Delcassé significantly that government censorship of the press kept public opinion dormant by forbidding any attack on the impending pledge to Russia. In dealing with the cabinet, Delcassé did not reveal the text of the notes exchange between him and Sazanov and simply adopted a predictable line of argument. The precipitous capitulation of the British, lamentable as it was, left them with no alternative but to follow suit. If England, for many years the principal adversary of Russia had chosen to cooperate, it would be hypocritical of the French, who professed to be Russia's sincerest friend, to continue to hold out. And in the process it would alienate the Russians and affect the war effort, possibly leading them to negotiate a settlement with Germany. Delcassé pointed out that Sazanov had declared that he did not think that Russia would be able to continue the war if the general public, excited at the prospect of gaining the country's historic objective as a means to compensate for their sacrifice, was denied fulfillment of their dream.[40] For three weeks the cabinet deliberated, explored different approaches to the question and arrived at the only possible conclusion. On 10 April Paris formally acceded to Russia's territorial claim in Turkey, subject to the war being fought to a successful conclusion and the realization by France and Britain of their own desiderata in the Middle East and elsewhere.

The Straits Agreement was a resounding diplomatic triumph for Sazanov. That the Russians extorted concessions in excess of what their strength justified must be attributed in large measure to the mediocre conduct of Grey's negotiations. Before hurrying to reach an accommodation with the Russians, he should have at least explored the possibility of establishing a common

---

38 Poincaré, *Au Service*, Vol. 6, pp. 87–88.
39 Poincaré to Paléologue, 9 March 1915 in Minstère des Affaires Étrangères, *Documents Diplomatic Français 1915*, tome 1 (Brussels: Peter Lang, 20002), pp. 418–20.
40 Ribot (ed.), *Journal de Alexandre Ribot,* pp. 56–58.

front with his French opposite number. Acting in unison, the two foreign secretaries might have induced Sazanov to delay the matter until the final peace settlement or, at the very least, moderate his country's demands. According to Lord Bertie, the Quai D'Orsay maintained that it would have been ready to resist the Russian demands if the Foreign Office, instead of being in a hurry to capitulate, had been inclined to stand alongside the French.[41]

The breach of a major principle of French foreign policy would remain a sore point with many high-ranking officials in the government until the Bolshevik Revolution in November 1917. It so troubled Poincaré that even two years after the country bowed to the Russian demands he would tell Viviani: "I have regretted more than anyone and I have not ceased to say so in Council that France was dragged into following England in a policy ... which ceded Constantinople to Russia and of which I only knew what was explained to us at the end of 1914 and in 1915."[42] What Poincaré and others in the government did not know at the time of the diplomatic negotiations was that secret talks were going on between British and Turkish emissaries with the object of ending the conflict between their two countries.

In January 1915 the Director of British Intelligence at the Admiralty, Captain Reginald Hall, dispatched two British agents to the remote Greek coastal town of Dedeagach to meet disaffected members of the Turkish government led by Talaat Bey (minister of the interior) to negotiate a peace treaty whereby Turkey would withdraw from the war, remain strictly neutral and open the Dardanelles to Allied shipping in exchange for the sum of £4,000,000. There were two meetings, one on 5 March and the other ten days later. The talks broke down because the British would not guarantee that Constantinople – which they had already promised to the Russians – would remain in Turkish hands. One of the British agents wrote after the war: "The whole country desired peace, and their leaders would have accepted any terms had we been able to assure them of the retention of Constantinople. They knew full well that signing away that city would also mean signing their own death warrants."[43] This strange and murky episode did not come to light until forty years later. Hall had acted on his own but informed Churchill and Fisher of his action on 19 March. They were incredulous that so important a step had been taken without their consent. They thought for a moment before ordering him to break off the talks. They doubted that the cabinet would approve the large sum of money involved, given that the naval attack, now going on, was expected to succeed.[44] Hall did as he was told but when the naval attack failed and he was asked to spare no expense to win over the Turks it was too late. Whether deliberate or not, the French were kept in the dark about the negotiations. Had the Viviani government been aware of the Anglo-Turkish talks before they ended, it is inconceivable that they would have agreed to turn over Constantinople and the Straits to the Russians.

When everything is said and done it clear that Poincaré and his colleagues resented the Straits Agreement, not the least because they anticipated a resumption of old rivalries during

---

41 Lennox (ed.), *Diary of Lord Bertie*, Vol. 1, p. 132.
42 Ribot (ed.), *Journal de Alexandre Ribot*, p. 131.
43 Capt. G.R.G. Allen, "A Ghost from Gallipoli," *Journal of the United Service Institution*, Vol. 101, May 1963, pp. 137-38; Patrick Beesly, *Room 40: British Intelligence 1914-1918* (New York: Harcourt Brace Jovanovich), 1982), pp. 81-82. Further details of the incident are available in Adm. Sir William James, *The Eyes of the Navy: A Biographical Study of Admiral Sir Reginald Hall* (London: Methuen, 1955), pp. 62-63.
44 Gilbert, *Winston S. Churchill*, Vol. 3, pp. 358-59.

the post-war period. But they were hardly unique among the Entente politicians to adopt such a view. That explains why the negotiations leading to the Straits Agreement had been drawn out and rather contentious. Once Russia's territorial aspirations were met, France and Britain looked to acquire their share of the Ottoman spoils. All three Powers were so concerned with achieving their Imperial objectives that they overlooked one vital factor. They first had to defeat Turkey.

6

Conduct and Aftermath of the Naval Attack on 18 March

As the month of March wore on, Carden's conduct of operations against the forts inside the Straits had only yielded minimal results. What was no less disconcerting was the inability of the ships to locate the hidden howitzers which continued to protect the vital minefields. The minesweepers were exposed to the enemy's guns not only during the daylight hours but also at night under the glaring rays of searchlights. The trawlers lacked armour protection and were manned by civilian crews who would turn back each time the enemy's fire became too intense. Spurred by an anxious Churchill willing to accept losses in return for success, Carden decided to shift his step-by-step approach to an all-out assault which he speculated would be carried out around 17 March. However the strain of command was too much for Carden and just before the naval attack he suffered a nervous breakdown and was replaced by Vice-Admiral de Robeck.[1] The new naval chief was well acquainted with Carden's plan and the change of command only pushed the start of the operation back by one day.

The ships coming together at the mouth of the Dardanelles were a tremendous spectacle and constituted the greatest concentration of naval strength which had ever been seen in the Mediterranean. Apart from an armada of cruisers, destroyers and lesser craft there were eighteen battleships at the disposal of de Robeck. The British had contributed fourteen battleships, most of which were semi-obselete but whose guns were superior to anything the Turks had on shore. Supplementing the British fleet were four French ships, all of ancient vintage. The French squadron was under the direction of Rear-Admiral Guépratte, a colourful character with a reputation for courage and audacity. It is probably safe to say that he was rather unique among the upper brass in the French navy.

Guépratte was born in Granville, near Cherbourg, on 30 August 1858, into a family steeped in naval tradition. He entered the *école navale* (Naval Training College) in 1871, became an officer in 1874 and was promoted *enseigne de vaisseau* in 1877. He saw service in Tunisia and Indochina, in addition to immersing himself in studies and becoming an expert on torpedo operations and anti-submarine defences. He rose rapidly, becoming *capitaine de vaisseau* in 1904 and entering the war in 1914 as a rear-admiral. In the early weeks Guépratte was in the

---

1   Marder, *From the Dreadnought*, Vol. 2, pp. 240-44; Victor Rudenno, *Gallipoli: Attack from the Sea* (New Haven: Yale University Press, 2008), pp. 44-49.

Mediterranean in command of a squadron of aged vessels assigned to escort convoys carrying troops between North Africa and France. In the aftermath of the escape of the *Goeben* and *Breslau*, he was sent with two battleships (in the fall of 1914) to join British naval forces guarding the Dardanelles.

Guépratte was a not an academic type of naval officer but a man of action with plenty of drive, determination and energy. A gifted leader with a firm grip of the technical side of his profession, he exuded confidence and possessed force of character. He believed in the old adage that attack was the best defence but at times he was aggressive and fearless almost to the point of overriding sound judgement. He was solid and dependable, if not intellectually brilliant and, with his dominant personality and consuming passion to win, eventually captured the public eye in France as few of its naval officers in recent history had.

A fire-eater like Guépratte was bound to rub some people the wrong way. He was accused of being vain, full of outward show, greedy for glory and possessing an erratic judgment. Among his most prominent detractors was the Minister of Marine. Professor Halpern wrote in his classic study on the naval war in the Mediterranean:

> Shortly after naval operations began at the Dardanelles in February, Auagagneur cabled Lapeyrère that he had received disturbing information that Guépratte's demeanour and attitude aroused fears that his mental equilibrium was likely to create a poor impression on the British. The minister asked if Guépratte appeared to be in a suitable state to continue his command and, if not, who would Laperèyre suggest. Lapyrère replied with the obvious, namely that Guépratte's relations with the British were excellent and that his health ... was also excellent and that he had given the officers and men of his division a remarkable élan which reflected honourably on the French navy, and in every respect there was no one more worthy to command. Augagneur shifted his ground with the customary skill of a politician and cabled that his query had only been to confirm from the C-in-C his own good opinion of Guépratte, and that he was glad to know the campaign of denigration whose echoes had reached him were not justified.[2]

Augagneur, however, continued to nurse doubts about Guépratte's fitness to command and, as will be seen in the next chapter, did not hesitate to act on them when the opportunity arose. In contrast to Augagneur, British naval leaders had the utmost confidence in Guépratte, liked him personally, and more often than not adopted his suggestions.

When Guépratte looked at the naval battle plan issued on 15 March he objected to the role assigned to the French ships. He disliked the idea of his old ships holding back and remaining stationary, partly because they would be easy targets and partly because it would be more difficult for them to zero in on the Turkish forts. He wanted his ships to close in and make a series of runs as they engaged the Turkish forts at short range. Although de Robeck acknowledged the strength of Guépratte's argument, he already had what he considered a sound battle plan in place and was reluctant to make last minute changes. Refusing to give up, Guépratte persuaded

---

2 Halpern, *Naval War*, p. 61.

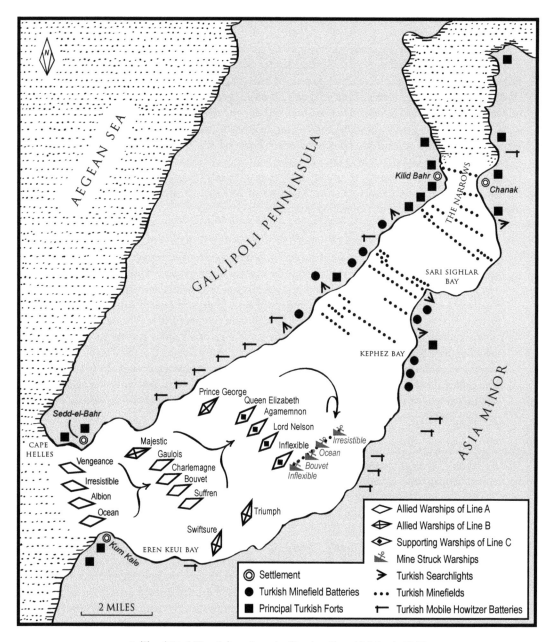

2. The Allied Naval Attack at the Dardanelles, 18 March 1915

three British captains to intercede on his behalf. Their intervention bore fruit and Guépratte was allowed to have his way.³

The plan of attack was simple and as good as could be expected under the circumstances. It was to be carried out in stages over a few days starting on 18 March. Steaming slowly up the waterway in daylight, the battleships would simultaneously hammer away at the forts inside the narrow Straits and the batteries protecting the Kephez minefield. Once enemy fire had been brought under control, the trawlers would be sent during the night to clear a channel through the minefield, allowing the fleet the next morning to advance into Sari Singhlar Bay to destroy The Narrow forts at close quarters. Thereupon the trawlers would proceed to sweep the minefield at The Narrows which would clear the way for the fleet to enter the Sea of Marmora.⁴

De Robeck deployed his fleet into three lines. The ships in Line A would initiate the action and consisted of the four most powerful battleships, *Queen Elizabeth, Agamemnon, Inflexible* and *Lord Nelson*, with the *Prince George* and *Triumph* guarding either flank and located slightly to the rear. The French ships named *Suffren, Bouvet, Charlemagne* and *Gaulois* made up Line B and were to follow and advance to within 8,000 yards of the shore to complete the demolition of the forts at close range. In Line C it was intended that the *Ocean, Albion, Irresistible, Vengeance, Swiftsure,* and *Majestic*, would act in support, "replacing damaged ships and allowing the attack to be pressed home without diminution of fire."⁵

Thursday, 18 March broke warm and sunny but the fleet awaited the morning haze to lift before proceeding up the Straits. The ships in Line A reached their station shortly after 11 am and 20 minutes later, while remaining in place but not anchored, opened a blistering bombardment against the intermediate defences and the forts at The Narrows. The ships scored repeated hits against the intermediate targets but their indirect long-range fire had little effect against the fortifications at The Narrows. The battleships were beyond the range of the Turkish guns in the forts but they were subjected to a continuous barrage from either side by mobile howitzers and light guns that formed part of the intermediate defences. Turkish fire was distressful but none of the ships had been hit seriously.

As Turkish fire from the intermediate guns slackened, de Robeck directed Guépratte a few minutes after midday to bring his squadron forward.⁶ Intent on carrying out, as he had expressly requested, a close-range attack on enemy defences, his ships swung around in a great arc and took a position about 9,000 yards from The Narrow forts before opening fire. Enemy guns came alive again as soon as the battleships came within range and a fierce cannonade ensued. The fire from the forts, added to that of the concealed batteries, began to take a toll. Both the flagship *Suffren* and the *Gaulois* took direct hits. The *Suffren's* power magazine was penetrated by a heavy shell and the battleship was a minute or two from being ripped apart with incalculable loss of life when it was saved by the quick thinking of a young gunnery officer. He then approached his commanding officer with some anxiety saying: "I hope I haven't overreached myself, but seeing

---

3   Vice-Amiral Émile-Paul Guépratte, *L'Expédition des Dardanelles 1914–1915* (Paris: Payot, 1935), pp. 57-58.
4   Corbett, *Naval Operations*, Vol. 2, p. 211; Halpern, *Naval War*, p. 76; Rudenno, *Gallipoli*, p. 49.
5   Peter Hart, *Gallipoli* (Oxford University Press, 2011), pp. 32-33.
6   The best accounts of the French action in my view are found in Guépratte, *L'Expédition des Dardanelles* and A. Thomazi, *La Guerre Navale aux Dardanelles* (Paris: Payot, 1926), old but reliable.

that the *Suffren* was in grave danger of explosion I've just flooded the magazine without orders."[7] François Lannuzel the young officer in question was not only complimented but awarded the military medal. Not long afterwards he was killed aboard the *Suffren*, the very ship that he had saved.

A shell exploded on the quarterdeck of the *Gaulois* and caused a few casualties but no serious structural damage. Far more serious was the next hit. A 14-inch shell fired from The Narrows struck the ship just below the waterline and opened a large hole, sending water rushing into the fore compartments. Guépratte was so concern by its strickened condition that he signaled the British light cruiser *Dublin*, in close support, to move forward and stand by in case it had to be abandoned. Captain Baird of the *Gaulois* declined an offer to have his ship towed and only requested from the English officers, who came on board to inspect the damage, for divers to repair the hole. A wooden partition covered the hole but there was no guarantee that it would remain in place under the pressure of water. With the ship in danger of sinking, part of the crew was removed but Baird chose to remain in the fray, only requesting from a midshipman his best uniform and a glass of port. Baird was setting an example of imperturbability but the young sailor misunderstood the order and thought that the captain was determined to poison himself rather than survive the loss of his ship.[8] He must have been both embarrassed and relieved when someone corrected his misimpression. The *Gaulois* did not go down but struggled to stay afloat and with a list to starboard and bows down, it was evidently unfit for further action. Hoping that the bulkhead was strong enough to hold up, Baird coolly and skilfully manoeuvred his slow-moving ship out of the Straits. Just outside the entrance, the *Gaulois* was successfully beached on a small island where it underwent emergency repairs before proceeding to Malta.

The severe struggle for the mastery of the Straits persisted with French bombardment increasing in intensity and volume and striking enemy targets repeatedly. The extent of the damage was usually hard to judge, impeded as it was by the thick smoke around the forts. Besides the forts would continue to fire, even if hit numerous times, unless their guns were permanently disabled. Still French action had been reasonably effective. It had gradually stifled the response from the intermediate forts but failed to put the guns located at The Narrows out of action. After nearly two hours of bombardment de Robeck, pleased by the sprited run of the French squadron, ordered it to withdraw to make way for the British ships in Line C. As the French ships turned down to exit the Straits, the *Bouvet*, travelling in Eren Keui Bay off the Asian shore, was rocked by a violent explosion slightly before 2 pm. Instantly a cloud of yellow and black smoke was observed trailing the crippled vessel. Most of the men aboard had no opportunity to escape. In about two minutes the old French warship heeled over, capsized and disappeared with only 66 survivors out of a crew of 724. The incredible speed with which the Bouvet sank sickened helpless onlookers. "If I live one hundred years, I will never forget the horror of watching the *Bouvet* sink", a French officer penned in his diary.[9] A British junior officer on the *Prince George* described what he witnessed after the explosion:

---

7   Guépratte, *L'Expédition des Dardanelles*, p. 66.
8   Peter Liddle, *Men of Gallipoli* (London: Allen Lane, 1976), p. 44.
9   Capitaine de Corvette X and Claude Farrère, "Journal de bord de l'expédition des Dardanelles", *Les oeuvres libres*, Vol. 17 (1922), pp. 218-29.

We saw a tremendous quantity of black smoke arise just abaft funnels on starboard side. Then she commenced gradually to roll towards us, we were about 400 yards to starboard of her. The roll steadily continued till she was keel uppermost then her stern steadily settled down and just as steadily she went under in about three minutes from when first struck. It was awful and unnerved us all in the top. There was no time to do anything... I never want to see the like again.[10]

To those on the scene it seemed that the *Bouvet* had received a direct hit on her magazine. Unfortunately, there was more bad news. Around 4 pm, as enemy guns fell practically silent, de Robeck sent in the minesweepers to clear a path to the Kephez minefield. Although protected by two warships they were greeted by such murderous fire from the mobile artillery that they turned and fled. At 4.11 pm the *Inflexible* hit a mine in a spot where the *Bouvet* had gone down and began to list as it struggled to move out of the range of Turkish guns. Several minutes later the *Irresistible* suffered the same fate and drifted towards the Asiatic shore. The cause of the devastating losses was not known for sure. It was believed that the area had been swept clean and the only plausible explanation for the disasters was that the Turks had fired torpedoes from undetected tubes across the Straits, or released floating mines down the rapid current.[11] It was not known until after the war that during the night of 7–8 March a small Turkish steamer had laid a fresh row of 20 mines, not across the Straits as was customary, but parallel to the shore in Eren Keui Bay where German onlookers had earlier observed that Allied ships passed through that location after their run.

The extensive damage incurred and the uncertainty of what had produced the mishaps led de Robeck to break off the engagement. Now the *Ocean*, in an attempt to tow *Irresistible* to safety, ran into the same minefield and both ships foundered in the night – but not before the crews in both ships had been removed. Out of 16 battleships three had been sunk and three disabled so badly that they were effectively out of service.

Although the naval attack had been an unmitigated failure, there was no thought at first to call a halt to the operation.[12] The idea that the ships would desist if difficulties were encountered, a condition without which the venture would not have gained official approval, disappeared the moment Churchill made his fateful announcement to the press. It was now felt in the War Council that it would be impossible to withdraw without loss of prestige which might spell trouble for Britain in parts of its Empire inhabited by Muslims.

On 20 March Churchill cabled de Robeck, promising to make good his losses and encouraging him to stay the course. He urged the naval commander not to suspend the attack or allow the Turks time to repair their forts. De Robeck, in telegrams sent on the 19th and 20th, showed that he too agreed with the general sentiment in the Admiralty. He expected a delay of several days until his plan could be revised to deal with the floating mines.[13]

The outcome of the naval attack appears to have left a deeper impression in Paris. It was over a German wireless on 19 March that the French learned the *Bouvet* had struck a mine and gone down. Shortly before the cabinet met, Auganeur confirmed the report to Poincaré, adding that

---

10 Cited in Robin Prior, *Gallipoli: The End of the Myth* (New Haven: Yale University Press), p. 56.
11 Marder, *From the Dreadnought*, Vol. 2, pp. 246-47.
12 BNA: Cabinet papers, CAB 42/1, Minutes of the War Council, 19 March 1915.
13 Churchill, *World Crisis*, Vol. 2, pp. 233-35.

he had no information yet about the results of the bombardment.[14] On the same day Augagneur received telegrams from the French naval attaché in London, telling him that the naval assault would be resumed as soon as the mines were cleared. At Churchill's request, Augagneur sent the coast defence ship *Henri IV* to replace the *Bouvet*.[15] The remaining ships – the *Suffren*, *Charlemagne* and *Gaulois* – were all damaged to varying degrees and temporarily pulled back for repairs. Consequently, the battleship *Jauréguiberry*, and two armed cruisers, *Latouche-Tréville* and *Jeanne d'Arc*, were directed at intervals to join the *Henri IV*.[16]

The cabinet met on 20 March and heard Augagneur provide further details about the naval attack as well as the loss of the *Bouvet* and the condition of the *Gaulois*. The praise accorded to Guépratte for his fearless conduct of the attack on the Turkish forts could not mask the unhappy result of the effort to force the Straits. Gone was the cautious optimism in which the Dardanelles had been seen as the key to a new Eastern strategy.

Back in London, the moment for action was permitted to lapse. The mood of resolution that de Robeck manifested in the wake of the naval setback on the 18th evaporated within 48 hours. What caused him to have second thoughts was his despondency over the loss of more than a third of his fleet, the uncertainty of what had caused the catastrophe, the presence on the scene of a military force and the fear of removal from command in case of another failure. On 22 March de Robeck suddenly announced at a conference with the generals that the navy could not do the job alone. Hamilton was of the same opinion and there was no further discussion.[17] The next day de Robeck signaled Churchill of a change to his plans and added that the army would not be ready to land until the middle of April.[18]

The unexpected announcement shocked Churchill. It must have taken him a few minutes to recover his bearing after which he drafted a reply ordering de Robeck to resume the naval attack at the first favourable opportunity. However he encountered fierce opposition from Lord Fisher (the First Sea Lord) who disapproved of the proposed telegram and was backed by professional members of the War Staff Group.[19] Fisher took the position that it was unthinkable to overrule the considered opinion of both the naval commander and general on the spot. Churchill admitted that "high words were used around the octagonal table" but at the end of the day he felt compelled to bow to the wishes of his naval experts.[20]

As was the case with anything affecting the enterprise, the decision to end the naval operation had been reached independent of the French. Churchill had made an effort to periodically keep Augagneur posted about the progress of the operations but he had not gone so far as to invite his opinion in formulating naval strategy. He may have deemed that as second fiddle, the French were not entitled to have a say. It is more probable, however, that he opposed including the French in discussions over high-level naval policy on the grounds that it would hamper his executive action. The operation was his brain child and his reputation and possibly his career,

---

14 Poincaré, *Au Service*, Vol. 6, p. 119.
15 SHD: AMM, Xa 3, Saint-Seine to Augagneur, two telegrams sent on 19 March 1915.
16 A. Thomazi, *Guerre Navale*, pp. 87, 106, 115, 144.
17 Marder, *From the Dreadnought*, Vol. 2, pp. 251-52.
18 Churchill, *World Crisis*, Vol. 2, pp. 236-37.
19 This body oversaw the conduct of naval operations and consisted of Churchill, Fisher, Rear-Admiral H. F. Oliver (Chief of Staff), Admiral Sir A. Wilson (Admiral of the Fleet), Sir William Graham Greene (Secretary to the Board) and Commodore C. M. de Bartolomé (Naval Secretary).
20 Churchill, *World Crisis*, Vol. 2, pp. 238-39.

rested on its successful outcome. At any rate Churchill had no reason to suspect that Augagneur was unhappy with the current arrangements. His proposals were accepted at the Ministry of Marine with scarcely a murmur, as were his requests for ships and minesweepers.

The check sustained by the navy on 18 March had shaken Augagneur but not to the extent that made him want to play a more active role in the decision-making process. He was deterred from doing so partly because in soliciting the advice of his naval experts after initially ignoring them, he would have to admit that he had made a serious error; and partly because he wanted to shield himself politically in case the operation ended in failure.

Predictably Augagneur expressed no displeasure when notified that the next effort would be in the form of a combined operation to be mounted around 15 April.[21] The news was also transmitted to Millerand who contacted d'Amade with suggestions for military landings (see next chapter). Both Augagneur and Millerand were on hand at the cabinet meeting on 25 March to announce the change in plans and, while a brief discussion followed, no dissenting voices were heard. A disgruntled Poincaré wrote: "The whole scheme is faulty having been insufficiently thought out in London. It was the conception of the Admiralty too rapidly put into effect without considering the military difficulties or diplomatic repercussions."[22]

No sooner had the Viviani cabinet been told that the nature of the Dardanelles operation had changed, then Saint-Seine delivered a bombshell. He revealed to his superior that Churchill had appealed personally to de Robeck to immediately resume the attack. De Robeck's reply, which coincided with the views of the British sea lords, had strongly advised against such action.[23] Several days later d'Amade seemed to lend credence to the report:

> "British Government and English Commander-in-Chief request that the fleet pursue its effort, without regard for the defeat of March 18, and maintain land forces ready to take advantage of an eventual success of the fleet in ensuring the freedom of passage of ships."[24]

In view of the new information the French authorities concluded that, contrary to the advice of the naval experts at the Admiralty, the First Lord, with the possible authorization of the British government, was contriving to induce de Robeck to make another assault by the fleet alone. Anxious to get to the bottom of the matter, the Quai d'Orsay cabled Cambon on 3 April:

> Following the operation of March 18, it was apparently understood that the co-operation of land and sea forces was essential in order to obtain more important results and achieve the aim of the campaign. However, it appears that the First Lord of the Admiralty, in a personal telegram, urged Admiral de Robeck to pursue vigorously operations against forts by naval means only.
>
> To this Admiral de Robeck allegedly replied that an immediate attack by the fleet on the Straits fortifications would be committing an error which might endanger the execution of a better and more ambitious plan.

---

21   SHD: AMM, Xa 3, Saint Seine to Augagneur, 24 March 1915.
22   Poincaré, *Au Service*, Vol. 6, p. 130.
23   SHD: AMM, Ed 109, Saint-Seine to Augagneur. The date inscribed on the document is 27 March 1915, but it is incorrect. The telegram was sent either on the 28th or 29th.
24   D'Amade to Millerand, 30 March 1915, in France, *Les armées françaises*, tome 8, Vol. 1, annexe no. 50.

The Government believes that what must be avoided above all is running the risk of a defeat which could have deplorable repercussions on current events – it would be better to wait a few more days and attack in force and with complete co-operation when we are sure of ourselves. It is impossible that this could not be the British Government's opinion.[25]

The French ambassador forwarded the text of the telegram to Asquith with a request that he verify the information with Churchill.[26] Asquith had been among the most vocal voices in the War Council for a resumption of the naval attack but not to the extent of defying Churchill's leading naval advisors. He knew that on 25 March, a day after Churchill had accepted the verdict of the Sea Lords, he sent a personal telegram to de Robeck with Fisher's reluctant consent. While de Robeck was free to act as he saw fit, the First Lord tried to encourage him to try once more by making his task less dangerous. Instead of sending the ships over minefields and past guns of undamaged forts to break into the Sea of Marmora, Churchill proposed limiting the objective to clearing the Kephez minefield. If successful, the stage would be set for the next deliberate advance.[27] De Robeck, however, concluded that a renewal of the naval attack could result in a disaster and jeopardize the success of a combined operation.[28]

Asquith was not sure of what to make of the communication from the Quai d'Orsay. Was the single-minded Churchill venturing to act behind the back of his sea lords? He had a private talk with Churchill and showed him the French note. Churchill denied there was any substance to the allegation, insisting that a week earlier he had accepted de Robeck's proposal for a combined operation. Churchill must have pointed out that the French had misunderstood the personal telegram he sent de Robeck, urging him to reconsider but leaving the decision in his hands. He assured Asquith, who was eager to still the fears of the French government, that he would set the record straight with its representatives in London.

Churchill immediately called in Saint-Seine, gently explained that it had been an unfortunate misunderstanding and convinced him that the moment for the ships to act alone had passed. Later in the day the naval attaché saw Cambon and informed him that, in light of de Robeck's opposition, Churchill had abandoned the idea of pursuing purely naval operations. Thereupon Cambon transmitted the information to Delcassé.[29]

The first stage in the great adventure was over. To sum up, the main selling point in Churchill's plan was that if the naval attack ran into difficulties it would be called off. This should have been the moment at which the operation was cancelled, and it would have if much of the world's attention had not been drawn to it by Churchill's inexcusable advance publicity. It was thus accepted in London that there was too much at stake to consider withdrawal and, if military operations on the Gallipoli Peninsula were necessary to finish the job, they must be carried through. It would prove to be much more difficult than anyone could have imagined. With the

---

25   AMAE: under the heading Opération des Dardanelles, carton 4, dossier 2, Delcassé to Cambon, 3 April 1915.
26   BNA: note in FO 371, no. 2470, 3 April 1915.
27   Churchill, *World Crisis*, Vol. 2, pp. 239-41.
28   Gilbert, *Winston S. Churchill, Vol. 3*, pp. 375-77.
29   AMAE: under the heading Opération des Dardanelles, carton 4, dossier 2, Cambon to Delcassé, 3 April 1915.

element of surprise gone, the army was now called upon to undertake a major campaign without adequate preparation or resources.

In assessing the naval plan to reach Constantinople there can be little doubt that it was terribly ill-conceived. Above all the ships lacked the means to deal with the land batteries, not the least of which were the hidden guns. Churchill maintained that if the naval assault had been renewed it would have succeeded because the Turkish forts had fired off most of their ammunition.[30] His contention is not supported by the available evidence. The Turkish forts appear to have had enough heavy and lighter calibre shells to hold off at least another attack on the scale of 18 March. Yet in the final analysis the issue is irrelevant. The main barrier that closed the Straits to the ships was the minefield and it was not only intact but defended by concealed howitzers for which there were an ample supply of ammunition.[31]

The old adage that errors committed in the original conception of a campaign is almost impossible to repair was never more apparent. At the outset the first thing on the mind of the Allies should have been to clearly define political as well as military ends. Forcing the Dardanelles should have been seen as only the preliminary step in accomplishing the military objective. None of the politicians in either London or Paris gave any thought to what would follow. They and especially their Russian ally appeared more concerned with laying rival claims to Turkish territory than with finding an appropriate solution to the enterprise. The alternatives were either total dismemberment of the Turkish Empire which would entail a very ambitious military operation and prior agreements amongst the major powers, or a campaign aimed at simply bringing about the overthrow of the pro-German administration and a separate peace. The second option might have proved more effective in helping the Allied war effort but it would not have fulfilled the Imperial ambitions of the powers.

Let us turn next to discuss the likely scenarios in the improbable event the fleet, or part of it, had managed to penetrate the Sea of Marmora. Right away it would have had to dispose of the Turkish navy which included the *Goeben* and *Breslau* before moving on to threaten Constantinople. It is useful to remember that the First Lord's plan was contingent on a revolution occurring in Constantinople and on the establishment of a friendly government that would seek peace. Churchill had been swayed by reports of public dissatisfaction and unrest inside Turkey but was he justified in staking everything on intelligence which cannot accurately predict what will happen.

From the moment the Young Turks freed the Ottoman state from the absolute and oppressive rule of Sultan Abdul Hamid in 1909, they had been plagued by intermittent warfare and internal crises. The democratic ideas and progressive reforms which they had professed to espouse were quickly forgotten as their energies became dissipated in a desperate struggle for their own survival. By 1915 Turkey was in desperate circumstances. Apart from the military defeats suffered in the Caucasus and in Egypt, the country was almost bankrupt, living conditions were deplorable and the Young Turk regime was badly divided, corrupt and extremely unpopular. To western observers, who were on the scene and steeped in Turkish affairs, the climate seemed

---

30 Churchill, *World Crisis*, Vol. 2, pp. 263ff.
31 Edward J. Erickson, *Gallipoli: The Ottoman Campaign* (Barnsley, S. Yorkshire: Pen & Sword, 2010), pp. 26-27; Prior, *Gallipoli*, pp. 57-58; Marder, *From the Dreadnought, Vol. 2*, p. 263.

ideal for another revolution.[32] But appearances can be deceptive. There is really no hard evidence that the Young Turk government was in danger of being overthrown. A successful revolution in Constantinople could have occurred only if the Turkish army had been withdrawn into the interior or mutinied and refused to obey orders. Neither requirement was likely to happen. Enver Pasha, the dominant member of the Ottoman regime, had made it quite clear that he intended to use every available soldier to defend the city at all costs.[33] The chances of a breakdown of military discipline before an enemy was highly remote when the very existence of the nation was at stake. Enver had been careful to weed out all the untrustworthy or undesirables from the army and to officer it with zealous and nationalistic young men.

It has been argued that the fleet could have taken the extreme step of compelling the Turks to surrender by a steady bombardment of Constantinople. Yet thinking along those lines is implausible. To begin with it was against international law to shell an undefended city. On the other hand if the army had remained in Constantinople, as seemed probable, it is conceivable that the ships would have attempted to give a display of force by blasting away at a number of selected targets such as the ammunition factories, the Turkish War Office, the army barracks on the hills and even the Sultan's palace; but to indiscriminately bombard harmless civilians, many of whom were Christians and friendly to the Entente, was unthinkable. If the expected revolution had not taken place within a fortnight, the ships, which needed to be resupplied and were certain to be subjected to relentless pounding from the guns in Asia that had escaped destruction, would have had no choice but to withdraw and again run the gauntlet of the Turkish batteries along the Straits.

Suppose by sheer good fortune a rebellion had swept the band of usurpers from office, the Allies would still have been confronted by at least two obstacles. In the first place the new ministry, though presumably desirous for peace, would not or could not have acquiesced in the partitioning of its own state, least of all the loss of Constantinople which was the nerve centre of all Turkish affairs – economic, political and industrial. The Allies had no means to coerce the Turks for no troops accompanied the fleet. On the other hand, if they had left Turkey intact in return for its pledge to withdraw from the war, they could not have satisfied their Imperial craving. How the Entente partners expected to coax Turkey out of the conflict and at the same time wrest from it enormous territorial concessions is a question they had obviously not considered. Secondly were the Germans simply to remain passive observers in the event of Turkey's defection? The Germans had extricated Austria from its difficulties in the past (and would continue to do so in the future), so what was to prevent them from coming to the rescue of Turkey. Was it not possible for them to make a deal with Bulgaria earlier than they actually did, overwhelm Serbia, and together with their new ally, pour into Turkey and restore their friends to power.

A strategic plan must be evaluated on the strength of its achievement, or at the very least on meticulous preparation, including responses to possible contingencies, and not on a rosy speculative premise. The naval operation was supposed to drive Turkey to the negotiating table,

---

32 Henry Morgenthau, *Ambassador Morgenthau's Story* (Garden City, NY: Doubleday, Page & Co., 1919), pp. 227-28; Lewis Einstein, *Inside Constantinople* (London: John Murray, 1917), p. xiv.
33 Morgenthau, *Ambassador*, pp. 204-05.

weaken Germany, and shorten the war. In this sense it was an utter failure. To quote Sir Gerald Ellison, "the underlining idea of the whole plan was Utopian in the extreme."[34]

From this resultant welter of confusion and illusion one thing emerges quite clearly. The Allies were trying to gain the advantages of a victory without providing for the means. Regardless from which direction the operation is viewed it was unlikely to have succeeded on any of the terms clearly available. Above all the Allies needed to agree on political ends that related, not to their Imperial ambitions, but to the defeat of Turkey.

---

34   Sir Gerald Ellison, *The Perils of Amateur Strategy* (London: Longman, Green & Co., 1923), p. *66*.

7

Kum Kale and Krithia

The decision to end unaided naval action had been made, not by the War Council, but by the men on the spot. As a withdrawal was deemed unthinkable, the only alternative was to land an army on the Gallipoli Peninsula. Although the campaign was to be essentially military in character, Kitchener was under the impression that the navy would cooperate in the next phase of the operation. De Robeck indicated that the navy would continue to be active but in fact he had resolved not to rush the Straits until the army was in control of the Peninsula. In the absence of specific orders from the Admiralty, de Robeck had laid down his own policy which was beyond the normal limits of his command.

In view of the army's new role the exact nature of its assignment was not only undefined but allowed to drift without direction – though it was hardly Hamilton's fault. At a conference with French military leaders at GQG in Chantilly on 29 March, Joffre asked Kitchener whether a scheme for a landing had been worked out. The Field Marshal replied that there was not enough information at home to prepare a detailed plan and that the task would have to be done by the Allied generals on the scene. He went on to say that the broad outlines amounted to the seizure of the high grounds overlooking the Narrows and later the occupation of the Bulair lines.[1]

Where then was the most advantageous place to disembark the troops to achieve the objective? Hamilton had been rushed to the Dardanelles without any provision made to supply him with reliable information about the disposition of the enemy, accurate maps of the area, a suggested plan of operation, or even the General Staff Memorandum of 1906 which had recommended that, owing to the great risks involved, even a large-scale military operation on the Gallipoli Peninsula was unlikely to attain decisive results. On arrival in March, Hamilton was faced with a serious problem, one which could have been avoided with a little foresight. British troops, supplies and war material had been loaded so swiftly on transport ships that they were hopelessly disarranged. As it was deemed impossible for the sorting out process to take place at Mudros owing to inadequate harbor facilities, Hamilton decided to transfer the main base of the expedition to the Egyptian port of Alexandria.[2] On the heels of Hamilton's

---

1   IWM: Wilson papers, entry in Wilson's diary of a summary of the meeting of 29 March 1915.
2   Aspinall-Oglander, *Gallipoli*, Vol. 1, p. 95.

decision, d'Amade received instructions from Millerand that he was to join the British troops in Alexandria with his major force, leaving only an advance guard at Lemnos.[3]

The reorganization of the army in Alexandria had several unfortunate consequences. It delayed the landing by a month and gave the Turks more time to improve their defensive arrangements. It prevented Hamilton from holding strategy sessions with de Robeck which would have strengthened the bond between the two men and almost ensured the navy's cooperation. Thirdly it eliminated the slightest remaining hope of preserving secrecy. The press made frequent announcements of the arrival and departure of ships and the concentration of more and more troops in the country as well as speculating freely on the impending operation. The height of indiscretion occurred when d'Amade gave an interview to an Alexandria newspaper in which, incredible as it may seem, he laid down the best way for the army to take control of the Gallipoli Peninsula.[4] All of this drew the attention of the horde of German and Turkish agents in Egypt who naturally reported their findings to the Intelligence centre in Constantinople.

Apart from attending to the administrative work associated with the enterprise, Hamilton had to select landing sites and draw up a plan of attack. His task was made more difficult by Kitchener's order to avoid a serious undertaking in Asia. This left only Bulair and the Peninsula.

Millerand had advised d'Amade on 16 March to suggest an advance south of Bulair to assault and capture Turkish fortifications running along the narrow neck of the Peninsula in order to sever the land communications of the Turkish army with Constantinople and Thrace.[5] At first glance there was much to be said in favour of this plan but Hamilton eliminated it as soon as he had made a reconnaissance along the coast of the Peninsula by ship. His appraisal was based on the following considerations. First the area was commanded by elaborate networks of trenches and rows of barbed wire, supported by guns in concealed positions. The only practical landing place lay to the east of the Bulair forts where the Allies ran the risk of attacks from Turkish forces in the south and by reinforcements in the north from Thrace. Second the main objective was to seize the guns at the Narrows to let the fleet through and, to that end, the army would have been forced to fight its way through 30 miles of difficult ground, without sufficient supplies, equipment and transport facilities. Third the two arms of the service would have been attacking from different directions – the navy from south to north and the army from north to south – so that effective cooperation would have been impossible. Fourth the Turks could still have continued the struggle in the Peninsula by drawing their supplies and reinforcements from the Asiatic side.

D'Amade did not dispute the result of Hamilton's investigation and, in fact, favoured avoiding the Peninsula entirely. As already mentioned he had in mind a landing in the Bay of Adramyti (opposite Mitylene) where the beach was wide and level and the water close in fairly deep. Little if any opposition was anticipated for it was reported that the region was very lightly held with no elaborate system of entrenchments. From Adramyti the object was to successively take possession of Belikessir and the port of Panderma, which he believed had excellent disembarkation facilities and, moreover, would pose a threat to Constantinople and

---

3 SHD: AMG, 5N 18, Graziani to d'Amade, 23 March 1915.
4 James, *Gallipoli*, pp. 79-80; Ian Hamilton, *The Happy Warrior: The Life of General Sir Ian Hamilton* (London: Cassell, 1966), p. 291; Great Britain, *The Final Report of the Dardanelles Commission* (London: HMSO, 1919), pp. 15-17; Marder, *From the Dreadnought*, Vol. 2, p. 238.
5 Millerand to d'Amade, 16 March 1915, in France, *Les armées françaises,* tome 8, Vol. 1, annexe no. 31.

3. Theatre of Operations

the Dardanelles. As a supplement to the northern manoeuvre, d'Amade suggested an attack on Smyrna by land. He maintained that the overall operation would allow the Allies to exploit control of a large part of the Straits as well as the lateral communications in the area. On 21 March d'Amade broached his concept to Hamilton who politely put him off with the excuse that he must await the arrival of all the troops before deciding on a course of action. In the interval d'Amade sought to convince the Minister of War of the merits of his scheme while arguing against the descent near Bulair: "Attempt on Bulair Peninsula, streaked with German trenches where we are expected by 75,000 men, and where we shall be blockaded by a force converging from Gallipoli, Adrianople, Constantinople, runs risk of bringing defeat to land forces, following that of fleet."[6]

The next day General Jean Césaire Graziani, then deputy chief of the general staff,[7] issued a sharp reprimand to d'Amade, expressing surprise that he had approached Hamilton with a strategic plan that was not authorized by the Ministry of War. He claimed that Amade's scheme, which he described as eccentric, was inconsistent with the objective of the Allied fleet and entailed a division of effort. He conceded that the French could reach Belikessir before Turkish units from Anatolia could arrive on the scene but to gain Panderma it would be necessary to overcome the resistance of these forces, possibly assisted by reinforcements from Thrace, in a battle that would decide the fate of the campaign. Even if all went well it would take about a month to attain Panderma, the acquisition of which would contribute nothing to forcing the Dardanelles. To maintain communications between Adramyti and Panderma the rail line would have to be extended or repaired. This would not only take many months but call for engineers and material resources that were unavailable. Adding insult to injury, Graziani described Panderma as a substandard port and maintained that the Allies would be able to establish better bases after they had gained control of the Dardanelles. Graziani insisted that in the future d'Amade show the greatest care and prudence before making suggestions. He added that the government would have found itself in an awkward situation if d'Amade had succeeded in persuading the English commander to share his views.[8] The manner in which Graziani lectured d'Amade was evidently a measure of the general staff's lack of faith in his judgement.

Acknowledging that an assault in the vicinity of Bulair was perhaps too hazardous, Graziani instead directed d'Amade to recommend to Hamilton the idea of a landing in the area of Besika Bay on the Asiatic side. Here the army in conjunction with the navy would undertake a deliberate sweep of the forts along the shore. Allied troops would be able to concentrate more rapidly than the Turks in the region, affording them a significant advantage in their initial clash. Graziani cautioned that the operation required to be organized carefully and secretly and executed at the same time as the fleet attacked the defences guarding the Straits.[9]

There is a division of opinion between the German commander of the Turkish forces in the Peninsula, General Otto Liman von Sanders, and the late Robert Rhodes James, an eminent historian of the campaign, as to whether the Besika Bay scheme would have been a worthwhile

---

6   D'Amade to Millerand, 21 March 1915, in France, *Les armées françaises*, tome 8, Vol. 1, annexe no. 41.
7   In July 1915, he was promoted chief of the general staff.
8   AN: Millerand papers, 470 AP/16, EMA, "Note au subject des propositions du Général d'Amade," 22 March 1915.
9   Graziani to d'Amade, 23 March 1915, in France, *Les armées françaises*, tome 8, Vol. 1, annexe no. 43.

enterprise. Von Sanders claimed that it represented the best opportunity for an Allied victory. He wrote:

> The most important works and batteries dominating the straits of the Dardanelles lay on the southern, Asiatic coast... As the works and heavy batteries of the fortresses were arranged only for a struggle for the possession of the waterway, an advance and attack against our rear after his landing on the Asiatic shore offered excellent chances to the enemy. Road communications here were tolerably good."[10]

On the other hand, Robert Rhodes James scoffed at Liman von Sanders' suggestion, accusing him of a serious error in judgement. Citing an American authority to support his contention, he maintained that the ground over which the Allied army would have had to traverse was so rugged and difficult as to prove a remarkable feat even for a large modern army. Moreover during the march both flanks would have been vulnerable, the left to artillery fire from the Peninsula and the right to attacks by Turkish forces.[11]

Whatever the benefits or disadvantages of a thrust by way of Besika Bay, Hamilton never gave it any thought as Kitchener had placed Asia off limits. D'Amade conveyed the information to Millerand on 30 March.[12] Thereafter the French Ministry of War made no further effort to press its views and left the conduct of the campaign entirely in the hands of Hamilton and his staff.

A draft plan was approved in principle on 23 March and with a few minor changes was the one adopted on the opening day of the landing. Hamilton elected to strike in the southern half of the Peninsula. Under cover of a feint at Bulair and a demonstration at Kum Kale, troops would disembark at five beaches (delineated S, V, W, X, Y) on Cape Helles, while another landing force further north aimed at cutting the waist of Gallipoli at Maidos to compel the defenders in the south to surrender or be taken in the rear. A division of force in battle is seldom justified, but in this case it was not possible to assemble all the troops in a single beachhead for a decisive push. Hamilton's strategy struck where the enemy expected it least and, in this respect, was in accordance with sound military principles. The Turks would be forced to hold back their reserves not knowing where the main attack would take place until it was too late and the Allies had secured a firm foothold on the Peninsula.[13]

As preparations were moving forward an incident occurred which threatened to embroil the Entente partners in another dispute and delay the attack. On 12 April Saint-Seine telegraphed Augagneur that quantities of oil intended for enemy submarines were being concentrated at Bodrum (a small town in the southeastern end of the Aegean).[14] The Minister of Marine immediately alerted a French squadron in the Mediterranean to stand-by. On 16 April, however,

---

10 Limon von Sanders, *Five Years in Turkey*, pp. 58-59.
11 James, *Gallipoli*, 74. The authority James refered to is Major Sherman Miles whose article "Notes on the Dardanelles Campaign" is in *US Coast Artillery Journal*, vols. 61-62 (1924–25). Miles went over the ground from Chanak to Kum Kale and concluded that the advantages of the Besika Bay plan "are not apparent."
12 D'Amade to Millerand, 30 March 1915, in France, *Les armées françaises*, tome 8, Vol. 1, annexe no. 50.
13 James, *Gallipoli*, pp. 88-89; Aspinall-Oglander, *Gallipoli*, Vol. 1, ch. 7; *Final Report of the Dardanelles Commission*. More recent accounts are critical of Hamilton's plan but it is easy to be wise after the event.
14 SHD: AMM, Xa 3, Saint-Seine to Augagneur, 12 April 1915.

a message arrived in Paris from across the channel that Churchill had ordered Admiral Peirse to draw a battalion of marines and two additional battleships from de Robeck's flag to raid Bodrum and destroy the oil.[15] Augagneur took exception to this directive for it violated an agreement London had struck with Paris two months earlier. It was understood, he reminded the First Lord, that the coast of Syria lay within the French sphere of command and, that no operations would be carried out in the region of Alexandretta without the consent of both governments.[16]

Churchill countered these arguments in a rather dismissive manner. He explained that "the operation in question being of altogether secondary importance and closely linked to that of the Dardanelles since its purpose is to protect ships operating in the area against submarine attacks and being furthermore under British command, it apparently could not be the subject of discussion between the two governments." Churchill ended by saying: "At any rate it can be fruitful only if it is conducted in a speedy manner and in the utmost secrecy."[17]

Augagneur was inclined to suspect and resent every unorthodox move attempted by the First Lord. It is not surprising, therefore, he felt that Churchill's explanation rang hollow, arousing in him fears that the English were trying to disguise their intent to establish themselves in the Levant. Additionally, the Marine Commission in March had fallen heavily on him for abdicating the naval command in the Mediterranean and he was in no mood to be enticed away from what seemed to him an incontestable right.[18] Augagneur was determined that the French navy should at all costs take the initiative in the operation. Before the dispute threatened to heat up an Allied agent sent to Bodrum indicated that the report was false. Consequently the Admiralty revoked the order to Admiral Peirse.[19]

Meantime, Hamilton and his staff had re-embarked at Alexandria on 10 April and set sail for Mudros ahead of the troops. By the 20th last minute preparations were completed and all the men detailed for the operation had assembled and were keen to be off. The operation was scheduled to begin on the 23rd but had to be delayed 48 hours because of the inclement weather.

The story of the British landings on 25 April is not relevant to this study but it bears repeating that it has been told innumerable times since the Great War ended. By contrast the French descent at Kum Kale on the Asiatic shore has been largely ignored by historians of the campaign. What is even more baffling, the operation drew only brief attention in the French official account.[20]

Originally, French forces were to be kept in reserve to support the attack at Cape Helles but their role was revised principally to prevent the Turkish Asiatic batteries from bombarding S beach. Besides Hamilton believed that a feint at Kum Kale might confuse the Turkish leadership long enough to delay sending its Asiatic troops to reinforce their comrades on the

---

15 SHD: AMM, Xa 3, Saint-Seine to Augagneur, 16 April 1915.
16 SHD: AMM, Xa 3, Augagneur to Saint-Seine, 17 April 1915.
17 SHD: AMM, Xa 3, Saint-Seine to Augagneur, 18 April 1915.
18 A.P. Bienaimé, *La guerre navale 1914–1915; fautes et responsibilities* (Paris: Jules Tallendier, 1920), pp. 171-74.
19 SHD: AMM, Xa 3, Saint-Seine to Augagneur, 20 April 1915.
20 France, *L'Expédition des Dardanelles*, tome 8, Vol. 1, pp. 43-45.

Peninsula until after the initial clash of battle.[21] As soon as the British had secured the beaches, the French troops would re-embark and head to Cape Helles where they would join the general advance against the Kalid Bahr plateau.[22]

Hamilton's instructions to d'Amade expressly limited the scope of the operation to clearing the region between Kum Kale and Yeni Shehr and west of the Mendere River. For the task Hamilton considered that one regiment and one battery of field guns would suffice as the information received indicated that the landing party was not likely to face much opposition.[23]

D'Amade selected Colonel Ruef, who commanded the Colonial Brigade, to oversee the entire operation and assigned him the 6th Colonial Regiment (consisting of one French colonial and two Senegalese battalions) totaling 2,700 men. A good number of the French contingent were raw recruits about to undergo their baptism of fire while the Senegalese, for the most part, had seen action in Morocco and at Ypres on the Western Front. Before leaving Lemnos, the men involved had practiced landings in canvas or rubber boats. They were not briefed, however, that their purpose ashore was to act as a diversion and that at some point they would be pulling out.[24]

Situated at the mouth of the Dardanelles, Kum Kale was two and a half miles directly across Sedd-el Bahr on the Gallipoli Peninsula. Ruef and his men would be operating over a strip of land about two miles long and 500 yards wide lying between the Aegean Sea and the Mendere River and dominated by two villages, Kum Kale in the north and Yeni Shehr in the south. The site of disembarkation was near Kum Kale, which had been reduced practically to ruins as a result of the earlier naval bombardment, and an old demolished fort adjacent to it. The ground in front of Kum Kale was low and sandy and in places marshy, rising slowly near Orkanie Mound and reaching a height of more than 60 feet at Yeni Shehr. A road crossing a bridge over the Mendere River exited near a cemetery halfway between Kum Kale and Orkanie Mound. The area around Kum Kale was flat and exposed to naval gunfire, which had led the British to conclude that the French landing would not be strongly contested.

Still Turks forces were expected to rush into the area once French concentration on shore had been detected. In fact Liman von Sanders was so apprehensive of an Allied landing in the vicinity of Kum Kale that, in addition to coastal defences, he had assembled nearby no fewer than three regiments belonging to the 3rd Turkish Division: one was deployed on the other side of the Mendere River and the other two further inland.[25] This was in keeping with standard Turkish tactics which called for keeping the main concentration of troops further back in preparation for counterattacks as soon as the enemy's landing had been located. Although the Turks outnumbered the French by a wide margin, they were hampered by the flat landscape and poor local leadership.[26]

In the pre-dawn hours of the 25th, the French naval squadron, reinforced by the British battleship *Prince George* and the light cruiser *Askold* – the lone Russian vessel to take part in the campaign – moved into position and at 5.15 am opened fire on the beaches and the villages of Kum Kale and Yeni Shehr. The terrifying bombardment took a deadly toll among the Turkish

---

21   Aspinall-Oglander, *Gallipoli*, Vol. 1, p. 133.
22   Hamilton to d'Amade, 21 March, 1915, in France, *Les armées françaises*, tome 8, Vol. 1, annexe no. 81.
23   Hamilton to d'Amade, 17 April 1915, *in Les armées françaises,* tome 8, Vol. 1, annexe no. 73.
24   Liddle, *Men of Gallipoli*, pp. 126-27.
25   Aspinall-Oglander, *Gallipoli*, Vol. 1, pp. 257-59.
26   For the details of the Turkish response to the French landing see Erickson, *Gallipoli,* pp. 81-86.

Kum Kale and Krithia 107

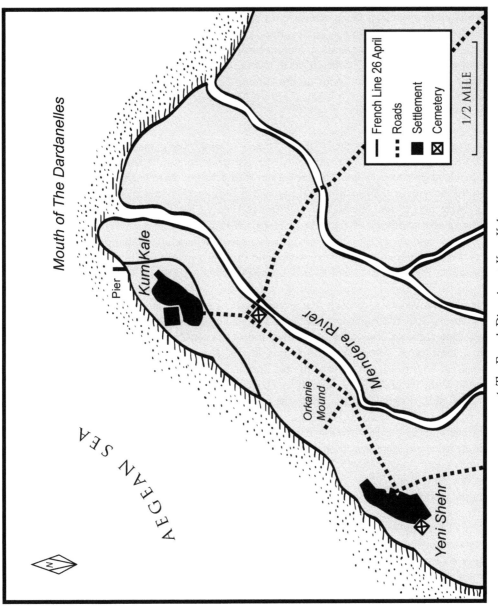

4. The French Diversion at Kum Kale

soldiers waiting in their trenches along the coast and provoked such panic in the survivors that they fled and joined their comrades behind the Mendere River. This meant that Turkish presence around Kum Kale was non-existent, except for small observation patrols.

At 6 am French troops, with knapsacks on their backs, crowded on the decks of the transport ships and 20 minutes later Guépratte gave the signal for the disembarkation to begin. The men descended on rope ladders to row boats ranged along the ships' side. Small steamships were on hand to tow the row boats towards shore. The steamers were expected to turn back about a 100 yards or so from shore, leaving the sailors to row the small boat the rest of the way. The warships did their part to protect the troops on the landing crafts from shore fire. Accompanying the invading party, a French senior medical officer, Major Joseph Vassal, witnessed the unfolding drama from the auxiliary cruiser *Savoie:*

> Our commandant orders the bugle-call "Stand to arms." The gunners are at their places. Powerful guns are at our disposal. A first shot is fired. Everybody is dazed. One's ears hurt; the blood goes to one's head. Before we can stuff cotton-wool in our ears a second and a third shot are fired. The outline of the village of Yenisher [Yeni Shehr] is now ragged. It is a destruction, certain, methodical, and regular. We see a big house with a red roof. A first shell marks it with a black fountain of smoke, which hides it for a minute from our eyes. It is ruined and one feels sad; for perhaps it has never sheltered other than peaceful people, perhaps … only absorbed in themselves and their own passionate embraces. The second shot, hitting it full, disembowels it, scattering it to atoms. The third shell ends in agony.[27]

The landing proved more difficult than anticipated. The current flowing from the Dardanelles was so strong that the tugboats were unable to make headway and more powerful transport vessels were required. The delay meant that it was not until 10 am that the first wave of the landing force came ashore near the ruined fort at Kum Kale. The French troops landed uncontested on the beaches, secured the old fort, and attacked the village, carrying it swiftly at the point of the bayonet. It was all over by 11.15 am and the good news was that the losses had been negligible. From a position inside the Straits, the *Henri IV* spotted two Turkish columns moving towards the Mendere River and opened fire. The battleship succeeded in destroying the bridge, forcing the Turks to move southwards in search of a ford to cross the river.

Throughout the afternoon French troops continued to come ashore with 75mm field guns and horses and shortly before 5.30 pm the concentration of all three battalions was completed. With the gunfire of the fleet providing cover, Ruef began his advance southwards shortly after 5.30 pm, sending two companies to occupy the cemetery on the outskirts of town and three companies against Orkanie Mound, preparatory to an assault on Yeni Shehr. By then the Turks had time to react and were entrenched in the two places. The French movements were met by stiff resistance, hindered also by an artillery battery east of the Mendere River, and the advance stalled. Aerial reconnaissance reported at 6 pm that hostile columns, presumably the ones which had attempted to cross the bridge and been obliged to move south, were close to Yeni Shehr. The French had reached about midway between Kum Kale and Orkanie Mound when Ruef abruptly called off the attacks. Remaining in place for the night, the men readied

---

27 Joseph Vassal, *Uncensored Letters*, pp. 49-50.

for defence: digging trenches, putting up barbed wire and bringing up the 75mm guns. The French line with the right flank resting on the coast stretched in a northeasterly direction until it arched around Kum Kale and continued to a point slightly above the wooden pier on the seashore.[28]

Although the ground in front of the French front was covered by periodic fire from the *Jauréguiberry* and illuminated by searchlights, it was not enough to prevent the reinforced Turks from concentrating in the area with the object of driving the invaders back into the sea. During the night at least three Turkish battalions made four furious attacks against the French positions on the eastern side of the village and each was hurled back with staggering losses. In the course of the fighting the Turks broke through at one place and furious hand-to-hand fighting followed before they were driven back. When morning broke French and Senegalese soldiers could see the result of their handiwork. In front of their trenches the bodies of dead Turkish soldiers littered the ground which was covered red with their blood.[29]

Still the Turkish counterattacks had exacted a significant toll on the French contingent. The *Savoie* had been converted into a makeshift hospital to attended to the masses of wounded soldiers transported from Kum Kale. Vassal described a terrifying scene:

> From twilight of the 25th till the first rays of dawn the next day we are leaning over wounded in an atmosphere of blood, of groans, and of indescribable horrors. We do not stop for a single minute. When suffering is quieted the infernal noise of firing returns to us from outside … The wounded still come in. They are mounted on the deck from the bottom of the boats, and form a long line of stretchers. We are able to put six wounded at a time on the big tables… Sometimes not even a groan is to be heard; the silence is impressive. Our fellows are admirable. The wounded of this night are, nevertheless, frightful. A sergeant-major comes back to us only to die. His chest was crushed by shrapnel; and for a moment we saw his heart, almost bare, still beating. There is a Senegalese with his head torn, a foot missing, and three fingers of a hand gone. Another black, waiting his turn on a chair, is asked, *"Beaucoup malade?" "Non il y en a un peu"* The doctor looks. Both legs have been torn off by a shell.[30]

Ruef had received orders in the middle of the night to resume his advance on Yeni Shehr in the morning. Before the fleet opened its preliminary bombardment a strange incident occurred. Around 7 am a party of about 80 Turkish soldiers – reported to be mostly Greeks and Armenians – waved a white flag, then advanced from the cemetery unarmed with their hands raised above their heads. The officer in charge of the 6th Regiment, Lieutenant-Colonel Charles Noguès, ordered his men to stop firing and the prisoners were led away. Behind them several hundred Turkish troops left their trenches and came forward, giving the impression that they too wanted to surrender. However they refused to lay down their arms unless the French agreed to do the same.[31] A French officer, Captain Rockel, who spoke Arabic fluently, took it upon himself to try to persuade the Turks to give up their arms. He was led to the cemetery to speak to the

---

28   French Diversion at Kum Kale, Map no. 5 in France, *Les armées françaises*, tome 8, Vol. 1.
29   Vassal, *Uncensored Letters*, p. 67.
30   Vassal, *Uncensored Letters*, pp. 56-57.
31   D'Amade, "Constantinople et les détroits", vols. 98-99, pt. 2 (1923), p. 307.

Turkish commander but the only thing we known for sure is that he disappeared and was never seen again.

Back within the French lines, the confusion grew steadily worse as tempers flared and there was much pushing and shoving with most of the Turks adamant about keeping their arms and some even tried to wrest the rifles out of the hands of the men of the 6th Regiment. During the scuffle, Private Marius Gondard suddenly found himself isolated from his platoon and was fortunate enough to have survived to relate what followed:

> The Turks came towards us and a great many surrendered, gave themselves up ... I don't know how many prisoners there were. And it was then I was taken, because, while disarming the prisoners more Turks arrived [presumably those that came after the first group] and over-ran us. I was taken by both arms by two Turks with a third walking behind me with a bayonet. I felt surprised. I was ready for anything: I expected I might be injured or killed, perhaps, but certainly not taken prisoner.[32]

Taking advantage of the disorder some Turks succeeded in making off with several machine-guns while others, estimated at between 80 and 100, slipped into the village and occupied empty houses. French troops closed in and hostilities resumed. The French made a serious effort to retrieve the machine guns from the Turkish purloiners who were concealed in several ruined houses. In so doing they suffered a number of casualties before a few salvos from a 75mm gun blasted everything that stood upright, causing the defenders to flee in every direction. In another part of town the French moved to dislodge the large party of Turks who had also barricaded themselves in abandoned houses. The Turks fought furiously and stubbornly for two hours, inflicting serious losses on the French. Captain Ferrero, the chief engineer, was among those killed and his colleague, Lieutenant Lefort, was spotted being dragged into a house. It was only when the French brought in a 75mm and levelled one house after another that the survivors (about 60) surrendered.

A search to determine what became of Lefort yielded no results. Noguès questioned some of the prisoners but none could or would provide any information. It was generally believed that Lefort had been beaten and shot. The enemy officer in command as well as eight of his men were executed in retaliation for the cruel fate that befell Rockel and Lefort in violation of the truce.[33]

While this was going on d'Amade, who had established his headquarters on the flagship *Jauréguiberry*, came ashore to survey the scene. Ruef briefed him on the progress of his troops, on stiffening enemy resistance and on the incident which had led to the loss of the two French officers.

Ruef reckoned that the first group of deserters genuinely wanted to surrender which is understandable since they were Christians, unwilling to die for their oppressive masters. What is less convincing is that he thought those that followed did not have perfidious intentions but that things got out of hand because of misunderstandings caused by communication difficulties. Ruef pointed out that the number of additional Turks surrendering that afternoon seemed to

---

32 Cited in Hart, *Gallipoli*, p. 74.
33 Vassal, *Uncensored Letters*, pp. 69-70.

confirm this opinion.[34] But he did not take into consideration the frightful inducement which had prompted so many Turks to abandoned the fight. A tornado of fire beating down on Orkanie Mound from the fleet's guns had proven so accurate that hundreds of Turks in the area panicked and either took to their heels or laid down their arms. A similar incident occurred while two companies of Senegalese launched a minor attack on the cemetery. The gunfire from the ships and a 75mm gun on shore inflicted such terrible damage on the defenders' positions as to break their spirit. A French second lieutenant of artillery, Raymond Weil, has left an account of the action:

> From our observation post we witnessed ... the Senegalese mount an attack on the Turkish trenches. We could clearly see the advance of our troops supported by the intense fire from our fleet and a 75mm gun which had been brought ashore ... The auxiliary cruiser *Savoie* approached the Asiatic coast and opened up a marvelous rapid fire on a covered Turkish trench which we had just discovered. It produced a veritable bloodbath when it took the trench in enfilade. That ended the battle... As evening approached we saw ... a minesweeper, loaded with prisoners, passed close by us. What an enthusiastic reaction.[35]

In the meantime Hamilton contacted d'Amade and directed him to transfer his Metropolitan Brigade from Lemnos to X Beach where there was a growing urgency to reinforce the troops of the 29th Division. In reply, d'Amade acknowledged the order and also indicated that his men could not advance further without reinforcements. An hour later Hamilton sent d'Amade a second telegram after conferring with Lieutenant-General Aylmer Hunter-Weston, commander of the 29th Division. He now wanted the Metropolitan Brigade to land at W, instead of X, Beach and for the remaining French infantry and artillery to be deployed at Cape Helles as quickly as possible. Since it was evident that no further French detachments would be available for the Asiatic operation, d'Amade feared for his isolated force in light of reports that the Turkish garrison at Yeni Shehr had been bolstered by new units during the night. He felt that he had fulfilled his mission and was now anxious to withdraw before it was too late.

At midday d'Amade set off to confer with Hamilton on board the *Queen Elizabeth*. He explained that he had given orders for his three remaining battalions on Tenedos to depart for W Beach and hoped that they would arrive in the afternoon. He added that he saw no point in remaining in Asia any longer as the Turkish force at Yeni Shehr had been significantly augmented overnight and he would require the full French division to attempt its capture. In view of the stalled efforts of the British on the Peninsula and Kitchener's directive ruling out the occupation of the Asian coast (owing to both lack of numbers and land transportation), Hamilton felt that he had no alternative but to grant d'Amade's wish to withdraw his force at nightfall. D'Amade immediately took his leave and returned to his headquarters to make the necessary arrangements. Offshore French transports were alerted at 3 pm and the orders for the re-embarkation of the troops reached Ruef two hours later.

---

34 "Rapport du Colonel Ruef", 28 April 1915, in France, *Les armées françaises*, tome 8, Vol. 1, annexe no. 99.
35 Raymond Weil, Extracts of his Journal reproduced in Association des Dardanelles, *Dardanelles Orient Levant* (Paris L'Harmattan, 2005), p. 26.

During the early evening Hamilton learned that the British position at Gallipoli had improved by the capture of key points and he came under pressure to reconsider his decision to evacuate Kum Kale. Both de Robeck and Major-General W.P. Braithwaite, his chief of the general staff, urged him to keep the French troops in Asia for another 24 hours. They argued that it would confuse the Turkish High Command as to where the main thrust would be delivered and delay the transfer of its troops to the other side of the Straits. Amidst the discussion, Guépratte came on board at 7 pm with good news from Asia. He revealed that several hundred Turks had approached the French lines in mid-afternoon and (for reasons already indicated) surrendered. Elated that the massive surrenders had eased pressure on the French, Hamilton signaled d'Amade that there was a change of plan and asked that he hold on at Kum Kale for another 24 hours. At 2 am on the 27th, Hamilton received a message that it was too late to stop the evacuation as it was already under way.[36] Aided by warship firepower, the re-embarkation – commencing at 11 pm and continuing throughout the night – proceeded without a hitch. The operation had achieved its purpose, not only in protecting the right side of the Cape Helles landings from the fire of the batteries in Asia and, even if only temporarily, tying down three divisions and delaying 11 others from crossing over to the Peninsula.[37] The fighting had been severe with the French sustaining 778 casualties but inflicting 1,730 on the Turks, in addition to taking 500 prisoners. Of the main Allied operations on land, Kum Kale had been by far the most successful.

On the 28th the French arrived at V Beach on Cape Helles and occupied the right of the line overlooking the Straits. Private A.R. Cooper, who had enlisted in the Foreign Legion under the alias Cornelius Jean de Bruin, was among the troops landing on the Peninsula. He described his first day in his new environment:

> Very soon the Turks started shelling from Fort Chanak. It was my first experience of shellfire and I did not like it very much. We started marching straight away. There was no camping; that night we rested on a hilltop. We had no idea where the enemy was. It was pitch dark and raining in torrents. The 1st Company was lost and Captain Rousseau detailed me, with four or five other men, to go out in different directions to find them and lead them back to the Battalion. I walked for about half an hour through the rain and darkness, stumbling over rocks and dead bodies, and, at last, scrambling up a hill, I saw a dim silhouette at the top. I was glad to see any living human being and went right up to him and spoke in French. With a yell the man dropped his rifle and fled, calling on Allah in Turkish. The best part of it that I was so startled that I did the same thing; that is, I dropped my rifle and ran.[38]

The French were left to their own devices and had to get along as best they could. The inconveniences they had to endure paled in comparison to what the British forces had just gone through. By an incredible act of courage, some 29,000 men had succeeded in landing on a series of narrow beaches at Gaba Tepe and Cape Helles on the 25th and, while they gained significant ground by nightfall, nowhere did they reach their objectives. There were many factors that

36   Aspinall-Oglander, *Gallipoli*, Vol. 1, pp. 262-64.
37   Rudenno, *Gallipoli, p.* 108.
38   Cited in Hart, *Gallipoli*, 206.

Kum Kale and Krithia 113

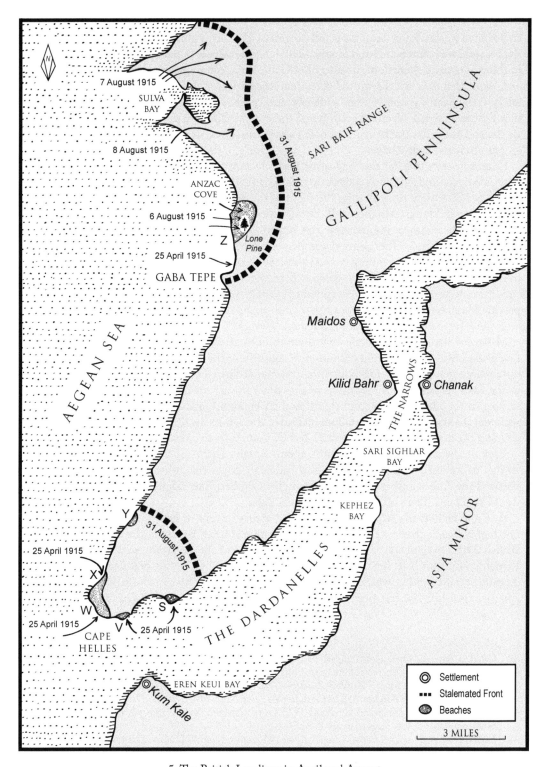

5. The British Landings in April and August

contributed to the slower than expected progress. The Turks almost always occupied the high slopes, were well entrenched and fought well; due to a mistake in navigation the Anzacs landed in the wrong place – north of, instead of at Gabe Tepe; communication between commanders and their men was not always reliable; the attacks were uncoordinated; orders were often unclear; the fleet was unable to provide effective cover as it had insufficient information about how far the men had advanced inland; and there was a failure to exploit uncontested landings. By the end of the day the British had taken severe casualties, were exhausted, short on food and ammunition and badly shaken.

Hamilton's awe of Kitchener had made him reluctant to reveal his difficulties and to request reinforcements. Indeed it was indirectly from Guépratte that Kitchener learned of Hamilton's urgent need for more men. During the night of the 26th the French naval commander alerted his superior at Malta: "All goes well, but in order to ensure continued success it is of utmost importance to reinforce immediately the Expeditionary Force which is insufficient for such extensive operations."[39] The telegram was forwarded to London on the 27th. Hamilton confirmed the announcement on the same day and in a subsequent cable, based on information supplied by d'Amade, told of a second French division being held in reserve for the Dardanelles and urged that it be despatched as well.[40] Responding to the appeal, Kitchener made arrangements to provide Hamilton with troops from Egypt and, at the same time, asked Millerand if he would send the reserve division to reinforce d'Amade's forces.[41]

Millerand had hoped to retain that division until after Hamilton had seized the Gallipoli Peninsula. Still he showed no hesitation to conform to the request and on 30 April he issued instructions to prepare the 156th Division commanded by General Maurice Bailloud for service in the Dardanelles. The composition of this division was similar to the contingent currently serving in the Dardanelles except that it had no Foreign Legionnaires and one of its colonial regiments had two European battalions instead of one. Under the title of the *Corps Expéditionnaire d'Orient* the first units of the (renamed) 2nd Division were to embark at Marseilles on 2 May.[42]

Back on the peninsula there was little enemy activity on 26 and 27 April which allowed the British to stabilize their front. Hamilton had high hopes that when the major attacks were renewed the Anzac units would stand triumphant on Sari Bari ridge and Anglo-French forces would sweep the Turks off the heights of Achi Baba.

At Cape Helles, the Allied sector extended across the entire Peninsula, from about a mile north of X Beach on the western coast to half a mile above S Beach on the eastern shore. The British 29th Division was in control of three quarters of the line from west to east while the French contingent held the eastern end. Hunter-Weston had drawn plans for an advance to a point beyond Krithia which he proposed to use as a launching pad against Achi Baba, a cone-shaped hill 700 feet high and intersected by deep ravines and ditches which formed a

---

39 Cited in Aspinall-Oglander, *Gallipoli*, Vol. 1, p. 304.
40 D'Amade had been informed of the availability of a reserve division and suggested to Hamilton that as c-in-c he should ask for it. Hamilton, *Gallipoli Diary*, Vol. 1, p. 174; AN: C7488, dossier 65, Viviani's testimony before the Foreign Affairs Commission, 11 March 1915.
41 De la Panousse, to Millerand, 29 April 1915 (copy obtained from Cambon), in France, *Les armées françaises*, tome 8, Vol. 1, annexe no. 101.
42 EMA, Note pour la 156em division, 30 April 1915, annexe no. 104; Millerand to d'Amade, 30 April 1915, annexe no. 105, both documents in France, *Les armées françaises*, Vol. 1, tome 8.

Kum Kale and Krithia 115

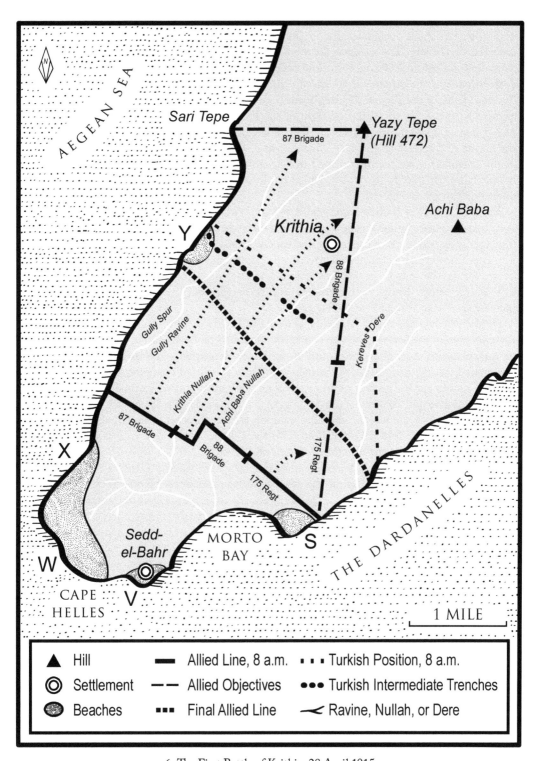

6. The First Battle of Krithia, 28 April 1915

natural barrier. As it dominated the ground to the south it was a useful observation post for the enemy's artillery. The idea was for the 87th Brigade to press forward on the far left about five miles in a relatively straight line and occupy Sari Tepe and Hill 472 north of Krithia. The 88th Brigade in the centre was to advance eastwards at a slower pace, then pivot sharply on the right flank of the French 175 Regiment (like a revolving door swinging from the left) and capture Krithia from the rear. The right of the French force would remain stationary, while its left moved up alongside the 88th. The overly complex plan was vague on details – such as the nature of the terrain ahead, the distance to be travelled and the strength and disposition of the defenders – and communicated to brigade commanders at 2 am on the 28th, just six hours before the start of the attack, which hardly allowed enough time for the men to clearly understand their assignment.[43]

The First Battle of Krithia commenced at 8 am with a desultory bombardment by the fleet and about two dozen guns on shore, followed by the weary British infantry's plodding advance. Good progress was made in the early going which seemed to herald the imminent fall of Krithia. The Turks, however, had fallen back to a new line of defence during the lull in the fighting a day or two earlier: they dug more trenches, placed machine guns in concealed positions and brought in reinforcements. Running into the main Turkish position, the British attack encountered increasing resistance and began to flag.

Hunter–Weston appointed Brigadier-General W.R. Marshall to coordinate the advance on the two-mile front. Arriving on the scene, Marshall had no headquarters and no telephone so he was unable to exert effective control as the attack developed. The lack of preparation and reconnaissance, the exhaustion of the men, and the difficulty of changing the direction of the forward movement in the face of an enemy whose strength and whereabouts were unknown, made themselves felt. Instead of moving together as a unified body, the units lost cohesion with some veering off in the wrong direction, merging with each other, even crossing paths, while others mistimed the turn and advanced with their flanks uncovered. Consequently the two British brigades were halted well short of their objectives.[44]

Within the French camp, it does not appear that either d'Amade or General Vandenberg, the officer he charged with conducting the advance, fully understood Hunter-Weston's plan. It is assumed that during the night Vandenberg received information that the Turks were dug in on high ground on the western bank of the Kereves Dere ravine and were in an advantageous position to enfilade the main advance of the 175th Regiment. Deviating somewhat from his instructions, he detached a small column on his right to occupy a plateau near the mouth of the gully, from where his men could dominated the Turkish posts and remove the threat to the 175th Regiment. The column set off in single file ahead of the main body shortly after 8 am and encountered no opposition until approaching the mouth of Kereves Dere and beginning the assent to the summit of the plateau. The men, conspicuous in their blue uniforms were spotted by Turkish sentries and a few moments later their artillery opened up with deadly effect. Caught in the open, the French ran back to seek shelter behind the cliffs but kept moving when they realized they were being pursued by Turks from the ravine. To their relief the guns of the

43 Aspinall-Oglander, *Gallipoli*., Vol. 1, pp. 285-86. .
44 Among the dozens of books that cover the British effort at the First Battle of Krithia I consulted the following: Prior, *Gallipoli*, pp. 133-35; Aspinall-Oglander, *Gallipoli*, Vol. 1, pp. 288-95; Hart, *Gallipoli*, pp. 206-08; James, *Gallipoli*, pp. 140-41.

British battleship *Albion* came to their rescue and broke up the counterattack. Still the incident delayed and impeded the French advance.

At approximately 10 am the left and centre of the 175th Regiment began to move forward and had only gone about 500 yards inland when they came under a hail of bullets from Turkish positions, especially those located on the western side of the Kereves Dere, which the column on the right sent earlier, had been expected to neutralize. The French continued to move forward, albeit slowly, and as they penetrated deeper into enemy territory they fell in greater numbers. Casualties among white officers in the Senegalese battalion were disproportionately high. They stood out among black troops and, wearing bright uniforms and distinctive white cork helmets, made inviting targets for enemy snipers. The Africans were not always reliable and, if hard-pressed or their officers were put out of commission, they were easily rattled and apt to flee. On the left of the French, Major A.J. Welsh of the 1/King's Own Scottish Borderers (87th Brigade) was both astonished and incensed at what he witnessed: "During the advance we passed … on the R. [right] some French Colonials, who were lucky not to be shot by being mistaken for advancing Turks, retired through us, … rearward bound."[45]

As the morning wore on the French drive ran out of steam and was gradually driven back. In the afternoon Vandenberg threw in his last reserve battalion in an attempt to reverse the course of the action but to no avail. The Turks then counterattacked with a fresh battalion which had just arrived from Bulair, obliging the French to give up practically all the rest of the ground won in the morning.[46]

When the Anglo-French assault was called off at 6 pm, the line had moved only slightly. The British gained a mile or so of territory and the French perhaps half that distance. Casualties had been heavy, further depleting the worn out British and French forces. Out of between 8,000 and 9,000 men engaged, the 29th Division reported losses of about 2,000. The French started the day with 5,000 men in the field and their casualties amounted to 1,000. Turkish killed and wounded were placed at nearly 2,400.

No longer concerned about defending the Asiatic side, the Turks had rushed reinforcements to the Peninsula and were poised to launch counterattacks against the Anzac and Helles sectors. Bottled up a mile from the sea, the Anzac contingent faced eight battalions of Turks who occupied the high ground with an excellent view of their front which they constantly peppered with shells and machine-gun fire. The Turks launched a major attack on 1 May but were turned back with terrible losses by the excellent marksmanship of the Anzacs. The next day the Anzacs unsuccessfully tried to break out of their precarious foothold and they too suffered heavily in killed and wounded and gained nothing. Thereafter the fighting in this sector degenerated into the all too familiar deadlock of trench warfare.

Further south at Helles, the Turks, with a force of 9,000 men (out of 21 battalions in the area), launched violent counterattacks against the Anglo-French front starting at 10 o'clock in the evening on 1 May. In the dark, Turkish hordes with cries of "Allah" swept across mostly open ground towards the Allied lines and, while they were mowed down in droves, still managed to

---

45 Cited in Patrick Gariepy, *Gardens of Hell: Battles of the Gallipoli Campaign* (Washington, DC: Potomac Books, 2014), p. 113.
46 For the account of the French troops in the battle see especially France, *Expédition des Dardanelles*, pp. 49-51.

118 Reluctant Partners

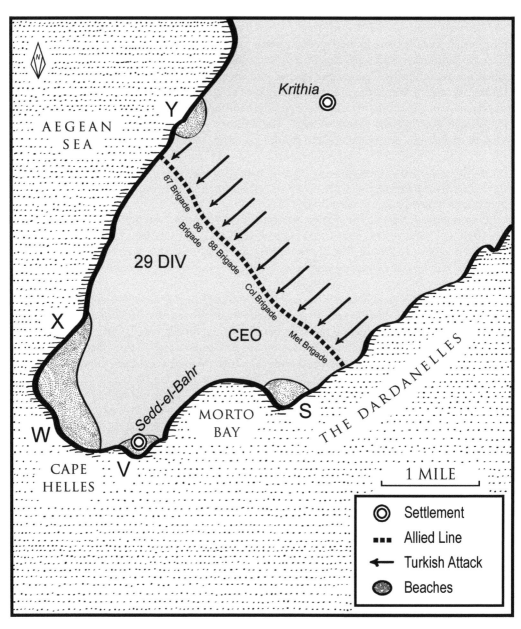

7. The Turkish Night Attack, 1–2 May 1915

break through the Allied line in several places. In the British sector they poured through a gap only to be met head on by reserve units of Royal Fusiliers and Royal Scots. In the confused and fierce struggle that followed the British drove back the Turks at the point of the bayonet and recaptured the trenches.

It was against the French holding the right portion of the line that the Turks carried out their heaviest and most sustained attack. Before the start of the action, the 2nd Colonial Brigade had been transported ashore and was deployed between the Metropolitan Brigade and the (British) 88th Brigade. The French did not have the time to dig their trenches deep enough owing to their recent arrival at Cape Helles, plus their participation in the First Battle of Krithia. The Turks opened with a severe bombardment, followed by an assault by masses of their troops screaming frenetically and charging straight ahead, uninhibited by the blistering fire of the defenders or the scores of fallen comrades. The chilling spectacle, exacerbated by the confusion in the darkness, was too much for a novice Senegalese battalion which bolted and ran. There was bitter hand-to-hand fighting and groups of Turks drove through openings in the front, overran command posts and reached as far as Morto Bay, threatening both British and French artillery. Rising to the occasion, a motley crew of British and French gunners picked up rifles and held off the advancing Turks until a reserve company (Worcesters) arrived on the scene. Together with their bayonets fixed, they raced towards the Turks who, isolated and caught in unknown country in the dark, hastily took to their heels. The fighting raged throughout the night and as dawn broke the breaches in the line had been plugged. The Turks made a last ditch effort to regain the initiative but were hurled back by reserve units of the 6th Colonial Regiment and melted away, leaving behind hundreds of their comrades strewn on the ground. With the advent of light the destructive fire of the fleet's guns came into play, pounding the ranks of the retreating Turks and adding significantly to their already devastating losses.[47]

The Turkish repulse encouraged d'Amade to attempt to capture the high ground above Kereves Dere which his men had failed to do on the day before. With the support of the 29th Division, the forward movement began at 10 am but there had been insufficient time for proper co-ordination or artillery support. On top of this, the Turks had managed to recover from their earlier debacle and reoccupied their previous defensive positions. The Allied advance made some headway here and there and captured a small number of prisoners but units in the lead ultimately were held up by the cross fire of concealed machine-guns. An hour or so later the entire Allied force broke off the engagement and except on the extreme French right, where appreciable gains had been made, withdrew in good order to their line. French casualties fending off the attack and during the subsequent advance had been considerably heavier than those of the British – about 2,100 as opposed to less than 700.

Taking stock, d'Amade became apprehensive about the strength of his front in the likelihood of further Turkish attacks. He asked Hamilton to lend him two or three British battalions until his reinforcements arrived. D'Amade's fears were confirmed on the night of 3/4 May when the seemingly indefatigable Turks mounted another blistering assault against his sector. Once again some of the Senegalese were unable to withstand the enemy's sledge hammer blows and fled in the direction of Morto Bay.[48] For a time there was no telling how the struggle would turn

---

47 Tim Travers, *Gallipoli 1915* (Stroud: Tempus, 2004), p. 120.
48 France, *Expédition des Dardanelles*, tome 8, Vol. 1, pp. 55-56.

out. The dangerous situation was restored thanks to effective counterattacks by reserves and a hastily assembled crew of cooks, staff officer and clerks. At daybreak French 75mm caught the retreating Turks in the open and wreaked death and destruction on a massive scale.[49] The artillery junior officer Raymond Weill wrote: "We had made a veritable slaughter of the Turks, but we also had heavy losses. And I had learned of a terrible thing, namely that we had no more shells left. The artillery park was empty and all that remained at the batteries were empty limbers and that was it. If the Turks attack this night we are done for."[50]

Fortunately for the French the Turks, other than lobbing occasional shells on their position, remained quiescent that night. It so happened that Liman von Sanders was so upset on receiving a report of the recent slaughter of Turkish troops that he ordered his commander in the area (that is south of Achi Baba) to put an immediate end to the attacks and to act on the defensive.[51]

Although the Turks had paid an absurdly high price for their reckless attacks, they had at the same time taken a significant toll on the French defenders. On 4 May d'Amade notified Hamilton that his position was critical. He pointed out that his men had not slept for several nights and were close to the breaking point; and that his units were severely weakened by heavy losses, especially among officers. He claimed the Zouaves and Foreign Legionnaire were exhausted and required rest and that the Senegalese were too unsteady to remain in the line. As he no longer had any reserves left, he urgently requested two battalions of the Royal Naval Division to replace his colonial troops. This time Hamilton acceded to his plea for assistance. The British had been enjoying a respite for a few days which allowed Hamilton to begin the process of relieving a section of the French front on the afternoon of the 4th.[52]

At that very moment Hamilton came under increasing pressure from Kitchener who was frustrated over the lack of progress. The Secretary for War wired him on 4 May, urging him to press on to Achi Baba before the Turks "bring up more reinforcements and … make unpleasant preparations for your reception."[53] Hamilton understood the importance of avoiding a delay and his first step was to reorganize his army to compensate for the heavy Allied casualties already incurred. He broke up units, arranged for artillery support and assembled a force – which included two brigades drawn from the Anzacs and the recent arrival of the 125th Brigade from Egypt – amounting to about 25,000 bayonets. The Allies had a numerical superiority of about 5,000 men but their adversary held formidable defensive positions carved out of higher ground and ridges. The time set to begin the advance was 11 am on 6 May, following a half an hour preliminary bombardment.

Hunter-Weston conducted several meetings with d'Amade and issued orders to him at 8 am on the 5th. The dividing line between the French and British forces would be east of Achi Baba Nullah (Kanli Dere). The first phase of the operation called for a general advance of about one mile across the Peninsula, ending with the French gaining control of the pivotal point on Kereves Spur – preparatory to an assault on Kereves Dere to its right. Once the spur had been

---

49 Aspinall-Oglander, *Gallipoli*, Vol. 1, p. 320.
50 Weil, cited in Association, *Dardanelles*, p. 29.
51 Liman von Sanders, *Five Years in Turkey*, pp. 70-71.
52 France, *Expédition des Dardanelles*, tome 8, Vol. 1, p. 56; Aspinall-Oglander, *Gallipoli*, Vol. 1, pp. 320-21.
53 Aspinall-Oglander, *Gallipoli*, Vol. 1, p. 321n2.

Kum Kale and Krithia 121

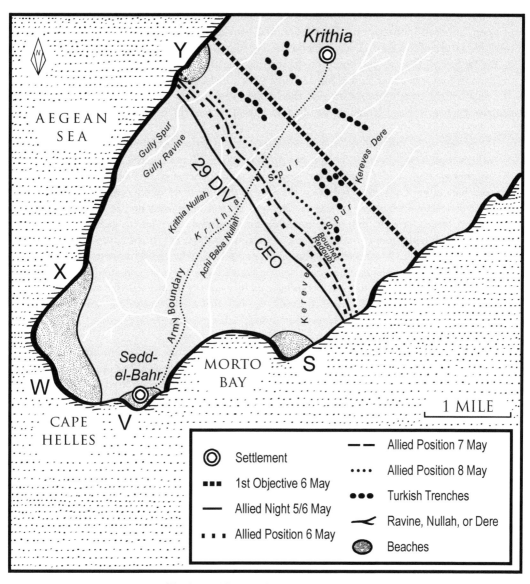

8. The Second Battle of Krithia, 6–8 May 1915

secured the French would remain in place and act as a pivot while British troops swung around to capture Krithia from the west, then pressing on to attack Achi Baba until it was taken. The plan was unrealistic and asked too much of men worn out by continuous fighting and lack of sleep, afforded ineffective artillery cover, and provided with insufficient details about the intricate nature of the ground over which they had to traverse.

The 1st French Division did not reach the starting line until 11.40 am because of the confusion over the precise role of the 2nd Naval Division which had been detailed to guard its left flank. The delay of thirty minutes meant that the French were unable to take advantage of artillery support, such as it was. Lieutenant Feuille had a good view of the early action:

> In perfect order our troops shook themselves out and set out to climb up the long hill which separates them from the enemy – no man's land. They advanced as if on exercise, our brave troops, and if it wasn't for gaps in the ranks punctuated by flashes of bayonets and blue glint of the rifles reflecting the rays of the sun at its zenith, one would think that they were on training ground ... This wall of steel stops, runs into an obstacle that it can't breach, remains indecisive, immobile for an instant. Then all the geometric lines disintegrate with groups coming together and running right, left, thrown into confusion. These mixed fractions of combatants lay on the ground in batches, many never to rise, while the crackle of Turkish machine-guns tearing through the air, fired non-stop into a wall of palpitating flesh. It is that our troops had run up against a barbed-wire network, hardly visible obstacles, harder to cross than a wall. It is that they try, in their desire to win, to get through nevertheless, despite the machine-gun which decimates them.[54]

Feuille's description sums up what happened to the entire French movement on the first day of the battle. The Metropolitan Brigade on the far right encountered little opposition until it reached the high ground overlooking the mouth of Kereves Dere when it was forced back by murderous fire from the opposing bank. In the centre and left some progress was made but resistance gradually stiffened and the drive staggered to a halt below the long slope leading to the pivotal point. Although Allied artillery concentrated on shelling Turkish trenches in the locality, the colonial units were unable to resume the advance. As the day wore on pressure build up against the French front, particularly on the extreme right. In reports to d'Amade the commander of the Metropolitan Brigade, Lieutenant-Colonel Charles Noguès, expressed concern about whether he would be able to maintain his position. He noted that his men were pinned down by rifle and machine-gun fire, that his losses had been severe, and that he had been required to use a reserve unit to bolster the 4th Zouaves who were depressed and exhausted.[55] Overall the French had gained several hundred yards but fallen short of the pivotal point, the capture of which would have aided the British advance.

The 2nd British Naval Brigade, acting in support of the French, was in-between the Senegalese of the Colonial Brigade on its right and the Composite Brigade on its left. The sailors got off to a good start and raced ahead of the French troops but mounting casualties, including their

---

54 Feuille, *Face aux Turcs*, pp. 53-54.
55 Noguès to d'Amade, 6 May 1915, in France, *Les armées françaises*, Vol. 1, tome 8, annexe nos. 144, 145, 146.

commanding officer who was killed, and the vulnerability of their right flank, forced them to withdraw.

The British in the other parts of the line had no better luck than their Naval Brigade. Nowhere did they make any appreciable headway. In fact they were not even close to the main Turkish defensive front when the attack was called off in mid-afternoon. The Allied effort had gained an average of 400 yards but, because overall casualties had been comparatively light, orders were issued for the assault to resume the next day.

The lines of advance laid down for the 7th were the same as on the previous day except that the 29th Division was not to wait until the French had secured the pivotal point but head straight for Krithia. A 15 minute bombardment was to precede the attack scheduled to begin at 10 am. After d'Amade received his instructions, he thought it would be helpful if his men captured the pivotal point before the British set out to assault Krithia. Accordingly at 4.45 am, he directed General Masnou, who commanded the 1st Division, to assign two battalions of the 8th Colonial Regiment (of the 2nd Division) which had arrived the previous evening, to carry out the task.[56] D'Amade changed his mind a few hours later and cancelled his order, presumably to conform to Hunter-Weston's plan. The new instructions called for the 1st Division to seize the western bank of Kereves Dere; and the 2nd Division to take control of the pivotal point on Kereves Spur and to remain there, pending the results of the attack.[57]

The bombardment which opened at 9.45 was so weak that it did absolutely nothing to disrupt the Turks. Under the circumstances there was little chance that the French could achieve significant progress. The Turks had at their disposal plenty of artillery which saturated the front of the 1st Division and prevented much of its infantry from even leaving the trenches. Noguès reported that it was impossible for his men to advance and that the capture of trenches on his front could only be achieved by a flank attack from the left.

The inability of units on the right to make any headway, practically ruled out what slender chance the newly arrived 2nd Divisions had of ejecting the Turks from Kereves Spur. The Turks anticipating the assault, had worked overnight to build up their defences all along the spur. They had dug well-positioned series of trenches, were supported by guns and their machine guns were so well hidden that they could not be detected even by the sound of their fire. In most places French infantrymen were met by a hail of enemy fire which cut deep into their ranks and the survivors, seeing the futility of pressing on, scrambled back to their line. The only success, albeit modest, was achieved by units in the centre which were directed to take control of the summit of the spur. They made a spirited rush and overwhelmed a group of Turks in a forward trench, coming to within 150 yards of attaining their objective when they reported that they could not continue until there was progress on their right. Nevertheless, as we have seen, that did not occur and a Turkish counterattack compelled them to abandon the trench.

The French had little to show for their effort at the close of the day's fighting. Practically everywhere they had not gotten beyond the starting line and the disappointment among the men was evident. "The moral [sic] is not good", Vassal wrote in his diary on 7 May. "Those who

---

56   D'Amade to Masnou, 7 May 1915, in France, *Les armées françaises*, Vol. 1, tome 8, annexe no. 150.
57   D'Amade to commanders of the 1st and 2nd Divisions, 7 May 1915, in France, *Les armées françaises*, Vol. 1, tome 8, annexe no. 154.

were hit did not hide their despondency, and the word retreat was often mentioned. The men were frightfully tired."[58] French losses for the 7th are unknown.

The Naval Division which took no part in the fighting sent a message to the 29th Division at 11 am: "Up to date no sign of any French movement beyond last night's line; "and another report at 3 pm was equally pessimistic, observing that "the French 2nd Division, allotted the task of seizing the pivot indicated yesterday, is not moving yet as its advance depends on the success of its right."[59]

The British for their part gained a little ground in a few places but nowhere did they come close to the main Turkish line. They had sustained about 800 casualties. After two dismal failures it would have made sense for Hamilton to call off the battle. The Turks were firmly entrenched and receiving daily reinforcements, had displayed courage and resolve, were supported by artillery which had registered its targets carefully and, fighting mostly defensively, had taken far fewer casualties than the Allies. Besides in the British camp, virtually all the troops were practically at their last gasp and the shells for the guns were almost exhausted. Still Hamilton, undoubtedly driven by Kitchener's directive, did not give it a second thought and at 10.25 pm on the 7th issued orders for the battle to resume next morning. As in the past two days the orders from Hunter-Weston went out late and by the time they passed through the chain of command there was not enough time to explain to company commanders or to the men what they were supposed to do.

Hamilton assigned a relatively minor role to the French on the 8th in contrast to the previous occasions. His instructions to d'Amade indicate that he was under the misimpression that the French had reached the pivotal point on the Kereves Spur. Thus the objective of the French left (2nd Division) was to consolidate its position in the pivotal point zone, while the right (1st Division) was directed to cross the Kereves Dere at the weakest defended spot. Further advance was to be governed by the progress of the attack on Krithia.[60]

The attack got under way at 10.30 am. The French, unlike the British, had an ample supply of high explosive shells with which they hammered the enemy's front but with little effect. Ordered to contest every inch of ground in the sector, the Turks had in the past few days converted their position on the high ground west of the ridge into a formidable system of defence while their eastern flank was amply covered by batteries from the Asiatic shore. D'Amade informed Hamilton that it was impossible for his men to advance until the British had capture Krithia. Hamilton was unaware of the extent of the difficulties facing the French. He resented, unfairly it would seem, that d'Amade was unwilling to encourage his men to make more of an effort.

By 3 pm the British attack had come to a standstill. Hamilton who had been following the events from his command post behind W and X Beaches intervened over the head of Hunter-Weston and decided to make a last ditch attempt to retrieve the day's fortunes. He ordered the men in the Allied line, reinforced by an Australian Brigade, to advance with fixed bayonets on Krithia at precisely 5.30 pm, following a 15-minute artillery bombardment. Hunter-Weston communicated Hamilton's decision to d'Amade at 4.30 pm. Thereupon d'Amade sent the

---

58 Vassal, *Uncensored Letters*, p. 84.
59 Cited in Aspinall-Oglander, *Gallipoli*, Vol. 1, p. 340.
60 Braithwaite (Hamilton's chief of staff) to d'Amade, 7 May 1915, in France, *Les armées françaises*, Vol. 1, tome 8, annexe no. 161; Aspinall-Oglander, *Gallipoli*, Vol. 1, pp. 341-42.

following message to his divisional leaders: "The Commander-in-Chief, Sir Ian Hamilton, expresses his conviction that the French troops are ready to take part in this forward movement. In consequence the general commanding the CEO directs that, at 5.35 pm, all along the French front the troops will advance and break down all opposition in front of them."[61] D'Amade, in his reply to Hamilton, made no mention of the extreme obstacles his men would have to overcome: "Your message received. I have ordered a general advance with the bayonet at 5.30 pm."[62] Before the start of the attack, d'Amade visited the front to inspire his men to vigorous action and to prevent the earlier failures.

All along the line the British and Australians, as they had done time and time again, conducted themselves with exceptional gallantry and self-sacrifice but it was all in vain. On the right the French divisional commanders were late getting their orders and it was not until 6 pm that, with drums beating and bugles sounding they charged, wave after wave of their men surged forward across Kereves Spur. The infantrymen showed great enthusiasm as they advanced in their bright, red and blue uniforms, and to British observers in the rear it seemed that they had overrun the enemy's defences and captured the entire spur.

Unfortunately that did not turn out to be the case, although they had made good progress until the Turks covered the spur with a storm of high explosive shells which exacted a huge toll on their ranks. "They were getting mowed", a British witness recalled. "I never saw such slaughter."[63] The brutal intensity of the fire stopped them dead in their tracks. The French wavered and fell back a short distance, then rallied and counterattacked in the course of which they captured a Turkish trench, later known as "Bouchet Redoubt", and made it their own until the end of the campaign. When the fighting died down in the early evening, the French were ordered to dig in as best they could. It had been another costly effort to no purpose. Vassal, who inspected the battlefield the next day, wrote:

> Wounded everywhere! The killed lay in confused heaps which increased as you advanced… Some were in postures of attack, others of defence. A little soldier of the 6th [Colonial Regiment] had his hands behind him. He had been shot from behind, and his skull was blown to bits. The bodies had swollen, and their uniforms were tight and narrow! It was awful![64]

After three days of incessant fighting the Second Battle of Krithia was over. The struggle had netted the Allies about 600 yards of worthless ground and they were still about half a mile from the objective initially set. They had suffered about 6,500 casualties or nearly one third of the forces involved in the battle. If the Allies learned anything from the two battles of Krithia it was that the Turks, far from being mediocre fighters as had been supposed, showed that they were tough, stubborn and prepared to die in defence of their homeland. The breezy optimism in London at the outset that the navy would require the help of only a small military force to breach The Narrows had disappeared. Given the new reality, Hamilton had no reason to be optimistic. Until he received a fresh supply of ammunition and reinforcements to replace his

---

61 D'Amade to Masnou, 8 May 1915, in France, Les *armées françaises*, Vol. 1, tome 8, annexe no. 166.
62 Aspinall-Oglander, *Gallipoli*, Vol. 1, p. 345.
63 Peter Fitzsimons, *Gallipoli* (London: Bantam, 2014), p. 372.
64 Vassal, *Uncensored Letters*, p. 88.

losses, he needed to worry more about maintaining his precarious position in the Peninsula than in trying to break through to the summit of Achi Baba.

The first Viviani Cabinet. Messimy is on the right at the end of the second row. (BnF)

Raymond Poincaré. (BnF)

Alexandre Millerand. (BnF)

Victor Augagneur. (Open source)

Théophile Delcassé. (BnF)

Aristide Briand. (BnF)

General Joseph Galliéni in civilian clothes while serving as Minister of War. (BnF)

French troops arriving in the Dardanelles pose for posterity. (BnF)

Rear-Admiral Émile-Paul Guépratte. (Open source)

Poincaré decorating two French soldiers near the front. (BnF)

A French soldier carrying a wounded comrade from the front line. (Open source)

Turkish captives marching to Sedd-el Bahr with a Zouave escort. (Open source)

A French 75 artillery gun at Cape Helles during the Third Battle of Krithia, 4 June 1915. (Open source)

Joffre chatting with a few members of the French delegation at the railway station in Paris, all of whom are waiting for the train which will take them to Calais for a conference with the British. (ILN)

French troops firing at Turks in an opposing trench. (BnF)

General Joffre acknowledges the cheers of the crowd on leaving the War Office with Lord Kitchener during his visit to London in October 1915. (ILN)

A French soldier surveying the scene behind barbed-wire. (Open source)

Admiral Guépratte boards a French destroyer prior to an offshore reconnaissance of the Gallipoli Peninsula. (*L'Illustration*, 6 May 1915)

French troops resting in a trench. (BnF)

General d'Amade. (Open source)

General Gouraud is standing with his foot resting on a gun and next to him is his successor General Bailloud. (BnF)

General Henri Gouraud with General Hamilton several days before he was seriously wounded. (ILN)

General Maurice Sarrail at his headquarters in Salonica with his chief of staff. (Open source)

Sedd-el Bahr French cemetery. (BnF)

8

Hanging On

The Dardanelles land campaign was proving more difficult and taking on far greater dimensions than had been anticipated. In Paris Millerand could not exclude the possibility that it was apt to cut significantly into French military resources before it was over. Given Joffre's intent on continuing his attrition policy in the west, Millerand was not anxious to move an infinite number of troops from France for what he viewed as little more than a colonial adventure in the eastern Mediterranean. The deepening involvement of the French in the Dardanelles with the decision to dispatch a second division, prompted Millerand to make a change in the command.[1] Bearing in mind that Millerand had reluctantly agreed to the appointment of d'Amade on the understanding that the army's role would be confined to minor operations. But this was no longer the case. Furthermore, in the few tough battles thus far, Millerand judged that the French division had suffered excessive casualties for which he evidently held d'Amade responsible.[2] Millerand wanted his action confirmed by experts lest he be accused of acting arbitrarily and risk offending Poincaré. He turned to his general staff (which he knew held little regard for d'Amade) to compile a report to conform to a decision he had already made.

In the preamble of the report, the general staff was highly critical of the British, especially deploring the long delay after the failure of the naval attack (imposed, it will be remembered, by the reorganization of the British army in Egypt). The lack of urgency, it pointed out, had allowed the Turks to build up their defences on Gallipoli and further prepare for the Allied land assault. Turning to the issue at hand, the general staff recommended the removal of General d'Amade, though it did not refer specifically to any serious mistake he had made. The reason given was that it would prefer the appointment of a reputable general, not only to serve the interest of the growing French contingent but to carry more weight and authority with Hamilton.[3]

Millerand had the official justification he needed to recall d'Amade. Yet even before receiving the general staff's memo, he had approached Joffre for his advice and assistance.[4] The French

---

1 AN: Millerand papers, 470 AP/16, Millerand to d'Amade, 4 March 1915.
2 Gaëtan Gallieni (ed.), *Les carnets de Galliéni*, (Paris, Albin Mitchell, 1932), p. 165.
3 AN: Millerand papers, 470 AP/16, EMA, Note pour le ministre de la guerre, 3 May 1915.
4 Millerand had notified d'Amade's successor at the end of April, several days before the general staff's report.

Generalissimo did not have to remind Millerand that the government had overridden his opposition to the campaign. He did not refrain from doing so, however, in his memoirs: "With a view to extricating themselves from the difficulties in which they had so light-heartedly engaged, the Government for the first time turned to me and asked me to nominate a general capable of bringing this difficult undertaking to a successful conclusion. General Gouraud … was at once placed at the disposal of the Minister."[5]

Hamilton did not rate d'Amade's professional ability any higher than Joffre or Millerand. He liked d'Amade as an individual, finding him selfless, open-minded and easy to work with. Still at the same time, he quickly formed strong reservations about his qualities as a commander. He wrote to Kitchener after the landings in April that d'Amade did not respond effectively under pressure, that he looked 20 years older since his arrival, and that he lacked initiative and resolve. That said he begged Kitchener "to take no action on this information" as it was possible that d'Amade was physically unwell.[6] On learning of the change in the French command, Hamilton was more forthcoming, although he told Kitchener that he thought a personal tragedy had exacerbated d'Amade's ineffective leadership:

> [D'Amade] … is, as you know, one of the most charming gentleman in the world. But he has lately lost a son, and the sorrow of this misfortune combined with the strain and responsibility of his present position has thrown him into an overwrought condition of mind. Directly any serious work begins I get nothing from him but pessimistic and usually quite inaccurate messages, even about the 29th Division. He appeals for help too, on the very smallest provocation.[7]

In contrast, Henri Gouraud would give Hamilton no reason to complain. At the age of 48 he had the distinction of being the youngest general in the French army. Like many young Frenchmen of his generation he was inspired to embark on a military career because of France's humiliating Second Empire defeat in the war against Prussia. He attended the military academy at Saint-Cyr in 1888 and received his commission as an infantry officer two years later. He was posted overseas during the prewar period and gained instant fame when in 1898 he stumbled upon the encampment of the rebel leader (Samory Touré) and captured him, marking the end of resistance to French colonialism in French Sudan. He continued to pursue his career across French Africa with postings in Niger, Chad and Mauritania before serving in Morocco and assisting General Louis Hubert Lyautey (the new resident-general) in the pacification of the country. He returned to France at the outset of the war and was placed in command of a division, then of a corps in the Argonne where he solidified his reputation. A solid, fearless and imperturbable soldier, he was affectionately called the "Lion of the Argonne" and idolized by his men.[8]

---

5   Joffre, *Personal Memoirs*, Vol. 2, p. 370. AN: C7532, dossier 1106, Augagneur's testimony before the Marine Commission, 11 May 1915.
6   BNA: Hamilton papers, 7/1/6, Hamilton to Kitchener, 30 April 1915.
7   BNA: Kitchener papers, 30/57/61, Hamilton to Kitchener, 5 May 1915.
8   On Gouraud see Pierre Lyautey, *Gouraud* (Paris: Julliard, 1949); H. Colin, "Gouraud", *Reuve historique de l'armée*, July - September, 1947, pp. 7-24; Julie d'Andurain, "Le général Gouraud, chef du corps expéditionnaire des Dardanelles en 1915", *Reuve historique de l'armée*, Vol. 258 (2010), pp. 46-56.

Gouraud was notified of his new assignment by phone several days before it was formally announced.[9] He could not have done any better when he selected as his chief of staff Colonel Pierre Girodon, a close friend who had served on his general staff in Morocco. During a skirmish in May 1914 Girodon had been stuck by a bullet which shattered his leg and he returned to France on crutches. He had not fully recovered when he was appointed to General Gallieni's general staff on the eve of the battle of the Marne. Indeed months later he still walked with a noticeable limp when he left France to take up his new assignment.[10]

Gouraud's instructions which he picked up on 5 May were practically a carbon copy of those given to d'Amade.[11] He wasted no time in gathering his belongings and set sail with Girodon, arriving at Mudros on 14 May. D'Amade was on hand to greet Gouraud and took him immediately to meet Hamilton. Although d'Amade was deeply upset by what he considered was an unwarranted dismissal, he showed no outward signs of bitterness and did what he could to help his successor. He briefed Gouraud on the strength and weakness of his former subordinates, on conditions in the Peninsula, on the reliability of the various units he had commanded and on the fighting quality of the Turks. His dignified conduct in the midst of his personal grief and disappointment did not go unnoticed. Millerand was very impressed and sent him a note acknowledging his graceful behavior: "At the moment you are about to leave the command of the expeditionary corps I want to express my thanks for the way you have carried on under conditions of extreme difficulty. I was particularly touched by the manner you acted in the transmission of power."[12] On 16 May, a day after formally turning over the command, d'Amade left the Peninsula amidst the thunderous applause of French troops who had turned out to pay him heartfelt tribute.[13]

Before and after Gouraud's arrival, dramatic events were taking shape in naval circles. The relative inactivity of the fleet during the landings of 25 April had produced a painful impression among de Robeck's senior naval officers. There was in the air a sense of guilt, a feeling that the navy had not pulled its weight. The Admiralty had laid down that the efforts of the navy on 25 April "will primarily be directed to landing the Army and supporting it till its position is secure, after which the Navy will attack the forts at the Narrows, assisted by the Army." As can be seen, the time to take the initiative was left to the discretion of de Robeck.

When the soldiers had secured a footing on the Peninsula and most of the ships were no longer required to provide covering fire, a strong feeling surfaced among a number of high-ranking naval officers that the ships ought to make another attempt to break through the Straits. The leading voice among them was Commodore Roger Keyes (chief of naval staff) who rejected the notion that the check on 18 March was proof that the Straits could not be breached.

Guépratte wholeheartedly embraced Keynes' line of thinking. He did not consider the minefield an impenetrable barrier and believed that the timing was right for bolder naval action. The fleet's losses had been replaced and the navy possessed advantages it did not have on 18 March. The trawlers, manned by untrained civilian crews and operating with difficulty against the current in the Dardanelles, had been exchanged for destroyers with efficient naval personnel

---

9   D"Andurain, "Le général Gouraud", p. 48.
10 Jérôme Carcopino, *Souvenirs de la guerre en Orient 1915-1917* (Paris: Hachette, 1970), p. 40.
11 Millerand to Gouraud, 5 May 1915, in France, *Les armées françaises,* tome 8, Vol. 1, annexe no. 125.
12 SHD: AMG, 5N 18, Millerand to d'Amade, 15 May 1915.
13 Aspinall-Oglander, *Gallipoli,* Vol. 1, p. 361.

capable of mine-sweeping at night. Then too it was believed that the enemy's supply of big shells was nearly depleted and that many of the mobile guns protecting the minefield had been moved inland to assist the land forces in opposing the Allied invasion.

Guépratte went over to see de Robeck on 3 May to air his views. During the talks he advanced a plan which consisted of sending four old battleships manned by volunteers in front of the main fleet to explode the mines and create a free channel. Guépratte maintained in a post-war study of the Dardanelles that de Robeck agreed in principle with the general outline of his scheme. But on 7 May de Robeck approached him with the news that the Admiralty had forbidden a resumption of independent naval action.[14] There does not appear to be any evidence to suggest that de Robeck informed Churchill, or even his own staff, of what Guépratte had in mind. The plain truth was that he opposed an attack on the Straits by the navy, irrespective of the plan. By pretending to blame the Admiralty for rejecting the idea he avoided the risk of straining his relationship with a man he liked and respected.

No sooner did de Robeck gently brush aside Guépratte's scheme, then he had to deal with members of his own staff led a combative Keyes. On 9 May de Robeck held a conference with them on board the *Queen Elizabeth*. Everyone present, save for de Robeck, was eager to renew the naval assault and accepted the fact that perhaps only half the battleships would reach the Sea of Marmora. De Robeck did not share their optimism and worried that a defeat at The Narrows, perhaps entailing heavy losses, would leave the army stranded on the Peninsula at the mercy of the enemy. With some reluctance he agreed to put the matter before the Admiralty.

After the conference broke up Keyes called on Guépratte to break the news to him. Keyes has the following entry in his memoirs: "Guépratte had not been summoned to the meeting, but I knew that he was of the same mind as I was, and ardently longed to renew the naval offensive, in fact, when I told him of my hopes, he said, 'Ah Commodore, that would be *immortalité*.'"[15]

Despite the unconfident tone of de Robeck's message to the Admiralty, Keyes and the others at the meeting fully expected to receive the green light to renew the naval attack. Excited at the chance of getting into the thick of battle again, Guépratte cabled Augagneur: "In order to assist army in its vigorous and violent action, we are contemplating active fleet participation in Straits with attack on fortifications. In these circumstances I need my battleships *Suffren, Charlemagne, Gaulois* as soon as possible." A second telegram soon followed, correcting the impression that it was to be a combined operation.[16]

The proposal met a hostile reception in Paris. Augagneur's career had already been compromised by the French navy's involvement in the unsuccessful naval action and he was unwilling to risk digging himself into a deeper hole. The navy's subsequent role had been confined to providing artillery support and he was content to allow the outcome of the operation to rest with the army unless, of course, it could be shown that the assault on the Straits was almost certain to succeed. He conveyed his thoughts to the Admiralty:

---

14   Guépratte in a paper written after the war discussed his plan with de Robeck but I was unable to locate it in the French archives. However, several unpublished works by young naval officers writing on the French side of the operation have referred to it. Their papers are in the library of the SHD.
15   Sir Roger Keyes, *Naval Memoirs of Admiral of the Fleet 1905-1915*, Vol. 1 (New York: Dutton, 1934), p. 336.
16   SHD: AMM, Ca 20, Guépratte to Augagneur, 12 May 1915.

If success is not absolutely certain, if conditions are not different from those of March 18th, I deem it foolhardy to involve the fleet in that enterprise. Apart from the risk of possible losses, defeat would have a deplorable moral effect. More realistically, instead of helping the land forces in an already difficult situation, the unfortunate intervention of the fleet would dangerously aggravate their position. I would appreciate your informing me of your views and intentions on the matter.[17]

Churchill, who was in the midst of a losing battle against his senior naval experts, replied cautiously on 13 May: "We have asked Vice Admiral [de Robeck] to explain what he intends to do before taking any decisive action." He added disingenuously: "I am generally in accord with your views."[18] Somewhat relieved, Augagneur next contacted Guépratte; "Your telegram ... refers to an impending operation to force [the Straits] while preceding telegram mentioned combined operation, apparently due to last some time. I cannot understand a return to a plan similar to the one of March 18 which had been abandoned."[19]

The naval scheme never proceeded beyond the talking stage. In London Churchill tried to persuade the Sea Lords to agree to a limited attack on enemy defences to provide cover for the trawlers sweeping the Kephez minefield. The First Sea Lord, however, flew into a rage and stated that under no circumstances would he be a party to such an attempt.[20] The Admiralty had received information that a German submarine was heading in the direction of the Dardanelles and on 12 May Fisher's apprehensions were confirmed when the old battleship *Goliath* was torpedoed in Morto Bay. Churchill was forced in the end to give way before the fiery First Sea Lord. On 13 May he signaled de Robeck that "the moment for an independent naval attempt to force the Narrows has passed and will not rise again under present conditions."[21] Churchill sent a similar message to Augagneur two days later.[22]

Until the second week in May neither Augagneur nor Vice Admiral Boué de Lapeyrère had sought to intervene in the conduct of naval operations or to impose orders on Guépratte contrary to those he had received from Carden and de Robeck. But Augagneur was no longer content to sit back and allow the Admiralty to dictate policy. Victory was nowhere in sight and the longer the operation dragged out the more he came under attack in political circles. To gain a decisive voice in planning future naval strategy he found a pretext to try to revise his earlier agreement with Churchill.

In a naval convention signed on 10 May Italy, as part compensation for joining the Entente, was promised four British battleships and an equal number of cruisers, plus certain French light units to reinforce its fleet in the Adriatic. As Churchill did not want to weaken British naval forces in the North Sea, he proposed to remove the cruisers from the Dardanelles division. The French, in turn, agreed to replace the British cruisers and increase the number of their battleships to six.[23]

---

17 SHD: AMM, Xa 32, Augagneur to Saint-Seine, 13 May 1915.
18 SHD: AMM, Xa 4, Saint-Seine to Augagneur, 13 May 1915.
19 SHD: AMM, Ed 108, Augagneur to Guépratte, 14 May 1915.
20 Churchill, *World Crisis*, Vol. 2, pp. 353-57.
21 Gilbert, *Churchill*, p. 429.
22 SHD: AMM, Xa 4, Saint-Seine to Augagneur, 15 May 1915.
23 Corbett, *Naval Operations*, Vol. 2, pp. 395-97; Halpern, *Naval War*, pp. 96-99.

132   Reluctant Partners

It should be noted that the French honoured their agreement and that the additional ships came on the scene singly, as soon as they could be spared. The battleships *Jauréguiberry*, *Henri IV* and *Saint Louis* were already in the Dardanelles when *Charlemagne*, *Suffren* and *Gaulois*, their repairs completed or nearly so, returned to action and were followed by *Patrie*. The *Suffren*, after its arrival, replaced the *Jauréguiberry* whose turret had been damaged. As cruisers, the Ministry of Marine despatched *Latouche-Tréville*, *Bruix*, *Dupleix* and *Kléber*.[24]

In view of the approaching increase in the size of the French squadron at the Dardanelles, Augagneur considered appointing a vice-admiral to take charge in the hope that he could wrest overall naval command from the hands of the British. He suggested to Churchill on 11 May that the present naval commander be superseded by a vice-admiral promoted to that rank before 1 January 1913.[25] Since all the French vice-admirals, (unlike de Robeck[26]) had received their promotions prior to that date[27] the implication was obvious. Churchill curtly swept aside the proposed arrangement:

> Under no circumstances would it be possible to replace for mere reasons of seniority Vice-Admiral de Robeck in whom we have the greatest confidence. That officer was selected for the immense task entrusted to him and his recall would compromise the success of the operations and would discourage the fleet. Moreover, by giving him the provisional rank of admiral would place him above Vice-Admiral de Lapeyrère, which is in no way desirable.[28]

Augagneur did not pursue the issue though he must have known even before he sounded out Churchill that the chances of placing his own nominee in charge of the naval operations were at best slim. Whether he still intended to appoint a vice-admiral remained up in the air. Events, however, forced him to make a decision. The next day (12 May) Augagneur, as already mentioned, learned from Guépratte of the navy's intention to renew the assault against the Straits. He was under the erroneous impression that de Robeck, as the naval commander, had been the moving spirit behind the plan.[29] To avoid any more unhappy incidents, he wanted someone he trusted to act as a check on de Robeck's supposedly adventurous impulses. In these circumstances the removal of Guépratte, in whom the Minister of Marine retained doubts about his mental stability, became inevitable. At Churchill's request Guépratte remained as second in command of the French squadron.[30]

The demotion stunned Guépratte who was not given any explanation for his fall from grace. He later wrote:

> The French government, deeming the situation incoherent and tired of my insistence and obstinacy in wanting to force the Straits, removed me from my command ... without the

---

24   Thomazi, *Guerre Navale*, pp. 150-51, 153.
25   SHD: AMM, Xa 37, Augagneur to Saint-Seine, 11 May 1915.
26   De Robeck became a vice-admiral when he succeeded Carden.
27   Lieutenant de vaisseau de Rivoyne, "L'Expédition des Dardanelles." The account in the unpublished paper written in 1923 can be found in the library at the SHD.
28   SHD: AMM, Xa 4, Saint-Seine to Augagneur, 11 May 1915.
29   AN: C7533, dossier 1126, Augagneur's testimony before the Marine Commission, 4 August 1915.
30   SHD: AMM, Xa 4, Saint-Seine to Augagneur, 12 May 1912.

courtesy of an explanation. I had to be satisfied with some vague rumours that my demotion was due to the alleged following complaints: "Daredevil and dangerous visionary."[31]

The qualities which had raised Guépratte so high in the French navy in the end proved to be his undoing. On the other hand, he continued to be held in the highest regard by British naval leaders. Robeck considered him "the most loyal of men" and was very troubled to see him replaced. In the months that Guépratte spent in the Dardanelles, thanks to his enterprising spirit and loyal cooperation, there was never an instance of friction. When Guépratte received orders in October to return to France to take up new duties he was given an impressive sendoff that went well beyond the bounds of simple courtesy and reflected the affection and esteem in which he was held.[32]

Augagneur selected as the new French naval commander Ernest-Eugène Nicol, promoting him to the rank of vice-admiral on the day of his official appointment (14 May). Augagneur gave Nicol his instructions on the same day, adding:

> I deem it useful to inform you that in the venturesome Dardanelles expedition, Admiral de Robeck shows great daring sometimes verging on temerity. While giving him your most faithful assistance and recognizing his authority, your rank and the size of the forces at your disposal will surely influence his decisions greatly. I trust your tact, your wisdom and your experience to temper his decisions, without clashes and friction, in a way which will be compatible with the honour of our flag and our commitments towards our Allies.[33]

Nicol arrived at Lemnos on 21 May. De Robeck's first impression was that he was "a little man of the most unprepossessing appearance", that he did not look like a gentleman and was unlikely to leave a striking mark on his profession.[34] In truth de Robeck would not have found any Frenchman able to measure up to Guépratte. Still the two men got along well, though their relationship was never warm.

By the time of the change in the French naval command, the army was still bogged down on the Peninsula and Hamilton could not hope to dislodge the Turks without significant reinforcements and a fresh supply of artillery ammunition. On 17 May he had telegraphed Kitchener that if the Russians could land troops on the shores of the Bosporus and if Greece or Bulgaria could be persuaded to enter the struggle against Turkey, two army corps would suffice to accomplish the task; otherwise he would require four. However no action was taken on Hamilton's request for three weeks. Britain was in the midst of a political crisis and other things were occupying the minds of politicians.

A controversy over a shell shortage on the Western Front in mid-May, compounded by Fisher's resignation, resulting from his differences with the First Lord over the ongoing Dardanelles campaign, forced Asquith to reshape the government on a non-party basis. Churchill was removed from the Admiralty and relegated to the sinecure post of the Duchy of Lancaster but

---

31 Guépratte, *L'Expédition des Dardanelles*, p. 238.
32 Halpern, *Naval War*, pp. 61, 160.
33 SHD: AMM, Ed 108, Augagneur to Nicol, 14 May 1915.
34 Halpern, *Naval War*, p. 160.

given a seat on the reconstituted War Council, now to be called the Dardanelles Committee.[35] The new government took office on 26 May with Arthur Balfour as the First Lord and Sir Henry Jackson as First Sea Lord. At the first meeting of the Dardanelles Committee on 7 June, Kitchener agreed to send Hamilton reinforcements (though not the number of divisions he had requested) in anticipation of another major offensive during the second week of July.

It was common knowledge throughout the country, even before attention centered on Fisher's resignation, that an ominous shadow had fallen on the Dardanelles campaign, a predicament for which Churchill was held directly responsible. With few exceptions the press was united in condemning the amateur strategist who had interfered in technical matters and had monopolized all initiative in the Admiralty. On 27 April 1915, the *Morning Post* went further when it published a full account of the events dealing with the Dardanelles and in the process excoriated Churchill for espousing an ill-considered scheme, overriding the First Sea Lord, winning over the government through misinformation and, above all, the abortive naval attack on the Straits. The article was so revealing that it immediately caught the eye of French officials in London. To Colonel de la Panousse it was even more surprising when reliable sources in the British government corroborated the story. Writing to Millerand, he cited excerpts from the article and concluded that the "First Lord thus appears to be entirely responsible for the failure [of the naval attack] and of its consequences."[36]

If Millerand retained any lingering doubts about the unsoundness of the naval plan, they were dispelled by d'Amade on his return to Paris. D'Amade maintained that if troops had co-operated with the navy on 18 March the Turkish forts would have been taken by *a coup de main*. He further explained that the Turks had used the lull between the naval strike and the military landing to fortify their system of inner defences. The Anglo-French force was now faced with the additional task of having to cut through elaborate wire entanglements and surmount earthworks before reaching the enemy in the trenches. During his talk on the operation, d'Amade digressed to comment on the British method of conducting war. He observed that London not only laid down the broad lines of military policy but also dictated the means to be employed.[37]

D'Amade overstated the extent of Kitchener's control over the Dardanelles operation. It is true that the British did not have a common military system in the Dardanelles and on the Western Front. The dissimilarity in the structural command stemmed from the different conditions in the widely separated fronts. The French, as the dominant partner on the Western Front, devised military policy and each time assigned the BEF a specific role, leaving Sir John free to work out the tactical means. Kitchener's hands for all practical purposes were tied and, although he occasionally offered Joffre a diverse opinion, did not put any pressure on its enforcement in order to preserve a united front. By contrast the British were in the driver's seat in the

---

35 The French made no secret that they wanted Asquith to retain Kitchener and Grey whilst excluding Churchill in the coalition government. CCAC: Esher papers, entry in Esher War Journal, 19 May 1915; BNA: PRO 30/57/59, Kitchener papers, Esher to Kitchener, 20 May 1915. As it happened the strong feeling in Paris against Churchill was no way connected to his demotion.
36 AMAE: under the heading Opération des Dardanelles, carton 4, dossier 3, de la Panousse to Millerand (copy), 28 April 1915.
37 Gen. Edmond Buat (Millerand's *chef de cabinet*) to Graziani, 25 May 1915, in France, *Les armées françaises*, tome 8, Vol. 1, annexe no. 216.

Dardanelles and made all the key decisions. Kitchener did maintain close supervision, gave advice and provided the requested reinforcements, but except for ruling out Asia as a possible landing site, left Hamilton free to formulate strategy and work out the broad lines of operations in the field. Hamilton wrote in his published diary (shortly before he was recalled): "I [am] indebted – very deeply indebted – to K. for having refrained absolutely from interference with my plan of campaign or with the tactical execution thereof."[38]

Fed inaccurate information, Millerand drew the conclusion that the War Office not only dictated strategy but had the final word in the tactics to be employed and so was acting contrary to all sound military principles. He informed Kitchener that it was the standard practice of the French government to devise the war plan and to allow the military commander freedom to carry out the operation as he saw fit. Millerand made his views known to the War Office, partly out of concern and partly as a means to exert influence over the future course of the Dardanelles campaign:

> I think it is opportune to call to your attention … our joint operations in the Dardanelles and to the regulations which control them.
>
> In France – whether it is a question of a Colonial expedition or a Continental War – the government chooses the Commander-in-Chief in whom it reposes confidence and whom it considers to be the best fitted to exercise supreme control; it then points out to him the object to be attained – and nothing more.
>
> The General Officer Commander-in-Chief enjoys full initiative in the conduct of operations for which he becomes *ipso facto* responsible.
>
> Thus General Joffre has always been left free to choose the moment, the force and the method of his attacks. The Government has confined itself to pointing out to him the main object – which is to beat the Germans and to oblige them, to start with, to evacuate the French and Belgian territories which they have invaded. Apart from such indication the Government only furnishes the Commander-in-Chief with all the information which it can obtain as to the enemy army.
>
> It is thus also that General Gouraud, while he should receive … from General Hamilton the directions necessary to co-operation and a clear indication of the object to be attained, has been left perfectly free to choose the means he will employ and the methods of utilizing his troops in that sector of operations allocated to him by the Commander-in-Chief.
>
> Now unless I am mistaken, the conception of the British Government differs from that of the French Government and Sir Ian Hamilton in the Dardanelles does not carry out operations according to his personal views but agreeably with instructions he received from the War Office, which are not simply general in character, but which state precisely the manner of execution.
>
> If that is so, and if the British Government thinks that matters should so continue, do you not think it would be advantageous that the instructions which you give to Sir Ian Hamilton should be the subject of preliminary exchange of views between the British and French ministers? These instructions could thus inspire the view of the two governments; they would take the exact account of the precise situation of the two Allied expeditionary

---

38 Hamilton, *Gallipoli Diary*, Vol. 2, p. 238.

forces; and they could, in particular, take into due consideration the opinion of General Gouraud in whose experience I have complete confidence.[39]

Kitchener must have wondered from where Millerand obtained his information as to how the British ran the campaign in the Dardanelles. One thing is certain. He did not for a moment consider Millerand's suggested arrangement that future military policy ought to be left to the two governments to decide. He did not bother to reply. Still the firm tone of Millerand's communiqué reflected the anxiety that had begun to develop in French political circles over the Dardanelles operation. As Bertie observed:

> The French are very sore on the subject of the Dardanelles Expedition. They say that the proposal was started by Mr. Churchill without proper consideration by the Military Authorities; that he obtained the concurrence of the French Ministry of Marine by flattery … The French also feel that the French and British Military forces sent to the Dardanelles might, more usefully … have been directed to the fighting lines in Flanders. The Dardanelles Expedition is regarded by ordinary Frenchmen as undertaken in the interests of Russia materially and of England politically, to secure her position in India and Egypt.[40]

Paris had anticipated that the expedition to the Dardanelles would, among other things, encourage the Balkan states to side with the Entente. So far none had made the move and there was an inclination to say that the "British Child", started without sufficient thought, preparation, and means had not yielded any results in spite of the effort and costs. Bertie heard comments like "cela ne marche pas bien" and nous avons des embarrass" in discussions with French political leaders.[41] Although d'Amade had expressed the conviction that inside a month the Allies would be in possession of the Peninsula the reports from the embattled area did not justify such optimism.

Gouraud arrived at a time when it was relatively quiet on the Peninsula and would remain so for the next three weeks. This afforded him the opportunity to personally reconnoitre the ground from his front-line trenches and to acclimatise himself to his new circumstances. The first thing he did was to identify the changes he deemed necessary in the organization of his army and front. He wanted the machine guns moved to different locations, claiming that they had been placed haphazardly. It was necessary to distinguish between the two uses of the machine guns. Those for the offensive were intended to clear obstacles in the enemy's front. On the other hand, the ones for defensive purposes were to be concealed and used only in case of an attack. He wanted the front to be dug in the shape of zigzags in stretches where it was too straight and apt to be enfiladed by the enemy. He requested greater spaces between the men in the front line. He observed that currently they were crammed in so tightly that they were practically shoulder to shoulder which inhibited fighting and day-to-day living. Similarly, the second line was too crowded as an artillery shell striking home would claim too many

---

39 BNA: Kitchener papers, PRO 30/57/57, Millerand to Kitchener, 30 May 1915.
40 BNA, Bertie papers, FO 800/181, Bertie note, 5 July 1915.
41 BNA: Grey papers, FO 800/ 57, Bertie to Marquis of Crewe (Secretary for India and a member of the Dardanelles Committee), 12 June 1915. Crewe had temporarily replaced the ailing Grey at the Foreign Office.

men.[42] To stabilize the Senegalese troops, he proposed to integrate them with seasoned units of the Metropolitan Brigade. Gouraud urged officers to arrange to bury the dead lying in the open, at least those in proximity of the trenches. That recommendation was never acted upon. Turkish snipers never relaxed and venturing only a few yards from the trenches would have meant almost certain death.

Gouraud found that after the recent fighting French troops were exhausted and dispirited by losses of comrades and the lack of progress. The struggle had degenerated into trench warfare with all of its attendant horrors. Men had to be wary of snipers; the horrid stench from the decomposing bodies sprawled where they had fallen hung permanently over the area; clouds of flies attracted to dead bodies and feces in open latrines carried a wide range of diseases; confinement to narrow and shallow trenches offered no shade from the intense heat; the anxiety and lack of sleep without the possibility of leave periods strained the mental health of soldiers with a growing number succumbing to nervous breakdowns; and finally random shelling was liable to occur without warning and not only got on everybody's nerves, but often killed or maimed.

When Gouraud surveyed and studied the ground opposite his frontline trenches, it became apparent that overpowering the Turks behind their intricate system of fortifications would present a challenge, more formidable than he had realized. In fact, as he would discover, it was the strongest part of the Turkish defences. Fearful of an Allied advance along the coast of the Dardanelles, the Turks had constructed two lines of trenches to protect their left flank, supported by four redoubts on the crest of Kereves Spur – which the French named Fortin Le Gouez, La Rognon, the Haricot and the Quadrilateral, the highest of the strongpoints which not only offered a commanding view of the area but was heavily defended by machine guns and barbed wire. On top of this the French extreme right and the entire back area were subject to a daily dose of shelling from the Turkish batteries on the Asiatic shore.

During the second half of May, Gouraud organized several local attacks to advance the French line. The first involved the colonial troops which twice attempted to storm the Haricot Redoubt and, while capturing it each time, were unable to hold it owing to heavy enemy bombardment and counterattacks. In all the French lost 31 officers and 1,442 men – 22 officers and 1,250 men wounded with 9 officers and 192 men killed. On the last day of the month, Gouraud's men launched a surprise attack which resulted in the capture and retention of Fortin Le Gouez.[43]

Looking at the broad military picture, Gouraud penned his thoughts in a memorandum dated 18 May which he submitted to Hamilton a day or two later. He observed that the Allied fleets had suffered substantial losses in trying to force the Straits and advised against a renewed attempt as long as the Turks were in possession of both banks of the waterway. Thus for the moment the principal role must be borne by the army with the navy providing assistance whenever it was able. He went on to explain that the Allies occupied roughly five kilometers of ground in the south and were in no danger of being pushed into the sea but that constant enemy shelling from the summit of Achi Baba wreaked havoc on their position. Gouraud considered the capture of the ridge a military necessity as well as a boost to the morale of the troops. Past experience had shown that the Turks were well armed and strongly entrenched and that plans

---

42 Gouraud to Millerand, 15 May 1915, in France, *Les armées francaises*, tome 8, Vol. 1, annexe no. 197.
43 France, *Expédition des Dardanelles*, tome 8, Vol. 1, pp. 77-79.

to rush the enemy's stronghold would have to be prepared with all the care of an attack on the Western Front. He advocated following the same tactics employed in the earlier battles of Krithia, that is, with the whole line pivoting on the French right – once it had gained a strong footing on Kereves Dere.

Gouraud cautioned against pushing beyond Achi Baba as the long march to The Narrows would take too long and allow the enemy time to adopt countermeasures. He thought that the least costly way to reach The Narrows was from Anzac Cove where, although surmounting resistance would be difficult; the distance was considerably shorter. Once Achi Baba was captured he proposed building a system of deep entrenchments to guard the southern end of the Peninsula. Leaving enough troops to hold the defensive positions there, the rest of the garrison would be transferred to join the arrival of fresh British divisions at Anzac, enlarging the Australian beachhead in preparation for a general thrust across the Peninsula along the Gaba Tepe – Maidos line. Such a movement would cut off the defenders in the south and open the way for the fleet to pass through the Straits.

As an alternative course, Gouraud suggested a landing in Asia near Besika Bay, followed by an advance on Chanak. He did not, however, recommend such a move. Along the lengthy attack route, strong defensive fortifications had to be overcome, and the Allied force would be exposed to flank attacks. If successful, it would clear the Straits for the fleet but an additional 100,000 men would be required for the task.[44]

Pending the arrival of large-scale reinforcements, Hamilton ruled out any major operation but one of Gouraud's option calling for a limited strike on a vital target caught his eye. By an odd coincidence Hamilton had arrived independently of the French general on the need to make another bid to capture Achi Baba, though this time he did not intend to do it in one day. The initial effort would be confined to overcoming the enemy's forward system of trenches across the Peninsula. Several factors encouraged senior Allied generals into believing that the outcome would be different this time. The Turks had just been repulsed at Anzac (19 May) which placed officers and men in a good frame of mind. Apart from their unsuccessful major assault, the Turks had only engaged in raids and minor attacks in May, giving the impression that their strength was ebbing away. Both the French and the English had received some reinforcements and many of the men and officers wounded slightly in earlier action were returning to duty. Hamilton would have preferred to await the arrival of 52nd (Lowland) Division from Britain but he deferred to the wishes of Hunter-Weston and Gouraud. The two generals were confident that they had enough troops on hand to eventually capture Achi Baba and saw that any delay would allow the Turks time to further fortify their defensive works.

Hunter-Weston and Gouraud produced the plan for the battle which was set to take place on 4 June. Officially designated the Third Battle of Krithia, it was the first on the Peninsula to be fought under the same conditions as those on the Western Front. The combatants faced each other in two lines of trenches stretching from the Aegean to the Straits, were supported by a lavish supply of machine guns, and the Turkish position was additionally protected in places by barbed wire and strong-points. In view of the changed conditions, the plans were more thorough and clear than the earlier battles. There were aerial photographs showing the exact location of enemy trenches. Advances at night with digging squads ensured that the Allied front

---

44 Gouraud memorandum, 18 May 1915, in *Les armées francaises*, tome 8, Vol. 1, annexe no. 201.

Hanging On 139

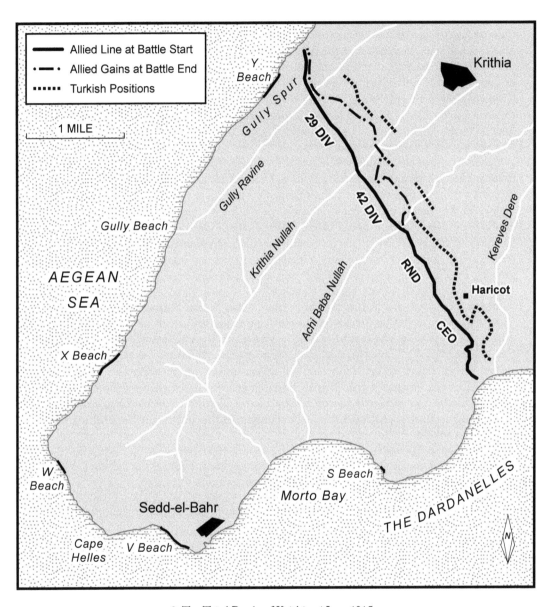

9. The Third Battle of Krithia, 4 June 1915

was only about 250 yards or less from the enemy, much closer than in the previous battles.[45] Instead of setting grandiose objectives the advance was limited to 800 yards. The actual attack would be carried out in broad daylight in two waves. The objective of the first was to capture the Turkish front trenches and that of the second passing through it 15 minutes later, was to secure the next main line, 400 to 500 yards ahead. Special digging parties were to advance on the heels of the second wave to consolidate the trenches against expected counterattacks.[46]

Prior to the assault, a two-and-one-half-hour artillery barrage would pummel the Turkish positions and the outlying strong-points. As the guns lifted, the troops would raise rifles with bayonets gleaming in the sunlight above the parapets to hopefully draw Turkish reserves into the forward trenches. The guns would then resume firing, concentrating on the enemy's front line. At noon the range of the guns would be extended whereupon officers would blow their whistles and the infantrymen would scramble over the parapet and surge forward.

Orders for corps commanders were issued on 2 June. The French 1st and 2nd Divisions were to storm the high ground overlooking Kereves Dere, an advance of between 400 to 650 yards. If all went well both divisions were to follow up and establish themselves on the west bank of the ravine. In the event that the operation was successfully executed the task of obtaining complete mastery over Kereves Dere would be greatly facilitated. On the other side of the French, the objective of the Royal Naval Division and the 42nd Division was limited to capturing and consolidating the enemy's front line but not to pass up any opportunity of gaining further ground. The 29th Division on the far left was to push forward between Krithia Nullah and the sea and capture the first three lines of trenches.[47]

Friday 4 June was a warm, sunny day with a strong breeze blowing from the north. The 20,000 British and 10,000 French troops participating in the attack would be facing between 25,000 and 28,000 Turkish defenders – although even an approximate number was unknown in the Allied camp. While the two sides were pretty evenly matched, it was the accepted doctrine that to have a chance the assailants required to outnumber the defenders by a margin of three to one. To make matters worse, British heavy guns were provided mostly with 18-pounder shrapnel shells – designed to detonate in the air and rain down showers of lead pellets – which were deadly against unprotected troops in the open but ineffective in demolishing trenches. Only high explosive shells could do the job.

Hamilton and his senior generals exuded a cheery optimism when the signal for the men to go over the top was given. For the French, things went badly from the start. Although they had plenty of high explosive shells in contrast to the British, the opposing lines were so close to one another (slightly more than 100 yards) that their gunners, fearful of hitting their own men had fired beyond the Turkish forward trenches. Thus Turkish defenders in the front line remained untouched by the preliminary bombardment and opened up with a withering hail of machine-gun and rifle fire that cut down the advancing French infantrymen by the hundreds. The slaughter terrified the African troops who wavered, turned and ran. Though they had a tendency to be unreliable under concentrated fire no amount of bravery would have accomplished anything in these circumstances. In a dozen minutes or so the French assault had

---

45   Prior, *Gallipoli*, p. 147.
46   Aspinall-Oglander, *Gallipoli*, Vol. 2, pp. 42-43.
47   Braithwaite, Instructions to General Officers commanding corps, in France, *Les armées francaises*, tome 8, Vol. 1, annexe no. 226; Aspinall-Oglander, *Gallipoli*, Vol. 2, pp. 44-45.

been halted in its tracks and the survivors crawled back to their original line. Lieutenant Weil described the grisly scene:

> We did not advance a step… I was informed by telephone: on the English side there was a little progress towards Krithia, but on our front it was a disaster. Our poor foot soldiers were slaughtered in the middle of the Turkish fortifications constructed precisely the night before as if they had been forewarned of our intentions… The enemy had taken advantage of the pause in our shelling, and the moment of hesitation by the infantry (who were wondering if it was really finished) to reoccupy the front lines that were hardly damaged and to set in place all their machine-guns. The result was that our unfortunate poilus, entangled in the barbed-wire and *"chevaux de frise"*[48] had to slow down and then were literally cut down by the machine-guns.[49]

British observers were outraged by the French infantry's seemingly lack of effort while their own men were pushing through in spite of encountering a tornado of enemy fire. However their view was partially obstructed by the dust and smoke that had blown back towards their line and, they were unaware that the French troops were confronted by difficult terrain and elaborate Turkish defences that included a plethora of well-placed machine-guns. All they could see was that the French had tested the waters, found it too hot and hurried back to the safety of their trenches. The fact that French forces had suffered 2,000 casualties after remaining sitting ducks for less than a quarter of an hour was proof that they had just cause to break off their attack.

Nonetheless, the French repulse would have a deadly effect on the Royal Naval Division after it captured the Ottoman front-line trenches. When its Collingwood battalion on the right attempted to continue the advance it was caught in enfilade fire from Kereves Dere and almost annihilated, losing 25 officers and 600 men out of total force of 850. The remaining battalions also ran into heavy fire and, with their position compromised by the collapse of their right flank, the shaken survivors were driven back to their original line. On the left of the line by the Aegean coast the 29th Division fared no better. The Indian Brigade got off to a fast start and, as it advanced along Gully Spur and up the narrow channel of Gully Ravine, it was cut up badly by Ottoman strong points which had been untouched by Allied bombardment. The one bright spot was in the centre where the 42nd Division had broken through the enemy's front to a depth of some 1,000 yards, captured 217 prisoners and was within reach of Krithia. Hunter-Weston had the choice of using his reserves to exploit the gap in the centre and secure Krithia or try again on the opposing flanks.

At first glance, the decision seemed obvious but Hunter-Weston worried that if the centre advanced too far it might be exposed to attacks from either side. He consulted with Gouraud and the two agreed to mount another attack on both flanks with the French on the right and the 29th Division on the left. A short time later Gouraud informed Hunter-Weston that his men were not fit to undertake another assault and he opted out of their arrangement.

---

48 A transportable wooden frame from which protruded rows of wooden or iron spikes.
49 Weil cited in Association, *Dardanelles*, p. 33.

The 29th Division was reinforced and went ahead on its own but accomplished nothing except endure more torment. Left out alone without reinforcements, the 42nd Division fell back, giving up most of the ground it had won during the day's fighting. At 5.15 pm Hunter-Weston ordered the units to dig in where they stood and to brace themselves for inevitable counterattacks.[50]

So ended the Third Battle of Krithia. The British had sustained 4,500 casualties and the French more than 2,000. The Turks fared even worse, admitting to losses of about 9,000 but it may have been a higher figure. The Allies had held such high hopes before the start of the battle but none of their objectives were achieved. Nor had they gained any ground that would have facilitated an untroubled advance on Krithia. On the contrary their position remained precarious. From the heights of Achi Baba, the Turks could observe the activities of the Allies below and their guns from there and Asia could continue to pound enemy trenches day and night. A French staff officer, Captain François Charles-Roux, expressed concern about the current outlook: "Theoretically our situation is untenable. I would say that if we were on manoeuvres the umpires would have declared us all dead a long time ago. That is ... the logical consequence of our troops living under the cross fire of Turkish batteries firing from Achi Baba to our front and the Asiatic coast to our rear. Happily, there is a difference between practice and theory."[51]

It remained to be seen what Hamilton's next move would be. Would he continue to order the Anglo-French expeditionary force to senselessly batter itself against an intricate system of Turkish defences or try something else? Presumably, much would depend on the advice of Lord Kitchener and the extent of reinforcements received.

50 France, *Expédition des Dardanelles*, tome 8, Vol. 1, pp. 84-87; Aspinall-Oglander, *Gallipoli*, Vol. 2, pp. 46-53.
51 François Charles-Roux, *L'Expédition des Dardanelle* (Paris: Armand Colin, 1919), p. 146.

9

Last Throw of the Dice

The disappointing results of the Third Battle of Krithia confirmed Gouraud's worst fears. To capture the enemy's lines would require siege operations and an even stronger force than the one currently at the disposal of the Allies. On 11 June he wrote to Millerand and, in assessing conditions on the Peninsula, did not attempt to minimize the challenge ahead. He pointed out that the deadlock on Cape Helles was as complete as on the Western Front. All along the line the Turks had constructed an elaborate system of trenches, flanked by machine-guns and protected by barbed wire. In clinging to the trenches, the Turks had shown that they were good soldiers, brave and tenacious, and well supported by artillery whose numbers and range had increased in the last three weeks. In some ways it was more difficult than in France as the soldiers had to endure intense heat, debilitating sicknesses and inadequate shelters. He went on to say that the process of disembarkation, starting in September when there were frequent storms on the seas, would be unpredictable. Thus Gouraud warned that advance in the southern part of the Peninsula would be slow and costly.[1]

It was after Gouraud sent off the telegram to the War Ministry in Paris that he learned the British Government had decided to send three new divisions to the Dardanelles for a major offensive in July – a short time later two more were added. Buoyed by the news, Hamilton invited Gouraud to state his views on where the troops could best be employed. "I look upon Gouraud more as a coadjutor than as a subordinate" Hamilton wrote in his diary, "so it is worth anything to me to find that we see eye to eye at present."[2]

Gouraud returned with his recommendations on 14 June, a day after he had compiled his paper. He noted in his prelude that the offensive of 4 June, notwithstanding the careful preparation involved, had not yielded the result commensurate with the vigorous and expensive effort of the Anglo-French troops. He repeated many of the observations he had made to Millerand three days earlier, in particular the fighting quality of the Turkish soldiers and the elaborate system of defence opposite the Allied line. Gouraud was struck by the possibility that the Turks had changed their strategy. Initially they wanted to throw the Allies back into the sea but, as a result of the huge losses they had suffered in the fighting in April and May, appeared to have

---

1 Gouraud tp Millerand, 11 June 1915, in France, *Les armées françaises* , tome 8, Vol. 1, annexe no. 238.
2 Hamilton, *Gallipoli Diary*, Vol. 1, pp. 295-96.

rejected this approach for the time being. Their current plan was to check the advance of the Allies, to hem them in along the narrow front from which they were forced to operate and to render their life unbearable by bombing their camps and landing beaches. In short the Allies were blocked in front and struck from behind. That being the case, Gouraud anticipated that conditions would worsen because of sickness resulting from the climate and the oppressive heat, the proximity of men in the encampment that might cause epidemics and, starting from the end of August, the turbulent weather which would make any landing very difficult.

When considering how to best use the impending reinforcements, Gouraud examined three possible landing sites. As he deemed it advisable to avoid Cape Helles, his first choice was to strike at Bulair which he considered would be unexpected and directly threaten Constantinople itself. If, however, the Admirals judged the naval difficulties insuperable, then the main blow should be directed from south of Gaba Tepe with the object of pushing across to a narrow part of the Peninsula at Maidos, a distance of eight kilometers. The successful execution of the plan would sever the enemy's communications, allow the formation of a base in Kilid Bahr for British submarines lurking in the Marmora and command the approaches to The Narrows. A third option was to disembark in Asia and seize the Yeni-Shehr heights, relieving the Allied forces on Cape Helles from shelling. This was a purely defensive measure and "would not bring victory a single step closer." He assumed that that the ships' guns would be able to neutralize the Turkish batteries in Asia.[3]

The next day, Hamilton thanked Gouraud for his appreciation, saying that his views were identical to those already reached by his general staff. Hamilton claimed that it was a source of great satisfaction to learn that such a unity of ideas existed between them.[4]

On 16 June Gouraud, accompanied by Hamilton, sailed to the island of Imbros[5] to see de Robeck to request that he turn the naval guns against the Turkish batteries in Asia. Gouraud pleaded his case during which he received strong support from Hamilton. De Robeck claimed that he could do nothing at the moment, but he gave assurances that with the adoption of new methods at the start of July the navy would again play an active role in the operation. De Robeck's implied promise of a concerted effort against the Asiatic guns, however, was never carried out.

Whilst at Imbros, Gouraud sat down with Hamilton to discuss the various military options he had advanced in his memorandum of 13 June. Hamilton ruled out a landing near Bulair, although it was an obvious danger area for the Turks. The capture of the communication lines would sever the land route between Constantinople and the Turkish army in the Peninsula. Still the objections to attempt to advance via Bulair were numerous. A short distance inland from the few narrow beaches, the ground rose sharply and would have presented an immense barrier to the advancing troops and, in addition, the Turks had constructed three defensive lines near the town. Then too de Robeck had expressed his opposition to a landing so far north as he could not guarantee that the supply ships could reach the troops owing to the presence of German submarines in neighbouring waters. Finally, even if the troops had managed through good fortune to take control of Bulair, it would not necessarily have entailed the surrender of

---

3   Hamilton, *Gallipoli Diary*, Vol. 1, pp. 296-301; Gouraud to Millerand, 13 June 1915, in France, *Les armées françaises*, tome 8, Vol. 1, annexe no. 240.
4   AN: Millerand papers, 470/AP/15, Hamilton to Gouraud, 14 June 1915.
5   The island is located in the Aegean at the entrance of Saros Bay.

the Turkish garrison or the opening of The Narrows. For one thing the Turks could still have supplied their army from Asia.

Turning next to the suggested strike from Gaba Tepe, Hamiltion recognized that it held attractive possibilities. He was discouraged from considering that proposal on account of the rugged terrain the men would have to traverse, especially on the side of the Australians, and their exposure to Turkish batteries located on Kilid Bahr plateau. As in any confined area the advance would be incremental, foot by foot, and the losses immense.

Hamilton observed that Asia alone provided an open field where the heavily reinforced and tenacious Turks could be outmanoeuvred and British cavalry employed. But such an operation would require greater forces than he could spare. A landing could only he made at Besika Bay and an advance against the defences at Chanak – approximately 45 kilometers distant– would entail crossing a country dominated by steep hills and intersected by a number of rivers. Along the way the troops would present an open right flank to Turkish forces in Anatolia and the long lines of communication would have to be protected.

Gouraud forward a memo to Millerand containing a summary of his talk with Hamilton. He noted that in order to defend the ground gained at Cape Helles and Gaba Tepe, Hamilton would require five divisions – three for Cape Helles and two for Gaba Tepe. This left Hamilton with only five divisions which was not sufficient to conduct the operation in Besika Bay without the risk of a serious mishap. It was therefore the lack of forces that decided the question of an expedition to Asia which Gouraud estimated would require 10 divisions, plus a number of cavalry units.[6]

It was not long before Hamilton entrusted Gouraud with yet another task. He wanted to keep pressure on the Turks in Cape Helles to deceive them into thinking that it was here that the next major attack would occur. Many writers of the campaign have questioned, and rightly so, Hamilton's policy of limited attacks which entailed heavy losses to achieve at best minor advances.[7] Be that as it may, Hunter-Weston and Gouraud were selected to work out the details.

The most important lesson Gouraud had gained from the Krithia debacle was that future attacks should be limited in scope and confined only to places where enemy trenches could be subjected to heavy bombardment.[8] As he saw it, the recent action in which the flanks had failed to advance – therby negating the loss of ground gained by the centre – was due to the neglect to bring Allied guns to bear on Turkish defences. The French general held a succession of meetings with Hunter-Weston and they ultimately came to the following conclusions: first the need to maintain steady pressure on the Turks through a series of local attacks conducted on a narrow front; second that the depth of the attack would be restricted only to the area covered by the artillery, simply put biting off a small section of the enemy's line, then fortifying it so as to fend off and inflict maximum losses on the expected counterattacks – the so called bite and hold strategy later adopted on the Western Front;[9] third that to capture Krithia and Achi Baba it was vital to overcome the Turkish strongpoints at Gully Spur on the left and the Haricot and Quadrilateral redoubts west of Kereves Dere on the right; and finally, as only one area could

---

6   Gouraud to Millerand, 18 June 1915, in France, *Les armées françaises*, tome 8, Vol. 1, annexe no. 250.
7   See for example James, *Gallipoli*, p. 217; Aspinall-Oglander, *Gallipoli*, Vol. 2, p. 111; and Hart, *Gallipoli*, pp. 272-74.
8   Rigoux, *Les Dardanelles*, p. 112.
9   Prior, *Gallipoli*, pp. 152-53.

be hit at a time owing to the limited availability of British guns and ammunition, the French would carry out the first experiment because they had the largest supply of heavy explosive shells. Hamilton approved of the arrangements and left Gouraud free to work out the tactical plan. The date fixed for the operation was 21 June.

The attack was to take place on a narrow front of 650 yards and be supported by the greatest concentration of artillery fire yet attempted on the Peninsula. In all there was roughly one gun for every 10 yards of front on which the advance was to be made. To obliterate the Turkish front lines, the French had allocated seven batteries of their rapid firing 75mm guns, two batteries of 155mm howitzers, 16 trench mortars, as well as seven howitzers borrowed from the British 29th Division. Moreover, there were six batteries of 75mm guns detailed to fire on the remainder of the Turkish trenches opposite the French, while a number of long-range guns, supplemented by the battleship *Saint-Louis*, were to target Turkish artillery on the Asiatic shore during the attack. The bombardment of the Turkish line began days before the 21st. Because the opposing lines were so close together French planners wanted to make sure that the shells did not drop short and strike their own men. The best way to avoid any such accidents was to shatter enemy front trenches so that their guns would extend their range the moment their men scrambled over the parapet. At 5.15 am on the day of the attack the bombardment intensified and lasted 45 minutes. A British artillery officer, 2nd Lieutenant Angus McCracken, described with amazement the fireworks from his vantage point:

> The 75s were going like machine guns and every now and again great columns would rise up and then a dull rumble, some gun about the size of our 6" firing HE. There were some wild shots, but on the whole the shooting was magnificent. Some bursts were too high, and you saw a long chain of 'spurts' from the ground extending across two lines of trenches. There was a battleship lying off Sedd el Bahr ... hurling shells into batteries in Asia or trying to do so anyway. The bombardment went on till 6.10 a.m. and then suddenly ceased and there was a moment's oppressive silence. There was a cloud of smoke hanging over the trenches and running right back to the beach.[10]

Gouraud had placed Colonel Girodon, his former chief of staff and now commanding the Metropolitan Brigade, in charge of the operation.[11] The French goal was to capture a stretch of Turkish held - ground that included the Haricot and Quadrilateral redoubts and the trenches overlooking Le Ravin de la Mort, an offshoot of Kereves Dere ravine.[12] It was to say the least a formidable task. The three participating units were the 6th Colonial Regiment on the right and the 176th Regiment on the left with the 2nd Régiment de Marche d'Afrique in reserve. The 6th Colonials were directed to take the trenches at the head of Le Ravin de la Mort. The assignment of the 176th was to drive the enemy off the Haricot and Quadrilateral redoubts, then swing right to link up with the Colonial troops. A reserve company was detailed to cover the left flank of the 176th Regiment. If the objectives were gained it would prevent Turkish enfilading fire on the centre of the Allied advance

10   Cited in Hart, *Gallipoli*, 256.
11   He was appointed to take charge of the brigade on 7 June after the previous commander was killed in action.
12   France, *Expédition des Dardanelles*, p. 89.

Last Throw of the Dice 147

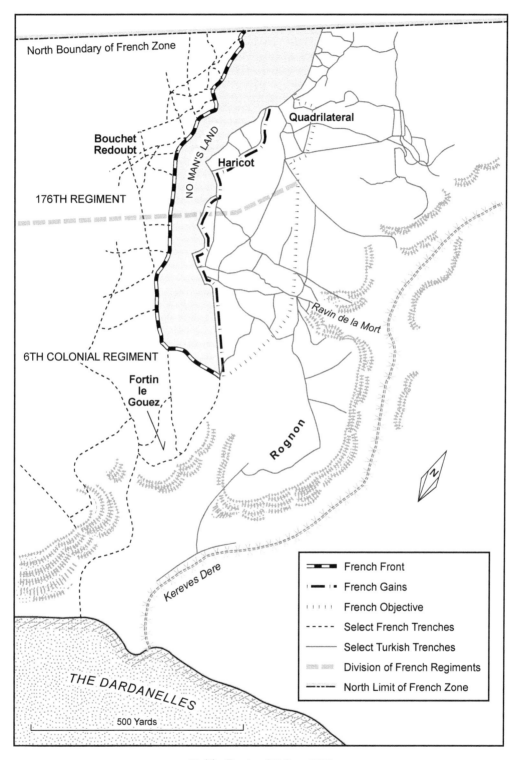

10. The Battle of 21 June 1915

Girodon had taken great pains to ensure that nothing was left to chance. He met with unit commanders and went over the various stages of the advance, gave each a definitive objective and stressed the need for their officers to instruct their men on the exact location of the Turkish trenches they were to take, and what to do after their gains. After rising on the day of the battle, the assaulting troops were given a hot breakfast consisting of soup, coffee and bread, supplemented by their wine ration. A generous measure of brandy was added to each man's canteen shortly before zero hour.

At 6 am the assault got under way. McCracken continued with his narrative just as the guns shifted to targets farther inland:

> And then a glorious sight – the French advancing through the smoke, a long line extended for the most part … On they came out of the smoke and then rifles and Maxims began to make music, but it struck me the Turkish artillery was very slow, perhaps they could not see for the covering black mantle of smoke. Then they came but the French were very near the first trench and only a few fell.[13]

The artillery had been so heavy and effective that the greater part of the 176th Regiment easily carried the Turkish second line trenches, including the Haricot redoubt, which had twice in the recent past been captured and lost. The men consolidated their position and beat back several violent Turkish counterattacks. French casualties had been light but one of the unfortunate victims was Girodon. As he watched his men surging forward from a parapet, he was struck in the chest by a bullet – and shortly thereafter was transported back to France. The one area where the 176th ran into difficulty was on the far left. Here the stubborn defenders resisted all attempts to dislodge them from the Quadrilateral redoubt, situated on the left (northeast) behind the Haricot.

The 6th Colonial, next to the sea, had little to show for their arduous effort during the day. They overran the first Turkish line because it had been leveled for the most part by artillery fire but could make no further progress. They fell back to what remained of the captured front-line trench which was over crowded and chocked with dead and dying Turks. As it offered little protection against Turkish artillery fire, its occupants suffered heavily and, among the mounting casualties, was Lieutenant-Colonel Noguès, commander of the regiment, who was badly wounded. It made no sense to remain where they were, so they raced back to their starting line. Gouraud sent them back into action twice, once at noon and again at 2.15 pm, following an intense barrage, but each time they were stopped well short of the second line of enemy trenches. Determined not to abandon the gains by the 176th on the left, Gouraud issued new orders that the position ahead must be captured at all costs before nightfall.

The assault was fixed for 6.45 pm but when the time came the new commander of the 6th Colonial Regiment, which had suffered heavy casualties, claimed it was unfit to attack again. Consequently, Gouraud turned to the Régiment de Marche d'Afrique which charged forward with great elan and gained a foothold in the Turkish defences, occupying and holding the ground overlooking Le Ravin de la Mort. Contact between the two brigades was reestablished. The day ended on a happy note.

---

13 Cited in Hart, *Gallipoli*, 256.

On the 23rd and for the next two days the French launched further attacks and, while there were slight advances in a few places, the main effort against the Quadrilateral, backed by insufficient artillery failed with significant losses. This meant that as long as the redoubt remained in enemy hands the Royal Naval Division, next to the French, could not advance without running the risk of an attack on its right flank.

Still Gouraud had to be pleased by the overall progress of the past four days. The French had improved their position, securing the Haricot and the trenches on the spur overlooking Kereves Dere and, as a result, would be staring down at the enemy for the first time. Moreover, the morale of the men was given a boost; dead enemy bodies lay everywhere and there was evidence that their losses had been severe (over 6,000 according to the Turkish official account). The experience proved that with adequate artillery support no Turkish position was inviolable. The cost to the French in killed and wounded was about 3,200.[14] It was a rare occasion when the defenders took heavier punishment than the attackers.

As was the case after every battle, French bodies were gathered for burial, although there were those blown to bits whose remains were collected in bags and laid in an anonymous grave. Lieutenant Weill was present when two French non-commissioned officers were at least given the dignity of a proper burial:

> This morning we had to bury the two non-commissioned officers killed yesterday at an observation post. Captain Michel selected me to represent the battery. It was a very sad mission. The poor devils yesterday were in full health, falling unfortunately so far from France without even allowing their families the consolation of burying them ... The ceremony was quick, awful in its simplicity. The chaplain recited the usual prayer. We rendered the honours in front of the two graves into which we would lower the unlucky pair. Captain Sainpère made a brief speech, interrupted at every moment by the explosion of 105mm very near us. But no one flinches. Each of us was thinking that at any moment he could be rejoining those who had gone to their last resting place, and the prospect of mouldering under two metres of Turkish soil near the sea, 900 leagues from France, is nothing to rejoice in.[15]

Along the coast of the Aegean Sea, the British carried out the other limited operation in the Gully Ravine area on 28 June in an attempt to outflank Turkish forces in front of Krithia. French heavy howitzers were moved to provide support as the British lacked ammunition for their artillery. Preceded by an artillery barrage, the attack on a 1,500-yard front met stronger Turkish resistance than expected and it was only on the left on Gully Spur that the line was pushed forward nearly half a mile. The results of the battle showed that trenches subjected to a thorough artillery pounding were easily captured but in places that were relatively untouched no progress was made, and casualties were high.

The French were determined to put to immediate use the lesson they had learned in their recent engagement about the decisive force of artillery on the battlefield. With everything in place, they set their sights on the Quadrilateral redoubt, assuming that the Turks had transferred

---

14 The number of casualties varies depending on the source, but the figure cited in this text is based on the French official history, p. 90.
15 Weil, cited in Association, *Dardanelles*, p. 36.

units facing them to bolster their forces still engaged on the British front. Gouraud selected the 7th Colonial Regiment to storm the redoubt while sending the *Suffren* to take a position inside the Straits to neutralize the Turkish batteries in Asia. After a fierce bombardment early on the morning of 30 June, the 7th Colonials scrambled out of their trenches and swept the enemy off the entire redoubt within an hour. Overcome with euphoria they pushed beyond the captured trenches until they ran into massive Turkish reinforcements and retreated with lightning speed. Weil recorded the event in his diary:

> Everyone is at his post. Like the 21 [June] we proceeded with a slow and methodically destructive bombardment. We had at our disposal shells with the new instantaneous fuses which exploded on impact and were much more effective in destroying trenches and fortifications than shells that delay before exploding. The result was that in our sector the opposing trenches were badly damaged and when the assault was launched at 5.30 it permitted our troops to take control of the Turkish first line with practically no losses. But carried away by their excessive enthusiasm they did not stop there and, by placing improvised bridges over captured trenches, continued to advance forward. I soon learned over the telephone that our men had gone so far that … they had clashed with a number of Turkish battalions arriving to the rescue and which almost surrounded our advanced elements. Isolated, waiting for reinforcements that never arrived and deprived of artillery support, the men hastily withdrew.[16]

The Turks counterattacked several hours later and regained some ground but the greater part of the Quadrilateral remained in French hands. At the end of the battle the *Suffren*, which had significantly restricted the level of Turkish fire from Asia, withdrew from the Straits and headed towards Mudros. With its departure, the Turkish guns from Asia became active again.[17] The jubilant feeling in the French camp over their success of 30 June was acutely dampened by a tragic event later in the day. Shortly before 8 pm Gouraud, on his way back from visiting a field hospital, was struck down by a 8-inch shell fired from a gun on the Asiatic shore. The shell landed very close and luckily none of shrapnel hit vital parts of his body but the concussive force of the explosion hurled him over a high wall. A fig tree broke his fall. Alerted by witnesses, several nurses and soldiers rushed to his aid and found him lying in a small garden, unconscious and covered with blood. He was placed on a stretcher and taken to the hospital where the doctors determined that he had suffered serious injuries to his left leg and right arm. While attending to his wounds, they gave him an injection of caffeine which allowed him to regain consciousness. In a dazed state he mumbled, presumably the standard question, and was told what had happened. The medical facility could not provide him with the necessary care and, once his condition stabilized, he was taken aboard the hospital ship *Tchad* which was set to leave for France that evening.[18]

As soon as Hamilton heard the bad news, he hurried over to the hospital but by the time he arrived Gouraud was already on the ship. Taken to see the patient, Hamilton was allowed to

---

16   Weil, cited in Association, *Dardanelles*, p. 37.
17   France, *Expédition des Dardanelles*, pp. 91-92.
18   AMAE: Gouraud papers, 399 PAAP 88-89, Account by J. Tourneix, a hospital worker, undated.

speak to him for about half a minute and found him "full of pluck." Doctors were not certain that Gouraud would survive but he pulled through thanks to his robust constitution.[19]

Along the way, the *Tchad* stopped at Mudros where Admiral Wemyss and General Baumann (French commander of the base on the island) came on board and did their best to bolster Gouraud's spirits. During the night he contracted a high fever and the next morning the chief of medicine, accompanied by a brilliant young surgeon, examined him after removing his bandages. Gouraud remembered that the odor was unbearable and that his shattered arm was causing him a good deal of pain. The leg, it turned out, was fractured and would heal in time but the damaged part of the lower arm could not be saved. The young doctor conveyed his medical diagnosis to Gouraud. His right arm was badly mangled and, to compound matters, gangrene had set in. He would die unless the arm up to the elbow was amputated at once.

Gouraud took the announcement without betraying any emotion, merely replying that like any one in similar circumstances he had no wish to die.[20] The operation was successfully performed after which Gouraud was evacuated to France. He would never return to Gallipoli but his career was far from over.[21]

Conversely, on the Dardanelles scene for six weeks only, Gouraud had been a tower of strength to his corps. His regular tour of the trenches, sharing the same dangers and hardships with the rank and file and, assuring them of the great value their continued presence at Cape Helles was to the main operation, had been instrumental in sustaining morale and affirming that the struggle was worth the sacrifice. His positive outlook, uncomplaining nature and ability to retain his equanimity in a crisis had endeared him to the British.

As reports of Gouraud's serious injury spread, the British monarch expressed his concern in a telegram sent to Hamilton on 2 July: "I very much regret to hear that General Gouraud was wounded yesterday by an artillery shell. I know how serious a loss he will be both to his own army and to you. I hope that his wounds are not serious and that he will recover soon." In a note addressed to the French war ministry, Kitchener echoed similar sentiments. He conveyed his sincere regrets on the loss of Gouraud, held high hopes for his speedy recovery and fully appreciated how his leadership would be missed during the length of his absence.[22]

By virtue of seniority, the post of acting commander of French forces devolved upon General Bailloud an old campaigner whose prewar career had taken him to widely scattered parts of the world, including terms of service in Madagascar, Algeria and China. Recalled from retirement in 1915, Bailloud was sent to the Dardanelles in charge of a division. He was dull, lacked vigour and tended to be ultra-cautious, giving the impression of timidity in contrast to his predecessor. In his defence he had a tough act to follow and this partly explains why he was unpopular with the British. Visiting the Gallipoli Peninsula in July, Maurice Hankey, the stalwart and influential secretary of the War Council and Dardanelles Committee, described him "as the

---

19 Hamilton, *Gallipoli Diary*, Vol. 1, pp. 259-60.
20 AMAE: Gouraud papers, 399 PAAP 88-89, Gouraud's post-wound account, undated.
21 After his convalescence, he resumed command of the 4th Army on the Western Front from December 1915 to December 1916. He left his command to replace General Lyautey, as resident–general in Morocco, and returned to the 4th Army in June 1917. By using the elastic defence strategy he played a pivotal role in stopping Luddendorf's last offensive in July 1918 which marked a turning point in the war. He was sent to Syria as High Commissioner in 1919 and on returning to France four years later became Governor of Paris, a post he held until his retirement in 1937. He died in 1946.
22 AMAE: Gouraud papers, 399 PAAP 88-89, Copies of the two notes in the collection were undated.

most confirmed pessimist I have met since the war began" and "an old stupid man" who "ought to be superseded."[23]

Hamilton was understandably sick at heart over the bad luck that had disabled his valued colleague. He knew that Gouraud would not be replaced by a man of his calibre.[24] He conveyed his dismay to Asquith:

> The ... loss of Gouraud, who is one of the finest commanders I have ever met, and whose loss to an impressionable set of people like the French, is, to my thinking at least equivalent to the loss of a Brigade ... The new General is not at all a man of the same calibre as Gouraud, and he is too old for the job (67) ... So for the moment, the French have cold feet and, as in the early days of d'Amade, we shall have to constantly act as big brother to them and try to get them to buck up.[25]

Hamilton's lack of confidence in the French was not entirely warranted. Admittedly certain colonial units like the Senegalese and Zouaves had proven to be unreliable, especially at night, but on the whole the French soldiers had given a good account of themselves, fighting with dash, spirit and courage. He only saw that the French lacked the same kind of persistence and determination as the British and Australians in the face of concentrated rifle and machine-gun fire, but he never seemed to appreciate that they were up against the most formidable part of the Turkish defences and had sustained heavy casualties.

In no place was Gouraud's misfortune felt as deeply as in Paris where events were rapidly moving towards a political crisis. His forced absence in the field was bound to affect operations in the Dardanelles and a victory at this time was badly needed. At home parliamentarians were increasingly restive at the manner in which the war was being fought. Most of the verbal attacks were levelled at Millerand. The chamber took him to task for failing to control Joffre and the Army Commission often complained that he fed them inadequate and incorrect information. It was evident from the growing level of political discontent that, unless Millerand was sacrificed or the Entente powers achieved a military victory somewhere soon, the Viviani Ministry would collapse under the strain.

Joffre's latest offensive in Artois, commencing on 9 May, limped along painfully until mid-June producing no worthwhile gains. Yet Joffre was inclined to discount the immediate results, fortified by the illusion that he had inflicted enormous casualties upon the Germans and that he was one step closer to a breakthrough. He intended to strike again at the enemy as soon as possible. Since the Marne he had fought a series of bloody and inconclusive engagements and, as a result, his reputation had suffered, allowing the government to regain a measure of control over war policy.[26] However both Joffre and Millerand were ready to wage an all-out fight to preserve the reigning war strategy, the former because he was convinced in its soundness and the latter out of his prolonged practice of unquestioned obedience.

---

23 Hankey, *Supreme Command*, Vol. 1, p. 381.
24 Hamilton, *Gallipoli Diary*, Vol. 1, p. 160.
25 Bodleian Library (Bod. L): Asquith papers, Vol. 13, Hamilton to Asquith, 7 July 1915.
26 The five unsuccessful battles Joffre engaged in since the Marne were as follows: First Battle of Champagne (20 December-7 March); Battle of Soissons (8-14 January); Battle of Neuve Chapelle (10-13 March); Second Battle of Artois (9 May-18 June); Battle of Festubert (15-25 May).

If Joffre was bent on pursuing the slaughter in the west, it was certain that he would receive no encouragement from the British authorities. Reviewing the general military situation in June, Churchill stressed the futility of further attacks on the Western Front, observing that since April Anglo-French forces had cleared a few miles of territory which was of little strategic value and, in the process, had suffered 320,000 casualties, believed to be three times greater than those of the enemy.[27] He urged that the Allies in France remain on the defensive and that every provision be made to achieve a victory in the Dardanelles.[28] Kitchener seconded Churchill's observation in a memorandum on 26 June. He wanted the next large-scale Allied offensive postponed until early 1916 when the New Armies would be fully trained and equipped and for such a movement to be coordinated with a Russian attack from the east. As the Russians were short of guns and ammunition, a synchronized advance at present was not possible. Thus the British requested a conference in order to persuade Joffre and the French government to delay mounting an offensive in the west until spring of 1916.[29]

The British delegation crossed over to Calais on 5 July and the Anglo-French conference got under way at 10 am the next day. Kitchener, who spoke French fluently, dominated the proceedings and made the case for adopting an active-defensive strategy in the west – that is confining activity to occasional local attacks – and giving priority to the Dardanelles campaign. The French representatives were won over for, like the rest of their colleagues in the cabinet, they had been inclined to follow Joffre's lead. Joffre was relatively reticent during the talks. Kitchener had met with him before the gathering and consented to send over additional divisions of the New Armies once their training was completed. Joffre had obtained what he wanted and took no notice of the arrangements that followed.[30] It was no secret in Paris that he considered Kitchener's concept of standing on the defence "as heresy", arguing that its adoption would invite massive and incessant enemy attacks.[31] He evidently had no intentions of complying with the results of the meeting.

On 7 July the first Inter-Allied military assembly was held at Joffre's headquarters in Chantilly with Millerand acting as chairman. Speaking before his audience, made up of military representatives from different Entente countries – Italy, Serbia, Russia, Britain and Belgium – Joffre emphasized the need to mount a major offensive in the west for three reasons: first to relieve pressure on the hard-pressed Russians; second to bolster the morale of the troops; and finally because he believed that the German line was weak. No one questioned Joffre's reasoning for the offensive which was set to begin in August.[32]

Millerand did not inform the French cabinet of Joffre's plan for an autumn offensive as it was incumbent on him to do so. He was aware, with just cause, that the idea would meet strong opposition. Buoyed by the agreement at Calais, opinion in the cabinet had begun to harden

---

27 The French had lost 222,000 men since May and recovered 1.5 miles of territory whereas the British had suffered 100,000 casualties and won back half the ground lost to the Germans in the Second Battle of Ypres.
28 Churchill, *World Crisis*, Vol. 2, pp. 420-28.
29 Cassar, *Kitchener's War*, pp. 209-10.
30 Cassar, *Kitchener's War*, pp. 210-11.
31 Poincaré, *Au Service*, Vol. 6, p. 281.
32 IWM: Wilson papers, entry in Wilson Diary, 7 July 1915. There is a somewhat different version in Brig-Gen. Sir James E. Edmonds, *Military Operations: France and Belgium 1915*, Vol. 2 (London: Macmillan, 1936), pp. 87-88.

against further attacks in the west. For several months evidence had been accumulating in Paris that the uneasiness in the country was due more to the dissatisfaction over costly and premature attacks than to impatience at remaining idle. On 5 July Poincaré wrote: "The war weariness which permeates certain quarters has produced a fresh flow of insulting and threatening letters addressed to me." Two days later while on an inspection tour at the front he indicated that a corps commander had taken him aside and pleaded "Mr. President, do what you can to put a stop to these local offensives. We are in the process of breaking our instrument of victory."[33] During the last attack at least one army corps had refused to leave the trenches and two battalions had gone over to the enemy singing *L'Internationale*.[34] Even Joffre's generals recognized that unless the Anglo-French armies were heavily reinforced there was not the slightest chance of smashing through the German lines. To the government, the abundant signs of disaffection suggested that if Joffre was permitted to continue his policy of frontal assaults the French army, which was in a state of complete exhaustion, might well mutiny.[35]

Within the cabinet the most questioning minds were probing to determine if there was a way out of the bloody stalemate in the west. While fully conscious of the importance of massing troops where decisive blows could be struck, they were no longer unanimous that France should be regarded as the only theatre of war. Even those who felt that ultimate victory rested on defeating the Germans in the west, there was a consensus that surplus troops should be sent to some other theatre where operations might lead to more productive results. When the cabinet began to search for an alternate strategy it did not have far to look. It fastened at once on the current campaign in the Dardanelles.

On 22 July and again two days later the cabinet had long and lively discussions regarding the Dardanelles. Viviani conducted a reappraisal of the Allied position on the Peninsula and pointed to the staggering casualties the French forces had sustained since the first landing. The ministers had the option of either abandoning the enterprise or, as some had suggested, sending three or four more divisions to seek the desired resolution. The mirage of the Bosporus and the capture of Constantinople seduced the imagination of the ministers. The success of the operation would restore communications with Russia, probably force Turkey to capitulate, open the door for the Balkans to join the Entente and assure for France those portions of the Ottoman Empire it valued. Poincaré, as described by one minister "led the orchestra", and hammered home the idea that the "road to Berlin passed through Constantinople."[36] He alluded to the important diplomatic and military interests that would accrue from breaching the Straits.[37] On the other hand, he argued against a continuation of further offensives in the west which was likely to produce nothing, but a continuation of extreme losses as shown in the previous attempts. Millerand, standing alone, was clearly uneasy at the mood in the cabinet. He observed that the war on the eastern front was going very badly and it was possible that, with the collapse of Russia, the Germans would be free to transfer numerous divisions to France for a gigantic assault on the Allied line. He reminded his colleagues that the safety of France must

---

33 Poincaré, *Au service*, Vol. 6, pp. 307, 313.
34 IWM: Wilson papers, entry in Wilson Diary, 22 June 1915; Poincaré, *Au service*, Vol. 6, p. 234.
35 Basil Collier, *Brasshat: The Biography of Field-Marshal Sir Henry Wilson* (London: Secker & Warburg, 1961), p. 228.
36 Ferry, *Les carnets*, pp. 101-2, 103-4.
37 Poincaré, *Au service*, Vol. 6, p. 335.

not be jeopardized by a secondary operation, no matter how important it seemed. Millerand tended to understate the inadequacy of the existing war policy, but the bare facts could not be concealed. Everyone was dejected over Joffre's recent failures, especially as there was nothing to show for the appalling casualties incurred. For them, as Poincaré maintained, the key to victory appeared to lie in the Dardanelles. If the English proved unequal to defeating the Turks, so the feeling ran, it should be up to the French to complete the job.

Thus far in the Dardanelles there were no signs that the defeat of the Turks was imminent, though it was not for want of trying. Before Gouraud was wounded he and Hunter-Weston had prepared a plan that would bring the centre in line with the advances on the flanks on 21 and 28 June. The idea was for the British to drive forward in the Achi Baba Nullah while the French, on their right, consolidated their earlier gains on the west bank of Kereves Dere.

French troops had been shaken by the severe injuries to Gouraud and Girodon and it was seen that they were not in the best frame of mind to overcome an enemy, protected by natural defences and a plethora of firepower. Nevertheless, Bailloud agreed, albeit reluctantly, to stand by the arrangement and carry out the French end of the operation, at least made easier by the capture of the Quadrilateral on 30 June which eliminated the threat of enfilading fire. The assault was originally set to begin on 7 July but delayed until the 12th to permit the French to move half of their artillery to support the British.

The appointed day was exceedingly hot and stifling even when the men woke up in the early morning hours. The attack on the French 700-yard front was to be conducted by eight battalions, four from each of the two divisions. The French artillery opened up at 4.35 am. The Turks were quick to respond and one of their shells caused absolute mayhem when it struck a dugout occupied by the staff of the 1st Division. Among the many casualties was General Masnou, the commander of the division, who was fatally wounded. Regarding the incident, Major Vassal wrote:

> We had a big fight on the 12th and I had all the wounded to evacuate ... Before the advance began at 7.15 a huge "105" shell fell on Post A of the Divisional command. Major Romieux, Chief of Staff, aged 45 was killed outright. General Masnou had his skull pushed in and his knee laid open. There were also wounded Colonel Bulleux, Captain Berge, Captain Boissonas, many non-commissioned officers and soldiers.

Romieux had been sitting next to Masnou and he was 43, not 45, when he was killed. Vassal had forged a special bond with Romieux and it was evident that he was shaken by his death. He wrote: "At first I got on rather badly with him because I held my own, but afterwards he loved our discussions. it is terrible to see a man like that die – a man of prodigious energy and unequalled activity and intelligence."[38]

At 7.35 am the infantry sprang out of the trenches and advanced in four lines as the artillery lifted to targets further inland. Sergeant D'Arnaud Pomiro, a member of the 175th Regiment (1st Division) was in the thick of the fighting before he was knocked out by a piece of flying rock. He survived the war and has left an account of the early action:

38 Vassal, *Uncensored Letters*, p. 154.

We leapt out without exception and at an athletic pace, under a thin rain of bullets and a few shrapnel shells, we were heading towards the second trench objective. The left got there a bit before me because, having to cover a longer distance, I had to go a few more meters. I arrived just the same and did not find a single Turk. But at the base of the ravine I saw at least three hundred of them swarming about, subject to a terrible sustained fire from us. For my part I fired eight rounds and killed four Turks, including an officer. I threw a grenade at a group of four who were creeping up to within 20 metres. Then I passed out. Regaining consciousness, I made my way … back to the rear, resting in areas less exposed to gun fire.[39]

As the French had lent much of their artillery to the British, they were unable to subject the Turkish positions to the usual intense bombardment. Nevertheless, enough damage had been done to leave the trenches in the first line half obliterated. The 2nd Division on the left, however, was unable to advance beyond the Turkish support line. The 1st Division on the right, despite meeting fierce resistance, captured two enemy lines blocking Le Ravin de la Mort. A second assault executed later in the day yielded the Rognon or most of it. Only one line of trenches located near the edge of the cliff overlooking the Kereves Dere remained in Turkish hands. Given the lay of the land the defenders were sheltered from bombardment and it helps explain why they were able to resist all French attempts to eject them.[40]

The British formations to the left of 2nd Division made little or no progress but that did not inhibit Hunter-Weston from renewing the attack in the afternoon. Bailloud agreed to cooperate along his entire front. At 4.50 pm, following an artillery barrage, the Allied troops moved forward as ordered. The results on the British side were pretty much the same as in the morning. They British passed over the crushed Turkish front trenches but soon after the advance was held up. The French for their part made slight gains on the left and in the centre.

Although the Allied units were exhausted and had been depleted by severe losses, Hunter-Weston decided to continue the battle the next day in order to forestall any attempt by the Turks to launch a counterattack. Bailloud was not keen on the idea but once more went along. As usual, Hamilton gave Hunter-Weston permission to go ahead. On the British front there were delays which resulted in the troops leaving their trenches 20 minutes after the bombardment had ceased. Consequently, the Turks were ready and the British attack was stopped dead in its tracks. The French fared much better. The objective of their two divisions, the 1st on the right and the 2nd on the left, was to capture the Turkish trenches on the west bank of Kereves Dere. Although the French made no headway on the left, next to the British, they were successful elsewhere. In the centre they drove the Turks back to their last remaining trench on the bank of the Kereves Dere, while on the right they seized a long trench at the mouth of the ravine and took 300 prisoners – making a total of 600 since the start of the battle.

The fighting during the two days had cost the French about 800 casualties and the British 3,100. Allied dead and wounded for the three battles on Cape Helles launched between 28 June and 12 July had totaled 12,300, 7,700 British and 4,600 French. It can be argued that the action had strengthened the Allied position and eased pressure on the Anzac front, but in the final

---

39   D'Arnaud Pomiro, *Les carnets des guerre* (Toulouse: Editions Privat, 2006), p. 183.
40   France, *L'Expédition des Dardanelles*, p. 96.

analysis the main objective, the capture of Achi Baba, was not achieved. The Turks suffered more heavily – reportedly over 30,000 men – but it should be pointed out that they could replace their losses more readily than the Allies.[41]

The bite and hold strategy ceased once the promised reinforcements arrived for the express purpose of launching an all out blitz later in the summer. As Hamilton concluded that the rugged terrain in Cape Helles was a formidable barrier to the capture of Achi Baba or Kilid Bahr, he decided that the main effort should be launched from Anzac. The French, however, preferred a landing in Asia, clearly reflecting the views of their successive commanders in the Dardanelles beginning, as we have seen, with d'Amade. Shortly before invalided home, Gouraud had urged a subsidiary landing on the Asiatic shore to silence the Turkish guns. The changing nature of the conflict had caused Gouraud to reverse an opinion expressed in his memo on 13 June. The arrival of German submarines had restricted the movement of Allied battleships in the area and allowed Turkish fire to increase dramatically. The relentless pounding from Turkish guns became unbearable and not only affected incoming traffic to Cape Helles but was seriously undermining the morale of French troops.[42] Bailloud went beyond his predecessor's proposal and wanted the landing in Asia to take the form of a major operation. He implored Millerand to insist that Hamilton divert two of his divisions for an offensive in Asia. "If a solution for this state of affairs is not promptly found", he warned, "it will mean the material and moral ruin of the French Expeditionary Corps."[43] Bailloud give a copy of his dispatch to Hamilton who glanced at it without reacting.

Hamilton never took into account the marked effect the constant shelling was having on the French troops, regarding it as mere inconvenience even though he had admitted earlier: "From the point of view of moral[e] one man killed by a shell from Asia is equivalent to ten men killed in action."[44]

He was confident that the shelling from Asia would be less troublesome once his forthcoming attack was successfully carried out. In the end he had no intention of abandoning his plan for the sake of what Gouraud himself conceded (in his memo on 13 June) would be a defensive measure which could not bring the Allies a step closer to victory.[45] In Paris, however, nothing short of decisive action in Asia would quell the unrest in the cabinet and pressure was exerted on Millerand to try to persuade the British to yield for once. Gouraud weighed in from his hospital bed. On 19 July he begged the Minister of War to intervene personally, stating emphatically that as long as the Turkish guns on the Asiatic side remain in place "the very existence of the French Corps is at stake."[46] The general had given the matter more thought and realized that the scope of the operation would have to be larger than he anticipated, requiring four divisions but no less than three.[47]

---

41   Aspinall-Oglander, *Gallipoli*, Vol. 2, pp. 111-12.
42   Gouraud to Millerand, 19 June 1915, in France, *Les armées françaises*, tome 8, Vol. 1, annexe no. 253.
43   Bailloud to Millerand , 4 July 1915, in France, *Les armées françaises*, tome 8, Vol. 1, annexe no. 269. See also annexes nos, 270 and 271.
44   Sir George Arthur, *Life of Lord Kitchener*, Vol. 3 (London: Macmillan, 1920), p. 158n.
45   Aspinall-Oglander, *Gallipoli*, Vol. 2, p. 146.
46   Gouraud to Millerand, 19 July 1915, in France, *Les armées francaises*, tome 8, Vol. 1, annexe no. 284.
47   Gouraud to Buat, 24 July 1915, in France, *Les armées françaises*, tome 8, Vol. 1, annexe no. 288.

Gouraud was no alarmist but he had become frustrated by Hamilton's attitude. On the same day he sent Millerand a note, he composed a personal letter to Major Marie Jean de Bertier, the French liaison officer with British Headquarters in the Dardanelles[48]: "I have been informed that Hamilton will not listen to anyone who favours a landing in Asia. I no longer understand him."[49]

The sense of urgency reflected in the appreciation by Gouraud finally drove Millierand to take matters in hand. On 20 July he appealed to Kitchener, claiming that the situation revealed by Bailloud, and confimed by Gouraud and d'Amade, called for the destruction of the Turkish batteries in Asia without delay. He observed that the daily shelling was eroding the strength and undermining the morale of the French Expeditionary Corps and he urged Kitchener to instruct Hamilton to take immediate measures consistent with the recommendations of Gouraud and Bailloud. [50] Kitchener, in turn, signaled Hamilton:

> The French state that the fire from the Asiatic side allow them no rest … They propose secondary operations on the Asiatic side to deal with enemy artillery, and suggest employment of 20,000 British assisted by French 75 monitors. Would the main scheme of our operation be jeopardized by thus detaching a considerable force, which may find itself employed with hostile forces of undetermined strength? [51]

Hamilton replied almost immediately: "I am sure you will agree, that a diversion if and when necessary, must be made at my own time, not at Bailloud's to whom I have not yet confided my plans."[52] Kitchener was satisfied with Hamilton's decision. He had from the beginning opposed involvement in Asia and, as he believed that Hamilton's attack, bolstered by five fresh divisions, would succeed, was unwilling to interfere in his plans. On 28 July he wrote to Millerand: "You will understand how difficult it is to impose upon a commander-in-chief an operation which does not fit in with his own carefully prepared plan."[53] To allow a military chief freedom of action in the field was a principle from which Millerand himself never deviated and he could hardly fault Kitchener from pursuing the same course. Still there was nothing to prevent Millerand from conducting an inquiry into whether it was feasible for the French alone to undertake an operation in Asia at a future date. Much would hinge on Hamilton's next attack.

On the Peninsula, Hamilton was busy making last minute adjustments before the great battle set to begin on 6 August. The plan that he adopted was similar to the one that he had carried out on 25 April the main difference was that the focal point of attack would take place at Anzac instead of Cape Helles. The idea was to break out from the Anzac beachhead and, after making a feint at Lone Pine to the south, converge on the Sari Bahr ridge. At the same time a complimentary assault would be mounted at Suvla Bay to the north to protect the Anzac flank

---

48 For de Bertier's background and his views on British and Australian led operations, see Elizabeth Greenhalgh and Col. Frédéric Guelton, "The French on Gallipoli and Observations on Australian and British forces during the August offensive" in Asley Ekins (ed.), *Gallipoli: A Ridge too Far* (Woombic, NSW, Australia: Exisle Publishing, 2013), pp. 221ff.
49 SHD: De Bertier papers, 7N 2170, Gouraud to de Bertier, 19 July 1915.
50 AN: Millerand papers, 470 AP/16, Millerand to Kitchener, 20 July 1915.
51 BNA: WO archives, tel. no. 1612, Kitchener to Hamilton, 21 July, 1915.
52 BNA: WO archives, tel. no. 1630, Hamilton to Kitchener, 23 July 1915.
53 SHD: AMG, 5N 132, Kitchener to Millerand, 28 July 1915.

and establish a base. There would also be a feint landing at Bulair and a diversionary attack at Cape Helles to hold the Turks there and attract some of their reinforcements from the Anzac sector. The plan was overly complicated, and its success was contingent on the proper execution of all the entities that were often interrelated. Then too the advance was not intended to push across the Peninsula but end with the capture of the Sari Bahr ridge. Presumably another operation, requiring more troops, would have to be mounted to overwhelm the Turkish defences on Kalid Bahr which guarded The Narrows.

Hamilton had arranged to use only British forces, recently augmented by five divisions, to execute the major part of his plan. The French remained at Cape Helles and were directed to extend their front as far west as Achi Baba Nullah which they carried out on the night of 31 July – 1 August.[54] Together with four British divisions of the VIII Corps, their role was to engage in feint attacks to assist the main offensive. Sickness and casualties had depleted three of the four British divisions and the two French divisions. The four British divisions (the 29th, 42nd, 52nd, and Royal Naval) had been reduced to 26,000 rifles against a war establishment of 46,000. The French divisions totaled 13,000 men out of an establishment of some 36,000.[55]

The VIII Corps objective was limited to an attack along a one-mile front in order to flatten a salient astride Krithia Nullah. On the afternoon of the 6th, the 29th Division started the diversionary assault after a brief and inadequate artillery bombardment. British intelligence had badly miscalculated the strength of Turkish defenders. Moving rapidly across No Man's Land, the units of the 29th were exposed to heavy artillery fire and cleverly concealed machine guns and suffered 2,000 casualties. The minor gains achieved were lost in counterattacks. In defiance of reason, the 42nd Division renewed the attack the next day and it too made no headway except to add 1,000 names to the casualty list. What is even worse the attacks continued for another week before Hamilton issued orders to end them lest it jeopardized the ability of the VIII Corps to hold its position without outside help.[56]

The day after the men of the 29th Division leaped into action, the French opened with an artillery barrage, preparatory to their assault against the western bank of Kereves Dere ravine. In view of the proximity of the opposing lines, gunners unwittingly fired shells that exploded behind the Turkish front trenches. They were understandably reluctant to shorten the range of their artillery pieces fearful of striking their own men. As a result, the Turkish front trenches were relatively undamaged when the French infantry surged forward. Still the French managed to break into Ottoman trenches with hand grenades and bayonets before counterattacks drove them back. Fighting continued sporadically until 10 August but the French failed to gain any ground. The operation had cost the French 703 casualties, including 5 officers and 230 other ranks killed.[57] The Turks had things so well in hand that they sent several reserve regiments north, precisely the reverse of what the Anglo-French diversionary attacks were meant to prevent.[58]

To repeat what was stated at the outset, this narrative was not intended to cover the movement of all the British units taking part in the various battles, only those, and briefly at that, which

54 Hamilton to Bailloud, 24 July 1915, in France, *Les armées françaises*, tome 8, Vol. 1, annexe no. 289.
55 Aspinall-Oglander, *Gallipoli*, Vol. 2, p. 141.
56 Aspinall-Oglander, *Gallipoli*, Vol. 2, ch.8.
57 France, *Expédition des Dardanelles*, tome 8, Vol. 1, p. 104n3b.
58 Erickson, *Gallipoli*, pp. 141-42.

had a bearing on French action. All that needs to be said about the offensive further north in August is that it ended in failure. Weary and disillusioned Hamilton admitted in a telegram to Kitchener on 17 August that his attack had not fared well, and he would require 95,000 more troops to give him the necessary superiority.

Kitchener was unable to meet Hamilton's request as (will be seen in the next chapter) he had already promised to support Joffre's plan for an autumn offensive. He told Hamilton that the best he could do under the circumstances was to supply him with drafts to replace his casualties. Hamilton replied that he would utilize the troops at his disposal to the best of his ability but unless reinforcements arrived shortly, he would have to consider reducing his front.[59]

In the days that followed, Kitchener and his colleagues searched painstakingly for a possible solution that would avoid the unpleasant option of admitting defeat and abandoning the Peninsula. Suddenly on 31 August the French government broke through the mood of despondency when it came forward with an offer to add four divisions to the two they already had in the Dardanelles. The British were delighted and yet puzzled by the French decision to assume a larger role in the operation. It was well known that the French had always opposed diverting large numbers of troops from the principal front. What had precipitated the change of heart which, it was assumed, had Joffre's acquiescence, if not approval. To this story we must now direct our attention.

---

59   Great Britain, *Final Report of the Dardanelles Commission*, pp. 51-52.

10

L'Affaire Sarrail

By the summer of 1915 there was growing dissatisfaction in the chamber of deputies over the manner in which the war was being conducted. Joffre drew most of the criticism. He was hammered for refusing to cooperate with the parliamentary commissions, for his series of abortive attacks which had resulted in staggering casualties but netted no significant gains, and for a belief that he was trying to set up a military dictatorship at Chantilly. Even the government had begun to lose faith in the Generalissimo's judgement but it was unthinkable to replace a soldier who was still popular with the press, idolized by the masses and the rank and file of the French army, and respected in the Allied countries. Joffre's strength was derived from the enormous prestige that he had gained as the "Saviour of the Marne" and sustained by denying subordinates public credit for taking action (as with Galliéni) which was apt to dim his own glory. In the first half of 1915 a popular rival appeared in the person of General Maurice Sarrail. In response to the challenge, Joffre provoked an incident which not only undermined his own position but triggered a return to prewar partisan politics that threatened to shatter the tenous *union sacrée*. This chapter in the French political account of the Great War is known habitually as *l'affaire Sarrail*.

Maurice Sarrail was born at Carcassone, near the Pyrenean border, on 6 April 1856 and reared in economically secure circumstances. He graduated from Saint-Cyr in 1877, ranking third in a class of 345. During his military ascent he pursued a course which set him apart from his brother officers. While orthodox French officers were apt to be devout Catholics and even harbor royalist sympathies, Sarrail was a free thinker, an anti-clerical republican and a Freemason. In the late 1890s Sarrail had been one of the few officers to have spoken in defence of Dreyfus and, upon the latter's vindication, found the door open for rapid advancement. In 1900 he went to the War Ministry and served under the reforming General André who appointed him the following year to command the infantry school at St. Maixent where men in the ranks were trained to become loyal republican officers. From 1904-7 he was commandant of the military guard at the Palais Bourbon – which housed the chamber of deputies – and used his time to strengthen social contacts with the leading politicians on the left. He became director of infantry at the War Ministry in 1907 and in 1911 his friend Joseph Caillaux promoted him *général de division*. When a left-wing government came to power in 1914 he was slated to replace Joffre in the autumn but the First World War broke out before the change in command could take place. Sarrail's rapid rise owed nothing to demonstrated ability on the battlefield, but was due partly to his administrative skill and partly to his political sympathies and ties to the parties on the left.

Aided presumably by his political connections, Sarrail entered the Great War as commander of the VI Corps, a unit of General Ruffey's Third Army. When given an opportunity it turned out that as a field commander Sarrail showed initiative and ability. In the Third Army's first encounter at the battle at Vitron in the lower Ardennes, the VI Corps gave a good account of itself but fell back to Verdun to avoid encirclement. Joffre, judging that Ruffy had lost his nerve, replaced him with Sarrail on 30 August, one week before the battle of the Marne. Attacked by a superior German force, Sarrail clung tenaciously to Verdun and ignored Joffre's order to retreat if pressure should become too great. By anchoring the eastern line while the main issue was decided further west, he was credited with contributing to the Allied victory at the Marne. He became a national hero and there were many on the left who began to promote him as a spectacular field commander and an ideal successor to Joffre.[1]

In February and March of 1915 some of Sarrail's most fervent admirers passed around two anonymous memoranda to certain parliamentary members, proclaiming the superiority of Sarrail over Joffre by drawing comparison between the two officers. The authors concluded that if Joffre were indisposed for a fortnight and the supreme command entrusted to Sarrail, the Germans would most assuredly be expelled from France as he would apply new strategic concepts "that would cost us less dearly than the war of attrition which we have endured for five months and which we shall go on enduring, leaving our richest regions of the north completely ruined."[2]

Whether or not Sarrail was in collusion with the authors cannot be determined. Sarrail's enemies maintained that the circulars contained sensitive military information and could only have been drawn up by members of his staff. Sarrail later replied that such a charge was absurd as Joffre's son-in-law was on his staff.[3] It is certain, however, that Sarrail was aware, and did not disapprove, of the movement to have him replace Joffre. It was one thing for Sarrail to take a jaundice view of Joffre's attrition policy, quite another to allow his idolaters to engage in underhanded methods of intrigue against his chief.

Not much escaped Joffre's notice in the army, whether of a military or political nature, and he was undoubtedly aware of the memoranda that denigrated GQG's leadership and urged his removal in favour of Sarrail. He referred to the incident in passing in his memoirs, observing that as soon as the front was stabilized, Sarrail became engrossed in "matters of a political and personal nature" instead "of purely military affairs which up to then, had suffice to engage his attention." Joffre went on to say that his rival "received all the Members of Parliament who passed near him, in particular M. Doumer"[4] who spread malicious rumours "about myself."[5] Joffre's star had begun to fade, and he was much more attentive to potential rivals. He worried

---

1 Tanenbaum, *Sarrail*, chs. 1-2; Palmer, *Gardeners of Salonica*, pp. 29-30; Paul Coblentz, *The Silence of Sarrail* (London: Hutchinson, 1930), pp. 23ff; Gabriel Terrail, *Sarrail et les armées d'Orient* (Paris: Ollendorff, 1920), pp. 17-19.
2 Terrail, *Sarrail*, p. 178.
3 Terrail, *Sarrail*, p. 192.
4 He was a senator and Galliéni's former secretary of civil affairs. He made a habit of visiting army commanders and informing them that it was inevitable that Galliéni, who was the real hero of the Marne, should replace Joffre. See Galliéni (ed.), *Carnets de Galliéni*, p. 131.
5 Joffre, *Personal Memoirs*, Vol. 2, p. 372.

much less about possible challenges from monarchists who rose to prominence in the army than popular republican generals as he understood that a majority of parliamentarians would back their cause. Joffre took what steps he could to safeguard his position from Sarrail and inevitably their relationship grew increasingly antagonistic.

The two generals were temperamentally incompatible and, to exacerbate their differences, held contrasting strategic views. Joffre was simple in manner and speech but he was authoritarian and a rigid disciplinarian. He had the utmost confidence in his reigning military policy and expected his leading subordinates to follow his lead without question. He required daily reports from his commanders in the field and insisted that they remain aloof from politics.

Sarrail was unconcerned about military precedence, neither respected nor admired Joffre, and showed a strong disposition for political intrigue. Impatient of delays and higher control, he preferred to chart his own course rather than strictly follow directives from Chantilly.[6] While dining with Poincaré on 28 March 1915, Sarrail was critical of Joffre's ongoing military policy in the Argonne where the attacks netted little gains at very high costs. He saw little chance of penetrating the German lines and expressed preference for an operation either in Belgium or Alsace. He blasted Joffre personally and complained about receiving from GQG a stream of orders and counter-orders.[7]

Joffre had his own list of complaints against Sarrail. He alleged that Sarrail often ignored directives from GQG, that he promoted men on the basis of his own political leanings and that his reports were sometimes deceptive, in particular when he failed to announce the loss of trenches in the hope of winning them back before it was discovered. By mid-1915 Joffre's personal relations with Sarrail had collapsed and he waited for the right moment to strike. A military setback on Sarrail's front afforded Joffre a pretext to get rid of his troublesome subordinate.

A two-month period of relative inactivity in the Argonne sector came to an end on 30 June when the Germans struck in force against the Third Army, now forming part of the Eastern Army Group. Accompanied by heavy artillery fire and poison gas, the well-coordinated German thrust, carried out on a wider front than previous attacks, drove in part of the Third Army's front and inflicted heavy casualties. Joffre sent two divisions of reinforcements to allow Sarrail to regain the initiative. Sarrail's counterattack was started too late and, despite two violent attempts to recapture the lost crest, the Third Army was thrown back to its starting line. Joffre saw his opportunity to intervene. On 14 July he called upon General Yvon Dubail, the supreme commander of the Eastern Army Group, to investigate Sarrail's conduct of the Third Army's operations in the Argonne. Joffre's knew what he was doing when he chose Dubail, a staunch republican and, like Sarrail, a favourite of the far left. If Dubail should call into question Sarrail's action the radical and socialist elements in parliament could not claim that his judgement was coloured by political bias. Joffre was not known for unusual astuteness, flexibility, or imagination in military matters, but as a politician he possessed an almost "Oriental" guile.

On 20 July Dubail submitted the results of his inquiry in the form of two long memoranda. In the first he was rather ambivalent about Sarrail's role in the recent operations in the Argonne,

---

6   Emile Herbillion, *Souvenirs d'un officier de liaison pendant la guerre mondiale*, Vol. 1 (Paris: Jules Tallandier, 1930), pp. 167-68; BNA: War Office archives, WO 159/11, Col. H. Yarde-Buller (Head of British Mission at GQG) to Kitchener, 26 July 1915.
7   Poincaré, *Au Service*, Vol. 6, pp. 136-37.

complimenting him in some instances but reproaching him for delaying the launch of a counter-attack. The second report, focusing on the state of morale within the Third Army and its headquarters, was more damaging. Dubail found that Sarrail had shown preferential treatment towards certain generals and was on bad terms with others, creating an intolerable spirit of unrest throughout the Third Army. Dubail recommended a change in the leadership of the Third Army and suggested that Sarrail be assigned to take charge of the less important Army of Lorraine.[8] Joffre could now justify on military grounds his move to dismiss or demote Sarrail. Although he may have felt he was on firm ground, he miscalculated the extent of Sarrail's political support. Joffre wasted no time in sending his liaison officer with a letter (on 21 July), informing Viviani that Sarrail would be replaced as commander of the Third Army. In making the announcement Joffre indicated that, instead of transferring Sarrail to take charge of another army, he proposed to appoint him a corps commander unless the government thought otherwise.

At the cabinet meeting on 22 July the matter of Sarrail's removal was presented as a *fait accompli*. There was agreement among the ministers on both the right and left, with Millerand a notable exception, that Joffre's action was unduly severe. Alexandre Ribot, the finance minister, echoed the general sentiment when he pointed out that it was unfair to discipline Sarrail for his questionable conduct of operations in the Argonne whereas General d'Urbal – known to be a reactionary and strong Catholic – had not been punished for a similar setback at Arras. The cabinet had the authority but did not dare to overturn Joffre's decision for to do so would certainly have arouse his anger and probably invited his resignation. It was thus decided to ask Joffre if he would soften his attitude and consider Dubail's recommendation of sending Sarrail to command the Army of Lorraine. Briand spoke out against the idea on the grounds that a discontented Sarrail would remain a centre of controversy if he remained in France. Colonel Edmond Buat, Millerand's *chef de cabinet*, had confided to Poincaré and presumably to the leading ministers, that Joffre would prefer to send Sarrail to the Dardanelles in succession to General Gouraud. This seemed like an ideal solution and the cabinet adopted Ribot's resolution, asking Joffre for a written statement of his views.[9]

That evening Sarrail received a telegram informing him of his dismissal and instructing him to report to the War Ministry the following day. On arriving in Paris on 23 July, Sarrail, in response to a telephone call, stopped by the office of Louis Malvy, the Radical Socialist Minister of the Interior, whose faith in the old soldier remained unaltered. Malvy revealed that the government was contemplating sending him to the Dardanelles to command the French expeditionary force.

After Sarrail took leave of Malvy, he went directly to the War Ministry where he was greeted somewhat stiffly by Millerand and Viviani. Grimly aware of what the two men were about to propose, he listened politely until they had their say and then turned down the new assignment, explaining that it was substantially inferior to the one he had been deprived of. Sarrail correctly discerned that Joffre and Millerand were anxious to throw him out of the country and he had no intention of playing into their hands. Humiliated that he had been unjustly cashiered from his post, or so he believed, he announced that he would retire from the army and return to his home

---

[8] The reports by Dubail are less critical than the version in Joffre's *Personal Memoirs*, Vol. 2, pp. 607-15.
[9] Poincaré, *Au service*, Vol. 6, pp. 336-37.

in Montauban.¹⁰ Contrary to what he said, it did not appear from his subsequent activities that he was prepared to leave the army quietly.

News that Sarrail had been deprived of his command rocked the chamber of deputies. The politicians had never fully discarded their mistrust of the army. They held a lingering fear that at the right opportunity the high command would instigate a *coup d'état* and bring an end to the republic. The intensity of feeling in the chamber over the fate of Sarrail brought old animosities to the surface and exacerbated tensions with the Viviani ministry and the leadership of the army.

The breaking of generals in the French army was not uncommon and rarely evoked outside interest. In the first six weeks of the war Joffre had retired three army commanders, 10 corps commanders and 38 division commanders, on the grounds that they were incompetent or had collapsed under pressure.¹¹ The royalist and clericalist generals may have been dominant in the upper echelons of the army but their support in parliament was negligible – "three dozen rattlepates", according to Clemenceau.¹² The same was not true of republican generals who commanded a large following in the chamber. And Sarrail was especially popular for he was viewed as a republican Maid of Orleans. Colonel Emile Herbillon, the liaison officer between GQG and the government, questioned Joffre's action: "Sarrail is a symbol [and] he should not have been touched. Removing him from his command is to slap parliament in the face by victimizing the only republican general."¹³ Although Caillaux was no longer in office to agitate for Sarrail's reinstatement, his numerous followers in parliament could be counted on to mitigate his fall from grace. Viviani had to tread warily if he had any hope of negotiating through the political minefield. The socialists in the chamber were becoming unruly despite all efforts to show that Sarrail's removal was founded on a report by Dubail. Joffre wrote in hindsight that they "refused to look upon it in any other light than a manifestation of spite."¹⁴ Viviani, never the most adept of politicians, was at his wits end to find a solution to the crisis. He knew that he could not afford to alienate the socialists whose departure from the *union sacrée* would spell the end of his ministry. He was in despair when he approached Poincaré on 23 July to inform him that Sarrail had turned down the command of the French expeditionary force in the Dardanelles. "Did you accept his refusal?" Poincaré inquired. Viviani replied: "What was I supposed to do? The Chamber is in an incredible state of agitation. Violette [a radical republican] on the one hand and the socialists on the other have been trying to see me all day to protest Sarrail's mistreatment. I managed to keep out of sight. But the situation is becoming impossible, since Parliament must be reckoned with."¹⁵

To avoid a rupture of the *union sacrée* the cabinet delegated three of its members – Gaston Doumergue, Albert Sarraut and Jean Malvy – to try to persuade Joffre to change his mind and appoint Sarrail to command the Army of Lorraine. It was subsequently decided to remove the two Radical Socialists, Sarraut and Malvy, from the delegation as they were known to

---

10   Maurice Sarrail, *Mon commandement en Orient 1916–1918* (Paris: Ernest Flammarion, 1920), pp. vii-viii; Coblentz, *Sarrail*, pp. 101-03; Poincaré, *Au service*, Vol. 6, p. 340.
11   Ferry, *Carnets Secrets,* annexe no. 7, p. 248. The journalist, Léopold Marcellin in *Politique et politiciens pendant la guerre*, Vol. 1 (Paris: La Renaissance du Libre, 1932), 1932), p. 98, claims that up to the Sarrail incident Joffre had sacked 138 generals.
12   Jean Martet, *Georges Clemenceau* (London: Longmans, Green & Co., 1930), p. 281.
13   Herbillon, *Souvenirs,* Vol. 1, p. 171.
14   Joffre, *Personal Memoirs,* Vol. 2, p. 376.
15   Poincaré, *Au service,* Vol. 6, p. 340.

be on intimate terms with Sarrail and only Doumergue, accompanied by Millerand, went to Chantilly. Here the two men learned that Joffre had already assigned General Augustin Gérard, a staunch republican, to the post. It was a move worthy of a consummate politician and confirmed Galliéni's observation that Joffre was the "the most cunning of men."[16] He had at one stroke disarmed many of his critics. Joffre added that he was quite willing to give Sarrail command of an army corps and he had no objections if he were placed in charge of the French troops in the Dardanelles.[17] Joffre secretly harboured the hope that Sarrail would be packed off to the obscurity of a colonial garrison.

The blaze in the chamber showed no signs of dying down and there was evidence that behind the scenes, Sarrail was intriguing with certain leftist deputies to keep stoking the fires until he achieved a measure of satisfaction. Different political groups had united and as one were centring their salvos on Millerand as a tool of the high command. Socialist editor Gustave Hervé wrote in *La Guerre sociale* that the left had been so exercised by the humiliating treatment of Sarrail, whom he referred to as the "pride of the whole Republican party", that they were prepared to leave the *union sacrée* unless certain conditions were met. The first was that Sarrail be given a new command as compensation for his earlier dismissal. The next was an arrangement that would reestablish government control over the army.[18] The inference on the latter point was that this was impossible to achieve as long as Millerand shielded Joffre and hindered investigating service commissions. Thus the only way to satisfy parliament's wishes was to replace Millerand with someone able to restrict the authority of the high command.

In the interest of restoring order in the chamber, the cabinet decided to send Sarraut with the aim to convince Sarrail to reconsider his decision and accept command of the French forces in the Dardanelles. The Radical Socialist Minister (of Public Instruction) was urged to stress the importance of the mission, the need to capture Constantinople post-haste and assurances that the size of the expeditionary force would be increased.[19] Sarraut tried his luck during the early evening of the 24th but found Sarrail unreceptive to his blandishments.

Following Sarraut's departure, Sarrail received the visit of two political supporters, Pierre Renaudel, leader of the Socialist party, and Henry Franklin-Bouillon, a prominent Radical Socialist deputy and vice president of the chamber Army Commission. They argued that he should accept the proffered assignment, making it clear that, in view of Joffre's refusal to rescind his decision, commanding an army on the Western Front was out of the question. Franklin-Bouillon went so far as to promise that everything would be done to induce the English to accept Sarrail as the supreme commander of the Anglo-French force.[20] At the end of the discussion the general began to waver, but he remained non-committal. Sarrail may not have been enthusiastic about going to the Dardanelles but in sober moments he must have realized that the general who entered Constantinople in triumph, to quote Col. H. Yarde-Buller, Kitchener's liaison officer at GQG, "would have a unique page in history."[21]

16 Galliéni (ed.), *Carnets de Galliéni*, p. 208.
17 Poincaré, *Au service*, Vol. 6, p. 341.
18 Tanenbaum, *Sarrail*, p. 60.
19 Poincaré, *Au service*, Vol. 6, p. 342.
20 Tanenbaum, *Sarrail*, p. 59.
21 BNA: War Office archives, WO 159/11, Yarde-Buller to Kitchener, 6 August 1915.

A late evening meeting was arranged between Briand and Sarrail. Briand believed that the best way to restore a semblance of political calm was to induce Sarrail to accept a post outside of France. He certainly had a personal stake in smoothing things over. He was eager to replace Viviani, if there was a change of ministry, and by conciliating Sarrail he would be strengthening his hand with the socialists and Radicals in the chamber. Briand reiterated Sarraut's message, confirmed that if the English were amenable he would be appointed supreme commander in the Dardanelles and that, away from France, he would no longer have to worry about Joffre's unwarranted measures against him. By using his famed powers of persuasion he succeeded in winning over Sarrail, subject to certain conditions. "I would accept the command offered if it were augmented but I would assume possession only after the increase had been carried out", declared Sarrail.[22] Viviani was encouraged by the sudden turn of events which he reported to the President the next day.[23]

With the expectation that a settlement with Sarrail was near at hand, Millerand turned his attention to laying plans for a landing in Asia which he considered was vital for the welfare of the CEO. He had concluded that the steadfast refusal of the British to intervene in Asia should not preclude the French from eventually acting on their own. On the 24th Millerand contacted Bailloud to request his opinion on the number of divisions that would be required for two types of operation under consideration by the general staff. It was to be assumed, he indicated, that regardless of which operation was chosen, it was to be executed entirely by French forces:

1. What effectives do you judge necessary and sufficient for an operation designed to occupy the battery emplacements on the shore [of Asia]?
2. Same question for an operation of greater scope, comprising the preceding but continuing along the coast of Asia to open the Dardanelles.
3. Do you believe that the first operation can be accomplished without entailing the second?[24]

Bailloud wasted no time in forwarding his appreciation to Millerand. In reply to the first question he considered that two divisions would suffice to silence the batteries in the Kum Kale region. As for the second query he felt that five or seven divisions would be needed, depending on which of the two schemes the government preferred: occupation of the area beyond Kum Kale (where the guns were located), followed by an advance along the shore in conjunction with the fleet; or a landing at Besika Bay and a march on Chanak away from the shore and outside the main line of Turkish defences but which would mean forsaking the assistance of the ships and require two more divisions. With regard to the last query, it was not only possible but advisable as preparations for the second operation would be rather lengthy when the need for rapid action was indisputable. Still Bailloud made it clear that another campaign must follow, as an extension of the first, to take control of Chanak; otherwise, if unimpeded, the Turks would concentrate their artillery at Chanak from where the relentless shelling would resume.[25]

22 Sarrail, *Mon commandement*, p. viii.
23 Poincaré, *Au service*, Vol. 6, p. 344.
24 Millerand to Bailloud, 24 July 1915, in France, *Les armées françaises*, tome 8, Vol. 1, annexe no. 287.
25 Bailloud to Millerand, 26 July 1915, in France, *Les armées françaises*, tome 8, Vol. 1, annexe no. 290.

It was in the hands of the cabinet to decide the next step when it met on the 27th. Viviani opened his remarks by observing that relations between parliament and the government had grown worse. It was apparent to everyone that a resolution could not be delayed much longer. A discussion followed and ended with a consensus to adopt the recommendation of Bailloud and Gouraud for an Asiatic operation and to augment the French force in the Dardanelles by three or four divisions. Since Millerand did not have an organized force from which to draw upon, it would be necessary to obtain the requisite reinforcements from Joffre's command. The cabinet left it up to Viviani and Millerand to make the necessary arrangements with the Generalissimo.[26]

The two ministers travelled on the same day to Chantilly where the talks with Joffre failed to produce any useful results. Joffre was not in a mood to entertain any suggestion that would decrease his striking power in France. He stiffened his back and outlined his position which he later confirmed in a long letter to Millerand.

Joffre's note was brought over to the minister of war while he was sitting at a cabinet meeting on 29 July. It covered a wide range of political and military issues, the central part of which ran as follows:

> The action now going on in the Gallipoli Peninsula should not be abandoned but should be carried on with the means required to bring it to a successful conclusion. At the same time care must be taken that the situation in France should not be compromised by untimely withdrawals from that theatre. At this period, the end of July, it seems to me impossible to withdraw any troops.
>
> It would be a different matter in September when the battle I propose to engage in Champagne and Artois has come to an end. Moreover, an interval of this duration appears necessary to enable a definite plan of operations against Constantinople to be drawn up, and for preparations to be made. It is clear that our setbacks in the East were due to defects in the general plan of operations, and to insufficiency of means. I, therefore, propose that a rational plan of operations be drawn up and that, with this end in view, an officer of my staff be sent to the Dardanelles to establish contact with the troops and obtain all necessary information.[27]

Millerand read out Joffre's comments, most of which he and Viviani had already revealed to the other members of the cabinet. There was nothing of consequence other than an inference that preparations for the proposed operation should be under the direction of GQG. If true, the cabinet needed to disabuse Joffre of that notion. Sarrail would never accept the Dardanelles command if he were subject to the orders of someone he hated as much as Joffre. To set the record straight, the ministers invited Joffre to confer with them at the Elysée on Saturday, 31 July.

Joffre arrived late in the morning and the interview with him, according to the President, was frank and cordial. Joffre made no reference to his paper and simply stated that it would

---

26   Poincaré, *Au service*, vol, 6, pp. 346-47.
27   Joffre, *Personal Memoirs*, Vol. *2, p. 371*. For the entire document see Joffre to Millerand, 29 July 1915, in France, *Les armées françaises*, tome 8, Vol. 1, annexe no. 296. The date on the document is 19 July but it is obviously a misprint.

be difficult for him to spare four divisions and especially their artillery and ammunition requirements. As others weighed in bit by bit he was brought around to the cabinet's way of thinking and it was decided that the question of the supplementary operation in Asia should be studied but that it would be carried out only if Hamilton's forthcoming assault failed. Joffre went on to talk about his plans for an offensive in five or six weeks which prompted Poincaré to remind him that before moving ahead he needed to consult with the cabinet.

That afternoon, the civil authorities reconvened without Joffre and agreed to appoint Sarrail commander of the French expeditionary force in the Dardanelles. He was to start to make arrangements immediately and would leave in a fortnight to take charge of the two divisions already on the Peninsula.[28] This was the first time since August 1914 that Joffre's views on military matters had been overridden. The government had begun the process of liberation from the role of Joffre's obedient servant.

Joffre's grip on power may have been slipping, but he was unwilling to yield to the dictates of the cabinet without a fight. It bothered him that he was being pressured to divert troops from his front for the benefit of a sideshow he despised. He recognized that his failure to block the despatch of reinforcements to the east could also have the effect of assisting his hated rival. Joffre was hoping that the offer to send Sarrail to the Dardanelles to command a mere two divisions would be considered so degrading as to invite his resignation from the army. Still he also realized that his nemesis might be enticed to accept the proffered post if the French contingent were enlarged to six divisions.

Sarrail was summon to the Ministry of War on 3 August for talks with Millerand. Asked to present his "desiderata", he listed three conditions: (1) an army would have to be constituted and take the name of the Army of the Orient; (2) unlike his predecessors, he did not want to be under the orders of an English general; (3) he would not leave without the extra four divisions. Sarrail was adamant about the last point, convinced that if he left France without the promised reinforcements, he would receive not "a rifle nor a cannon" and consequently would be unable to accomplish anything.[29]

When the cabinet gathered on 5 August, attention was first directed to Millerand's recent interview with Sarrail. Many members were nervous about doing anything that would appear to humiliate a republican general. To cross that line, one member declared, would result in the collapse of the cabinet. The ministers as a group were eager to come to terms with Sarrail. Poincaré interjected to say that their ultimate decision should not be influenced by personal considerations.[30] The President did not express his true feelings in the cabinet but from what he told others he was not anxious to see Sarrail depart for the Dardanelles. To be sure he wanted an end to the political crisis, but he seemed to think that Sarrail would not be pacified if he were banished to a remote outpost. He suspected that Sarrail would not fit easily into this narrowed groove in the eastern Mediterranean and that nothing could stifle all the bitterness he would feel at being transferred to a secondary theatre. In these circumstances Poincaré had grave doubts that the General would be able to collaborate with the English, work in harmony with his subordinates, or provide inspirational leadership to his men. Similar views had been

---

28 Poincaré, *Au service,* Vol. 6, pp. 350-51.
29 Sarrail, *Mon commandment*, p. viii.
30 Poincaré, *Au service,* Vol. pp. 7, 11.

expressed by Gouraud and Bailloud, the latter had reportedly indicated that he would prefer to return to France rather than serve under Sarrail.[31]

A new issue was unfolded when Millerand read a letter he had received from Joffre two days earlier, explaining it would be injudicious to send four divisions to the Dardanelles as requested by the government. He pointed out that the operation had been a dismal failure and that it would require more than four division to reverse the tide. To compound matters there were no plans setting forth the objectives, the landing spots or difficulties likely to be encountered. According to Joffre, France did not possess the military strength to reduce its front by four divisions at a time when it must take action to assist the Russians who had suffered serious reverses. He pointed out that he was bound by the protocol of the Allied conference of 7 July at which all the representatives had approved of an offensive aimed at lessening the pressure on the Russians.[32]

As indicated earlier, the full results of the conference were not communicated at once to the members of the government. In fact it was just before the cabinet met that day (5 August) that a copy of the minutes of the conference was distributed. Poincaré and the other members of the cabinet were livid that Joffre's plans had been deliberately concealed from them. It had been understood at the Anglo-French meeting held the previous day that there would be no more major offensives for the remainder of the year. It was evident, moreover, that the decision to mount attacks in the west would quash the cabinet's proposal to send reinforcements to the Dardanelles – which everyone agreed had been Joffre's goal all along. Millerand sat uneasily as he came under renewed criticism for failing in his duty to the government and for his continued self-effacement before Joffre. In recent months Poincare's relations with Millerand had become strained and after the cabinet meeting broke up, he immediately went to his office and wrote him a sharp note:

> What is this? What are these contemplated operations? Is it to be a repetition of Champagne, Woevre, Eparges or Souchez? Joffre told us himself, in his long letter relative to the Dardanelles, that the wear and tear of our forces has surpassed his predictions. I must formally ask you that no new offensive be undertaken without revealing to me its conditions and objective, or without my being able to consider whether, in a war which will surely extend until next year, anything like premature action may not constitute a dangerous squandering of strength. When I am fully informed, we will consider, you and I, the situation, and if there is a good reason, lay the matter before the government. Until then no definite or irreparable step must be taken. The question must not only be based on military consideration for it also affects our diplomatic and national concerns.[33]

Millerand had been through an exhausting cabinet session on the 5th but the day for him was not yet over. After considering Sarrail's demands, Millerand had set up another meeting with him which took place at the Ministry of War late in the afternoon. Millerand opened the discussion by announcing that Sarrail had formally been named commander of the Army of the Orient.

---

31 BNA: Grey papers, FO 800/58, Bertie to Grey, 3 August 1915; BNA: War Office archives, WO 159/11, Yarde-Buller to Kitchener, 8 August 1915.
32 SHD: AMG, 20 N/87, dossier 13, no. 8, Joffre to Millerand, 3 August 1915.
33 Poincaré, *Au service*, Vol. 7, p. 14.

He made no reference to Sarrail's status, whether he would be independent or subordinated to Hamilton. Millerand was rather vague about the question of reinforcements as it was still up in the air. Evidently the government could not keep its promise to Sarrail as long as Joffre was unwilling to release the requisite divisions. Millerand simply stated that Sarrail would not be sent to the Dardanelles without an increase in the expeditionary force. Meantime, he invited the General to express his views on what "a French army ought to do in the Orient." It was an irregular request since it was the responsibility of the government, not the commander, to set the aims of the mission. However these were unusual times and Millerand deemed it politically expedient to keep Sarrail busy so as to deter him from intriguing with his left-wing supporters. As Sarrail was about to leave, Millerand warned him not to "associate with parliamentarians."[34]

On 11 August, Sarrail submitted a written appreciation of how he viewed what the French army might do in the eastern Mediterranean. He observed that the two French divisions currently on Gallipoli were crowded into vulnerable positions and reduced to fighting under conditions of trench warfare and that progress would be difficult slow and costly. He suggested leaving the English to pursue operations in the Peninsula, while his own forces, including the two presently under Hamilton, be used in another theatre. He put forward a number of schemes. These included establishing a firm beachhead in Asia opposite Tenedos and a march along the coast to silence the enemy's batteries; a more ambitious operation to begin farther south in the Bay of Adramyti with the object of marching on Chanak; landings at Smyrna, possibly at Alexandretta, or, as he preferred, an advance into Serbia by way of Salonica. The first two schemes would contribute to the original idea of capturing Constantinople while the remaining three represented a radical change in strategic objectives. On seizing control of Smyrna, the idea was to dig in and defend the city port against Turkish attacks until the end of the war. The only benefit to what otherwise appears to be a useless exercise would be to relieve some pressure on the British in the Peninsula. A similar action at Alexandretta would place the French in a position to capture the important Baghdad-Bahn railway at a future date, incite the Arabs to revolt, and assist the advance of the British in Mesopotamia. At Salonica, the presence of French troops would induce the wavering Balkan states to side with the Entente. The French and the Balkan forces could then link with the Serbian army, preparatory to a great offensive against Austria-Hungary.[35]

As might be expected Joffre, to whom the memorandum was sent, dismissed outright Sarrail's proposed operations. He considered the various schemes too sketchy, with no thought of problems that were likely to be encountered, the extent of enemy resistance and the chances of success and rejected them all as either impractical or posing excessive risks and, in the case of the Balkan enterprise, anticipating results based on uncertain diplomatic arrangements.[36] Sarrail admitted that the criticism was probably valid but, as he correctly remarked, "the duty of deciding where an army should be sent and what it should do is the task not of the soldier but of the government."[37]

---

34 Sarrail, *Mon commandement*, p. ix; King, *Generals and Politicians,* pp. 76-77.
35 Sarrail, Note au suject de la question militaire en Orient, 11 August 1915, in *Les armées françaises*, tome 8, Vol. 1, annexe no. 315.
36 Joffre to Millerand, 18 August 1915, in France, *Les armées françaises*, tome 8, Vol. 1, annexe no. 318.
37 Sarrail, *Mon commandement*, p. x.

Whilst Sarrail showed no signs that he was in a rush to accept a new assignment except on his own terms, some of his more fervent admirers were anxious to speed up the process. A handful of deputies, acting more or less on their own, engaged in subtle ways to make Sarrail's appointment as supreme commander in the Dardanelles more palatable to the British government by lobbying its representatives in Paris. They circulated reports hailing Sarrail's contribution to the victory at the Marne and decrying as unjust his removal from his post which it attributed to Joffre's jealousy. Chief among these lobbyists was Franklin-Bouillon who collared any eminent Englishman he ran into, regardless of whether he had any political influence back home. He spoke to Lord Alexander Murray of Elibank whose political career ended in 1912 when he was forced to resign after being accused of insider trading in the Marconi scandal. It is difficult to assess how much weight Murray's opinion would have carried at the ministerial level for, although his reputation had taken a hit, he was on close terms with Eric Drummond, private secretary to Sir Edward Grey and Asquith. Franklin-Bouillon did not scruple to play upon British fears that the French might soon be forced to seek a release from the war. He hinted that the French were gaining the impression that the English did not have the ability to wrap up the conflict in the eastern Mediterranean. He claimed that France was on the verge of a crisis – presumably because of the series of military defeats on the Western Front with the resultant staggering casualties – and that, unless the Dardanelles expedition succeeded, there would be such a serious revulsion of opinion that it could lead to a movement for a separate peace. Not surprisingly, Franklin-Bouillon held that a much-needed victory in the Dardanelles could best be assured by a competent leader like General Sarrail.[38]

Franklin-Bouillon adopted much the same line when he talked with Lord Bertie, the British Ambassador. Brimming with self-assurance, he maintained that Russia was beaten and would undoubtedly conclude a settlement with Germany. France was near exhaustion, one-eighth of its territory was occupied by the enemy and, as things stood, could not continue for more than a year. The anxiety in the country could be dispelled if the Allies, by executing a bold coup in the Dardanelles, drove the Turks out of the war before the end of the summer. According to Franklin-Bouillon, Allied fortunes in the Dardanelles would change if General Sarrail were appointed supreme commander. He reasoned that "such command ought not be governed by the number of troops furnished by each of the two Allies, nor questions of national pride." He added: "National safety should be the sole deciding factor."[39]

Bertie had no interest in Sarrail's fate – anymore than the British government which would not have intervened in a purely internal policy – but he was concerned over Franklin-Bouillon's claim that France was approaching the limit of its endurance. He called on Briand and related his encounter with the Radical Socialist deputy. Briand dismissed Franklin-Bouillon as a "busy-body" with an inflated sense of his own importance and currently in search of a portfolio. He maintained that this politician carried no weight outside the rue de Valois (site of Radical Socialist headquarters) party and that he had no authority. He stated unequivocally that there was no substance to the allegation and that the French government intended to fight to the end. Moving on to another relevant topic, he indicated that as far as Sarrail was concerned, it was decided to appoint him to take charge of the French troops in the Dardanelles but that there was

---

38 BNA: Grey papers, FO 800/60, Murray to Drummond, 4 August 1915.
39 BNA: Bertie papers, FO 800/181, Bertie to Grey, 4 August 1915.

no question of proposing to London that he be placed in supreme command.[40] Bertie received a different response when he went over to the Quai d'Orsay. He gave a brief summary of his interview with Delcassé in reporting the incident to the Foreign Office:

> I enquired of M. Delcassé as to the truth of the report which I had heard from Socialist quarters that General Sarrail is to succeed General Gouraud at the Dardanelles. Delcassé said: "not that I know of." On coming out of his room I read in *Le Temps*: *"Le conseil des ministers a désigné le Général Sarrail comme commandant en chef de l'armée d'Orient."* I suppose that Delcassé must be deaf or an awful liar.[41]

Another approach taken by the left was to spread gossip, undoubtedly designed to promote Sarrail's case by underlining British bungling. One such yarn was that the French had consented to join the expedition on the strength of assurances from London that the Turkish commanders in the forts had been bribed and would allow the Allied ships to pass through the Straits. The story went on to say that Enver Pasha discovered the plot shortly before the naval attack on 18 March and brought in German officers to replace his own commanders.[42]

Bertie could find no concrete evidence that the incident had taken place in discussions with the leading French political authorities and he concluded, erroneously as it turned out, that the scraps of gossip had been spread about town "partly to shield Augagneur from responsibility for a failure."[43] Unknown to Bertie, however, there was some basis for these rumours. As we have already mentioned, secret talks were held with the aim of negotiating a peace treaty between Britain and Turkey. But the event was never communicated to the French authorities. How Franklin-Bouillon and others of his group found out that the British had tried to buy off the Turks is unknown.

In the end the various ways individual left-wing politicians outside the chamber adopted to promote Sarrail's cause had little effect. On the other hand, the parliamentary commissions produced more significant results. Conscious of their strength and fed up at being denied military information to which they were entitled, they began to assert themselves by challenging the pretentions of the high command. On 13 August the chairmen of the three commissions, all friends of Sarrail, visited Poincaré to urge that reinforcements be dispatched immediately to the Dardanelles.[44] The President was non-committal, replying that he could not offer views independent of the cabinet or engage in debate with parliamentarians.[45]

Here again, the President thought to himself, was further evidence that the country desired to shift the main scene of the fighting to a theatre which offered greater prospects of success. The next day Poincaré, accompanied by Millerand and Viviani, motored to Chantilly to confer with Joffre. The Generalissimo had prepared a paper for the occasion and in the first part

---

40   BNA: Grey papers, FO 800/58, Bertie to Grey, 6 August 1915.
41   BNA: Grey papers, FO 800/58, Bertie to Grey, 6 August 1915.
42   BNA: Grey papers, FO 800/58, Bertie to Grey, 4 August, 1915. There is a brief reference to this incident in Lyautey, *Gouraud,* p. 125.
43   BNA: Grey papers, FO 800/58, Bertie to Grey, 4 August 1915.
44   J.M.G. Pédoya, *La commission de l'armée pendant la grande guerre: Documents inédits et secrets* (Paris: Flammarion, 1921), p. 353. Select documents on the investigations.
45   Poincaré, *Au service,* Vol. 7, p. 30.

stressed the need for complete freedom of action in the future conduct of his operations. A single sentence summed up his views on the issue: "A single man must conceive, decide and command."[46] Once Joffre had defined his role as c-in-c, he announced his intention to mount an offensive in Champagne in September but that it would be broken off immediately if the contemplated element of surprise failed to make a difference. The President disputed Joffre's assumption that he could ignore the right of the government to control policy and there followed a rather sharp exchange of words between the two men. Joffre held the opinion that an Allied offensive was needed to honour France's commitment to Russia. Poincaré interjected to remind him that he should not be concerned about matters outside the purview of his responsibility: "No the questions of alliance are for the government, not the soldier, to decide. You must judge matters only from the strategic point of view, the rest concerns us, the ministers and me." Joffre repeated his absurd claim that from purely military considerations it was necessary to keep the men active, otherwise they would deteriorate "physically and morally."

When the discussion turned to the Dardanelles, Joffre maintained that he could not spare the four divisions until his offensive was over. At the end he commented tartly: "What is to be done at the Dardanelles? Prepare an expedition for a factitious general?" He proceeded to tear into his nemesis, only to be reminded by Poincaré that it was not Sarrail but Gouraud and Bailloud who thought that the expeditionary force should be increased and that their appraisal had been supported by the parliamentary commissions and government. After considerable prodding Joffre promised that he would release two army corps in September but not sooner. The civil authorities gained the impression that Joffre would resign if they tried to force his hand.[47]

While Joffre's threat of resignation had allowed him to ride roughshod over the cabinet, he held no such trump card when he tried to persuade Sir John French, the British commander, to cooperate in his impending attack. French rejected Joffre's request for he was convinced that the fall offensive would fail. Consequently, Joffre arranged to invite Kitchener to Chantilly, hoping that his proposal might fall on more sympathetic ears.

On 15 August Kitchener crossed the channel and held talks with Joffre and Millerand. By then signs were not wanting that the German drive on the eastern front was meeting with great success. Warsaw had fallen on 4 August and the Russians were in full retreat. Joffre claimed that, unless vigorous action were taken at once in the west, the Russians might be defeated and forced to make a separate peace. The General went so far as to hint that with so much of the country under the control of the German invaders the appearance of inactivity on the main front might drive the war weary French themselves to seek a way out of the war. This was confirmed the next day by Sir Henry Wilson, British liaison officer with GQG, who asserted that Joffre's failure to attack would bring a new government bent on making peace with the enemy.[48] An ardent Francophile, Wilson believed that the sun rose and set on Joffre. It is true that the idea of a negotiated peace had begun to spread among the parties on the left but Wilson vastly exaggerated the extent of the movement.

---

46 Charles Bugnet, *Rue St Dominique et GQG* (Paris: Plon, 1937), p. 76.; J.M. Bourget, *Gouvernement et commandement: Les leçons de la guerre mondiale* (Paris: Payot, 1930), p. 139.
47 Poincaré, *Au service*, Vol. 7, pp. 36-38.
48 IWM: Wilson papers, entry in Wilson's diary, 16 August 1915.

Kitchener had long since realized the futility of large-scale attacks, but he had to face a disastrous commitment only because he saw no way of avoiding a rupture with the French.[49] He instructed the British High Command to "act with all our energy, and do our utmost to help the French, even though, by doing so, we suffered very heavy losses indeed."[50] It is a safe bet that Kitchener would have acted differently if he had known that Joffre's views were contrary to the declared policy of the French government. Joffre actually used Kitchener's assent to his advantage in dealing with the cabinet. It was no secret in Paris that Kitchener had hitherto advocated an active-defence in the west, at least for the rest of the year, and so his change of heart was all the more significant.[51]

As Joffre was concluding his private understanding with Kitchener, the cabinet met (17 August) and delegated Viviani to ask Sarrail to produce another appreciation, studying closely how the Dardanelles could be forced and leaving aside the extraneous schemes he had examined earlier. When Sarrail reported to the Prime Minister's office, he was told to focus exclusively on the possibilities of a landing at Bulair, Gaba Tepe or in Asia. Sarrail complied with the request and returned a week later to submit his findings. It was a vague and superficial survey, confined to discussing the pros and cons of striking out from possible landing sites in the region of the Dardanelles.[52]

A day later the parliamentary commissions, in an unusual gesture, made written representations to the President and to all the ministers, manifesting frustration at the inadequate attention given to their concerns. Whilst acknowledging that they had no right to discuss war policy, they were emphatic in their request for regular sessions with Viviani so that he could keep them posted on important issues. They expressed concern at the indecision to send reinforcements to the Dardanelles. They urged that the process be expedited on account of the approach of bad weather after 15 September which would make a landing in Europe or Asia uncertain; also, because the threat of a German attack on Serbia would open a direct route between Berlin and Constantinople.

Failing to receive an answer, the commissions passed a resolution on the 27th which they addressed to the Prime Minister. They reiterated their desire for periodic meetings with government leaders, as well as their conviction of the need to press on at the Dardanelles, alluding to the great benefits that would accrue from the capture of Constantinople. This time Viviani replied to the motion. He recognized the right of the commissions to be kept informed and asserted that henceforth all-important matters would be discussed with them in advance.[53]

Events were now moving rapidly at long last towards a resolution on the matter of the Dardanelles. On 26 August the French military attaché (among others) in London disclosed that in a recent telegram Hamilton admitted that his attack had definitely failed and that he would be compelled to remain on the defensive without significant reinforcements.[54] Two days

---

49 BNA: Cabinet papers, CAB/42/3, Minutes of the Dardanelles Committee, 20 August 1915.
50 Robert Blake (ed.), *The Private Papers of Douglas Haig* (London: Eyre & Spottiswoode, 1952), p. 102.
51 Aspinall-Oglander, *Gallipoli*, Vol. 2, p. 372.
52 Sarrail, Opérations dans la région des Dardanelles, 24 August 1915, in France, *Les armées françaises*, tome 8, Vol. 1, annexe no. 323.
53 Pédoya, *Commission de l'armée* , pp. 354-59.
54 AN: Millerand papers, 470 AP/15, de la Panousse to Millerand, 26 August 1915. Cambon and Bailloud sent similar letter to their superiors.

later the French cabinet convened to decide what step it should take to improve Allied fortunes in the Dardanelles. All the ministers were in agreement that the British setback rendered indispensable the dispatch of French troops.[55]

Millerand read a report by the general staff (at the War Ministry) which recommended a renewed effort in the Dardanelles before the onset of bad weather. It discouraged pursuing operations on the Gallipoli Peninsula because of the impossibility to manoeuvre and the build up of enemy defences. Instead it favoured a French landing in Asia, anticipating better results with less loss of life. The first objective would be to establish a base at Kum Kale, followed by an advance on Chanak, the capture of which would open the waterway to the Allied fleet. The general staff believed that six divisions would suffice to accomplish the mission.[56]

That afternoon Joffre made his way to the Elysée to keep an appointment with Poincaré, Viviani, Millerand and Augagneur. He was told on arrival that events dictated the immediate dispatch of reinforcements to the Dardanelles. Caught by surprise, the Generalissimo seemed upset and claimed that he would need the requested divisions either for an offensive or possibly to hold back a German attack. When reminded of his earlier promise Joffre clasped his head with his hands and his only comment was that he could not abdicate his responsibilities as commander-in-chief. To which Poincaré replied that the government too had obligations and he proceeded to define the respective responsibilities between civilian and military authorities. If the offensive Joffre was preparing was inspired by military considerations he was within his right to go ahead. However if it was based on France's relations with its Allies "please let me say that the opening of the narrows is of far greater importance, affecting as it does Russian opinion and the supplies to the Russian army then the gain of a few kilometers on our front." The upshot was that Joffre half-heartedly consented to release the reinforcements by 20 September, or the 22nd at the latest, if he failed to achieve a breakthrough on the main front.[57]

After returning to Chantilly, Joffre read Sarrail's second memorandum which had just arrived and found it no more informative than the first one. He then turned to the secretariat of the Superior Council of National Defence (*Conseil Supérieur de la défense nationale*) to study the propositions of Sarrail as well as those of Gouraud and Bailloud, in evaluating the whole undertaking. The Superior Council of National Defence, was a new body, created at the suggestion of Joffre. It was reconstituted from the defunct Superior Council of War which had not convened since the outbreak of the war. Presided over by Poincaré, this committee was originally composed of Joffre, Millerand, Delcassé and Augagneur but after the early meetings its membership tended to increase in size. To guard against possible leakage of classified information, no official minutes of the sessions were kept. The Superior Council of National Defence was in theory a purely advisory body but in practice, as its members constituted a powerful voice in the cabinet, its recommendations were usually acted on at once. It could best be described as a supplement to the cabinet, charged with exploring major questions of policy, rather than a device for meeting the day to day emergencies of the war. It was the government's main instrument – until late in the war – for the correlation of political and military aims.

---

55 Poincaré, *Au service*, Vol. 7, p. 64.
56 SHD: AMG, 7N 2170, Graziani, Note pour M. le Ministre au sujet de la situation aux Dardanelles, 18 August 1915.
57 Poincaré, *Au service*, Vol. 7, pp. 68-69.

The Superior Council had a permanent secretariat (known at first as the *Section d'études de la défense nationale)* which lay outside the jurisdiction of GQG and functioned at the War Ministry under the direction of General Graziani, now chief of the general staff. The other members consisted of William Martin (minister plenipotentiary representing the Quai d'Orsay), *capitaine de vaisseau* Grasset (representing the Ministry of Marine), and Lieutenant-Colonel R. Alexandre (representing GQG and also serving as secretary). Summoned only when Joffre or Millerand deemed it desirable, the role of the *Section d'études* was to examine questions relating to the war in its entirety, forward its reports to the Superior Council, draft the final decisions and supervise their execution.[58]

Graziani returned with the recommendations of the secretariat on 31 August. Rejecting the idea altogether of a new assault in the Peninsula, the report would do no more than cast a net in Asia. It was seen that Sarrail's estimate of six divisions would be inadequate and that an additional four would be required as the Turks could assemble at least 165,000 men by the 10th day after the landing. As a basis for this calculation it was alleged that Gouraud himself had asserted that the operation should not be attempted with less than 10 divisions. Since it was obvious that the high command could not spare that many divisions it was suggested that the Italians should be approached and requested to make up the difference and that a French general be placed in supreme command of the entire Allied force in the Dardanelles, the army as well as the navy. Still even the assurance of Italian assistance, the *Section d'études* pointed out, would not eliminate the dangers and difficulties connected to the enterprise, from transportation to the nature of the challenge and enemy submarines lurking in the Aegean Sea. Taking everything into consideration it advised against a renewed effort in the Dardanelles unless important results could not be achieved on the Western Front. This would mean that for the time being the Allies on the Peninsula would have to adopt a defensive strategy and cling to their existing positions.[59]

The appreciation could not have been more to Joffre's satisfaction than if he had written it himself. On 1 September he forwarded it to Millerand, along with a memo of his own, and a rather childish covering note. Joffre opened his argument in his paper by urging that no action be taken in the Dardanelles until a precise plan had been drawn up in concert with the British. At his last cabinet meeting (28 August) he had been led to believe that such a plan existed and for that reason, agreed to detach the four divisions from his front after 22 September to help carry it out. Since then he had received Sarrail's memorandum which merely considered a number of possible landing on the coasts of Europe and Asia without coming to a final conclusion and no detailed analysis either of the troops required to complete the mission or the prospects of success. He warned that the country could not afford to be caught in an ill-prepared enterprise which would incessantly absorbed men, munitions and other resources vital for the defence

---

58 I provided more details on the workings of the Superior Council of National Defence and its secretariat than I normally would have on a related matter because there is very little data about them in print. Much of what appeared in this text was kindly supplied to me by the late eminent French historian *M. le doyen* Pierre Renouvin while I was doing research for my first book. There is some information on one or both of the two bodies in Gen. R. Alexandre, *Avec Joffre d'Agadir à Verdun* (Paris: Berger-Levrault, 1932), pp. 191-92; Renouvin, *Forms of War Government*, p. 83; and France, *Les armées françaises*, tome 8, Vol. 1, annexe no. 332n.

59 Section d'études, Note au sujet des Dardanelles, 31 August 1915, in France, *Les armées françaises*, tome 8, Vol. 1, annexe no. 332.

of the national soil. Joffre requested that the dispatch of troops be postponed until the early days in October, by which time he would have a clearer picture of conditions on the Western Front. Meantime, a thorough study of the projected operation should be made in collaboration with the British and the issue of a supreme commander settled; and Sarrail should go to the Dardanelles to make a reconnaissance on the spot.

In the covering note Joffre asked the ministers to consider the political ramifications of a conceivable defeat in the Dardanelles: "It was the English who took us to the Dardanelles. Today the abandonment of the attack would be an English defeat. Tomorrow, if we were to send reinforcements and claim the chief command, we should be faced, in case of failure, by a French disaster."[60] Joffre was evidently willing to go to any length if it would further his chances of scuttling the projected operation.

Millerand at once sent the reports to Poincaré who presumably distributed copies to the members of the cabinet. But Joffre's latest démarche arrived too late to have any possible effect. The cabinet, weary of Joffre's delaying tactics, had decided on the previous day (31 August) that the four divisions should be ready to start for the Dardanelles on 20 September and, if necessary, these would be followed by an additional four. After the meeting Delcassé telegraphed the Foreign Office that the French government was prepared to send reinforcements to the Dardanelles, subject to four conditions: that the expeditionary force led by a French general be allowed to operate in a new theatre, independent of, but in close liaison with the English on Gallipoli; that the Royal Navy assist in transporting the new divisions; that the Allied fleet together cover the disembarkation of the French forces; and that the French be permitted to establish a separate base at Mudros or Mitylene.[61] A subsequent message from the Quai d'Orsay requested that the English replace the two divisions under Bailloud at Cape Helles with their own units.[62]

The arrival of large-scale French reinforcements in the Dardanelles was expected to breathe new life into the flagging operation. But would the troops be allowed to leave France? Would Joffre accept that his period of dictatorship had run its course and submit to civilian rule, or would he redouble his efforts to regain his former position of strength? The fate of the expeditionary force hinged on the outcome of the struggle between the high command and the government over the strategic conduct of the war.

60   Joffre to Millerand, 1 September 1915, in France, *Les armees françaises,* tome 8, Vol. 1, annexe no. 336.
61   SHD: in section under the heading Engleterre, carton 70, AMG, Delcassé to Cambon, 31 August 1915.
62   Millerand to Delcassé, 31 August 1915, in France, *Les armées françaises,* tome 8, Vol. 1, annexe no. 331; SHD: AMG, under the heading Opération des Dardanelles, carton 6, dossier 1, Delcassé to Cambon, 1 September 1915.

11

Dardanelles or the Balkans?

The French announcement in London was unexpected – in view of the planned offensive on the Western Front in September – and "caused a great sensation in the Dardanelles Committee."[1] Spirits were lightened. Kitchener stated that he would gladly arrange to relieve the two French divisions on the Peninsula, while Balfour began the process of assembling the necessary transport ships. Even the conservative leader, Bonar Law, who had constantly opposed diverting troops to the east, joined Churchill in urging the dispatch of additional British troops "to make a good job of it."[2] Seldom since the opening months of the war had the English acted with such singleness of purpose and alacrity.

Kitchener contacted Millerand to lend his support to the idea of opening a new theatre in Asia, though in truth he could hardly have done otherwise. In a rare mood of optimism, especially astonishing in light of his warning to Hamilton to avoid military operations in Asia, he maintained that an expedition made up of four divisions would be adequate to take in reverse the Turkish forts commanding The Narrows and open the way for the fleet. He urged haste in getting the operation under way before the onset of bad weather and that preparations for it be kept in absolute secrecy in order to deny the Turks time to concentrate more divisions in Asia. Kitchener explained that the two divisions he proposed to send to relieve the French contingent on the Peninsula would be withdrawn from the Western Front but that these would be replaced by two fresh divisions from England. He added that he would be happy to meet Millerand, if that was his wish, to discuss the details of the operation.[3] As the British eagerly looked forward to the French effort to unlock the Dardanelles, Joffre was doing what he could to ensure that the attempt never occurred.

On 2 September Joffre, together with Viviani, Millerand and Delcassé, came to confer with Poincaré at the Elysée. Joffre thought it would be prudent to put off his attack until 25 September as several of his subordinates had indicated that they could not be ready by the 15th. He claimed that the offensive was necessary to help the Russians and that it was likely to be successful. He recognized that if it failed, he must try somewhere else. As for the Dardanelles, he threatened

---

1 Hankey, *Supreme Command*, Vol. 1, p. 410.
2 Churchill, *World Crisis*, Vol. 2, p. 492.
3 AN: Millerand papers, 470 AP/15, de la Panousse to Millerand, 2 September 1915.

to resign if ordered to detach a single division from his front before October. He went on to say that four divisions would be available after that date but considering the investigations by the secretariat (*Section d'études*) of the Superior Council of National Defence and also, recently by Colonel Alexandre, one of his staff officers, he doubted that theses troops would be sufficient to clear the way for the fleet to get through The Narrows. He repeated that it was vital that Sarrail assess the Allied position on the spot and report back on what he proposed to do in the Dardanelles. On the last point there was unanimity among the ministers and President and it was confirmed by the full cabinet the next day.[4]

It was left to Millerand to convey the cabinet's decision to Sarrail. On 2 September Sarrail attended a meeting at the Ministry of War with Millerand and Augagneur in order to determine the size and work out the basic plans of the Army of the Orient. The following decisions were taken: 1. that the Expeditionary army sent from France be composed of four divisions; 2. that the two divisions under Bailloud join the Expeditionary army which would be concentrating at Lemnos or Mitylene; 3. that the entire French contingent disembark at a single place; 4. that the navy assure the supply of stores.[5] Before the meeting broke up, Millerand tried to persuade Sarrail to journey to the Dardanelles to personally inspect possible landing sites. Sarrail was adamant in resisting the pressure. He would leave with the divisional reinforcements or not at all. He later wrote: "It was the continuation of the same idea: my removal at any price. I absolutely declined to leave, wanting to stay in order to arrive at something; the Minister of War wanted me to leave to arrive at nothing. The war of attrition persisted."[6]

Sarrail assumed that time was on his side, that his influential political allies would keep his case in the forefront of French politics and that in the end the cabinet would be compelled to accept his terms. The cabinet, however willing to resolve the issue, felt powerless to meet Sarrail's conditions as long as Joffre pulled from the opposite direction. The Generalissimo could not openly flout the wishes of the government but he could stall and allude to all sorts of obstacles, whether legitimate or not, ready to exploit any opportunity to his advantage. The Viviani ministry was caught between the irreconcilable conditions laid down by the high command and Sarrail. The government's task was rendered many times more difficult by the absence of a trusted body of experts who could offer reasoned and impartial advice on the general conduct of the war. The Superior Council of National Defence had been created near the end of August 1915 but it did not start to operate until November.[7] For want of professional unbiased recommendation, France's wavering war policy in the summer of 1915 violated every principle of sound strategy.

As the battle of wits between Joffre and the Viviani ministry continued, Poincaré wrote a letter to Millerand on 7 September to report a recent conversation he had with Gouraud. He noted that the General walked deliberately and with some discomfort but that he hoped to be fully recovered in a month. It seemed that Gouraud had no recollection of mentioning anything like 10 divisions, which according to Colonel Alexandre (a member of the secretariat of the Superior Council of National Defence), he is said to have judged indispensable for the

---

[4] Poincaré, *Au service*, Vol. 7, pp. 78-79, 83.
[5] SHD: AMM, Ed 108, Résultats de la conference de 2 Septembre 1915.
[6] Sarrail, *Mon commandement*, p. xi.
[7] Greenhalgh, *French Army*, p. 127.

proposed operation in Asia.[8] Although Gouraud would not commit himself, he thought that four divisions would suffice to sweep the forts along the Asiatic shore and open The Narrows to the fleet. At any rate the General persisted in his belief that it was sheer folly to leave the French troops on Cape Helles without trying to silence the Asiatic batteries. For this limited undertaking he estimated that one infantry and one cavalry division would be required and stressed that these should be sent out no later than the first week in October.[9]

The same day that Millerand received Poincaré's missive, he directed Joffre to have four divisions ready to embark at Marseilles in the first week in October.[10] Joffre replied that he could not spare the units in question by that date and implored the government to reconsider carefully the findings of his appreciation of 1 September before adopting a course of action that would seriously hinder the execution of his impending offensive.[11] Joffre's acolyte Henry Wilson wrote in his diary on 9 September: "Joffre has temporarily stopped the business until some proper plan of operation is drawn up. Here is the whole thing. Joffre would crush it altogether if he could, but he can't do more than he has done."[12]

At this juncture, the English learned through Sir John French that Joffre intended to go ahead with his offensive in the fall. French maintained that on no account would Joffre allow the levy of any troops from his command until the results of his attack were known. The news came as a surprise. The British government assumed that the French would postpone their grand offensive on the main front in order to concentrate more resources in the Near East for a decisive push. Since it was unthinkable of attacking simultaneously in France and in the Dardanelles, the cabinet concluded that a delegation led by Kitchener should cross the channel to find out the precise designs of Paris.[13]

On 11 September, the Anglo-French conference was held at the Hotel Terminus in Calais. The French were represented by Millerand, Joffre and Sarrail; and the British by Kitchener, Hankey, French and Wilson. The meeting got under way at 9 am with Kitchener invited to take the chair. The first order of business concerned the planned dispatch of reinforcements to the Dardanelles. Joffre rose from his seat and made an impassioned plea against removing any troops from his front. He declared that he did not mind parting with four divisions as much as he feared that if the drive in Asia stalled, it would require more men and munitions which he could not spare without endangering the safety of France. Kitchener remarked that he did not anticipate a far-reaching military commitment in Dardanelles. As he saw it, the army's role would be confined only to helping the fleet get through The Narrows after which its mission would be completed.[14] Instead of opening up a new dialogue, his comments failed to elicit any

---

8   Gouraud's memory betrayed him for his earlier estimate of the required number of divisions was on record. See his memorandum on p. 145 in this text.
9   AN: Millerand papers, 470 AP/15, Poincaré to Millerand, 7 September 1915.
10 Millerand to Joffre, 7 September 1915, in France, *Les armées françaises*, tome 8, Vol. 1, annexe no. 348.
11 Joffre to Millerand, 8 September 1915, in France, *Les armées françaises*, tome 8, Vol. 1, annexe no. 351.
12 IWM: Wilson papers, entry in Wilson's diary, 9 September 1915.
13 J.A. Spender and Cyril Asquith, *Life of Herbert Henry Asquith, Lord Oxford and Asquith*, Vol. 2 (London: Hutchinson, 1932), pp. 183-84; Hankey, *Supreme Command*, Vol.1, p. 410; Cassar, *Kitchener's War*, p. 237.
14 Kitchener's statement in the minutes of the conference ran as follows: "The scope of the operation was to open the Dardanelles for the fleet and he had no intention of committing himself to further operations."

reaction from the French. It is apparent that they did not fully comprehend the implications of his statement. What exactly he now had in mind cannot be ascertained for sure but it would seem that he had given up any thought of further involving the army in the attempt to seize Constantinople.

The operation had turned into a nightmare for Kitchener and, while he rarely complained, he must have frequently reproached himself for trusting Churchill and accepting too willingly his optimistic scenario at the outset. Wilson left an account of his private talks with Kitchener at Calais: "Kitchener's one idea is to get out of the mess he is in, and he said so specifically, and that there was now no intention of going to Constantinople."[15] The British Field Marshal was opposed to an immediate withdrawal partly because of the effect such an admission of failure would have on the Muslim population in the east and partly because he believed that it could not be carried out without appalling losses. He confided to Wilson that he would be thankful if the Allies could gain possession of the high ground west of Maidos from where it would be possible to dominate, not only the principal defences of The Narrows but the Asiatic guns as well.[16] Possession of the waterway would allow the Allies to provide assistance to bolster the crumbling Russian armies and facilitate re-embarkation when the time came. Thus it appears that Kitchener's main objective was to link up with the Russians and leave Constantinople in Turkish hands. It should be noted that Kitchener's change of heart was inconsistent with the declared policy of the Dardanelles Committee. It meant modifying the scope of the campaign, scaling down the objective to merely reopening communications with Russia. With ammunition barely sufficient to supply the British armies, Kitchener had to know that, even if a sea route could be opened to the Black Sea, little could be done to resuscitate the Russian armies. But in his mind, the idea of avoiding defeat in the east and its possible consequences, overshadowed all other considerations.

Throughout the meeting Joffre made no secret of his dislike of the whole affair and refused to fix a date when it would be possible to remove the divisions from his front. It was hoped that the troops would be ready to leave on 10 October and that operations could begin around the middle of November. Still nothing was definite. If the grand attack in the west succeeded the decision to send the four divisions to the Dardanelles would be cancelled to permit Joffre to use them to follow up initial gains. In the interim the assembled members requested that Sarrail draw up a detailed plan of operations for his new mission.

Millerand wanted Sarrail appointed supreme commander of the Allied forces in the Dardanelles, but Kitchener firmly objected on the grounds that Hamilton had more troops at his disposal, possessed greater experience and was senior in rank. A compromise was reached under which Sarrail could operate independently in Asia but in close liaison with the British on the Peninsula. The two governments would be called upon to resolve any differences that might arise between the two generals.[17]

After the conference was over, Joffre told Kitchener in private that the Asiatic scheme was ill-advised and that in any event it would require more than six divisions. He lashed out at Sarrail's personal conduct and placed grave doubts on his fitness to command. Kitchener

---

15 IWM: Wilson papers, entry in Wilson's diary, 11 September 1915.
16 IWM, Wilson papers, entry in Wilson's diary, 10 and 11 September 1915.
17 BNA: Cabinet papers, CAB 28/1, Minutes of the Anglo-French and Allied Conferences, 11 September 1915.

learned that the French offer to send an expedition to the Dardanelles had been driven as much by political consideration as by military necessity. The French government had tried to kill two birds with one stone – send a force large enough to complete the mission in the Dardanelles and find a job for Sarrail who had been sacked by Joffre but was immensely popular with left-wing politicians. Kitchener had occasion to chat with Sarrail and did not find him very sympathetic. At Hankey's suggestion Kitchener invited Sarrail to visit the Dardanelles for several weeks to make a personal inspection. However the General politely declined, saying he could not absent himself from the country.[18]

The inconclusive nature of the conference could not have disappointed Joffre. Wilson surmised that, even if the troops sailed from France around 10 October, "the whole thing will fall down of itself, because it will be impossible for Sarrail to land with six divisions before the end of November, beginning of December and the weather will decide the question then."[19] Joffre did not have a practical policy of what to do in the Dardanelles. He was torn between a desire to concentrate all Anglo-French troops in the west and a realization that withdrawal would entail loss of life and badly damage Entente prestige in the Balkans and Muslim world. Wilson provides us with a glimpse of his views: "I had a long talk with General Joffre about the Dardanelles. It is quite clear he is opposed to the landing in Asia Minor. He is equally opposed to a landing in Gallipoli and he thinks K's idea of sending out six divisions in order to bring the whole lot away … ridiculous … He agrees we are in a morass, but his plan is to dig in and stick it out."[20]

No sooner had the Viviani cabinet been briefed on the results of the Anglo-French conference than it was presented with a second memorandum produce by the secretariat of the Superior Council of National Defence. In it the author(s) urged that, owing to the critical importance of the approaching attack in the west, Joffre be permitted to employ all available troops until the outcome had been decided. It was conceded that the initial projection of the number of divisions required for the Asiatic operation was perhaps excessive and that six might suffice if the landing was carried out rapidly and energetically and if the enemy was kept in the dark until the last moment. The report did not minimize the dangers involved and assumed that the English would launch another assault on the Peninsula while the French fell on the Asiatic forts from the rear. For the French the ultimate object was still to occupy Constantinople, though no attention was given as to how this would be accomplished.[21]

The note revealed little that was not already known or introduced earlier, except it was the first time that a body of experts, under the influence of GQG – if technically outside its authority – admitted that an operation of moderate means had a reasonable chance of getting the job done. Any lingering doubts in the cabinet about the feasibility of an enterprise in Asia were dispelled. On 14 September Millerand reminded Joffre that, in accordance with the decision reached at Calais, he was to assemble four divisions at Marseilles by 10 October.[22]

18   Hankey, *Supreme Command*, Vol. 1, p. 411.
19   IWM: Wilson papers, entry in Wilson's diary, 11 September 1915.
20   IWM: Wilson papers, entry in Wilson's diary, 4 September 1915.
21   Section d'études, Note aux sujet des Dardanelles, September 1915, in France, *Les armées françaises*, tome 8, Vol. 1, annexe no. 354. The date listed on the document is 20 September, but it is a misprint. It was likely written on 10 September.
22   Millerand to Joffre, 14 September 1915, in France, *Les armées françaises*, tome 8, Vol. 1, annexe no. 358.

The recent events had not narrowed the differences between the separate parties. The republican General was straining with impatience at the endless cat and mouse game between the government and the high command. He passed the time at his home in Montauban, occasionally travelling to Paris on business or to confer with his socialist political cohorts on a political strategy that would force the government's hand. There was fleeting talk in the cabinet of creating for Sarrail a new post, president of the Superior Consul of National Defence, at first glance seemingly prestigious, but little more than a sinecure. The idea was never considered as it was recognized that such dubious compensation would only infuriate Sarrail. If anything, Sarrail's terms had hardened in recent days and he now reportedly demanded as a condition for departing for the Dardanelles 100,000 men and supreme command of the Allied force. When Millerand observed that he had set his sights too high, Sarrail reportedly exclaimed, "You have merely to put me in the place of that old goat Joffre."[23]

Before the cabinet could finalize an arrangement that would be acceptable to Sarrail, it needed from him (as previously stated) a thorough plan that would focus on his recommendation for a landing site, the objective to be sought, the difficulties likely to be faced and the number of divisions required to complete the task. Millerand referred the wishes of the cabinet to Sarrail and asked him whether he preferred to do the work at home, or confer on the spot with Hamilton and Bailloud.[24] Not surprisingly the General chose the former option.

Whilst cabinet ministers sat back and awaited further developments, Jean Cruppi, a deputy was back in Paris after a visit to Russia with a stopover in the Dardanelles. He conveyed alarming news. At Mudros he held long discussions with General Baumann as well as several other officers. He feared that unless reinforcements arrived shortly, the Allied force was likely to be thrown into the sea.[25]

At the next cabinet meeting, Poincaré was sufficiently concerned to make an issue of Cruppi's report in the hope it would break down the barriers of listlessness and inertia. He was fast losing heart at the cabinet's ability to make a decision and enforce it. He recognized that as long as the ministry allowed itself to be checkmated by Joffre, Allied strength would continue to be siphoned away on the Western Front by fruitless and costly attacks.

Although the military reasons for going to the Dardanelles had not changed, the political inducements had been weakened when Russia ran away with the main prize. Stamped with the old traditions of French foreign policy, Poincaré could not bring himself to accept the Straits Agreement. To hand over to Russia the most cherished possession of the Sultan's realm after the French and English had shed rivers of blood did not make any sense. The President remained convinced that the assurances given to Petrograd had been premature and went beyond what the Russians themselves had anticipated. He hoped, however, that the presence of Anglo-French troops in Constantinople would offset the promise made to the Russians. The Entente partners could remain in Constantinople until satisfactory terms had been arranged with the Tsarist government after consultation with all the interested powers. As far as Poincaré was concerned, the commitment to Italy of a share of Ottoman spoils as part of the compensation package for joining the Allies, and, especially the failure of Russia to contribute forces to land operations in the Dardanelles, had nullified the Straits Agreement. Poincare's attitude was shared by Lord

---

23 Stanford University Library (SUL): William Martin, "Notes de guerre", 13 September 1915.
24 SHD: AMG, 7N 2170, Millerand to Sarrail, 15 September 1915.
25 Poincaré, *Au service*, Vol. 7, p. 103.

Bertie who admitted that the Straits Agreement had been a mistake as it adversely affected relations with Bulgaria and Romania. Poincaré reminded him that it was his government that had been in a rush to appease Petrograd. As the Russian people, their hearts firmly set on acquiring Constantinople, were accusing their partners in the west of inertia, the President did not think it was the right moment for their governments to go back on their word.[26]

Poincaré was amongst the most vocal of a growing trend in many quarters in France over the uneasiness of the Straits Agreement. On 15 September Gabriel Hanotaux, former Minister of Foreign Affairs, told Bertie that he hoped Constantinople and the Straits would be internationalized.[27] The *Journal des débats* declared that unless Russia co-operated more fully in the war against Turkey, France and England would have to revise their position in regard to the Straits question.[28] Isvolsky reported to Sazanov on 12 October that the absence of Russian troops in the Dardanelles campaign had provoked "a growing agitation against Russia … in French Parliament, press and even Government circles."[29] In the latter part of October, the Vatican inspired *Corriere d'Italia* advised that "for the diplomacy of the Triple Entente to succeed in the Balkans, it was essential for Russia to renounce her Byzantine dreams."[30]

It is curious that throughout the summer months Joffre never alluded to the Straits Agreement to reinforce his arguments in his bid to dissuade the French government from pressing ahead with its proposed operation. It was no different when he replied to Millerand's earlier note (of 14 September) six days later. Considering it "his duty to protest once more", he produced his third document on the Dardanelles and gave the standard line that, in view of the pending operations on the Western Front, he could not promise that the requested divisions would be in Marseilles on time. He warned that the expedition ran the risk of being held up and lead to a call of additional troops. He pointed out that France's manpower resources were limited and to keep the army on the same footing it might become necessary in 1916 to call up the young men of 1917. He lied or at best stretched the truth when he alleged that after the Calais Conference Kitchener had confided to him that the Asiatic campaign would be hazardous and that Hamilton had disapproved of it. He again appealed to national pride, saying that a fresh attempt in the Dardanelles would get the English off the hook but in case of a defeat, the responsibility and consequences would have to be borne entirely by the French.[31]

The memo caused considerable consternation amongst cabinet ministers the next day for it was interpreted as a ploy on the part of Joffre to wriggle out of a promise he had twice made to them. "You see", cried an emotional Viviani, "it is as I told you. The Dardanelles operation will not materialize. GQG will not allow it because Sarrail is to command."[32] The atmosphere in the cabinet was somber and the day's session ended leaving open the question of how to overcome Joffre's obstinacy.

26 BNA: Grey papers, FO 800/58, Bertie to Grey, 27 August 1915; BNA: Bertie papers, FO 800/172, Bertie to Grey, 26 August 1915; and Bertie papers, FO 800/181, Bertie to Grey, 18 September 1915.
27 Lennox (ed.), *Diary of Lord Bertie*, Vol. 1, p. 236.
28 Cited in Gottlieb, *Studies in Secret Diplomacy*, p. 130.
29 Isvolsky to Sazanov, 12 October 1915, in Russia, *Constantinople et les détroits*, Vol. 1, p. 233.
30 Cited in Gottlieb, *Studies in Secret Diplomacy*, p. 130.
31 Joffre to Millerand, 20 September 1915, in France, *Les armées françaises*, tome 8, Vol. 1, annexe no. 365.
32 Poincaré, *Au service*, Vol. 7, p. 111.

A day later, Sarrail returned to the Ministry of War to hand over his detailed plan of operation. Arguing that a campaign in Asia was the most practical of the three he considered – the others were landings at Bulair and Gabe Tepe – he selected the Bay of Yukyesi as a place which could accommodate a large landing. Since French forces would have to cross difficult terrain and fight a resourceful enemy, he recommended the dispatch, not of four divisions, but two corps. Leaving a minimum number of troops to guard against an attack from Smyrna, the rest of the force would march rapidly towards Chanak and on a front large enough to overwhelm positions of Turkish resistance. He deemed it indispensable that the English mount an attack simultaneously on the Peninsula, claiming that without control of both shores the fleet could not get through. He noted that his appreciation had been drawn up in Paris and saw no advantage in traveling to the scene of action until he could leave with his troops.[33]

However the hour to again attempt to open the Dardanelles had passed. In late summer 1915, General Erich von Falkenhayn, chief of the German general staff, decided that in order to keep Turkey in the war, he must dispose of Serbia and open a direct route to the Ottoman capital so that supplies and reinforcements could move freely. To achieve that objective, he needed to coax Bulgaria to join the Central Powers.

Since the opening days of the conflict, Bulgaria had wavered back and forth in tantalizing fashion, weighing competing offers of territory from the two coalitions and biding its time when its services would command a higher price. The Allies were reluctant to promise territory belonging to an ally (Serbia) and to a neutral state (Greece) and Sofia was not attracted to a promise of Turkish regions contingent on their victory. The Germans, however, were in position to make good their commitments.

Lured by the old dream of a Greater Bulgaria, together with a belief that the Russian disasters on the eastern front and the failure of the British at Suvla Bay presaged the ultimate triumph of the Central Powers, prompted Sofia to sign a secret military convention with Germany and Austria on 6 September. Bulgaria was promised, in return for its pledge to declare war on Serbia, a loan of 200,000,000 francs, Serbian Macedonia, and restoration of lands lost to Greece and Romania in the Second Balkan War (1913) should their former enemies align themselves with the Entente. On 23 September Sofia decreed general mobilization and it was apparent that an attack on Serbia was only a matter of a week or two. Greece was directly affected by what happened to Serbia as a defensive alliance existed between the two countries in the event either was attacked by Bulgaria. By the terms of the treaty, Serbia had to provide 150,000 men to defend its eastern frontier. Since the Serbs would have their hands full protecting their northern front against an Austro-German onslaught, they could not supply the 150,000 men needed to fight the Bulgarians. The Greeks had an army of about 150,000 men and Venizelos, back in power after an electoral victory, was unwilling to take up arms against Bulgaria unless supported by an equivalent force from outside. While the Serbs made frantic appeals to London and Paris for aid, Venizelos asked the Entente partners for 150,000 men to enable Greece to honour its treaty obligations to its northern neighbour.

In light of the new developments, the French cabinet was faced with a difficult choice when it assembled on 23 September. The Greeks wanted a quick reply. To be sure the French were

---

33   Sarrail to Millerand, 21 September 1915, in France, *Les armées françaises*, tome 8, Vol. 1, annexe no. 366.

anxious to save Serbia but, with Joffre's offensive set to begin on the 25th, its quota of 75,000 men could be met only by abandoning the Dardanelles venture.

The prospect of a Balkan campaign, which the French cabinet had briefly entertained on two separate occasions at the start of 1915, was revived with Briand taking the lead. Disparaging a fresh attack in the Dardanelles as likely to end in heavy losses with nothing achieved, he was wildly optimistic in calculating the benefits of a Balkan enterprise. Here was the surest means to succour Serbia, frustrate Germany's dream of establishing a *Mitteleuropa* and unite the Balkan states in a common front against Turkey and Austria. Left unsaid but grasped at once by most ministers was the opportunity to further France's imperialism in the eastern Mediterranean and to assist in its post-war recovery. With the British in Egypt and Russia's eventual occupation of Constantinople and the Straits, a foothold in the Balkans would better ensure France's control of Syria and other areas of interest in the region.[34]

There were other motives, some quite obvious, which helped sway the cabinet's precipitate decision to open a new theatre in the Balkans. Serbia was not only an important prewar purchaser of French armaments but weighing heavily upon the ministers was the feeling that its abandonment would be fatal to Allied prestige throughout the world. The helplessness of three great powers to save from destruction a small state that relied on their protection would deter neutrals from joining the Entente. Moreover, since the start of the war, Serbia's stubborn and gallant resistance against heavy odds had inspired overwhelming sympathy in France and public opinion approved the idea of rendering some form of assistance to their ally. Lastly there was anxiety in ministerial circles of a possible revolt by parliament – its relations already strained with the country's civil leaders – over their inaction in dealing with a potentially dangerous military development. Since the middle of 1915, Parliamentary Commissions had repeatedly warned the government to take measures against what they viewed as an impending Austro-German attack on Serbia only to be assured each time that such a threat was premature.[35] If the parliamentarians discovered that the cabinet had been caught by surprise and no plan existed to counteract the Austro-German offensive against Serbia, their confidence in its capacity to conduct the war would vanish. It was obviously the hope of the Viviani ministry that the hurried adoption of a Balkan based project might yet set everything right.

In short, the cabinet readily grasped the idea of a Balkan campaign as a solution to its immediate and long-range problems. The lone dissenter was Delcassé who questioned the wisdom of embarking upon an adventure so uncertain that it was apt to lead to a dangerous dissipation of manpower and material resources. Yet by this time there was a growing mistrust of Delcassé's judgment in view of the collapse of his foreign policy – as will be seen in the next chapter – and his arguments had lost all power to convince. Poincaré was as keen as Briand to accept the Greek offer, despite his earlier enthusiasm for a renewed offensive in the Dardanelles. The promise of disengagement from an inconvenient commitment to Russia, together with Bailloud's recent warning of the dire consequences that Bulgarian entry in the war might have on the French expeditionary force, had presumably changed his perspective.

---

34 David Duttom, "The Balkan Campaign and French War Aims in the Great War", *English Historical Review*, Vol. 94 (1979), pp. 97-113.
35 See especially the scathing attack by Georges Leygues (President of the Foreign Affairs Commission) at the Government for misleading parliament and for taking no timely action. AN: C 7488, dossier104, Foreign Affairs Commission, 19 October 1915.

Before the cabinet broke up for the day it agreed to dispatch a force to the Balkans and, as Serbia had no seaport, requested that Millerand study the possibility of a landing either at Salonica or Dedeagatch in Greece.[36] In deciding to send an expedition to the Balkans the French cabinet had not even consulted the English who were expected to supply the other half of the quota requested by Greece.

After waging a war of nerves for months against Joffre, the cabinet's sudden reversal of attitude is striking evidence of how completely it had lost confidence in the need or successful conclusion of the Dardanelles adventure. Yet to embark on a new campaign without definite objectives, adequate preparations and a precise plan of action, after having blasted the ill-conceived British operation in the Dardanelles as a lamentable succession of improvisations, revealed a shocking lapse of judgement. Here was another example of politicians determining the benefits to be derived from a successful drive in the Balkans before considering the necessary means to achieve that victory.

In a previous chapter, the logistical difficulties that a French army would encounter if it proceeded northwards after landing in Greece was mentioned. Since the operation was about to get underway, it may be useful to review them. The terrain was mountainous, the few roads that existed were in poor condition and only a single rail line connected Salonica to the interior and, in case of war, it could be easily demolished. Even in the best of circumstances, it would be almost impossible to supply a sizeable army any distance from Salonica, the most convenient place to disembark.

The second difficulty was that the element of surprise was unattainable. By using the utmost caution and by sheer good fortune secrecy might be maintained to a point, but once the troops got off the ships there could be no further concealment. Greece was neutral and dozens of German agents milled about the city port, complete with notebooks in which to record details of units, their equipment and probable destination. It would take several weeks before the Allies were ready to march inland, by which time the enemy would know what to expect. This introduced a third problem. As soon as the Allies began to march into the interior, the Central Powers would have ample time to decide on a strategy and, if circumstances warranted, make adjustments. Unlike the conditions at the Dardanelles where the Turks had to cling to their defences or open the way to Constantinople, Germany and its partners did not have to hold any ground south of the Danube. They could attack immediately or withdraw north and wait for a more favourable opportunity. From a military point of view the Central Powers were clearly in a dominant position.[37]

It is apparent that Briand and his colleagues had rushed into the Balkan imbroglio without carefully weighing the risks involved. After all they knew little or nothing about logistics, the quality of the transportation system and the topography which not only favoured the defence but inhibited the wide sweep of armies. It was extremely irresponsible for the cabinet to have neglected to consult the general staff at the Ministry of War as to the feasibility of an operation in the Balkans before reaching its decision. It can be argued that the military experts, as

36 Poincaré, *Au service*, Vol. 7, pp. 116-18.
37 Gen. C. R. Ballard, *Kitchener* (New York: Dodd, Mead and Co., 1930), pp. 305-6; Field Marshal Sir William Robertson, *Soldiers and Statesmen 1914–1918*, Vol. 2 (London: Cassel, 1926), p. 88; General Erich von Falkenhayn, *General Headquarters 1914–1916 and its Critical Decisions* (London: Hutchinson, 1919), pp. 190-92.

Westerners, would not have approached their study objectively, but surely they could have been trusted to point out the myriad obstacles that lay ahead following the landing at Salonica. That might have been enough to give the cabinet pause before it blindly pursued what turned out to be a dangerous and foolhardy course.

Traditionally disdainful of "sideshows", Joffre shuddered at the prospect of opening another front in the east. This would have been the proper moment for him to counter the government's proposal with the same dogged resistance he had shown in preventing the Asiatic landing from materializing. But outwardly Joffre fell in line with the government's new policy and, according to Henry Wilson, did so to ensure the demise of the Asiatic landing.[38] He found the diversion in the Balkans less objectionable than the Dardanelles campaign for, in his mind, it would at least serve to draw German reserves from the Western Front.

In a memorandum dated 23 September, Joffre advocated that, as France did not have the resources to sustain three fronts, the defence of Serbia must be achieved at the expense of the operations in the Dardanelles. He maintained that the attack in the Dardanelles had been initiated to open a direct route to Russia but, that having failed, it was necessary to establish communications via Salonica and the Danube. He considered that the first installment of forces should consist of four divisions, two French and two British. He observed that the requisite French divisions should be drawn from Gallipoli which would also give the impression – ridiculously naïve if he actually believed it – that their movement was a "manoeuvre and not a withdrawal."[39]

Joffre's acquiescence sealed the government's decision. The French had left the domain of discussion, such as it was, and were ready to set their plans in motion. Their reckoning, however, assumed that London would move in the same direction.

Across the channel the English were livid that the French had made a huge commitment without reference to them. They were straining every nerve to meet the needs of their four fronts – besides France and the Dardanelles, Egypt and Mesopotamia – and were far less in a hurry to overreach themselves. Kitchener calculated that, in addition to Greece's estimated 180,000-man army, the Allies would require no fewer than 300,000 men if they hoped to save Serbia from annihilation. He had no surplus troops on hand, and none could be diverted from France until the end of the month. As a last resort, drafts could be withdrawn from Hamilton's army but at the expense of evacuating Suvla. Kitchener saw no immediate threat to Egypt even if Serbia fell and, as he was still fuming over the French cancellation of their projected Asiatic operation, his first instinct was to wait upon events. Still nothing less than swift action would satisfy Paris. The British had serious reservations but in the interest of preserving unity, in the words of Asquith, "it was impossible for us in the circumstances to hold back."[40]

Kitchener had no option but to turn to Hamilton to supply England's portion of troops. However, Hamilton, seconded by de Robeck, pleaded against retirement from Suvla, claiming that such a course would lead to disastrous consequences. Hamilton's fear of a possible withdrawal from Gallipoli deepened upon the receipt of a message from Bailloud on 25 September that

---

38 IWM: Wilson papers, entry in Wilson's diary, 6 October 1915.
39 Joffre to Millerand, 24 September 1915, in France, *Les armées françaises*, tome 8, Vol. 2, annexe no. 43.
40 BNA: Cabinet papers, CAB 37/35/1, Asquith to George V, 2 October 1915; Hankey, *Supreme Command*, Vol. 1, pp. 417-18.

Paris had instructed him to prepare one of his divisions for service elsewhere.[41] There was no indication of its destination or reason for its departure. During the night Hamilton received a cable from the War Office, explaining the ramifications of the Bulgarian mobilization and directing him to arrange the despatch to Salonica of two British divisions and one French division or brigade. The General replied that he could get along without the two divisions (identified as the 10th and 53rd) and no more than a French brigade, otherwise he would be unable to maintain the front at Suvla. No sooner had the telegram left, then Hamilton received a message from Bailloud, saying that he had been told to concentrate a French division at Mudros to serve in the Balkans under his command. The other French division was to remain on the Peninsula under General Brulard (his second in command).[42] Hamilton answered that no such notice had arrived and, as his instructions were specific, he could not permit the departure of a division from the Peninsula. A directive from the War Office confirming Bailloud's mandate ended the dispute.

Relations between Hamilton and Bailloud, civil but never cordial, were strained by events during the latter part of the summer. From the very beginning Hamilton had taken a dim view of Bailloud, judging him to be timid, an inveterate complainer, duplicitous, and unfit to command. Bailloud, for his part, had no use for Hamilton either. He resented that his proposals to silence the Turkish batteries in Asia, which were taking a heavy toll on and affecting the morale of French troops on Helles, had been ignored by Hamilton. Another sore point with Bailloud was Hamilton's refusal, on security grounds, to divulge information concerning his forthcoming operations in August until the last moment. When de Bertier had approached the British to learn about the plan, he was told bluntly that "a shared secret was no longer a secret."[43] Bailloud accused the British of selfishness and inconsideration in a confidential letter to Millerand on 1 October as he was about to leave Gallipoli. While he conceded that on the surface his working relations with Hamilton and his commanders were excellent, he added that it was wholly different when the interests and prestige of the British were at stake.[44]

In truth seldom, if ever, in the conduct of a coalition war do the separate parties always see eye-to-eye on the major issues. That differences sometimes sprang up between the two military partners in the Dardanelles should not have come as a surprise. After months of working together, at times under strained circumstances, both Bailloud and Hamilton were tired of one another. The increasingly troubled relationship was perhaps more difficult for Bailloud to bear because he no longer had any faith in the eventual success of the Dardanelles operation. In fact, he looked forward to leaving in the mistaken belief that he would be in charge of French troops in the new theatre.

On 30 September Kitchener asked Hamilton to comment on Bailloud's claim that the remaining French division on Cape Helles could resist any attack on its line. Hamilton could not conceal his anger. In reply he maintained that Bailloud had fed false information in order to suit his own ends: "He is perfidious and determined to play entirely for his own hand the moment a

---

41 BNA: War Office archives, WO tel. no. 2204, Hamilton to Kitchener, 25 September 1915.
42 Hamilton, *Gallipoli Diary*, Vol. 2, p. 225.
43 SHD: De Bertier papers, 7N 2170, De Bertier to Hamelin (chief of the African section which was a component of the French army's general staff), 10 August 1915. For the body's role overseas see Greenhalgh and Guelton, "The French on Gallipol", in Ashley Ekins (ed.), *A Ridge too far*, pp. 221-22.
44 AN: Millerand papers, 470 AP/16, Bailloud to Millerand, 1 October 1915.

cloud shows above the horizon." Hamilton charged that Bailloud had "leaped at the prospect of getting away from a position which I have had the greatest difficulty in persuading him to hold with two divisions, and which he now thinks can be held with one division, comprised largely of unreliable black troops; this is startling enough to need no comment." Hamilton went on to say: "If you want to get at his real opinion, suggest that he stays here with one division while Brulard goes to Salonica."[45]

In Paris there were no signs that the drama surrounding *l'affaire Sarrail* was winding down. Sarrail, under the impression that he was heading for the Dardanelles, remained unaware of the cabinet's change of plans until Alphonse Aulard, a good friend and famed historian of the French Revolution at the Sorbonne, alerted him on 25 September that the cabinet had decided to send one of the French divisions in the Dardanelles to Salonica.[46] Four days later Millerand formally informed Sarrail of the new destination of the Army of the Orient and asked him to draw up a note on the subject of French intervention in the Balkans. Sarrail complied at once and in his memo dated 2 October pointed out that the suggested force of three brigades – one assigned from France and Bailloud's division – would have no real impact and could not be regarded as anything more than a gesture. Rather than adopt a role at best limited to protecting a section of the Nish-Salonica railway, he suggested a more ambitious project if the size of the army was comprised of three corps. While 30,000 British troops – the full number was as yet unknown – held the line of communication between Salonica and the Serbian border, French forces would pour into Serbia and mount a massive offensive in the direction of Sofia to knock Bulgaria out of the war. He thought that in order to avoid delays and misunderstanding the British force should be subordinated to the French commander.[47]

The following day, the Viviani government appointed Sarrail commander-in-chief of the French army operating in the Balkans. His assignment was initially to cover the communications between Salonica and Serbia against any threats from Bulgaria and eventually to cooperate with the Serbian army in fighting its enemies.[48] To say that Sarrail's instructions were vague would be an understatement.

On 5 October, Millerand and Augagneur journeyed to Calais for a meeting with Kitchener and Balfour. The object of the conclave was to determine the number of troops each side would provide and the exact role of the Balkan expedition. Millerand explained that Joffre had agreed to send 37,000 men at once – which included a division from the Dardanelles – with an additional 27,000 once his offensive was over. Kitchener, in turn, expressed reservations about the whole affair but he agreed to match the 64,000 men – one infantry and one cavalry division immediately, plus three more after Joffre's offensive was over – the French promised to send. This still fell short of the number of troops the Greeks requested by 22,000. Millerand wanted the British to make up the difference, but Kitchener deferred for the time being, pointing out that the troops would have to be drawn from Sir John French's command. On the issue of a supreme commander, Millerand suggested that both the French and British commanders should be coequals and operate under the direction of the c-in-c of the Serbian army. Balfour

---

45 BNA: War Office archives, WO tel. no. 2274, Hamilton to Kitchener, 1 October 1915.
46 Sarrail, *Mon commandement*, pp. xiv-xv.
47 Sarrail, Note au suject de l'intervention françaises dans les Balkans, 2 October 1915, in France, *Les armées françaises*, tome 8, Vol. 2, annexe no. 96.
48 Millerand to Sarrail, 3 October 1915, in France, *Les armées françaises*, tome 8, Vol. 2, annexe no. 100.

agreed to provide transportation, not only for the British contingent, but for some of the French troops as well.

A disagreement arose when the dialogue shifted to the purpose of the Balkan expedition. Kitchener pointed out that before leaving London he and his colleagues were under the impression that the Allies were to assist the Greeks fulfil their obligation to the Serbs but on arriving at Calais he discovered that the French objective was to go to the aid of Serbia. He claimed that 150,000 would be insufficient to save Serbia and was adamant that British troops would not leave Salonica unless Greece entered the war.[49] This is how matters stood when the talks ended.

The Allied dissension over a military strategy was further complicated by the sudden turn of events in Greece. On the same day of the Calais conference, the Germanophile King Constantine repudiated the invitation issued to the Allies and announced Greece's intention to remain neutral, leaving Venizelos with no option but to resign. The British and the French reacted differently to the Greek refusal to take the field. For the British it eliminated the reason for Allied intervention in the Balkans, but it had no effect in Paris. The French cabinet, except for Delcassé, remained convinced that it was vital to save Serbia. But where were the troops to come from? The Russians had been approached for a contribution but sent their regrets. Joffre, needless to say, would never permit to supply more than a token force from his front. Under the circumstances the Viviani cabinet's only recourse was to turn to the British government and try to persuade it to significantly augment its allocation to the expedition. On 6 October Augagneur and Viviani were chosen to journey to London that evening to present the French case, emphasizing that the abandonment of Serbia would allow Bulgaria to cut communications with Russia and for the Germans to open the road to Constantinople; and if the war in the Near East were lost, German leaders would divert the divisions on that front to the west and, together with the main body of their army's forces, finish off the French.[50] No less important for the cabinet than the assumed benefits of sending an expedition to Salonica was the need to end the political crisis at home. If the Balkan operation were cancelled, Sarrail would be left without a prominent field command.

Following the cabinet meeting, Millerand notified Sarrail that he was to leave immediately for Salonica to take command of three divisions (two of which would be from the Dardanelles), far fewer than the three corps he had requested. On the previous day Sarrail had sought to learn the exact aim of his mission. Unable to receive clarification from the Quai d'Orsay, he had called on Poincaré who proved equally unhelpful. Sarrail's political admirers, concerned about the inadequacy of his forces, rallied around him and advised him not to leave the country. Léon Blum, *chef de cabinet* of the Ministry of Public Works, recommended an exchange of posts with Franchet d'Espèrey, who commanded the Fifth Army and was known to be familiar with the terrain in the Balkans. Paul Benazet, a leftist deputy, warned Sarrail not to hurl himself into an "Oriental wasp nest." Even Georges Clemenceau became involved, telling Sarrail that he could still change his mind. The Tiger was convinced that that the Allied operation in the Balkan

---

49 Compte rendu de la conference tenu à Calais le 5/10/15, in France, *Les armées françaises,* tome 8, Vol. 2, annexe no. 108.
50 Poincaré, *Au service,* Vol. 7, pp. 158-59.

would never materialize because the French had no surplus troops and the British were unlikely to support such a mad scheme.[51]

Still Sarrail wearied of enforced inactivity and concluded that he could not advance his career by remaining at home. Yet in accepting his new assignment he understood that he would be playing into the hands of his enemies who wanted him out of the country at almost any cost. Sarrail maintained that his reason for taking control of the French forces at Salonica was so that "it might not be said that I had evaded a most thankless task." To add to his woes, he went on to say: "I did not have the requested reinforcements; I did not have a supply chief, having been denied the one that I had demanded; graver yet, I still had no directive."[52] Matters would not improve after his arrival in Salonica.

Contrary to expectations, the departure of Sarrail from Marseilles on 7 October did not ease the political pressure on the Viviani ministry. On the previous evening a group of prominent leftist parliamentarians met with Viviani and insisted that the force under Sarrail was ridiculously undersized and tantamount to sending him to the "slaughter-house." They wanted the number of divisions substantially increased regardless of whether it was in harmony with the views of the British or Joffre. As they were about to leave, one member issued a warning: "If you want to avert real trouble, you haven't a minute to lose in order to correct the mistake of our diplomacy and to shake off your inertia and show some energy."[53]

It had been an exhausting day for the besieged Viviani, and it was not yet over. A train took him and Augagneur to Calais where they boarded a steamer and crossed the channel in the early hours of the 7th. If Viviani hoped to gain some relief at home, he needed to wrest the desired concessions from the British. It would not be an easy task.

Already overburdened, the British were about to be asked to take on another major commitment. If they agreed to accommodate the French, they would be unable to meet Hamilton's appeal for reinforcements. The fate of the Dardanelles rested on the outcome of the negotiations between London and Paris.

---

51 Sarrail, *Mon commandement*, pp, xiv-xv; Coblentz, *Silence of Sarrail*, p. 108; King, *General and Politicians*, pp. 80-81.
52 Sarrail, *Mon commandement*, p. xv.
53 Cited in Tannenbaum, *Maurice Sarrail*, p. 69.

12

End of the Adventure

On the morning of 7 October Viviani and Augagneur arrived in London and in the afternoon conferred with Asquith, Kitchener, Balfour and Grey at 10 Downing Street. Viviani argued on the necessity of mounting a major Allied campaign in the Balkans and, to that end, proposed that the British supply 333,000 of the 400,000 men required.[1] The British position had hardened since the resignation of Venizelos and they had already repudiated the agreement concluded at Calais on the 5th so they were in no mood to entertain Viviani's implausible suggestion.

It turned out that in disclosing their agenda, the French ministers had not consulted Joffre. It was well known that Joffre had always resisted efforts to deploy large numbers of troops outside of France. Thereupon Kitchener hurried over to Chantilly to hold talks with the Generalissimo on 8 October. What Kitchener did not realize was that under political pressure Joffre's attitude had begun to change. During the meeting Joffre underlined the need to assist Serbia, for which he intended to allocate 60,000 men with Britain, given its greater available manpower resources, supplying the balance of the 150,000 required total. Kitchener estimated that the Allies would need to concentrate 250,000 men to avert Serbia's defeat and 400,000 to launch a major offensive against Austria. Joffre dismissed all thoughts of undertaking a major campaign in the Balkans. While he admitted that it was too late to save Serbia, he believed that 150,000 men would suffice to play a defensive role: that is securing the base at Salonica, keeping the railway open to Uskub, fending off the Bulgarians, and, if necessary, covering the Serbian army's retreat to the sea. Kitchener saw no point in risking 150,000 men to carry out an enterprise that had no rational basis. But Joffre would not yield an inch and the meeting ended with Kitchener agreeing to the earlier plan to send 150,000 men to Salonica.[2] In the interest of preserving a semblance of unity, Kitchener had reversed his government's decision against sending any British troops to Salonica.

The Dardanelles Committee on 11 October essentially repudiated Kitchener's accord with Joffre at Chantilly. As Joffre's offensive was virtually over and not likely to be renewed for some months, the discussion centered on whether British troops should be sent to the Dardanelles or

---

[1] Hankey, *Supreme Command*, Vol.1, p. 428.
[2] AN: Millerand papers, 470 AP/15, Compte renu de la conférence tenu à Chantilly, 8 October 1915; Hankey, *Supreme Command*, Vol.1, 429.

the Balkans. The majority of the members favoured mounting another assault on Gallipoli but a few, led by Lloyd George, argued vigorously that abandoning Serbia would send the wrong message to the rest of the world. To break the impasse, the committee accepted the Prime Minister's proposal that substantial forces should be withdrawn from the Western Front and sent to Egypt to await their ultimate destination; and that a specially selected general should be despatched to the Near East to study and advise the most advantageous place the troops should be used.[3]

Britain's foot-dragging was deeply resented in Paris where the *union sacrée* was in danger of collapsing. As if *l'affaire Sarrail* was not bad enough, more trouble had been brewing ever since Delcassé fell out of the government's Balkan policy. In the beginning Delcassé opposed opening a new front in the Balkans but he had been brought around to the idea when it was pointed out that, with the Greeks, Russians and possibly Italians providing troops, only a token force would be removed from French soil. But the expected outside aid never came and he grew increasingly uneasy at the prospect of draining the Western Front and jeopardizing the security of France. Although his diplomatic triumphs in the early years of the 20th century had raised his standing to lofty heights at home and on the international stage, his last tenure in office, apart from helping entice Italy to fight alongside the Allies, was marked by one failure after another. He was reproached for consenting to Russia's annexation of Constantinople and the Straits at the end of the war, an act made even more unpopular in France by the conviction that it had driven Greece, Romania and Bulgaria away from the Entente, and by Petrograd's unwillingness to provide aid either in the Balkans or in the Dardanelles. His efforts to create a block of Balkan states that would join the Entente in the conflict had been a disaster. He nursed the illusion that Bulgaria would form the mainstay of such a league and went to extraordinary limits to win it over, confident that Romania and Greece would follow suit. He ignored early warnings that Bulgaria was practically in Germany's orbit and to distrust the promises of its King Ferdinand. The folly of his Balkan policy became apparent when Bulgaria came into the war on the side of the Central Powers during the second week in October.[4]

During the latter half of 1915, Delcassé's health began to fail, in part due to agonizing over the possible fate that awaited his aviator son, shot down and captured by the Germans – the name Delcassé was despised in Germany. Showered with criticism in parliament for and shaken by his diplomatic reverses, at loggerheads with his colleagues over Salonica, ill and worried, the daily duties of his office became unbearable. Finally on 12 October Delcassé tendered his resignation over the protest of Poincaré who wanted him to remain at the Quai d'Orsay to uphold French prestige among the Allies.[5]

The resignation of so prominent a figure as Delcassé, as one well-known historian has written, "inevitably shook the Viviani government to its foundations and caused widespread misgivings throughout France."[6] Viviani met the emergency by assuming the portfolio of foreign affairs and

---

3   BNA: Cabinet papers, CAB 42/4, Minutes of the Dardanelles Committee, 11 October 1915; Hankey, *Supreme Command*, Vol.1, pp. 429-30.
4   A secret treaty between Bulgaria and Germany and Austria-Hungary had been signed on 6 October 1915.
5   Zorgbibe, *Delcassé*, pp. 327-28; Claeys, *Delcassé*, pp. 275-76; Porter, *Théophile Delcassé*, pp. 330-34; Poincaré, *Au service*, Vol.7, pp. 174-75; Wright, *Raymond Poincaré* pp. 157-58.
6   Dutton, *Politics of Diplomacy*, p. 52.

attempting to reshuffle his cabinet but the announcement that Joffre's offensive in Champagne had faltered let loose all the complaints that had been accumulating since the middle of 1915. The calamitous and endless loss of life for no apparent gain was laid at the doorsteps of the high command and produced a spirit of disillusionment in the country. Beneath the military bungling the fabric of the nation was being torn apart. France was straining to make good its losses and could not continue at the present pace much longer. There had to be a change in policy. Yet how could this be done? Joffre had been at liberty to manage the war as he pleased. Cloistered in the small town of Chantilly he struck back at those who sought to diminish his authority and dismissed with disdain and outrage any advice which conflicted with his own plans. Such methods would have been tolerated, much as they infuriated the politicians, had they shown to be effective against the enemy. But the so called "nibbling attacks" throughout 1915 had consumed huge manpower resources without producing any tangible results and the laurels that Joffre had won at the Marne were rapidly receding into the pages of history.

The growing despair in the nation was reflected in the chamber where parliamentarians freely castigated the government for its want of grip in managing the war, for its rosy prognostications that failed to materialize and for allowing GQG too much independence. If the country was to fight on to victory, leaders with new ideas were needed to chart a different course and maintain close supervision over the army.

Beyond the usual complaints, another recent one was added by left wing deputies whose concern about the fate of Sarrail found expression in relentless attacks against the government. It did not help that Viviani, at his wit's end to find a solution to appease them, made an obviously disingenuous announcement in the Chamber on 12 October to the effect that Britain and France were working together to send assistance to Serbia and, acting on the advice of military experts, agreed on the number of men required.[7] As a consequence he received no respite and, in fact, things got worse after the nation's attention was drawn to the Balkans where fighting had broken out. On 11 October Bulgarian troops clashed with Serbian units and two days later each country declared war on the other. On the 13th the Bulgarians also came into contact with Sarrail's forces. On that day, Viviani was subjected to the most blistering attack in the chamber, accused of sending Sarrail on a suicide mission and of failing to provide him with sufficient divisions when he was sent out. Teetering on the edge of a precipice, the Viviani ministry survived a vote of no confidence by a tally of 372 to 9. The appearance of faith in Viviani's leadership was deceiving as over 150 deputies abstained from voting.[8]

The facade of political harmony did not relieve left-wing pressure on the Viviani ministry, determined as they were to ensure that Sarrail was not left in the lurch. Viviani responded by sending Millerand to London on the 15th to urge that the British commit several additional divisions to the Balkans. Millerand was unable to see Asquith (who was ill) but he held interviews with the other leading ministers. Grey told him bluntly that Britain would provide no more than the one division (10th) already at Salonica. Kitchener was only slightly more encouraging, saying that he would not exclude sending there additional troops destined for Egypt if circumstances so warranted. Millerand engaged in discussions with other members of the cabinet, only to find that they supported the hardline position with such conviction

[7] Tannenbaum, *Maurice Sarrail*, p. 71.
[8] Dutton, *Politics of Diplomacy*, p. 53.

and passion that he believed that his mission had failed completely. His despair was relieved somewhat by Lloyd George who indicated that there were others in the cabinet who, like him, saw merit in the Balkan expedition. Still Millerand had to fight an uphill battle to try to overcome the general sentiment in London that there was no military rationale for sending more troops to the Balkans as it was too late to save Serbia. His most compelling argument was that, unless left-wing radicals in the chamber were pacified, Viviani would be forced to resign and the alliance itself would be imperiled if the peace-seeking Caillaux should be thrust into power. After much give and take Millerand settled for a compromise. The resolution adopted was couched in the following terms:

> The two Governments consider that one of their principal objectives in the Balkan Peninsula is to oppose the passage of the Austro-German troops to Constantinople. Consequently they agreed to send the necessary contingents to constitute a force of 150,000 men.
> If, however, particularly at the moment of the landing of the British troops in Egypt … a new examination of the military situation should appear to be necessary to one or other of the two Governments, such examination will be undertaken in agreement by the two Governments with a view to arrive at an understanding as to the manner in which their troops shall be deployed.[9]

The arrangement Millerand worked out with the British was scrutinized by Viviani, Poincaré and Joffre on the 20th, a day or two after his return from London. No one, not even Millerand, was happy with the accord. All immediately recognized that it left the British a way out if they should have second thoughts. There were other factors weighing heavily on Viviani's mind which made the pressure on him almost unbearable. He was concerned with Millerand's statement to parliament, which contradicted his understanding with the British. The Prime Minister feared that as soon as the details were known, Millerand would be held accountable for lying and may have to go.[10] On the previous day Viviani had appeared before the Commission on Foreign Affairs where he was given a severe dressing down by hostile inquisitors. The chairman (Georges Leygues) warned Viviani that there would be ominous political repercussions unless Sarrail was reinforced by several hundred thousand men.[11]

The news from the Balkans did not alleviate the anxiety in Paris. On 22 October the Bulgarians advanced across the railway south of Uskub, severing the communications of the Serbian army with Salonica. Consequently Paris directed Sarrail to march inland to join hands with the Serbs, but the British were unwilling to plunge headlong into the Balkan theatre without Greece's commitment to join the war.

Viviani met with Joffre on 23 October and explained that his ministry was tottering and that unless the demands of Sarrail's fervent supporters could be met, he might be forced to resign in which case his post as commander-in-chief would be endangered. Joffre realized that in the event Sarrail suffered a military reverse, even a minor one, he might becaome a victim of the political fallout and that prospect drove him to take a more active role to induce the British, not only to follow France's lead but to contribute the majority of the forces for the Balkan

---

9 SHD: Millerand paperts, 470 AP/15, Millerand to Viviani, 19 October 1915.
10 Poincaré, *Au Service*, Vol.7, pp. 187-88.
11 Tannenbaum, *Maurice Sarrail*, pp. 71-72.

expedition. He urged London that the six British divisions removed from France should be sent, not to Egypt, but to Salonica to prevent the destruction of the Serbian army. On top of this, he wanted the British government to transfer all of its troops in the Dardanelles to the Balkans so that the entire Allied contingent there would be raised to 250,000 men.

London would not consider Joffre's formula but agreed to discuss the matter. An Anglo-French military conference held at Chantilly on the 27th failed to break the impasse. Joffre was so upset with the results that he hurried over to London to make a personal plea. At a meeting at 10 Downing Street he explained that if the British were unwilling to concentrate 250,000 men in Salonica they could at least agree to 150,000 – about half the number that Sarrail, once on the scene, estimated would be required to save Serbia. Joffre indicated that their task would be confined to guarding the Nish-Salonica railway, while Sarrail with his three divisions would try to establish contact with the Serbian army. He intimated that a British refusal to join the French in sending adequate reinforcements to the Balkans would place his own position and even the alliance itself in grave jeopardy. The Dardanelles Committee had already received information from the British embassy in Paris confirming Millerand's earlier warning about the political chaos in the capital and the frail state of the Viviani ministry. The last thing the British wanted to see was a new administration headed by Joseph Caillaux whom they strongly suspected favoured a compromise peace with Germany. Thus for the sake of preserving the alliance, the British bowed to what Churchill termed "this outrageous threat." Kitchener consented to send four additional divisions to Salonica on the understanding that if it proved impossible to reopen and maintain communications with the Serbian army, the Anglo-French force would be withdrawn.[12]

Joffre's arrangement with London arrived too late to save the Viviani administration. As violent scenes in parliament had persisted, Viviani concluded that his days were numbered and informed the President that he could no longer continue in office. After accepting Viviani's resignation on 29 October, Poincaré entrusted the formation of the new cabinet to the outgoing Minister of Justice, Aristide Briand, a durable and experienced politician with a proven ability to reconcile persons of widely different beliefs and temperament. Briand went to work assigning the various portfolios, retaining some of the former incumbents and taking on the added responsibility of assuming control at the Ministry of Foreign Affairs. The difficult task of finding a suitable replacement for Millerand was complicated by the unusual request of the British Monarch, George V, that he be retained in the new government in the interest of Anglo-French harmony. The King, acting on the advice of Lord Bertie, had appealed directly to Poincaré who was known to interfere in the selection of cabinet ministers. The much maligned Millerand was considered "dead weight" and an obvious liability to any incoming ministry. Poincaré replied to George V that regretfully Millerand could not be included in the new cabinet.[13] To assume the duties at St. Dominique, Briand turned to General Galliéni. The old soldier clearly did not

---

12   BNA: Cabinet papers, CAB 28/1, Anglo-French and Allied Conferences, Notes of a Conference held at 10 Downing Stree on 29 October 1915; BNA: CAB 42/4, Minutes of the Dardanelles Commission, 29 and 30 October 1915; Cyril Falls, *Military Operations: Macedonia*, Vol.1 (London: HMSO, 1933), pp. 44-45; Dutton, *Politics of Diplomacy*, pp. 55-57; Tannenbaum, *Maurice Sarrail*, pp. 72-74; Prete, "Imbroglio par excellance,"pp. 64-67; Churchill, *World Crisis*, Vol. 2, pp. 504-06.
13   CCAC: Esher papers, Vol.5, under the heading Letters and Memoranda, Esher to George V, 23 October 1915; and George V to Esher, 25 October 1915.

want the post but an appeal to his sense of patriotism overcame his resistance.[14] Authoritative, stubborn and blunt, Galliéni was nonetheless a judicious and clever professional soldier and, in keeping with his strength of character, was unafraid to make critical decisions. As he was never on the best of terms with Joffre, his arrival at the Ministry of War was likely to initiate a new phase in the relationship between GQG and the government. In another key change, Augagneur, tarred by the charge that he had been duped (*roulé*) by Churchill, was dropped in favour of the much respected Admiral Marie Jean Lacaze at the Ministry of Marine.

The new government, consistent with the spirit of the *union sacrée*, included figures from the entire political spectrum.[15] It was slightly more to the right than the previous one, but it was not expected to produce any radical change in the conduct of state affairs. Briand himself was a stronger personality then Viviani and a skilled political operator, raising hopes that he could keep the bond holding men of different political persuasion from fraying. He was among the most fervent advocate of a diversion in the Balkans as a means to strike the Central Powers from the rear and establish a base to secure French post-war aims in the eastern Mediterranean. In his first speech to the chamber on 3 November he promised unequivocally that he would not abandon Serbia. He might have chosen his words more carefully for at that very moment the Bulgarians were driving towards Skopje and Veles, forcing the Serbs to retreat to the southwest. It did not augur well for the prime minister whose political survival was linked to the fate of the adventure in the Balkans.

Since Joffre had been unwilling to allocate more than three divisions to the Balkan theatre, it was assumed in London that the French were going to concentrate exclusively on their new interest and wash their hands of the Dardanelles. Unknown to the British, however, Paris, which still had troops under Brulard on the Peninsula, had not made a final decision. Even before Briand's ascendency, the matter had been debated in the French war councils. The *Section d'études* adopted the line that, if the enemy front in the Balkans were reinforced, the withdrawal from the Dardanelles was inevitable. Such a move, it insisted, would not directly affect the interests of France.[16] The Superior Council of Defence considered the recommendation when it assembled for the first time on 4 November. It interviewed Colonel Girodon, who had been invalided home after a serious lung wound and was currently attached (again) to Galliéni's staff. Girodon was adamantly opposed to withdrawing from Gallipoli where he observed that the Allied troops were tying down the bulk of the Turkish army. Without an Allied presence on the Peninsula, he felt that the Turks would be free to send large forces to the Balkans or even Belgium. Admiral Lacaze was equally convinced that the retirement of Anglo-French troops could lead to a disaster. By attempting to pull out, much of the artillery would be lost and there was no assurance that the men could be safely removed from the Peninsula. Joffre, on the other hand, was dead set against transferring new divisions from France, repeating that it was on the main front that the German army would be beaten. In the end the Superior Council rejected

---

14 For behind the scenes details see P.H. Gheusi, *Guerre et théâtre 1914-1918* (Paris: Berger-Levrault, 1919), p. 229; Marius-Ary Leblond, *Galliéni parle* , Vol.1 (Paris: Albin Michel, 1920), pp. 87-89; Lyautey, *Galliéni* , p. 274.
15 See Appendix I for the composition of the 5th Briand ministry.
16 SHD: AMG, 3837 GOG, Section d'études, Notes pour M. le ministre, 24 October and 3 November 1915.

the arguments of the *Section d'études* and resolved to cling to Gallipoli, at least for the time being.[17]

Besides the testimony of Girodon and Lacaze there were other factors that influenced the conclusion of the Superior Council. In the first place General Lyautey had warned his civilian chief that an acknowledgement of defeat in the Dardanelles would be the signal for the Turkish Government to encourage its co-religionists to rise against the French in North Africa, in which case, unless substantially reinforced, he could probably hold Morocco but doubted that Algeria could be retained.[18] Second, the French were eager to foster Arab nationalist movements in Syria and elsewhere but they had no available troops to support it. They worried that all these movements would have little chance of succeeding if Gallipoli were evacuated.[19]

On 5 November Kitchener stopped for two days in Paris on the way to the Near East. There had been new developments in the British camp in the last few weeks. Hamilton who had lost the confidence of the Dardanelles Committee after his last defeat in August was replaced by General Monro who was to report "fully and frankly," on the military prospects in the Dardanelles. After Monro landed at Mudros on 28 October, he took charge of the expeditionary force. He spent six hours inspecting all three fronts on Gallipoli and, after conferring with the local commanders, wrote a 700 word report advocating evacuation. As a confirmed Westerner hostile to sideshows, it cannot be claimed that he came with an open mind but he undoubtedly made the right decision. Kitchener was extremely upset by the report. On 3 November the new War Committee – which replaced the Dardanelles Committee – put off making a decision on Monro's recommendation. Instead it decided that Kitchener should proceed to the Near East to survey the scene himself and render a second opinion. When Kitchener left London on the evening of the 4th, his spirits could not have been much lower.

On arrival in Paris, Kitchener was surprised and delighted to discover that the new French government was opposed to the evacuation of Gallipoli. He received the first intimation when he met Gallién and found out that he thought it would be sheer folly to withdraw from the Peninsula. The two soldiers were inclined to think along the same lines except for differences on the merits of the Salonica venture. In the early days of the deadlock in the west Galliéni had been one of the few generals who favoured striking the enemy from the Balkans and thereafter brought up the idea in discussions with politicians. On each occasion the government, unwilling to invite Joffre's wrath, had turned thumbs down, explaining that it did not have the means to supply another theatre. The right moment had slipped by and now Galliéni admitted to Kitchener that the relief force would arrive too late to save Serbia. Nonetheless, like his colleagues in the cabinet, he was reluctant to face the consequences of disengagement from the Balkans. This provoked Kitchener into remarking brusquely: "Your Government seems to have no plans, only aspirations."[20] No statement better fitted the circumstances and the French War Minister could only shrug his shoulders.

The interview with Galliéni set the tone for Kitchener's subsequent talks with French leaders. Kitchener explained to Briand that the continued presence of the Allies on Gallipoli tied down

17 Poincaré, *Au service*, Vol. 7, pp. 220-21. See also Girodon, "Note pour M. le ministre," 4 November 1915, in France, *Les armées françaises*, tome 8, Vol.1, annexe no. 376.
18 British Library (BL): 49726, Vol. 44, Balfour papers, Kitchener to Balfour, 6 November 1915.
19 BNA: Kitchener papers, PRO 30/57/66, Kitchener to Asquith, 5 November 1915.
20 Esher, *Tragedy of Lord Kitchener*, p. 170; Lyautey, *Galliéni*, p. 272; Leblond, *Galliéni parle*, Vol. 2, p. 109.

large Turkish forces which otherwise would be free to advance on Egypt. While understanding the effect the evacuation of Gallipoli would have on Muslim feeling in North Africa and elsewhere, Briand was more concerned on sending massive reinforcements to Salonica to rescue the Serbian army and possibly tempt Greece and Romania into abandoning their neutral status. Kitchener replied that for the moment he could not remove any more troops from Gallipoli and tried in vain to dissuade Briand from pursuing his Balkan policy. Kitchener was frustrated with the French government's tendency to base its plans on imaginary results and to have lost its bearing. He wrote to Asquith that evening: "They simply sweep all military dangers and difficulties aside and go on political lines … I could get no idea when the troops could come out [from Salonica]: they only said they must watch events."[21]

At the British embassy Kitchener expressed a strong wish to meet Colonel Girodon after informed of his service on Gallipoli and his outstanding qualities as a soldier. The French Colonel was contacted and on his arrival at the embassy was escorted to a room which Kitchener occupied on the upper level. Kitchener liked him immediately. Girodon spoke English as though it were his native tongue and shared Kitchener's fears about the adverse consequences of withdrawing from the Dardanelles.

Interestingly, Girodon had previously encountered Kitchener under unusual and less than pleasant circumstances in January 1897, although in hindsight, he probably chuckled in relating the incident to friends. Both he and his cousin Adophe Messimy (the future minister of war) had just graduated from the military academy at Saint-Cyr and were spending part of their holiday as tourists in Egypt, visiting ancient sites. During their stay, they decided to journey to Wadi Halfa where the Anglo-Egyptian army was concentrating, preparatory to its invasion of the Sudan. They acquired a little steam boat and travelled at night because they were told that a stretch of territory of some 200 kilometers before reaching the base was off limits to tourists. On the morning of the second day's journey, they were stopped by a British vessel and taken on board as prisoners. Arriving at camp they were led to see Kitchener whose busy schedule was suddenly interrupted and, as he was in a surly mood, proceeded to give then a severe tongue lashing. As Kitchener paused they reminded him – a tale told to them at the French consul in Cairo – that in 1870 he had joined the French army without even asking authorization from his own government.[22] Girodon followed up by saying, "Do we look like spies?" Kitchener's demeanor changed and he told them they were free to leave which they did hurriedly.[23]

Girodon was no ordinary officer. He had won his laurels by displaying exceptional skill and courage on the battlefield. He held definite opinions and was not afraid to express them even when they conflicted with government policy. He was charming, handsome, alert and held in high regard by all his superiors, as well as officers and soldiers with whom he worked or came

---

21   BNA: Kitchener papers, PRO 30/57/66, Kitchener to Asquith, 5 November, 1915.
22   Passing out of Woolwich in December 1870, Herbert Kitchener joined his father who had remarried and was living in Dinan (in Brittany), France, which was approaching the end of a disastrous war with Prussia. Young Herbert was eager to gain first-hand experience of war and, with his father's encouragement, joined the army of General Chanzy. He was attached to an ambulance unit and saw plenty of harrowing sights but no action. After Paris capitulated in January 1871, he returned to England where he was severely reprimanded by the Duke of Cambridge, the commander-in-chief of the British army. His commission had been issued on 4 January 1871 while he was in France. As a serving officer he had violated his country's strict policy of neutrality when he joined Chanzy's army.
23   Messimy, *Mes Souvenirs*, pp. 272-75.

into contact. An accomplished professional, full of fire, he never shrank from an assignment, no matter how difficult. Nonetheless he was aggressive and fearless to a point where he had no regard for his personal safety. While in action he had already been wounded twice. As a newly commissioned general in 1916 at the age of 46, the youngest in the French army, he was killed by an artillery shell during reconnoitering at the Somme in September.

Kitchener and Girodon spoke at length about the future prospects in the Dardanelles. Kitchener was anxious to bring Girodon along to the Dardanelles in order to have someone who could supply him with first-hand information. Before Girodon rose from his chair to leave, Kitchener asked him whether he would accompany him on his journey as a member of his staff. Girodon was startled by the unusual invitation and, after some hesitation, replied that it would be up to his superior. Kitchener laughed and said, "I shall see you at the station to-morrow evening."[24]

On 6 November, Kitchener lunched with Galliéni and after some coaxing prevailed upon him to temporarily release Girodon. If Galliéni was at first reluctant, it was because he had an assignment already planned for Girodon, not to mention that he was aware that his young subordinate had not fully recovered from his lung injury. But he understood Kitchener's dilemma and proved generous in other ways as well. He indicated that, if Girodon deemed it necessary once he arrived on the spot, he would divert two French brigades destined for Salonica to Gallipoli. No less important, he was willing to send fresh troops from France to the eastern Mediterranean provided an equal number of battle-weary soldiers from Cape Helles or Suvla went to Salonica.[25] These arrangements revived Kitchener's hope of staving off evacuation. With fresh troops on hand it would be possible not only to dig in for the winter but even take the initiative if the British navy agreed to cooperate by rushing the Straits.

On the last leg of his stay in Paris, Kitchener motored to Chantilly where he was warmly greeted by Joffre. The two men engaged in private conversation for several hours. Surprisingly Joffre did not deviate from the announced government policy. He seemed as set on the campaign in Greece as he was on the need to hang on to Gallipoli and had no objection to the exchange of troops as long as the numbers were kept up at Salonica.[26] In truth, the French general intensely disliked both projects. He had fought too long and hard to keep the focus on the Western Front to suddenly change his views. Still as a good politician he towed the government line and paid lip service to the Dardanelles operation lest he offend Kitchener on whom he depended to continue to send newly trained British divisions to France. Somehow he extracted from Kitchener a promise that Britain would supply 90,000 of the 150,000 men for the expedition to the Balkans.

During the voyage Kitchener discussed with Girodon the two theatres that were foremost on his mind. With regard to the Balkans he maintained that it was necessary to land 400,000 men or abstain altogether. The 150,000 troops committed to the Balkans were insufficient to make a difference and at any rate would arrive too late. He did not conceal his resentment against the French government for making the decision to send troops there without consulting him and

---

24 Esher, *Tragedy of Lord Kitchener*, pp. 172-73.
25 BNA: Kitchener papers, PRO 30/57/66, Lord Kitchener's report to the Cabinet on his East Mediterranean Mission in November 1915, 2 December 1915; BNA: Bertie papers, FO 800/172, Bertie to Grey, 6 November 1915.
26 BL: Balfour papers, 49726, Vol.44, Kitchener to Balfour, 6 November 1915; Sir George Arthur, *Life of Lord Kitchener*, Vol.3 (London: Macmillan, 1920), p. 186.

he had half-heartedly agreed to go along only in the interest of the alliance. He was adamant that it was vital to be vigilant and that the troops needed to pull back once they ceased to be of help to Serbia, lest their communications in the rear be severed. Kitchener also dwelled on the Dardanelles where he thought it was necessary to hang on as long as possible, otherwise it would liberate the Turks to attack Egypt and the Suez Canal.[27]

Kitchener arrived at Lemnos on the evening of 9 November and in the days that followed held a series of conferences with divisional and corps commanders, in addition to personally inspecting the fronts on the Peninsula. He saw that the terrain was much more difficult than he had imagined and he was further disheartened by the almost impregnable nature of the Turkish defences. Additionally he had committed five divisions to the Balkans and had no troops to spare for the Dardanelles and, just before leaving France gained the impression that the Admiralty would not sanction another naval attack on the Straits.[28] He began to have second thoughts about the rationale for persisting in the Dardanelles. The more he thought about it the more he realized that the most practical course was to adopt Monro's advice. Thus he telegraphed home and provisionally recommended the evacuation of Suvla and Anzac but that the front at Helles should be retained for the present.

To cushion the impact of retirement on Muslim opinion, Kitchener proposed a new landing in Ayas Bay, near Alexandretta, to cut rail communications and, by preventing the flow of Turkish troops east and south, ensure the protection of Egypt and assist British operations in Mesopotamia. It was his belief that the evacuation of Suvla and Anzac should be preceded by the Ayas Bay landing with two divisions. Once established the garrison was to be reinforced by two British divisions from France, followed by troops from Gallipoli when the evacuation was over.[29]

Girodon kept Galliéni informed of Kitchener's activities, the results of his conferences with the military leaders, the evolution of his thoughts and his meeting with General Brulard. As far as Girodon was concerned, he unequivocally supported the Ayas Bay project as a means to offset the moral effect of evacuating the Dardanelles and to protect Egypt where there were reports that the Germans were planning to capture the Suez Canal. He explained that it was vital to deny the Turks a propaganda victory which might ignite a holy war and threaten French

---

27 Girondon to Galliéni, 11 November 1915, in France, *Les armées françaises*, tome 8, Vol.1, annexe no. 382.
28 An aggressive coterie of naval officers, led by Roger Keyes, urged a resumption of naval activity in the Straits. De Robeck remained unconvinced that the ships could produce decisive results but allowed Keyes to plead his case personally to the Admiralty. Keyes arrived in London on 28 October and in a series of meetings with the naval authorities found them well disposed to a naval strike if the army advanced simultaneously against the forts at The Narrows. Kitchener could not meet that condition as he had already promised the French that he would reinforce the British contingent at Salonica. But in Paris Kitchener's hopes were revived by Galliéni's offer to lend a hand. Accordingly he asked Keyes to meet him at Marseilles on his way back to the Dardanelles so that they could discuss the naval plan. Keyes never received the message as the secretary to the First Lord did not think he could arrive in Marseilles before Kitchener left. When the Commodore failed to show up at Marseilles, Kitchener concluded that the naval scheme had fallen through and decided to leave without him.
29 Arthur, *Lord Kitchener*, Vol.3, pp. 189-91; Aspinall-Oglander, *Gallipoli*. Vol.2, pp. 414-17; James, *Gallipoli*, pp. 330-31.

possessions in North Africa. Girodon observed that Kitchener assured him that Britain had no designs on Syria and that personally he was opposed to such a move.[30]

The French government brooded about Kitchener's suggestion for an alternate operation in Ayas Bay. As we have already noted earlier in the year, the French had considered a landing of their own in the region before their involvement in the Dardanelles campaign. When William Martin, a member of the *Section d'études,* went over to London on 12 October, key elements in the British government and War Office, confided in him that they were considering occupying Alexandretta as a means to cover Egypt against a Turkish attack. To encourage their partner across the channel to join the enterprise, they were willing to recognize Syria and Cilicia as lying within the French zone of influence.[31] Consequently the general staff at the French War Ministry as well as the *Section d'études* were requested to study the feasibility of such an undertaking. Both bodies felt strongly that France did not have the resources to become involved in a new operation which they claimed would not advance the Allied cause, either in the Dardanelles or in the Balkans, or pose a threat to Turkey.

The general staff calculated that two divisions would suffice in the first phase to gain control of Alexandretta and its environs as Turkish defenders were small in number. It harboured serious concerns, however, about the aftermath. It acknowledged that the Germans might succeed in establishing a direct link with Constantinople and pour in reinforcements and supplies. With the security of the Dardanelles practically assured, there would be nothing to prevent the Turks from detaching forces and sending them by rail to recover Alexandretta. In such an eventuality, the two divisions, certain to be outnumbered, would find themselves in precarious circumstances.[32]

The *Section d'études,* whilst mindful of the benefits that were likely to accrue, saw that collecting a force for the venture could only be achieved at the expense of the other two fronts. That being the case, the consequences would be devastating. It would mean the abandonment of the Dardanelles as the garrison there would be too weak to hold the line. The withdrawal from the Dardanelles would free 150,000 Turks and constitute a moral defeat. In the Balkans the Allies would have to adopt a defensive strategy which would lead to the defeat of Serbia and drive away Greece and Romania. The *Section d'études* concluded that "an expedition to Alexandretta, beset with all sorts of difficulties and risky from the point of execution, would necessitate a dispersal of our forces which, for the sake of secondary results, would prevent us from operating effectively on the main theatres of operations in the Orient."[33]

The matter was left in abeyance until Kitchener raised it again the following month. Apart from the military demands and risks, there were political implications to consider. Although the Ayas Bay landing was really beyond the French sphere of influence, it was too close to Syria for comfort. The French cabinet simply did not trust the British, notwithstanding Kitchener's pledge. Accordingly on 13 November the French military atttaché was directed to lodge a protest against the British government. The note advised that before the British disembarked

---

30   SHD: AMG, 7N 2170, Girondon to Galliéni, 6 lettters between 11 and 16 November 1915.
31   Alexandre, *Avec Joffre,* p. 213.
32   AN: Millerand papers, 470 AP/16, EMA, Note sur un projet d'opération dans la région d'Alexandrette, 22 October 1915.
33   AN: Millerand papers, 470 AP/16, Section d'études, "Rapport sur un projet d'opérations à Alexandrette", 23 October 1915.

troops in the region of Alexandretta it would behoove them "to take into consideration not only the economic interests, but also the moral and political situation held by France in these countries." It went on to say:

> French public opinion could not be indifferent to anything that would be attempted in a country that they consider already as intended to become part of the future Syria, and they would require of the French Government that, not only no military operations in this particular country could be undertaken before it has been concerted between the Allies, but even that, in the case of such an action being taken, the greater part of the task would be entrusted to the French troops and the Generals commanding them.[34]

The French note served to buttress the British general staff's objection to the contemplated landing. It maintained that the operation would require 10 or 12 divisions, that Britain was already overextended and that Egypt could best be defended along the line of the canal rather than at the enemy's point of concentration.[35] On 14 November Asquith informed Kitchener that the French were resolute in opposing his scheme.[36] The next day the War Committee passed a provisional resolution that the Ayas Bay project should be dropped.

In view of the danger of adding another military commitment whilst confusion surrounded the Balkan enterprise and the fate of the campaign in the Dardanelles remained uncertain, the French government requested a conference to review and coordinate Allied policy in the Near East. The British and French delegations assembled at the Quai d'Orsay in Paris on 17 November. Discarding the idea of an Ayas Bay landing almost immediately, the greater part of the discussion centred on the Balkan operation. The British fared poorly in the debate. Kitchener was still in the Dardanelles and none of his colleagues present – Asquith, Balfour, Grey and Lloyd George – could speak French with any semblance of clarity. To make matters worse, Lloyd George, an ardent supporter of the Balkan enterprise, lined up behind the French and helped neutralize his comrades' disjointed arguments. The upshot was that the French more or less coerced the British into sending as quickly as possible, not only the earlier promise of 90,000 men but two extra divisions as well. To mollify the British, Briand pledged that, if juncture with the Serbs proved impossible, the French government would consider pulling out of the Balkans. It was an empty gesture for Briand was guided by domestic political consideration, not by the course of the military conflict.

On the Dardanelles issue, nothing was settled. Galliéni considered it imperative that the Anglo-French troops remain on Gallipoli as long as possible. He alluded to appreciations by Brulard and Girodon to the effect that the Allied force, even with minimal help, could withstand any Turkish attack. They did concede, however, that in case the Turks were reinforced by German forces and heavy artillery their position would be untenable. It was decided to defer the question of evacuation pending the final reports of Kitchener and Girodon.[37]

---

34 BNA, Cabinet papers, CAB 42/5, A copy of the document was appended to the minutes of the War Committee on 13 November 1915.
35 Aspinall-Oglander, *Gallipoli*, Vol.2, p. 415-16.
36 Bod L: Asquith papers, Vol.121, Asquith to Kitchener, 14 November 1915.
37 BNA: Cabinet papers, CAB 28/1, Anglo-French and Allied Conferences, procès-verbal de la conference tenue a Paris, 17 November 1915.

It appeared strange to the British representatives that, while the debate over the Dardanelles was going on, Joffre had not been afforded an opportunity to say a word. Whenever Joffre's opinion was invited, Galliéni would interject and answer for him. After the conference Lloyd George asked Joffre in private for his personal views on the future of the Dardanelles. The General unhesitatingly came out in favour of evacuation, basing his opinion on the absence of fresh divisions to relieve those on Gallipoli, the widespread sickness among the troops, and the possible arrival of heavy German artillery and poison gas.[38]

The French appeared oblivious to the fact that in improvising the conduct of the Balkans campaign, they were repeating the same mistake as the British had committed in the Dardanelles. It should not have required exceptional perspicacity to determine the results. Sarrail advanced about 40 miles into Serbia when he confronted much larger Bulgarian forces and, denied the expected reinforcements, gave the order to fall back into Greece. Sarrail was unaware that Joffre intended to place a limit on the number of troops he intended to dispatch to the Balkans until informed by Kitchener who had crossed over from Gallipoli to pay him a quick visit. The unhappy news, later confirmed by Galliéni, stunned Sarrail who later wrote: "General Joffre had stated that he would not give me one man more than those I had; he had persuaded the French and British ministers that 150,000 men would be enough for the Balkans."[39] Just as the retreat got under way, the Serbs, having managed to escape encirclement, crossed into Albania and began their perilous flight through the snow clogged and frigid mountain passes that would end on the Adriatic coast.[40]

Whilst this was going on, Kitchener cabled home his long-awaited final report on 22 November. He maintained that with German aid practically available to the Turks it was pointless to continue to hold on to Gallipoli. He proposed that the evacuation of Suvla and Anzac be carried out but that Cape Helles should be retained provisionally. The next day Asquith replied that the War Committee favoured totaled evacuation, including Cape Helles and that the decision had been referred to the cabinet for confirmation.[41]

The French Government had been informed of Kitchener's recommendations but not the War Committee's stand for total evacuation. In discussing Kitchener's report, the cabinet came to a tentative and informal agreement to cling to Cape Helles. It reasoned that to abandon Gallipoli completely would leave the Germans free to develop their plans in the east and throw the Arabs into their arms, igniting the torch of revolt against the French in North Africa. It hoped that the 60,000 or so troops removed from Suvla and Anzac would be used to retrieve Allied fortunes in the Balkans.[42] The *Section d'études* followed up with a memorandum in support of Kitchener's concept of partial withdrawal. This solution, it argued, would liberate approximately 60,000 troops from a precarious position while continuing to immobilize the greater part of the Turkish army. Additionally it would remain a threat to seize the forts at The

---

38 IWM: Wilson papers, entry in Wilson's diary, 18 November 1915.
39 Sarrail, *Mon commandement*, p. 44; Galliéni to Sarrail, 19 November 1915, in France, *Les armées françaises*, tome 8, Vol.2, annexe no. 379.
40 From there Allied ships transferred the survivors – less than 150,000 men – to the island of Corfu. Within eight months they were moved to the Salonica front.
41 Great Britain, *Final Report of the Dardanelles Commission*, pp. 56-7; Hankey, *Supreme Command*, Vol.2, p. 459; Cassar, *Kitchener's War*, p. 254.
42 SHD: AMG, carton 70, under the heading Engleterre, Briand to Cambon, 25 November 1915.

Narrows, deny the enemy an opportunity to establish a submarine base in the vicinity, facilitate the evacuation of Suvla and Anzac and mitigate the blow to Allied prestige in the east.[43]

On 29 November, Kitchener and Girodon, having returned from the Dardanelles, arrived in Paris. Shortly after they alighted from the train they parted but only briefly. Girodon planned to see Kitchener again at the British Embassy later in the day to bid him farewell. In the meantime Kitchener made the rounds to visit key French members of the government. He spent part of the morning with Poincaré at the Elysée. The French President recorded that Kitchener remained unbending about Salonica and expressed concern over the safety of Egypt, fearful that it might be attacked in January (1916) by a German division and some 200,000 Turks. He thought it was vital to reinforce the garrison in Egypt which was currently defended by only 20,000 mostly mediocre Indian troops. As the divisions that could he evacuated from Gallipoli were worn out, he deemed it indispensable to bring away some of the British troops at Salonica. Poincaré ventured to ask if "the Germans and Turks were to fling themselves on Salonica are you not afraid of the effect a Franco-British defeat would have on Greece and Romania." To which Kitchener replied somewhat impatiently: "That I do not know. This is a political matter but we cannot stay at Salonica if we want to defend Egypt and if we lose Egypt, we will lose the war." Kitchener saw Egypt, apart from its indispensable strategic value, as the linchpin to keeping Muslim opinion in check in the Middle East, North Africa and India. Any turmoil in that country would set off an explosive chain reaction in the other Muslim states under French and British control.

Kitchener remained convinced that a landing at Alexandretta was an important step to ensure the safety of Egypt. He thought that such an operation was still feasible as a recent reconnaissance of the area by a British naval officer had shown that as yet there were no organized enemy defences. Poincaré, out of courtesy, replied that the Field Marshal's views would be considered by the French cabinet and Joffre but he pointed out that they expected the British government to carry out its promise to send 90,000 men to Salonica.[44]

It remains unclear whether Kitchener's interviews with Briand and Galliéni followed or preceded his talk with Poincaré. What is known is that during the discussion with the two men he laid down the reasons for recommending the abandonment of Suvla and Anzac, adding that he had reached a similar conclusion with regard to the Balkan adventure. He absolutely refused to consider Briand's plea that the forces about to be released join the operations in the Balkans. He reminded the Prime Minister that, with the failure to gain contact with the Serbs, the extent of his commitment had been reached and he was now at liberty to cancel Britain's involvement.[45]

That evening, Kitchener left for London. He had tried, without much success, to bring the French politician leaders around to a reasonable frame of mind. Whilst Galliéni had given him a sympathetic hearing, both Briand and Poincaré, although in support of the evacuation of Suvla and Anzac, adopted a different attitude towards the expedition in the Balkans. Defying military logic, each had his own reason for wanting to retain a presence in Greece. For Briand it was a matter of political survival. Disengagement from Salonica would be interpreted as a

---

43　SHD: AMG, 3837 GQG, dossier 3, Section d'études, Rapport sur un project soumis par Lord Kitchener, 26 November 1915.
44　Poincaré, *Au service*, vpl. 7, pp. 288-89.
45　Esher, *Tragedy of Lord Kitchener*, p. 180; BNA: Bertie papers, FO 800/172, summary of events 29 November – 4 December 1915.

defeat and leave Sarrail humiliated and without a command in which case the Radical Socialists and other left-wing groups would withdraw their parliamentary support from his government. Poincaré had his differences with Briand but trying to find a replacement would have kept him awake for nights on end. The most obvious choice was Georges Clemenceau with whom he was not even on speaking terms.[46] Besides his personal feelings, he was frightened that a government headed by the irascible "Tiger" might turn out to be so reactionary that, rather than tolerate it, the nation would insist on a political settlement to the war.

As for Galliéni, he was caught in forces over which he seemingly had no control. He wondered how the country could pull itself out of the Balkan quagmire. Yet he felt that he had no option but to subject his military logic to political considerations. He was too fine a soldier to think that a puny force of 150,000 men could accomplish anything significant in the new theatre and only a deep sense of loyalty compelled him to uphold the government's policy.

There is no record when Girodon reported back to Galliéni or what passed between them during what must have been a brief interview. Galliéni had his hands full at the time, as will be discussed below, and he may simply have told Girodon to submit a memorandum on his activities and thoughts on the unfolding events in the Near East. In a long paper, Girodon echoed nearly all aspects of Kitchener's position and gave his reasons for doing so.[47] The appreciation is undated and appears to have been written a week or two later. It helps explain why Girodon believed that it was now too late to undertake an expedition to Alexandretta which he had firmly supported when Kitchener recommended it before departing from the Dardanelles. It may also account for the lack of interest in circulating the appreciation to the cabinet. Presumably by the time it was submitted to the War Minister, the cabinet had already reached decisions on the main issues.

Girodon's return to Paris coincided with a crisis in which Galliéni was personally involved. The War Minister's strained relationship with Joffre, a former subordinate, had nearly reached a breaking point.[48] At the root of their differences was the question of who should control the direction of the war. As Minister of War and with greater seniority than Joffre in the army, he was adamant that the reins of command should rest firmly in his hands. Joffre, for his part, felt suffocated by an arrangement that denied him freedom of action and he threatened to resign unless granted the same authority he had enjoyed under Millerand. Gaining the ear of both Poincaré and Briand, Joffre made a further effort to increase his power by stressing the importance of assigning a single individual to direct operations in France and the Near East.

Galliéni resented the support lent to Joffre by Briand and Poincaré. In fact nothing would have given him greater pleasure than to see Joffre resign. He was convinced that a shake-up at Chantilly was long overdue and had even toyed with the idea of adding the command of the army to his existing office in order to formalize his responsibility for the supreme conduct of the war. However he could not overcome the opposition of Briand and Poincaré, neither of whom, it must be added, had much use for Joffre. However, the two seasoned politicians contended that Galliéni, who was 66 years old, could not effectively combine the onerous duties of a commander-in-chief with those of a minister of war. They gave other reasons. To force Joffre's

46 Gabriel Terrail, *Joffre, la première crise du commandment* (Paris: Ollendorff, 1919), pp.89-90; Wright, *Raymond Poincaré*, p. 166.
47 SHD: AMG, 7N 2170, Girondon, Note sur La Guerre en Orient, undated.
48 Joffre had served under Galliéni at Madagascar.

resignation would not only shake public confidence in the army, but it would also make Galliéni responsible for operations in the field, exposing him to constant harassment from the chamber and parliamentary commissions. Finally it was unlikely that the French could gain ascendancy in the Entente coalition without Joffre's prestige and authority. Confronted by these arguments, Galliéni grudgingly deferred to Joffre's wishes on condition that he dismiss a number of "Young Turks" at Chantilly as it was suspected that they had undue influence over their chief's thoughts. and action.[49]

On 2 December, Poincaré and Galliéni issued a decree appointing Joffre supreme commander of the French armies – though his authority did not extend over the colonial units in Algeria, Tunisia and Morocco.[50] This arrangement had been carefully conceived and implemented by Briand who saw an opportunity to address a number of issues at one stroke. By enlarging Joffre's command, the Prime Minister would raise his standing with the general's coterie of admirers. Furthermore, Joffre who had been dragged into releasing the barest number of divisions to his arch-rival would now be responsible for attending to the needs of the Army of the Orient. Then too the radical groups in the chamber would accept Joffre's promotion once they realized that Sarrail would be supplied more readily with reinforcements if the Generalissimo were responsible for the Balkan campaign.[51]

What seemed like an ideal political solution had, in fact, extended Joffre's once uncertain chances of survival in the bitter power struggle with the government. During the middle and latter part of 1915 the accumulated failures of Joffre's Western Front strategy had given rise to growing dissatisfaction with his leadership in government circles and it appeared that his days as commander-in-chief were numbered. In view of his string of military setbacks, he was forced to bite the bullet and make concessions. In so doing he slipped further and further down from his high perch and at some point could have been removed without causing much of a public outcry. Still Joffre used his remaining political capital to gain a march on the politicians and before the close of the year was again back on top. It is true that Joffre's resuscitated powers were temporary and he would never return to the days immediately following the Marne but in the short term he would exercise preponderant influence over the conduct of operations in France and the Near East.

Momentarily pushed into the background by the events surrounding the settlement with Joffre, the fronts in the Near East emerged once more to recapture centre stage of political interest. By now the French were aware of the War Committee's decision in favour of total evacuation. Galliéni had reluctantly arrived at the same conclusion. He reckoned that, as Cape Helles could not be held in isolation for long, complete evacuation was preferable to being driven into the sea. Not surprisingly, Joffre concurred with his assessment. The cabinet could not bring itself to recommend a withdrawal, though it did agree to convey the views of Galliéni and Joffre to the British authorities. On the other hand the administration showed no such hesitation in its resolve to remain at Salonica and to request that the British send further reinforcements to bring up the strength of the Allied force to 300,000 men.[52]

---

49 Bugnet, *Rue St Dominique*, pp. 106-08; Wright, *Raymond Poincaré*, p. 198; Doughty, *Pyrrhic Victory*, pp. 229-31.
50 King, *Generals and Politicians*, p. 86; Joffre, *Personal Memoirs*, Vol.2, pp. 401-2; Terrail, *Joffre*, pp. 87-88.
51 King, *Generals and Politicians*, p. 85; Bourget, *Gouvernement et commandement*, p. 145.
52 Poincaré, *Au service*, Vol. 7, p. 295.

Far from considering the French request, the War Committee had unanimously decided to withdraw from the Balkans – even before fulfilling Britain's commitment to send 90,000 troops there. The news caused great consternation in Paris and especially to Briand who feared that without British support he would face a political crisis similar to the one that drove Viviani from office. He used every argument he could think of to dissuade the British from moving ahead but to no avail.[53] In London, the firm resolve to abandon the Salonica enterprise, renewed interest in exploring the possibility of mounting another assault in Gallipoli. Although the War Committee had unanimously agreed to withdraw completely from the Dardanelles, the opposition in the cabinet blocked its ratification. The proponents of the Dardanelles campaign received a boost when Kitchener changed his mind. He announced on 2 December that since his telegram on 22 November the British abortive attack on Baghdad made it imperative that the Turks should not be allowed to claim a victory in the Dardanelles. Given the expected political and military consequences that would follow the evacuation of the Peninsula, the War Committee inclined to Kitchener's view. It authorized him to inquire if an offensive could be launched at Suvla with four divisions from Salonica. The next day it was agreed that a final decision could not be reached without consulting the French.[54]

On 4 December, Briand, Galliéni, Lacaze and Joffre made their way to Calais to confer with the British representatives. It is interesting to note that the British delegation consisting of Asquith, Kitchener and Balfour did not include Lloyd George, a fiery advocate of the operation in the Balkans. Touching on the subject of the Dardanelles in the early dialogue, it was evident that a final decision must await settlement of the Balkan scheme. Given the floor, Kitchener pointed out that the conditions of British participation in the expedition had not been met and, with the Allied force in great danger, the only sensible course was to withdraw. Briand did much of the talking on the French side as he marshalled a host of arguments on the importance of remaining in the Balkans. A disengagement now would allow the Central Powers to dominate the region, turn Salonica into a base for enemy submarines, drive Romania and Greece into German arms, cause Russia to lose faith in its allies and prevent the eventual conversion of the Serbian army into a force to assist the Allies. But the British had dug in their heels and remained steadfast, unaffected by Briand's arguments. Joffre weighed in to suggest that the Allies could hold on to Salonica by strengthening its defences and in the spring break out in a broad sweep with 400,000 to 500,000 men. Evoking sharp rebuttals from Kitchener and Gallieni, the Generalissmo was jarred from his reverie. Kitchener shook up the French when he suddenly announced that if it was decided to remain at Salonica he would have no option but to resign as he had no wish to shoulder the responsibility for a military catastrophe.

The French delegates were caught off guard and during a brief recess they almost certainly discussed the damaging effect Kitchener's departure from the War Office would have on France's security. Britain had not yet adopted conscription. It was no secret that the British authorities relied on Kitchener's name to bring in the unending flood of recruits for the New Armies and without him they could not remotely match the exceedingly high level of popular enthusiasm that he inspired. At some point they must have decided that it would be contrary, possibly fatal, to the interests of their country if they forced Kitchener's resignation. The assembly having

---

53 Dutton, *Politics of Diplomacy*, pp. 67-68.
54 Hankey, *Supreme Command*, Vol. 2, pp. 453, 462; Aspinall-Oglander, *Gallipoli*, Vol.2, p. 436.

reconvened, Asquith read a formal statement, declaring that in the opinion of the British general staff the retention of Salonica with a force of 150,000 men was not only dangerous but likely to lead to a military disaster and therefore strongly advocated that preparations for evacuation be made without delay. Exasperated but with little room to manoeuvre, Briand saw that it was useless to continue the discussion and conceded defeat.[55]

Briand had barely set foot in Paris in the evening when he found himself trapped in a political minefield. While he was in Calais news arrived in the capital that the Bulgarians had struck a hard blow against Sarrail's forces. The chamber was in an uproar with the socialists blasting the government for leaving Sarrail practically defenceless. At 1 am on 5 November, Philippe Berthelot, Briand's influential *chef de cabinet*, submitted a four-page memorandum, in which he underlined the folly of withdrawing in the face of an imaginary threat, thereby abandoning control of the Mediterranean and opening the way for Germany to dominate the Near East. Given the political implications, he urged the Briand administration to absolve itself of all responsibility for the decision reached at Calais by making it public that, while the two governments differed on the issue of Salonica, the French had accepted the British position to avoid fracturing the Alliance. He castigated the British, describing them as shortsighted, infantile and selfish, unwilling to look beyond northern France and Egypt. He warned that their war policy would lead to their defeat and drag France along with them.[56]

Taking an opposite view was Denis Cochin, who had just returned from a mission to Greece. Cochin reported on his interview with King Constantine and on his own investigation, concluding the Allied force was in a precarious position and that its presence at Salonica no longer served a practical purpose. It was, as Poincaré wrote in his memoirs, "a summing up which fairly startled us."[57]

On the morning of 5 December, Poincaré presided over a tumultuous cabinet meeting that lasted two hours. Split almost down the middle, the cabinet was unable to agree on what course to adopt in the Balkans. Pulling in the direction of evacuation stood Lacaze, Cochin, Galliéni, Charles de Freycinet, Alexandre Ribot and Jules Méline (the last two were former exponents of the Balkan expedition). Those arrayed on the other side included Poincaré, Leon Bourgeois and two prominent socialists, Marcel Sembat and Albert Thomas. The pro evacuation group led by de Freycinet, with strong support from Lacaze, argued that as the objectives of the Balkan expedition had not been achieved, namely saving Serbia and maintaining communications with its army, it followed that the Allied troops should be withdrawn for urgent service elsewhere.

---

55 BNA: Cabinet papers, CAB 28/1, Anglo-French and Allied Conferences, minutes of the meeting of 4 December 1915; Hankey, *Supreme Command*, Vol. 2, pp. 453-54 H.H. Asquith, *Memoirs and Reflections*, Vol. 2 (London: Cassell, 1928), p. 111; Poincaré, *Au service*, Vol.7, pp. 310-11. Some of the dialogue, excluded from the minutes of the meeting, can be found in Galliéni (ed.) *Carnets de Galliéni*, pp. 226-28. There are accounts, like Suarez, *Briand*, Vol.3, p. 213 and Joffre, *Personal Memoirs*, Vol.2, p. 290 , which claim the decision to evacuate Salonica had been postponed at Calais but that is inaccurate. Briand added to the confusion by editing the minutes of the conference to make it appear that a final decision had been deferred, pending consultation between the British and French representatives and their respective governments.

56 A. Bréal, *Philippe Berthelot* (Paris: Galliard, 1937), p. 144; Jean-Luc Barré, *Le Seigneur Chat: Philippe Berthelot 1866–1934* (Paris: Plon, 1988), p. 287: Dutton, *Politics of Diplomacy*, p. 71.

57 David Dutton, "The Calais Conference of December 1915", *The Historical Journal*, Vol.21, no.2 (1978), pp. 143-56; Poincaré, *Au service*, Vol.7, pp. 308-09.

The chief spokesmen for the opposite group were Sembat and Thomas, who maintained that retirement, coming at the end of a long series of defeats for the Entente, would have a devastating effect on what remained of their prestige in the Balkans and in the Levant. They insisted that retention of Salonica could still influence the attitude of the Balkan states and permit a resumption of a forward military movement at a later date.

Briand stood poised between the two groups, notwithstanding his own personal attachment to the Balkan enterprise and the need to placate the socialists in order to eliminate the dangerous threat to his government. He could not, however, overlook his agreement with the British, much as he hated it. Displaying an attitude of frantic indecision he was afforded several day's grace when the cabinet unanimously accepted Bourgeois' proposal that a final decision be deferred to allow the other interested parties, the Russians and the Italians, to join the discussions.[58] Neither belligerent was directly involved in the Balkans but both had a stake on what happened there. Russia was massing for operations in Bessarabia while Italy was making arrangements to send an expedition to Albania and it was reasonable to assume that they would both support the continued effort in the Balkans as lessening the pressure on their own fronts.

Few actually believed that the British could be pressured into retreating in view of their rock-like stand at Calais. But to Albert Thomas the assumption that opinion among the ministers in London in support of the evacuation of Salonica had been unanimous did not square with the information passed on recently by his friend Lloyd George and he suspected that there was a division in the cabinet.[59] He held a conversation with Briand on the 5th and received permission to go to London to personally urge the case for remaining at Salonica. It was the start of French efforts to reverse the verdict reached at Calais.

In London, Thomas, accompanied by Lloyd George, "attended more than one prolonged meeting" with various British ministers on 6 December. Everywhere he went he repeated the same scenario. The Briand ministry was deeply committed to the Balkan operation and would surely fall if it became known that it had consented to a withdrawal. If the government were voted out of office, Poincaré would be obliged to turn to Georges Clemenceau to assume the mantle of prime minister. This would mean the end of the *union sacrée* as the socialists would rebel against the old tyrant and resume their factious criticism in the chamber. Would England allow its ally to fall into factional strife, the consequences of which would deal the Allied military effort a crippling blow?[60]

Lloyd George did his part in the War Committee and cabinet to compliment Thomas' plea. Instead of arguing on the military merits of the enterprise, he focused on the need to avoid a breach in the Alliance. He claimed that any impression that the British were deserting the French would lead to the collapse of the Briand administration and precipitate a political crisis that would endanger France's continued participation in the war. Lord Bertie, often told by French officials that the political crisis was approaching a climax, gave a boost to Lloyd George's observations. He warned the Foreign Office on 6 December that a British withdrawal from

---

58 Cambon, *Correspondance*, Vol. 3, p. 91; Leblond, *Galliéni Parle*, Vol. 2, p. 195; Georges Louis, *Les carnets de Georges Louis*, Vol.2 (Paris: Rieder, 1926), p. 232; Poincaré, *Au service*, Vol.7, pp. 311-12.
59 Lloyd George admitted that he told Thomas of his opposition to abandoning Salonica and it is not unreasonable to assume that he revealed the names of other colleagues who shared his opinion. See Lloyd George, *War Memoirs*, Vol.1, p. 453.
60 Marcellin, *Politique et politiciens*, Vol. 1, p. 164; Hankey, *Supreme Command*, Vol.2, p. 453.

Salonica would be seen in Paris as deserting the French and probably result in the fall of the Briand ministry.[61] The resolve of the British authorities began to weaken.

Much would depend on the results of the discussions between Joffre and the Allied chiefs of staff currently taking place at Chantilly to define a concerted policy for all the theatres of war. Joffre dominated the conference from the start and, when it came time to evaluate the reason for remaining at Salonica, his resolution echoing the French government's line carried the day with the British representative as the lone dissenter.[62]

The news from Chantilly greatly troubled the British ministers who had expected a different result – given Joffre's known support of his government's Balkan policy and his dislike of the Dardanelles campaign, it should not have come as a surprise. By all accounts it was judged to be a significant blow and together with the ongoing ministerial crisis in Paris, probably was enough to cause them to lose heart completely. If there was any doubt, the Russians sealed the matter. At the instigation of the French, Petrograd cabled the Foreign Office to urge that Salonica should on no account be abandoned. Nearly fifty years later Hankey would recall: "The risks of so serious a quarrel with our Allies were too grave to be run, especially on an issue on which opinion in the Cabinet itself was divided."[63] It would become a familiar theme during the war for the British to reverse their own policy in deference to the dictates of French domestic politics. For Briand the sudden turn of events had given him a new lease on life, just when defeat seemed inevitable.

Once it became evident that British troops would not be released from the Balkan front the Asquith administration gave up the idea of reinforcing Suvla. The French, with their focus on Salonica, had accepted the recommendation of the Allied military conference, or Joffre to put it bluntly, that the Dardanelles should be evacuated. There was no reaction in Paris when the British decided on 7 December to evacuate Suvla and Anzac, retaining Cape Helles for the immediate future to avoid the admission of total failure. It is interesting to speculate whether the British would have stuck to their guns on the matter of Salonica if they had known that, on the very day they gave up on the Dardanelles, Sarrail informed his government "that, with the forces currently at his disposal, no meaningful result was possible and that, diplomatic and political considerations aside, evacuation seemed the logical conclusion."[64] At any rate the die had been cast and the evacuation of Suvla and Anzac began in the second week of December. The plan, based on deception and sound logistics, called for a gradual and secret withdrawal, leaving only a hand-picked corps behind as a covering force. The sick and the wounded, the prisoners of war and finally the infantry began leaving in small boats. The weather was favourable and the Turks, unaware of what was happening, were quiescent. By 15 December the program was well advanced; by the 18th half the force had been removed; and by the 20th the evacuation was completed. A week later the cabinet agreed to give up Cape Helles. Again plans were prepared with utmost care and skill. This was to be a three-staged operation with the final withdrawal fixed for 8 January, 1916. Here too the entire undertaking was carried out

---

61 BNA: Bertie papers, FO 800/172, Bertie to Grey, 6 December 1915.
62 Doughty, *Pyrrhic Victory*, pp. 234-36; Joffre, *Personal Memoirs*, Vol. 2, p. 390; Poincaré, *Au service*, Vol. 7, pp. 315-16.
63 Hankey, *Supreme Command*, Vol. 2, p. 462.
64 Dutton, *Politics of Diplomacy*, p. 75.

without mishap. With the evacuation of so many men, it is remarkable that not a single life was lost.[65]

Wars and campaigns are not won by retreating but credit should be given where it is due. The evacuation of the Gallipoli Peninsula was far more competently conducted than any other phase of the campaign and stands out as one of the great retreats of history. It has always been asserted that if the same level of thought had gone into the preparatory stage of the Dardanelles operation, the outcome might have been different. Whether a victory would have shortened the war, as was the justification for undertaking the sideshow, is not so certain.

---

65 Aspinall-Oglander, *Gallipoli*, Vol.2, chs 31 and 32; James, *Gallipoli*, pp. 338-47; Michael Hickey, *Gallipoli* (London: John Murray, 1995), pp. 329-34.

13

General Review and Reflections on the Dardanelles Campaign

The Anglo-French withdrawal from Gallipoli had ominous repercussions in Europe and the Muslim world. It hardened the determination of Greece and Romania to remain neutral and damaged Allied prestige in the Near East, though in Muslim states under their control there were no serious internal disturbances as had been feared. More importantly it lifted the stigma of inferiority which had marked the Ottoman armies in light of their stinging defeats in the Balkan Wars and in the early First World War battles. Able to defeat two European powers boosted the confidence of the Ottoman regime and, to its ever-lasting discredit, intensified its brutal and pitiless campaign to exterminate the Armenians. With visions that the Empire could be revitalized, the Ottomans became a more formidable foe in the Near East. In Mesopotamia they drove back a British expedition and at Kut-al-Amara forced it to surrender in April 1916. From southern Palestine they drove into the Sinai with the object of capturing the Suez Canal and expelling the British from Egypt. The British eventually turned the tide, but the war in the Near East was a drain on men and resources badly needed elsewhere. Instead of shortening the Great War, the Dardanelles campaign probably extended it.

The fighting on Gallipoli ended over a century ago but the lengthy passage of time has not ended the controversy over the strategy of attacking Turkey through the Dardanelles. Apologists have justified the campaign on the grounds that the defeat of Turkey would have brought about a turning point in the war. They have attributed the defeat to so-called "lost opportunities." In reality the operation was doomed from the start. It was launched in haste and without enough resources to ensure victory, proper intelligence, a coherent plan, realistic goals, and much regard for the fighting quality of the Turks. As the architect of the plan to force the Straits by ships alone, Churchill was under two major misconceptions. In the first place he lacked the technical expertise to understand the difference between land defences and naval guns with flat trajectory firing many miles away from their target. Secondly he assumed that the appearance of the fleet off Constantinople would cause mass panic among the population, leading to the collapse of the Young Turk government and bringing to power a new regime favourable to the Entente. But relying on hope or chance is not a proper way to conduct a campaign. Churchill never gave any thought to what would happen to the fleet if it should blast a way through the Dardanelles and yet became powerless to influence events in the Ottoman capital. Bottled up in hostile territory, it would have to confront the enemy without the support of the army.

As British desire to command the naval operation rested on working out an arrangement with Paris, Churchill invited Victor Augagneur, the Minister of Marine, to London. At the end of the talks Augagneur willingly abdicated the right to appoint a naval commander in exchange for Britain's promise to abandon the idea of seizing control of the Alexandretta region. Paris viewed with fear any action on the part of Britain which would imperil its future control of Syria. Augagneur was sufficiently impressed by Churchill's glowing picture of the political and military benefits that lay beyond The Narrows that he committed the French navy to support an operation plan he had not seen – and for which he would later come under fire at home. Augagneur was not as sanguine as Churchill about the fleet's prospects of victory but, as was understood from the start, the naval attack could be broken off without reproach if progress was found to be difficult.

The diplomatic talks leading to the Straits Agreement focused the attention of the Allies on the future dismemberment of Turkey, rather than on ensuring that they had sufficient resources on hand to force its capitulation. The Allies were guilty of tunnel vision and overlooked the fact that a purely maritime enterprise did not have the capacity to fulfil their post-war imperial ambitions. Since they expected the fleet to break through the Dardanelles and political change to follow in the Ottoman capital, it is difficult to imagine how they could have ignored the reaction of the new government to their imperial demands. It goes without saying that no Ottoman government, however strong its feelings for peace, would seriously have considered giving up major portions of its territory unless of course forced to do so. Without troops on hand, the Allies would not have been in a position to bring any pressure to bear on the Ottoman government. Their only alternative would have been to leave Turkey alone in exchange for its promise to withdraw from the war. If the powers wanted to satisfy their imperial aspirations, they required to undertake an operation on a much broader scale. It was the familiar story of wanting the ends without providing the means.

By the late April, the chances of the military operation to achieve its objective were remote at best. Conditions had changed since the opening months of the year. The element of surprise had been forfeited and on Gallipoli the Turks had strengthen their fortifications, brought up more troops and occupied the heights opposite the probable landing sites, limiting penetration. The operation should have been called off after the failure of the naval attack but early on Churchill's reckless announcement to the press had removed that option.

Throughout most of the Dardanelles campaign, French political authorities showed little disposition to look beyond the security of France. They had been attracted to the sideshow not so much because of their confidence in the success of the enterprise as for a desire to protect their interests in the Near East. As they were unenthusiastic about coping with the difficulties of a distant theatre, they were content to follow Britain's lead. They responded to the needs of the operation as though it were an illegitimate child, providing only such troops as were available without weakening the front in France or arousing the ire of GQG. Yet it was only natural that, with the Germans occupying large sections of the country's sacred soil, every effort should be made to drive them out.

The French high command was confident that through attrition it could wear down the Germans and ultimately achieve a breakthrough. Joffre was too obtuse to understand that frontal daylight charges, far from wearing out the enemy, took a greater toll on the attacking forces than on the defenders. It was a senseless strategy to adopt given that France had a considerably smaller population than Germany. Each offensive started with high hopes and ended the same way, with casualties out of all proportion to the gain of a mile or two of worthless ground. With no signs that a breakthrough could be achieved in the near future, gloom and frustration settled over the country. The politicians came to the conclusion that further offensives in the west would only increase the butcher's bill and that some new approach had to be found. Late in the summer they looked to build up their forces in the Dardanelles and take the lead from the British who seemed incapable of wrapping up the campaign. What galvanized them into action was the political fallout from *l'affaire Sarrail*.

As Joffre's famed dimmed with each bloody inconclusive battle and there was talk of finding a replacement, the name of General Maurice Sarrail invariably surfaced. Joffre, ever jealous of his authority, looked for a way to eliminate his rival. His opportunity came when Sarrail made an error in judgement during a German attack at the end of June. Immediately after the conclusion of an investigation criticizing Sarrail's conduct, Joffre relieved him of command of the Third Army. It so happened that Sarrail was one of the few high-ranking military officers in the French Army who was an anti-clerical republican and, as a result, was wildly popular with the parties of the left. His supporters protested and claimed that he had been the victim of a witch-hunt, insisting that he be given a new command. With the Viviani ministry in danger of collapsing, Sarrail was offered the leadership of the French contingent in the Dardanelles in succession to General Gouraud. Sarrail was conscious of his strong position and among the conditions he listed before leaving for the Dardanelles was an adequate increase in the number of French divisions and an independent command. The government was ready to accommodate him, seeing an opportunity to play a more active role in the Dardanelles where a stalemate had set in after Hamiliton's second major offensive in August had failed.

Joffre, who viewed any sideshow with scorn, tried his best to block the dispatch of reinforcements overseas. But the failure of his strategy in the west had allowed the government to reestablish some degree of control over war policy since its abdication in the months following the Marne. Friction between Joffre and the government, confined to relatively minor matters in the first half of 1915, escalated to near-explosive dimensions during *l'affaire Sarrail*. While the government sought to appease Sarrail and preserve the Sacred Union, Joffre was determined to ease his nemesis out of the army or at least dispatched to a secondary outpost overseas. The politicians were careful not to push Joffre too far lest he resign. Given enough latitude, Joffre raised one obstacle after another to frustrate the government's design and in the end succeeded in making it a condition that no troops would be levied from his front until the results of his impending offensive in the fall were known. He would release the reinforcements no sooner than the second week in October which meant that they were unlikely to affect the operations in the Dardanelles before the onset of winter.

The ongoing struggle between the government and high command, however, was overtaken by the rapid developments in southeast Europe. Weighing offers from both coalitions, Bulgaria decided it had more to gain by aligning itself with the Central Powers and decreed general mobilization on 22 September. The moment it became evident that Bulgaria would soon be joining its new partners in a concerted attack against Serbia, the French cabinet seized upon the idea of an expedition to Salonica – such as had been discussed at the turn of 1915 – instead of renewing the effort in the Dardanelles. The change in plans by the politicians was decided on the spur of the moment without reference to London, an indication of how anxious they were, not only to rescue Serbia but to find a suitable post for Sarrail as well. There were other less immediate goals. The politicians expected that the expedition would serve as a lever to extend

French economic and territorial interests in the eastern Mediterranean and possibly lead to their long-cherished vision of a Balkan coalition.

Joffre became a late convert to the Balkan enterprise out of self-interest. He found it distasteful to detach troops from his front almost as much for the venture in the Balkans as for the one in the Dardanelles. But his reputation and prestige were on the wane and he was astute enough to realize that, if the Viviani ministry collapsed, his own position would be endangered. He thus felt that he had no choice but to endorse the government's new commitment.

Once Paris had decided on opening a new front in the Balkans, it was presented to the British government as a matter of course. The British were already involved in four theatres and were horrified at the prospect of increasing their back-breaking load. More importantly they were convinced that the contemplated force was neither adequate enough nor arrive in time to succour Serbia. Nevertheless the French were persistent and in the interest of preserving the alliance, London reluctantly gave way and consented to contribute the major portion of the expeditionary force of 150,000 men. The British authorities extracted a promise from their partner, however, that if the Anglo-French force failed to establish contact with the Serbs it would be withdrawn from the Balkans.

The lack of planning and forethought, plus an undersized force, crippled the expedition from the outset. The French committed the same mistake as the British whom they criticized for blindly leaping into the Dardanelles miasma. The expected help from the Greeks never arrived as Athens refused to honour its prewar treaty with Serbia and declare war on Bulgaria. Predictably the Anglo-French force was too small and too disorganized to advance very far inland and was forced to fall back to Salonica. Logic would seem to dictate that it proceed to withdraw, but the French refused to leave. As justification for going back on their word, they claimed that an admission of defeat would bring down the new ministry under Aristide Briand. The British had no way of knowing that Briand, quite apart from his political survival, had an ulterior motive for remaining in the Balkans. He knew that Sarrail would not be able to contribute to winning the war but his presence in Salonica would ensure France's post-war dominance in the eastern Mediterranean. The British were wary that the fall of Briand might thrust into power a ministry headed by someone like Joseph Caillaux who would try to reach an accommodation with Germany. Just as it happened two months earlier, the British caved in. This would not be the last time that French internal politics dictated the course of Britain's action in the war.

The entrenched camp that the Allies established around Salonica grew exponentially during the following months with the addition of Serbs, Russians, and Italians. The conglomerate force had no defined mission and it remained relatively inactive until the last few months of the war. By 1917 the size of its garrison had swelled to over 600,000, draining men and resources which could have benefited more important theatres. As this huge and unproductive army was contained by a mere 150,000 Bulgarians, it is no wonder that German commentators jokingly referred to Salonica as the "largest Allied internment camp."

The French decision to divert their effort in the Near East to the Balkans signaled the death knell of the Dardanelles campaign. Dragged into a new undertaking against their better judgment, the British, lacking the resources to maintain another front, were compelled to liquidate the one in the Dardanelles. Whether the projected French offensive to open the Straits to the fleet in the fall would have borne fruit is a matter of conjecture. I am inclined to believe, that if the Allies had been unable to defeat Turkey when it was isolated, they were unlikely to do so when a direct link with Germany had been forged.

The Dardanelles campaign had originally been conceived as a purely naval attack, designed to achieve a major victory with minimum losses. Poorly planned, it evolved into a full-scale military operation lasting 260 days (25 April – 9 January 1916) and ended in failure after replicating the losses of many of the battles on the Western Front. The French contribution to the ill-fated enterprise did not come close to matching British resources but it was as extensive as the defence of its national soil would permit. From the outset the French accepted to place their naval and military forces under the command of the British and, while there were occasional instances of friction and bruised feelings, no serious disagreements broke out during the entire campaign.

The French initially supplied four pre-dreadnoughts battleships to the Dardanelles, all of which participated in the naval attack on 18 May. During the action the French squadron under Rear-Admiral Guépratte closed in and boldly engaged the Turkish forts and in the process one ship was sent to the bottom of the seas and another seriously damaged. To replace the vessels temporarily withdrawn for repairs, Augagneur despatched a battleship, a coast defence ship and two armoured cruisers. There were additions to the fleet in the weeks that followed so that by the time Nicol replaced Guépratte, the French had at least six battleships and four cruisers in the Dardanelles, as well as a host of auxiliary vessels that included minesweepers and submarines. French naval losses during the campaign included the 600 sailors who drowned with the sinking of the battleship *Bouvet*, plus an undetermined number of men serving on the other ships and vessels.

The French contributed a total of 79,000 men (two divisions drafts inclusive) to the land operations. Although French forces were inexperienced and their quality varied, on the whole they fought reasonably well. Out of the many British and Australian forces involved in the first landings on 25 April, the French contingent was the only one which attained its objective at Kum Kale. Transferred to Cape Helles, French troops had to deal with the Turks in front of them, acted in support of the British in the three Battles of Krithia and took part in diversionary action during Hamilton's last major offensive in August. It must be remembered that on Cape Helles they faced the most formidable part of the Ottoman front and additionally were subjected almost daily to long-range shelling from Turkish batteries in Asia. In all the military action, the number of French killed, wounded or missing in action, was placed at about 27,000, disproportionately higher than the British (70,775). If the evacuation of some 20,000 men sick or dying of disease are included, the number of casualties rose to 47,000 while those of Britain and its colonial contingents totaled 205,000.[1] Many western commentators speculate that the Turkish government's official statement of 251,000 casualties is probably an underestimate of the actual figure because its records were loosely kept. Lieutenant-Colonel Erickson has categorically refuted that assumption, observing that Turkish authorities in fact maintained detailed and complete records. Thus the losses on both sides were approximately equal.[2]

It has often been argued that if an amphibious operation had been planned at the outset a victory with far-reaching strategic and political benefits could have been achieved. But thinking

---

1 Brig.-Gen., C.F. Aspinall-Oglander, *Military Operations: Gallipoli*, Vol. 2 (London: William Heinemann, 1932), p. 484.
2 Erickson, *Gallipoli*, p. 198.

along those lines is unrealistic. At the start of 1915 the small British army could not have supplied anywhere near the necessary troops to carry out a full-scale military operation and the recruits in the training camps would not have been ready to take the field until late in the spring of 1915. Nor would it have been possible to meet the army's critical needs. In fact munitions and heavy artillery were actually insufficient to take care of the needs of the regular divisions in France. Before Churchill persuaded the War Council that the navy alone could bring Turkey to its knees, Kitchener estimated that 150,000 troops would be required to overcome resistance on the Gallipoli Peninsula. Even then it was based on the assumption that Turkish soldiers were second rate and would not put up much of a fight. If Kitchener had known that the Turks in defending their homeland and their religion would prove to be courageous and tough adversaries, he undoubtedly would have judged even such a force as inadequate.

For the sake of argument, supposing it would have been possible to organize a combined attack at the outset. What would have happened if the military operation to open the Straits had bogged down, necessitating the Allies to keep sending reinforcements at the expense of the Western Front to prevent a disaster? Was an amphibious operation worth the risk? There is no guarantee that even the fall of Constantinople would have yielded the anticipated benefits. The evidence would seem to suggest that Turkey would not have capitulated but rather continued to fight from Anatolia. The prospect that the Balkans would unite in a common front against Austria was in fact based on wishful thinking, failing to take into account their long-standing and internecine hatred for each other, the absence of a common language and woefully inadequate communications. The most practical route to Russia would have been opened but to what end? Neither the French nor the English could have shipped much in the way of armaments and munitions to their ally as they could barely meet the needs of their own armies.

The Allied rationale for embarking on the sideshow in the Dardanelles was to obtain a cheap victory and shorten the war. It is difficult to see how either could have been achieved in the best of circumstances. What then should the Allies have done to deal with Turkey? The brief response was nothing. The Turks were hardly a dangerous foe as the few options open to them almost certainly would have invited their defeat. They could have mounted attacks against the Russians or the British in Egypt, as they had done earlier in the war, but the results would have been the same. The most sensible course for the Allies would have been to allow the Turks to take the initiative until they revealed their intentions before striking back – like a skilled boxer counter-punching to break down an awkward and slow moving opponent. At some point the Turkish leaders would have wearied and recognized that they their army was overmatched. Their only hope to remain in power in view of the deepening discontent at home and rising Arab nationalism, would have been to seek a peace settlement. With the Turks no longer a factor, Anglo-French forces would have avoided the bloody campaigns in the Dardanelles, Mesopotamia, and Palestine, concentrating their resources instead on defeating the Germans on the Western Front and accelerating an end to the war.

Appendix I

Viviani's First Ministry, 13 June –26 August 1914

René Viviani – President of the Council and Minister of Foreign Affairs
Adolphe Messimy – Minister of War
Louis Malvy – Minister of the Interior
Joseph Noulens – Minister of Finance
Maurice Couyba – Minister of Labour and Social Security Provisions
Jean-Baptiste Bienvenu-Martin – Minister of Justice
Armand Gauthier de l'Aude – Minister of Marine
Victor Augagneur – Minister of Public Instruction and Fine Arts
Fernand David – Minister of Agriculture
Maurice Raynaud – Minister of Colonies
René Renoult – Minister of Public Works
Gaston Thomson – Minister of Commerce, Industry, Posts, and Telegraphs

Viviani's Second Ministry, 26 August 1914 – 29 October 1915

René Viviani - President of the Council
Théophile Delcassé – Minister of Foreign Affairs
Alexander Millerand – Minister of War
Louis Malvy – Minister of the Interior
Jean-Baptiste Bienvenu-Martin – Minister of Labour and Social Security Provisions
Aristide Briand – Minister of Justice
Albert Sarraut – Minister of Public Instruction and Fine Arts
Fernand David – Minister of Agriculture
Gaston Doumergue – Minister of Colonies
Maurice Sembat,– Minister of Public Works
Gaston Thomson – Minister of Commerce, Industry, Posts and Telegraphs
Jules Guesde – Minister without Portfolio

Briand's Fifth Ministry, 29 October 1915 – 12 December 1916

Aristide Briand – President of the Council and Minister of Foreign Affairs
Joseph Galliéni – Minister of War
Louis Malvy – Minister of the Interior
Alexander Ribot – Minister of Finance
Albert Métin - Minister of Labour and Social Security Provisions
René Viviani – Minister of Justice
Lucien Lacaze – Minister of Marine
Paul Painlevé – Minister of Public Instruction and Fine Arts
Jules Méline – Minister of Agriculture
Gaston Doumergue – Minister of Colonies
Marcel Sembat – Minister of Public Works
Étienne Clémentel – Minister of Commerce, Industry, Posts, and Telegraphs
Léon Bourgeois – Minister of State
Denys Cochin – Minister of State
Émile Combes - Minister of State
Charles de Freycinet – Minister of State
Jules Guesde – Minister of State

Appendix II

Order of Battle

Corps Expéditionnaire d'Orient
Commanders
Gen. Albert d'Amade
Gen. Henri Gouraud
Gen. Maurice Bailloud
Gen. Jean Brulard

1st Division

1st Metropolitan Brigade
    175th Regiment
    1st Régiment de marche d'Afrique (2 Bns. Zouaves, 1 Bn. Foreign Legion)
    Foreign Legion Battalion (2 Coys.)

2nd Colonial Brigade
    4th Colonial Regiment
    6th Colonial Regiment
6 Batteries of Artillery (75-mm)
2 Batteries of Artillery (65-mm)

2nd Division

3rd Metropolitan Brigade
    176th Regiment
    2nd Régiment de marche d'Afrique (3 Bns. Zouaves)

4th Colonial Brigade
    7th Colonial Regiment
    8th Colonial Regiment
9 Batteries of Artillery (75-mm)

Corps Artillery

1 Heavy Battery, 120-mm
3 Heavy Batteries, 155-mm
2 Siege Guns, 240-mm
Naval gun battery

Bibliography

Archival & Unpublished Sources

*France**
AMAE, La Courneuve
AMG, Service historique de la Défence, Vincennes
AMM, Service historique de la Défence
Bertier papers, Service historique de la Défence
Briand Papers, La Courneuve
Cambon papers, La Courneuve
Commission de la Marine, Archives Nationales
Commission de l'armée, Archives Nationales
Commission des Affaires Etrangères, Archives Nationales
Commission du Buget, Archives Nationales
Delcassé papers, La Courneuve
Gouraud papers, La Courneuve
Martin, "Notes de guerre," Stanford University Library
Millerand papers, Archives Nationales
Poincaré papers. His journals are on-line and his personal collection is at the Bibliothèque Nationale

*Great Britain***
Admiralty archives, British National Archives
Asquith papers, Bodleian Library, Oxford
Balfour papers, British Library
Bertie papers, British National Archives
Cabinet papers. These consist of the Minutes of the War Council, Dardanelles Committee, War Committee and Allied Conferences between 11 September 1915 and 16 November 1916, all found in the British National Archives
Churchill papers, Churchill College, Cambridge
Dardanelles Commission Report, British National Archives
Esher papers, Churchill College, Cambridge

* The following collections, except the one designated, are housed in Parisian archival repositories.
** London-based repository unless otherwise indicated.

Foreign Office Archives, British National Archives
Grey papers, British National Archives
Kitchener papers, British National Archives
Wilson diary, Imperial War Museum

Published Government Sources & Official Histories

Aspinall-Oglander, Brig.-Gen. C.F. *Military Operations: Gallipoli*, 2 Vols. London: William Heinemann, 1929, 1932.
Corbett, Julian S. *Naval Operations*, Vols. 1-2. London: Longmans, Green and Co. 1920, 1921.
Dardanelles Commission, *First and Final Report*. London: HMSO, 1917, 1919.
Edmonds, Sir James E. *Military Operations: France and Belgium 1915*, Vol. 2. London: Macmillan, 1933.
Falls Cyril. *Military Operations: Macedonia*. Vol. 1. London: HMSO, 1933.
France, Assemblée nationale, *Annales de la chamber des députés, débats parlementaires, sessions ordinaires et extraordinaires de 1915*. Paris, 1918.
France, Assemblée nationale. *Journal official de la république française, Comité secret, juin 1916-Octobre 1917*. Paris, 1919.
France. Ministère de la Guere, État Major de l'Armée. Service historique. *Les armées françaises dans la grande guerre*, tome 8, Vol. 1 (Official History). Paris: Imprimerie Nationale, 1923.
France. Ministère de la Guerre, État Major de l'Armée. Service historique. *Les armées françaises dans la grande guerre*, tome 8, Vol. 1, annexes 1-2. Paris: Imprimerie Nationale, 1924- 1926. Official documents relating to the Dardanelles and Balkan Operations.
France, Ministère des Affaires Etrangères. *Documents diplomatiques français 1915*. Brussels: Peter Lang, 2002.
Great Britain, Foreign Office. *British Documents on the Origins of the War*, ed. by George P. Gooch and Harold Temperley, Vol. 10, pt. 2. London: HMSO, 1938.
Russia. *Constantinople et les détroits*, 2 vols., trans. by S. Volski, G. Gaussel and V. Paris; ed. and annotated by G. Chklaver. Paris: Les Éditions Internationales, 1930.
Russia. *Documents diplomatiques secrets russes, 1914–1917*, trans. by J. Polonsky. Paris: Payot, 1928.

Books & Articles

Alexandre, G. R. *Avec Joffre d'Agadir à Verdun*. Paris: Berger-Levrault, 1932.
Allen, Capt. G.R.G. "A Ghost from Gallipoli." *Journal of the United Service Institution*, Vol. 101, May (1963). pp. 137-38.
Amade, Albert d'. "Constantinople et les détroits." *Revue des questions historiques*, vols. 98-99, Parts 1 & 2 (1923), pp. 5-35; 290-326.
Andrew, Christopher M. and S. Kanya-Forstner. *The Climax of French Imperial Expansion 1914-1924*. Stanford: Stanford University Press, 1981.
Andurain, Julie d'. "Le géneral Gouraud, chef du corps expéditionnaire des Dardanelles en 1915." *Reuve historique de l'armée*, Vol. 258 (2010), pp. 46-56.

Arthur, Sir George. *Life of Lord Kitchener*, Vol. 3. London: Macmillan, 1920.
Asquith, H.H. *Memories and Reflections*, Vol. 2. London: Cassell, 1928.
Association des Dardanelles. *Dardanelle Orient Levant*. Paris L'Harmattan, 2005.
Azan, Paul. *Franchet d'Espèrey*. Paris: Flammarion, 1949.
Ballard, Gen. C.R. *Kitchener*. New York: Dodd, Mead and Co., 1930.
Barré, Jean-Luc. *Le Seigneur Chat: Philippe Berthelot 1866–1934*. Paris: Plon, 1988.
Beesly, Patrick. *Room 40: British Intelligence 1914-1918*. New York: Harcourt Brace Jovanovich, 1982.
Bell, Christopher M. *Churchill and the Dardanelles*. Oxford: Oxford University Press, 2017.
Benoist, Charles. *Souvenirs*, Vol. 3. Paris: Plon, 1934.
Bienaimé, A.P. *La guerre navale 1914–1915: Fautes et responsabilités*. Paris: Jules Tallendier, 1920.
Blake, Robert. (ed.). *The Private Papers of Douglas Haig*. London: Eyre and Spottiswoode, 1952.
Bobroff, Ronald P. *Roads to Glory: Late Imperial Russia and the Turkish Straits*. London: Tauris, 2006.
Bonham Carter, Lady Violet. *Winston Churchill: An Intimate Portrait*. New York: Harcourt, Brace and World, 1964.
Bourget, J. M. *Gouvernement et commandement: Les leçons de la guerre mondiale*. Paris: Plon, 1930.
Bréal, A. *Philippe Berthelot*. Paris: Gallimard, 1937.
Brock, Michael and Eleanor. (eds.). *Margot Asquith's Great War Diary 1914–1916*. Oxford: Oxford University Press, 2014.
Bugnet, Charles. *Rue St Dominique et GQG*. Paris: Plon, 1937.
Cambon, Henri. (ed.) Paul Cambon: *Correspondance 1870–1924*, Vol. 3. Paris: Bernard Grasset, 1946.
Carcopino, Jérôme. *Souvenirs de la guerre en Orient 1915–1917*. Paris: Hachette, 1970.
Cassar, George H. *Kitchener as Proconsul of Egypt, 1911–1914*. London: Palgrave Macmillan, 2016.
_____. *Kitchener's War: British Strategy From 1914 to 1916*. Washington, DC: Potomac Books, 2004.
Challener, Richard D. *The French Theory of the Nation in Arms 1866–1939*. New York: Russell and Russell, 1965.
Charles-Roux, François. *L'Expédition des Dardanelles*. Paris: Armand Colin, 1919.
Charteris, Brig.-Gen John. *At GQG*. London: Cassell, 1931.
Churchill, Winston S. *The World Crisis*, Vol. 2. New York: Charles Scribner's Sons, 1951.
Claeys, Louis. *Delcassé*. Pamiers: Acala, 2001.
Coblentz, Paul. *The Silence of Sarrail*. London: Hutchinson, 1930.
Colin, H. "Gouraud". *Revue historique de l'armée*, Vol. 41 (1937), pp. 7–24.
Collier, Basil. *Brasshat: The Biography of Field-Marshal Sir Henry Wilson*. London: Secker and Warburg, 1961.
Curran, Tom. *The Grand Deception: Churchill and the Dardanelles*. Newport, NSW: Big Sky Publishing, 2015.
Dossant, Serge. *Le général André*. Paris: Éditions Glyphe, 2013.
Doughty, Robert A. *Pyrrhic Victory: French Strategy and Operations in the Great War*. Cambridge: Cambridge University Press, 2005.

David Dutton. "The Balkan Campaign and French War Aims in the Great War." *The English Historical Review*, Vol. 94 (1979), pp. 97–113.
_____. "The Calais Conference of December 1915." *The Historical Journal*, Vol. 21, no. 1 (1978), pp. 143-56.
_____. *The Politics of Diplomacy*. London: Tauris, 1998.
_____. "The Union Sacrée and the French Cabinet Crisis of October 1915". *European Studies Review*, Vol. 8 (1978), pp. 411–24.
Einstein, Lewis. *Inside Constantinople*. London: John Murray, 1917.
Ellison, Sir Gerald. *The Perils of Amateur Strategy*. London: Longmans and Green, 1926.
Erickson, Edward J. *Gallipoli: The Ottoman Campaign*. Barnsley, S. York. : Pen and Sword, 2010.
Esher, Reginald Viscount. *The Tragedy of Lord Kitchener*. London: John Murray, 1921.
Eubank, W. K. *Paul Cambon, Master Diplomastist*. Norman: University of Oklahoma Press, 1960.
Farrar, Margorie, M. *Principled Pragmatist: The Political Career of Alexandre Millerand*. Oxford: Berg, 1991.
Ferry, Abel. *Les carnets secrets 1914-1918*. Paris: Bernard Grasset, 1957.
Feuille, Henri. *Face aux Turcs: Gallipoli 1915*. Paris: Payot, 1934.
Fitzsimons, Peter. *Gallipoli*. London: Bantam, 2014.
Flandin, Étienne, "Nos droits en Syrie et Palestine." *La revue hebdomadaire*, 29 May, 1915, pp. 17-32.
French, David. *British Strategy and War Aims 1914–1916*. London: Allen and Unwin, 1986.
Galliéni, Gaëtan. (ed.). *Les carnets de Galliéni*. Paris: Albin Michel, 1932.
Galliéni, Joseph-Simon. *Mémoires*. Paris: Payot, 1920.
Gariepy, Patrick. *Gardens of Hell: Battles of the Gallipoli Campaign*. Washington DC: Potomac Books, 2014.
Gheusi, P. B. *La vie prodigieuse du maréchal Galliéni*. Paris: Plon, 1939.
Gilbert, Martin. *Winston S. Churchill: The Challenge of War 1914–1916*. Boston: Houghton Mifflin Co., 1971.
Gorce, Paul Marie de la. *The French Army; A Military-Political History*. New York: George Braziller, 1963.
Gosa, Pierre. *Un Maréchal Méconnu: Franchet d'Espèrey*. Paris: Nouvelles Éditions Latines, 1999.
Gottlieb, W.W. *Studies in Secret Diplomacy during the First World War*. London: Allen and Unwin, 1957.
Greenhalgh, Elizabeth. *The French Army and the First World War*. Cambridge: Cambridge University Press, 2014.
Greenhalgh, Elizabeth and Col. Frédéric Guelton, "The French on Gallipoli and Observations on Australian and British forces during the August offensive in Asley Ekins, ed., *Gallipoli: A Ridge Too Far*. Wollombic, NSW, Australia: Exisle, 2013.
Grey of Fallodon, Viscount. *Twenty-Five Years 1892–1916*, Vol. 2. London: Hodder and Stoughton, 1925.
Guépratte, Vice-Amiral Émile-Paul. *L'Expédition des Dardanelles 1914–1915*. Paris: Payot, 1935.
Hale, William. *Turkey's Foreign Policy 1774–2000*. London: Frank Cass, 2000.

Halpern, Paul G. *The Mediterranean Naval Situation, 1908–1914*. Cambridge: Cambridge University Press, 1971.

_____. *The Naval War in the Mediterranean 1914–1918*. Annapolis: Naval Institute Press, 1987.

Hamilton, Sir Ian. *Gallipoli Diary*, 2 Vols. London: Edward Arnold, 1920.

Hamilton, Ian. *The Happy Warrior: A Life of General Sir Ian Hamilton*. London : Cassell, 1966.

Hankey, Lord. *The Supreme Command 1914–1918*, 2 Vols. London: Allen and Unwin, 1961.

Hart, Peter. *Gallipoli*. Oxford: Oxford University Press, 2011.

Herbillon, Émile. *Souvenirs d'un officier de liaison pendant la guerre mondiale*, 2 Vols. Paris: Jules Tallandier, 1930.

Hickey, Michael. *Gallipoli*. London: John Murray, 1995.

Horne, Alistair. *The Price of Glory*. New York: Harper Colophon, 1967.

Howard, Harry N. *The Partition of Turkey 1913–1923*. New York: Howard Fertig, 1966.

Howard, Michael, (ed.) *Soldiers and Governments*. Bloomington: Indiana University Press, 1959.

James, Robert Rhodes. *Gallipoli*. London: Batsford, 1965.

Jobert, Aristide. *Souvenirs d'un ex-parlementaire 1914-1919*. Paris: Figuière, 1933.

Joffre, Field Marshal Joseph. *Personal Memoirs*, 2 Vols. trans. by Col. T. Bentley Mott. New York: Harper, 1932.

Keiger, J. F. V. *France and the Origins of the First World War*. London: Macmillan, 1983.

_____. *Raymond Poincaré*. Cambridge: Cambridge University Press, 1997.

Keyes, Sir Roger. *Naval Memoirs of Admiral of the Fleet 1905–1915*, Vol. 1. New York: Dutton, 1934.

King, J. C. *Generals and Politicians*. Berkeley: University of California Press, 1951.

Larcher, Commandant Maurice. *La grande guerre dans les Balkans*. Paris: Payot, 1929.

Laurens, Adolphe. *Le Commandement navale en Méditerranée 1914-1918*. Paris: Payot, 1931.

Leblond, Marius-Ary. *Galliéni parle*, 2 Vols. Paris: Albin Michel, 1920.

Lennox, Lady Algeron, (ed.) *The Diary of Lord Bertie of Thame*, Vol. 1. London: Hodder and Stoughton, 1924.

Liddle, Peter. *Men of Gallipoli*. London: Allen Lane, 1976.

Liman von Sanders, Field Marshal Otto. *Five Years in Turkey*. Annapolis: United States Naval Institute, 1929.

Lloyd George, David. *War Memoirs*, Vol. 1. London: Odhams Press, 1938.

Louis, Georges. *Les carnets de Georges Louis*, Vol. 2. Paris: Rieder, 1926.

Lyautey, Pierre. *Galliéni*. Paris: Gallimard, 1959.

_____. *Gouraud*. Paris: Julliard, 1949.

Macfie, A.L. *The End of the Ottoman Empire 1908–1923*. London: Longman, 1998.

Marcellin, Léopaul. *Politique et politiciens pendant la guerre*, Vol. 1. Paris: La Renaissance du Libre, 1932.

Marder, A. J. *From the Dreadnought to Scapa Flow*, Vols. 1-2. London: Oxford University Press, 1961, 1965.

Martet, Jean. *Georges Clemenceau*, trans. by Milton Waldman. London: Longmans, Green and Co., 1930.

Mayer, Émile. *Nos chefs de 1914*. Paris: Stock, 1930.

Mayer, Jean Marie. *La vie politique sous la Troisième Republique*. Paris: Seuil, 1984.

Messimy, Adolphe. *Mes souvenirs*. Paris: Plon, 1937.

Morgenthau, Henry. *Ambassador Morgenthau's Story*. New York: Doubleday, Page and Co., 1919.
Paléologue, Maurice. *An Ambassador's Memoirs*, Vol. 1. trans. by F.A. Holt. London: Hutchinson, 1924.
Palmer, Alan. *The Gardeners of Salonica*. New York: Simon and Schuster, 1965.
Pédoya, Jean Marie Gustave. *La commission de l'armée pendant la grande guerre: Documents inédits et secrets*. Paris: Flammarion, 1921.
Pierrefeu, Jean de. *French Headquarters 1915–1918*, trans. by Maj. C. J. C. Street. London: Geoffrey Bles, 1924.
Pingaud, Albert. *Histoire diplomatique de la France pendant la grande guerre*, Vol. 1. Paris: Éditions Alsatia, 1938.
Poincaré, Raymond. *Au service de la France*, Vols. 5-7. Paris: Plon, 1928, 1930, 1931.
Pomiro, D'Arnaud. *Les carnets de guerre*. Toulouse: Éditions Privat, 2006.
Porch, Douglas. *The March to the Marne: The French Army 1871-1914*. Cambridge: Harvard University Press, 1981.
Porter, Charles W. *The Career of Théophile Delcassé*. Philadelphia: University of Pennsylvania Press, 1936.
Prete, Roy A. "Imbroglio par excellence: Mounting the Salonica Campaign, September-October 1915." *War and Society*, Vol. 19 (20001), pp. 47-70.
_____. *Strategy and Command: The Anglo-French Coalition on the Western Front 1914*. McGill and Kingston, McGill-Queen's University Press, 2009.
Prior, Robin. *Gallipoli: The End of the Myth*. New Haven: Yale University Press, 2009.
Puntous, Jacques. "Albert d'Amade: Portrait Intime." *Mondes et Culture*, Vol. 66, no. 1 (2006), pp. 596-610.
Ralston, David B. *The Army of the Republic*. Cambridge, MA: MIT Press, 1967.
Renouvin, Pierre. *La Crise européenne et la grande guerre 1914–1918*. Paris: Félix Alcan, 1934.
_____. *The Forms of War Government in France*. New Haven: Yale University Press, 1927.
Ribot, Alexandre. *Lettres à un ami: souvenirs de ma vie politique*. Paris: Bossard, 1924.
Ribot, A. (ed.) *Journal de Alexandre Ribot et correspondances inédites 1914–1922*. Paris: Plon, 1936.
Rigoux, Pierre. *Les Dardanelles 1915*. Paris: Economica, 2013.
Rivoyne, Lieutenant de vaisseau de. "L'Expedition des Dardanelles 1914–1915" (1923).
Roberts, Stephen H. *The History of French Colonial Policy 1870–1925*. London: Frank Cass, 1963.
Roth, Francois. *Raymond Poincaré*. Paris: Fayard, 2000.
Rudenno, Victor. *Gallipoli: Attack from the Sea*. New Haven: Yale University Press, 2008.
Salaun, Henri. *La Marine française*. Paris: Les Éditions de France, 1934.
Sarrail, Maurice P. *Mon commandement en Orient*. Paris: Flammarion, 1920.
Sazanov, Serge. *Fateful Years 1906–1916*. London: Butler and Tanner, 1927.
Semur, François-Christian. *MacMahon*. Paris: Gawsewitch, 2005.
Smith, C. J. *The Russian Struggle for Power 1914–1917*. New York: Philosophical Library, 1956.
Soltan, R. *French Parties and Politics*. London: Oxford University Press, 1930.
Spender, J. A. and Cyril Asquith. *Life of Herbert Henry Asquith, Lord Oxford and Asquith*, Vol. 2. London: Hutchinson, 1932.

Stuermer, H. *Two Years in Constantinople*. London: Hodder and Stoughton, 1917.
Suarez, Georges. *Briand: sa vie-son oeuvre*, Vol. 3. Paris: Plon, 1939.
Tanenbaum, Jan K. *General Maurice Sarrail 1856–1929*. Chapel Hill; University of North Carolina Press, 1974.
Taylor, A.J.P. *Politics in Wartime*. London: Hamish Hamilton, 1964.
Taylor, A.J.P. (ed.). *Lloyd George: A Diary by Frances Stevenson*. New York: Harper and Row, 1971.
Terrail, Gabriel. *Joffre: la première crise du commandement*. Paris: Ollendorff, 1919.
_____. *Sarrail et les armées d'Orient*. Paris: Ollendorff, 1920.
Thomazi, Auguste. *La Guerre navale aux Dardanelles*. Paris: Payot, 1926.
Travers, Tim. *Gallipoli 1915*. Stroud, Tempus, 2004.
Unger, Gérard. *Aristide Briand*. Paris: Fayard, 2005.
Valentin, Jean-Marc. *Rene Viviani 1863-1925*. Limoges: Pulim, 2013.
Vassal, Joseph. *Uncensored Letters from the Dardanelles*. London: William Heinemann, 1916.
Wright, Gordon. *Raymond Poincaré and the French Presidency*. New York: Octagon, 1967.
Captaine de Corvette X et Claude Farrère. "Journal de bord de l'expédition des Dardanelles." *Les oeuvres libres*, Vol. 17 (1922).
Zorgbibe, Charles. *Delcassé*. Paris: Éditions Olbia, 2001.

Also by the same author

The French and the Dardanelles: A Study of Failure in the Conduct of War (London, 1971)
Kitchener: Architect of Victory (London, 1977)
The Tragedy of Sir John French (Newark: 1984)
Beyond Courage (Ottawa, 1985)
Asquith as War Leader (London, 1994)
The Forgotten Front: The British Campaign in Italy (London: 1998)
Kitchener's War: British Strategy From 1914 to 1916 (Washington DC, 2004)
Lloyd George at War, 1916-1918 (London, 2009)
Hell in Flanders Fields: The Canadians at the Second Battle of Ypres (Toronto, 2010)
Trial By Gas: The British Army at the Second Battle of Ypres (Washington DC, 2014)
Kitchener as Pronconsul in Egypt, 1911-14 (London, 2016)
A Survey of Western Civilization
World History

Index

Achi Baba, 114-15, 120, 122, 126, 137-38, 142, 145, 157, 167
Adramyti, Bay of, 74, 101, 171
Alexandre, Lieut.-Col. R., 177, 180
Alexandretta, 45, 46, 48, 50 -51, 61, 203, 204, 207, 216
Alexandria, 100-2, 105
Amade, Gen. Albert d', 69, 101
    attends conference on board *Queen Elizabeth*, 74
    character and earlier career, 66-67
    instructions, 73
    and Kum Kale, 106, 111-112
    participates in the First and Second Battles of Krithia, 116-17, 122-25
    relieved of command, 127, 129
    unsure of his role in operations, 73-74
    works on plan for employment of Allied forces, 101-3, 110
André, Gen. Louis, 20, 161
Anzac front, 117, 159
Argonne, 128, 163
Arras, Battle of, 164
Artois, Battle of, 152
Asquith, Herbert H. 41, 60, 72, 96, 189, 201, 205
    reads statement at Calais warning of impending military disaster in the Balkans, 210
    reshapes government on a non-party basis, 133
Aubert, Vice-Adm. Marie-Jacques-Charles,
    considers Carden's plan of attack flawed, 57
    opposes purely naval operation, 51,
    strained relations with Augagneur, 52, 55
Augagneur, Victor, 43, 176
    accompanies Millerand to Calais for a conference with Kitchener and Balfour, 191
    attempts to wrest naval command from the English, 131-32
    concern over French rights in the Mediterranean, 45-46, 48
    confers with Churchill in London, 49-53, 216
    discloses results of meeting with Churchill, 54-55
    earlier career and character,45
    excluded from the new ministry, 199
    gives a brief interview to *Petit Parisien*, 65
    ignores the opinion of French naval authorities, 52
    insists on taking the initiative at Bodrum, 104-5
    journeys to London with Viviani to wrest concessions from the British, 193-94
    opposes resumption of independent naval action, 95-96, 130-31
    questions Guépratte's mental stability, 89, 132
    removes Guépratte as naval commander, 132-33
    requests Carden's plan of operation, 56
Ayas Bay, 203-5

Baghdad Railway, 34, 171
Bailloud, Gen. Maurice, 114, 187
    carries out French end of operations on Cape Helles, 155-56, 159-60
    earlier career, 151
    favours an offensive in Asia, 158, 167-68
    instructed to prepare one of his divisions for service elsewhere, 189-90
    relations with Hamilton, 190
Balfour, Arthur, 134, 179, 191-92, 205
Balkans, 36-37, 199, 200-3, 207
    debate on sending troops to, 39-40, 41, 59-60 187-88
    debate on staying in, 191-93, 194-95, 196-98, 205-6, 209-11, 212-13
    difficulty of waging a campaign in, 188
    counterproductive campaign in , 218
Baumann, Gen. 151, 184
Benazet, Paul, 192
Benckendorff, Count Alexander, 77, 83
Berthelot, Philippe, 211
Bertie, Sir Francis, 61, 198
    admits that Straits Agreement was a mistake, 184-85
    assesses French feeling over the Dardanelles, 136

concerned about rumours spread by leftists, 172-73
confirms fraigile state of Briand ministry, 212
Besika Bay, 103, 145, 167
Birdwood, Lieut.-Gen, William, 69, 73-74
Blum, Léon, 192
Bodrum, 104-5
Bonar Law, Andrew, 179
Bordeaux, 32-33, 37
Boué de Lapeyrère, Vice-Adm. Augustin, 46, 131
  Allied Naval Commander in the Mediterranean, 43-44
  discovers Allied plan to attack the Dardanelles, 55-56
Boulanger, Gen. Georges, 18-19
Bourgeois, Lèon
  proposes that a settlement on Salonika be deferred,211
Braithwaite, Maj. Gen. W. P., 112
Breslau, 40n43, 43, 97
Briand, Aristide,
  applies pressure on Galliéni to conciliate Joffre on Balkan expedition, 39-41, 187, 210-211
  becomes prime minister, 198-99
  character and early career, 30
  faces ministerial crisis, 211-12
  gives assurances of France's determination to fight to the end, 173
  interviews with Kitchener in Paris, 200-201, 207
  opposes turning Constantinople and the Straits over to the Russians
  persuades Sarrail to accept the Dardanelles command, 167
  succumbs to British pressure to evacuate the Balkans, 211-12, 220-21
British general staff
  prewar surveys on feasibility of an attack on the Dardanelles, 42
  opposed to Ayas Bay landing, 205
Brulard, Gen. 190, 203
Buat, Col. Edmond, 164
Buchanan, Sir George, 77-78, 79-80, 81
Bulair, 70,100, 101, 103-4, 144, 175, 185
Bulgaria, 60, 186, 195-197, 217

Caillaux, Henriette, 28
Caillaux, Joseph, 25, 161, 165, 197-98
  character and pre-war career 21
  settlement with Germany over Moroccan crisis leads to fall of his ministry, 21-22
Calais, conferences at, 153, 181-2, 191-92, 210-211
Cambon, Paul, 46, 54, 62, 65, 96

endorses Churchill's proposals, 47
investigates rumour that de Robeck plans to resume naval attack,
on need to maintain secrecy, 54
reports Kitchener's views on the subject of a c-in-c in the Dardanelles, 68
suspects real English motive for sending troops, 65
visits Grey to obtain details of British plan, 71
Cape Helles, 104, 105, 106, 112, 114, 119, 144-45, 156-57, 206, 213
Carden, Vice-Adm. Sackville H. , 51, 74, 88
  opens naval attack on Turkish forts, 63
  outlines naval plan for forcing the Dardanelles, 43, 56
  suffers nervous breakdown, 88
Champagne, Battle of, 196
Chanak, 57, 145, 167, 171, 176, 186
Chantilly, 100, 168, 173, 176, 194, 196, 198, 202, 213
Churchill, Winston, 35, 59, 182, 198
  character, 41
  consequences of his reckless announcement to the press, 63-64
  and Dardanelles operation, 63, 93, 94-95, 153, 215
  differences with naval advisors, 59, 94, 131
  encounters French resistance to his scheme, 48-49
  is excluded from the coalition government
  mistaken assessment of the naval attack, 97-99
  orders ships to Bodrum, 104-5
  proposes plan to force the Dardanelles by ships alone, 43
  presses for a continuation of naval attack, 94
  reaches an accommodation with Augagneur, 50-53, 216
  resists Augagneur's move to place his own nominee in charge of the naval operations, 132
  relations with Fisher, 94, 131
Clemenceau, Georges, 29, 165 192-93, 207-8
Cochin, Denys, 211
Commission on Foreign Affairs, 197
Conseil supérieur de la défence nationale, 176, 180, 183, 199-200
Conseil supéieur de la guerre, 24, 32
Constantine I, King of Greece, 81, 82, 192, 211
Constantinople, 34-36, 43, 55, 57, 65, 76-86, 97-98, 166, 182, 184, 192, 204
Cruppi, Jean, 184

Dardanelles, 42, 60, 61, 103, 114
  bombardment on outer and inner defences, 63

Churchill makes a case for a naval attack, 43
consequences of Allied withdrawal from, 215
description of, 42
evacuation, 200, 225, 226, 213-14
French interest in Asiatic landing, 157-58, 178,
Goeben and *Breslau* pass through, 36
Hamilton appointed to command expeditionary force, 72
Hamilton's plan for landing in April, 104; in August, 158-59
Kitchener requests a military demonstration in, 42
military campaign, 112-14, 116-117, 122-25
minefields, 92-93, 97
mobile batteries, 97
naval plan of operation, 43, 91
Turkish resistance, 117-20
Dardanelles Committee, 134, 194-95
Delcassé, Théophile, 66, 72, 173, 176, 179, 192
and Constantinople and the Straits, 77, 82-85
distrusts the British, 79
endorses idea of naval attack, 54
failure of his foreign policy and resignation, 195
inquires if attack will be delayed until arrival of troops, 62
mixed feelings about accepting Greece's offer to land troops on Gallipoli, 81-82
notifies London that French government intends to send four divisions to Dardanelles, 178
opposed to campaign in the Balkans, 187, 192
previous career and character, 31
seeks Russia's active participation in the operations, 78-79
tries to place a French general in overall command of land operations, 68
De Robeck, Vice-Adm., J. M., 112, 189
succeeds Carden, 74
on naval attack on 18 March, 88, 91, 93
opposed to resumption of naval activity, 94, 130,
Doumergue, Gaston, 165-66
Dreyfus Affair, 19, 23
Dubail Gen. Yvon, 163-64
Duckworth Vice- Adm. Sir John, 42

Egypt, 41, 44, 45, 46, 61, 97, 114, 127, 189, 203, 204-5, 207
El Arish, 45
Ellison, Maj.-Gen. Sir Gerald, 99
Enver Pasha, 98, 173
Eren Keui Bay, 92-93
Esher, Lord, 69

Falkenhayn, Gen. Erich von, 186
Ferdinand I, King of Bulgaria, 195
Fisher, Lord
opposes resumption of naval attack, 94
relations with Churchill, 94, 131, 133
Foreign Affairs Commission, 197
Fortin Le Gouez redoubt, 137
Franchet d'Espèrey, Gen. Louis, 39
character and experience, 36
favors opening a new front in the Balkans, 36-37,
Franklin-Bouillon, Henry, 167, 172
French, Sir John, 174, 181, 191
French contribution to the Dardanelles campaign, 219
French Expeditionary Corps
1st Division, 66, 122, 123, 140, 155, 156, 159
1st Metropolitan Brigade, 111, 119, 122, 123
175th Regiment, 116-117, 155
1st Régiment de marche d'Afrique, 159
Foreign Legion Battalion, 112
2nd Colonial Brigade, 106, 119
4th Colonial Regiment, 159
6th Colonial Regiment, 106, 119, 146
2nd Division, 114, 123-24, 140, 156, 159
3rd Metropolitan Brigade, 159
176th Regiment, 146
2nd Régiment de marche d'Afrique, 146, 148
4th Colonial Brigade, 159
7th Colonial Regiment, 150
8th Colonial Regiment, 123
French general staff, 44-45, 59, 103-4, 176, 204
French naval units
Bouvet, 91-92, 93-94, 219
Bruix, 132
Charlemagne, 91-92, 94, 132
Dupleix, 132
Gaulois, 91-92, 94, 132
Henri IV, 94, 108, 132
Jauréguiberry, 94, 109, 110, 132
Jeanne d'Arc, 94
Klèber, 132
Latouche-Tréville, 94, 132
Saint Louis, 132,
Savoie, 109
Suffren, 91-92, 132, 150
Freycinet, Charles de, 211

Gaba Tepe, 112, 138, 144-45, 175 186
Galliéni, Gen. Joseph, 37, 39, 161, 166
appointed Minister of War, 198-99
attends conference at Calais, 205-6, 210-11
on Balkan expedition, 200, 211
on Dardanelles campaign, 200, 202, 205

interviews with Kitchener in Paris, 200, 202, 207
part played at the Marne, 33
relations with Joffre, 205-6, 208
agrees reluctantly to appoint Joffre supreme commander of French forces, 208-9
Gallipoli (see Dardanelles)
George V, King, 70, 80, 151, 198
Girodon, Col. Pierre, 155
  accompanies Kitchener to the Dardanelles, 202-3
  character, 201-2
  as Gouraud's chief of staff, 129
  invalidated home, 148
  keeps Galliéni informed of Kitchener's activities on Gallipoli, 203
  opposes evacuation of the Dardanelles, 199
  placed in command of the Metropolitan Brigade, 146-47
  submits his report to Galliéni, 208
  supports Kitchener's Eastern policy, 203, 208
  visits Kitchener at British embassy in Paris, 201-202
Goeben, 40n43, 43, 46, 97
Gouraud, Gen. Henri, 152, 155, 164,
  advocates a landing in Asia, 157-58, 168
  assists in planning and execution of Third Battle of Krithia, 138-41
  earlier career and character, 128
  examines possible landing sites in Dardanelles, 137-38, 144
  participates in operations on Cape Helles, 145-50
  reorganizes army and front, 136-37
  severely wounded and returned home, 150-51
Graziani, Gen. Jean Césaire, 103, 177
Greece, 59-60, 189, 192, 195, 206
  on implementing alliance with Serbia, 186-88
  offers to send troops to Dardanelles, 80-2
Grévy, Jules, 17
Grey, Sir Edward, 46, 61, 65, 71-72, 77, 80, 205
  and negotiations over the fate of Constantinople and the Straits, 77, 84, 85-86
Guépratte, Rear-Adm. Emile-Paul, 55, 74-75, 108
  approves of Carden's plan, 56
  eager to renew naval attack, 129-30
  earlier career and character, 88-89
  joins Carden's fleet at the entrance of Dardanelles, 43
  part played in Allied naval attack on 18 March, 90-92
  replaced as naval commander, 132

urges reinforcements for army, 114

Hall, Capt. Reginald Hall, 86
Hamid, Abdul, 64, 97
Hamilton, Gen. Ian, 74, 106, 111, 124-26,
  appointed c-in-c of expeditionary force, 72
  approves of bite and hold strategy in Cape Helles, 156
  attends meeting on board *Queen Elizabeth*, 74-75
  calls for large-scale reinforcements, 160
  devises plan for landing in April, 104
  devises plan for landing in August, 158-59
  dismayed over loss of Gouraud
  pleased with change in French leadership, 128
  opposed to the evacuation of Suvla, 189
  relations with d'Amade, 128
  relations with Bailloud, 190-91
  relations with Gouraud, 143,
  relieved of command, 200
  rejects French request for a landing in Asia, 158
  reorganizes his army, 120
Hankey, Lieut.-Col. Maurice, 151-52, 181, 183
Haricot redoubt, 137, 145-46, 149
Herbillon, Col. Emile, 165
Hervé, Gustave, 166
Hunter-Weston, Lieut.-Gen Aylmer, 111, 123, 155-56
  and the Three Battles of Krithia, 114-16, 122-25, 138-142

Imbros, 82, 144
Inflexible, 93
Inter-Allied Military Conference, 153, 213
Irresistible, 93
Isvolsky, Alexander, 77, 82, 83
Italy, 131

Jaffa, 46, 51
James, Robert Rhodes, 103-4
Joffre, Gen. Joseph, 66, 70, 176, 193, 196, 197, 207
  appointed supreme commander of the French army, 208-9
  on the Balkans, 40, 60, 189, 198, 202, 206, 210 218
  clashes with government over conduct of the war, 176, 180
  at conferences in Calais, 100, 153, 181-83, 195, 210
  conflict with Sarrail, 162-63
  on the Dardanelles, 65-66, 100, 127-28, 168-69, 170, 202
  declining reputation, 161, 169, 196,

Index 235

defines his role as c-in-c, 174
determined to preserve war strategy, 152-53, 169, 174, 199, 176
early career and character 24
faulty strategy to deal with trench warfare, 38-39, 216-17
induces Allied chiefs of staff at Chantilly to adopt his military policy, 213
on landing in Asia, 182-83, 185
Marne, Battle of the, 33
meets Kitchener at Chantilly, 194, 202
Plan XVII, 26-27, 32
prestige after the Marne, 37-38
refuses to release the divisions until after his fall offensive is over, 174, 176, 182, 185, 217
rejects Sarrail's first appreciation, 171; and the second, 176, 177-78
removes Sarrail from command of Third Army, 164

Kereves Dere ravine, 116 -117, 119, 122-24, 140, 145, 149, 155-56, 159
Kereves Spur, 137
Keyes, Commodore Roger
presses for a renewed attack on the Dardanelles, 129-30, 203n28
Kilid Bahr, 57, 106, 144, 157
Kitchener, Field Marshal Horatio Herbert, 66, 185, 206
accompanied by Girodon on visit to the Dardanelles, 202-3
advocates evacuation of Peninsula, 203, 206
appoints Hamilton c-in-c of the expeditionary force, 72
on the Balkans, 59, 189, 191-92, 194, 196, 198, 200-1, 202-3, 210
character, 41
and Churchill, 43, 46, 63, 153, 182
at conferences in Calais, 100, 153, 181-83, 191-92, 210
on the Dardanelles, 43, 60-65, 68-69, 72-73, 100, 181-82, 200
favours an active-defence in the west, 153
insists that a British general lead the Allied force, 68
interviews with French political leaders in Paris, 200-1, 207
meets Joffre at Chantilly, 194, 202
recalls Hamilton, 200
recommends a landing in Ayas Bay, 203-5
reluctant to talk with French leaders, 69-70
rules out a descent on Constantinople, 182
supports opening a new theatre in Asia, 179
and western front, 153, 174-75, 181-83

Krithia, 149
First Battle of, 116-17; Second Battle of, 122-25; Third Battle of, 138-42, 143, 145
Kum Kale, 167
French feint at, 105-112

Lacaze, Vice-Adm. Marie Jean, 210
favours remaining in the Dardanelles, 199
opposed to remaing in the Balkans, 211
replaces Augagneur at the Ministry of Marine, 199
La Rognon redoubt, 137
Lemnos, 61, 79, 100-1, 105 111, 151, 178, 203
Le Ravin de la Mort, 146, 148, 156
Leygues, Georges, 197
Limon von Sanders, Gen Otto, 103, 106, 120
Lloyd George, David,
supports operation in the Balkans, 41, 60, 195, 197, 205, 212
Loubet, Paul, 19
Loyzeau de Grandmaison, Col. Louis, 24-25
Lyautey, Gen. Louis, 66, 200

MacMahon, Field-Marshal Patrice de, 16-17
McMahon, Sir Henry, 44
Maidos, 104, 138, 182
Malvy, Louis, 164-65
Marine Commission, 50-51, 52-54, 105
Marshall, Brig.-Gen. W.R., 116
Martin, William, 177, 204
Maucorps, Lieut.-Col.
opposes purely naval attack, 70-71
Maxwell, General Sir John, 61, 71
Méline, Jules, 211
Messimy, Adolphe, 201
earlier career, 25
makes radical changes in the high command, 26
removes Michel from post of designate c-in-c, 25.
Michel, Gen. Victor, 25, 26
Millerand, Alexandre, 39, 45, 54, 59, 95, 153, 173, 176, 178, 179
at a conference with Kitchener and Balfour in Calais, 191-92
decides to replace d'Amade, 127-28
earlier career and character, 31
excluded from new ministry, 198
investigates the possibility of a Syrian expedition, 44-45, 59
and Joffre, 37, 127-28, 152
and Kitchener, 68-69, 71, 72-73, 191
meetings with Sarrail, 164, 170, 180, 184
plea for landing in Asia is rejected, 158

requests information from London on key
  questions, 71-73
seeks additional British troops for Western
  Front, 60
selects d'Amade as commander of the CEO,
  66-68
tries to take part in determining strategy in the
  Dardanelles, 135-36
views on landing sites in the Dardanelles, 101
under criticism for unwavering support of
  Joffre, 166,
Mitylene, 101, 178
Monro, Gen. Charles, 200, 203
Mudros (see Lemnos)
Murray of Elibank, 172

National Assembly, 15-17,
Naval convention of February 1913, 22-23, 43; of
  August 1914, 43, 49
Nicholas, Grand Duke, 42, 51, 78, 79
Nicholas II, Tsar of Russia, 76, 80
Nicol, Vice-Adm. Ernest-Eugène, 133
Noguès, Lieut-Col. Charles, 109, 110, 122-23

Ocean, 93
*Offensive à l'outrance (*cult of the offensive*)*, 24-25
Ottoman Empire, 76, 82, 83, 87, 97, 99
  alliance with Germany, 35
  best Allied approach to deal with, 220
  consequences of Allied withdrawal from
    Dardanelles, 215
  French extensive interests in, 34-35
  French territorial interests in case of partition
    of, 48
  its army is fighting harder than expected,
    119-120, 122-25, 137, 140-42, 143, 215
  offers to an ally a wide-range of strategic
    possibilities, 33-34
  unlikely to surrender in the event ships entered
    into the Sea of Marmora, 98

Paléologue, Maurice, 77-78, 79-80, 81, 83, 85
Panouse, Col. Arthus de la, 62, 68, 72, 175-76
Paris Commune, 16
Parliamentary Commissions, 38, 173, 175, 187
Peirse, Rear-Adm. Richard, 45, 46, 50, 105
Plan XVII, 26-27, 32
Poincaré, Raymond, 32, 36, 39, 173, 178, 192,
  197, 211
  against further offensives on main front, 154,
    170
  applies pressure on Galliéni to yield to Joffre,
    208-9
  on Balkan expedition, 39-41, 187

calls for a *union sacrée*, 29
coordinates war effort 30
on Dardanelles expedition, 54, 95, 154
earlier career and character, 22
instrumental in the appointment of d'Amade as
  commander of the CEO, 67-68
meets Parliamentary Commissions, 173
objects to giving Russia Constantinople and the
  Straits, 84-85, 86, 184-85
at odds with the idea of sending Sarrail to the
  Dardanelles, 169-70
prewar policy to strengthen France 22-23
receives a visit from Kitchener, 207
relates to Millerand a discussion with Gouraud,
  180
tries to dissuade Delcassé from resigning

Quadrilateral redoubt, 137, 145-46, 149-50, 155
Queen Elizabeth, 52, 74, 91, 111, 130

Radical Socialist Party, 19-20, 23, 207
Renaudel, Pierre, 166
Ribot, Alexandre, 164
  favours evacuation of Salonica, 211
Rohrbach, Paul von, 34
Romania, 59, 186
Ruef, Colonel, 106, 108, 110-11
Russia, 182, 184, 187, 195, 212
  and Constantinople and the Straits, 76-87
  on Dardanelles operation, 78,
  experiences setbacks on eastern front, 70, 170,
    174
  favours retention of Salonica
  feeling in France against, 84
  opposes Greek offer to send troops to the
    Dardanelles, 80
  requests a demonstration against Turkey, 42

Saint-Seine, Comte de, 46, 47-48
Salaun, Henri (*capitaine de vaisseau*), 50-51
Salonica (see Balkans)
Sari Bair, 114, 159
Sarikamish, Battle of, 42
Sarrail, Gen. Maurice, 184, 217
  in Balkan theatre, 197, 206, 211
  at Calais, 181--83
  has insufficient troops to accomplish anything
    meaningful, 214
  leaves for Salonica
  on meetings with Millerand, 169, 170-71, 186
  memoranda on use of French troops in the
    Mediterranean, 171, 175
  is offered a new assignment in the Dardanelles,
    164 -67,

previous career and character, 161-62
relations with Joffre, 162-63
removed from command of the Third Army, 164
setback in the Argonne, 163
is visited by Kitchener in Salonica, 206
Sarrault, Albert, 165-66
Sazanov, Serge, 84
brilliant diplomatic achievement, 85
on Dardanelles Operation, 78-79
formally lays down Russia's territorial claims, 82
resists Greek offer to send troops to the Dardanelles , 80
Section d'études de la défence nationale, 177, 183, 199, 204, 206
Schlieffen Plan, 25, 33
Sembat, Marcel, 84, 211
Serbia, 36-37, 59, 60, 79, 81, 171, 175, 186-87, 188, 192, 194-195, 196-98, 200, 203, 206
Souchon, Adm. Wilhelm, 36-37
Straits Agreement, 84-85, 216
Suvla, 189

Tenedos, 74, 82
Thomas, Albert
opposes evacuation of Salonica, 211
goes on a mission to London to reverse the decision reached at Calais, 212
Thompon, Gaston, 221
Turkey (see Ottoman Empire)

Vandenberg, Gen., 116-17
Venizelos, Eleutherios, 59, 80, 186,
Viviani, René, 39, 165, 167, 173, 179, 195-96,
on Balkan expedition, 39-41
character, 30
on Dardanelles campaign, 154, 185
endorses idea of a naval assault on the Straits, 54
fall of his ministry, 198
meetings with Sarrail, 164
on a mission to London with Augagneur to wrest concessions from the British , 193-94
under attack, 165, 193, 196, 197

War Committee, 200, 205, 206, 209
War Council, 41, 43, 46, 49, 60, 64
Wemyss, Rear-Adm. R. E. 74-75, 151
Wilson, Lieut.-Gen. Sir Henry, 174-75, 181-82, 189

Yeni Shehr, 106, 108, 111
Yukyesi, Bay of, 186

Zola, Emile, 19

Milton Keynes UK
Ingram Content Group UK Ltd.
UKHW050030230424
441476UK00001B/3